Careers in Nursing

Careers in Nursing

SALEM PRESS

A Division of EBSCO Information Services, Inc.

Ipswich, Massachusetts

GREY HOUSE PUBLISHING

Cover Image: Nurses consulting records on a digital display. Image by sturti (iStock).

Copyright © 2019 by EBSCO Information Services, Inc., and Grey House Publishing, Inc.

Careers in Nursing, published by Grey House Publishing, Inc., Amenia, NY, under exclusive license from EBSCO Information Services, Inc.

∞ The paper used in these volumes conforms to the American National Standard for Permanence of Paper for Printed Library Materials, Z39.48 1992 (R2009).

Publisher's Cataloging-In-Publication Data
(Prepared by The Donohue Group, Inc.)

Title: Careers in nursing.
Other Titles: Careers in--
Description: [First edition]. | Ipswich, Massachusetts : Salem Press, a division of EBSCO
        Information Services, Inc.; Amenia, NY : Grey House Publishing, [2019] |
        Includes bibliographical references and index.
Identifiers: ISBN 9781642650501 (hardcover)
Subjects: LCSH: Nursing--Vocational guidance--United States.
Classification: LCC RT82 .C37 2019 | DDC 610.73069--dc23

First Printing

PRINTED IN THE UNITED STATES OF AMERICA

CONTENTS

Specialties

Industries

PUBLISHER'S NOTE

Careers in Nursing contains thirty-seven chapters organized into five sections. The first section of the book provides an overview of education options for nurses and describes the various levels of education and certification nurses acquire and how those degrees and certifications relate to specific types of nursing careers, from aides and assistants to nurse practitioners and nurse researchers.

The next section of the book details various levels of nursing practice in nine profiles, including emergency medical technicians and paramedics, home health aides, medical assistants, medical and health services managers, licensed practical and vocational nurses, nursing assistants and orderlies, nurse anesthetists, nurse midwives, nurse practitioners, registered nurses, and surgical technicians. These career profiles offer details about a particular career path by providing:

Snapshot details including the most current data about
- Median Pay
- Typical Entry-Level Education
- Career Cluster
- On-the-job Training
- Number of Jobs
- Job Outlook
- Employment Change
- Holland Score

Career Overview includes a description of the career in terms of its
- Duties
- Examples of titles for positions in that specific career
- Work environment
- Work schedules

Each profile provides details about **How to become**… that explain how to begin and grow a career within a specific career profile by describing
- Important qualities
- Education
- Licenses, certifications, and registrations that may be required
- Advancement opportunities

Profiles also include the most current details about pay compared to other career clusters as well as a look at pay by industry as well as a description of **Similar Occupations** that lists specific jobs that are related in some way to the nursing career being profiled.

Job Outlook and **Job Prospects** describe current and anticipated rate of growth for a specific career, and compares the rate to other jobs in areas in the same career cluster, as well as to career growth taken as a whole.

Each profile concludes with **Contact information** to additional resources such as specific associations or certifying bodies for further details.

In the third section of the book, we examine eleven settings where nursing care is provided, including
- Assisted living facilities
- Case management
- Clinics
- Critical care
- Emergency rooms
- Extended care
- Home care
- Hospice
- Intensive care unit (ICU)
- Internet medicine
- Telehealth nursing

The fourth section of the book reviews ten areas of medical specialties and the fifth section takes a look at six industries where nurses find work.

Merging scholarship with occupational development, this single comprehensive guidebook provides students passionate about finding a career in nursing with the necessary insight into the wide array of options open to trained nurses. The book offers guidance regarding what job seekers can expect in terms of training, advancement, earnings, job prospects, working conditions, relevant associations, and more. Careers in Nursing is specifically designed for a high school and undergraduate audience and is edited to align with secondary or high school curriculum standards.

Scope of Coverage

Understanding the wide scope of jobs, settings for providing care, and industries where nurses typically work is important for anyone preparing for a career in nursing, from hospitals and clinics to public health and alternative care.

Careers in Nursing is enhanced with numerous charts and tables, including projections from the US Bureau of Labor Statistics, and median annual salaries or wages for those occupations profiled. Enhancements, like Fast Facts, Famous Firsts, and dozens of photos, add depth to the discussion. Additional highlights in the book include twenty-two interviews—Conversation With...—featuring a professional working in a related job who offers insight into specific areas of nursing such as palliative care, home nursing, school nursing, public health nursing, occupational nursing, military nursing, geriontological nursing, and more. The respondents share their personal career paths, detail potential for career advancement, offer advice for students, and include a "try this" for those interested in embarking on a career in their profession.

Special Features

Several features continue to distinguish this reference series from other career-oriented reference works. The back matter includes:

- Appendix A: Guide to Holland Code. This discusses John Holland's theory that people and work environments can be classified into six different groups: Realistic; Investigative; Artistic; Social; Enterprising; and Conventional. See if the job you want is right for you!
- Appendix B: General Bibliography. This is a collection of suggested readings, organized into major categories.
- Appendix C: A glossary of some terms related to nursing career paths.
- Appendix D: Organizations & Resources. This is a comprehensive list of organizations and societies and web addresses to provide further information about membership, training, certification, examinations, and more.
- Subject Index: Includes people, concepts, technologies, terms, principles, and all specific occupations discussed in the occupational profile chapters.

Acknowledgments

Thanks are due to Allison Blake, who took the lead in developing "Conversations With," with help from Alicia Banks, and to the professionals who communicated their work experience through interview questionnaires. Their frank and honest responses provide immeasurable value to *Careers in Nursing*. The contributions of all are gratefully acknowledged.

INTRODUCTION TO
CAREERS IN NURSING

The Role of Nursing

It is difficult at times to distinguish nursing from medicine, since there are so many ways in which they interrelate. Whereas some people think that nursing began with Florence Nightingale (1820-1910), nursing is as old as medicine itself. Throughout history, there have been periods when the two fields functioned interdependently and times when they were practiced separately from each other. It seems likely that the role of the mother-nurse would have preceded the magician-priest or medicine-man. Even the seeds of medical knowledge were sown by the natural remedies used by the mother. Over the course of human history, the words *nurse* and *nursing* have had many meanings, and the connotations have changed as tribes became highly developed and sophisticated nations.

The word nurse comes from the Latin *nutrix*, which means "nursing mother." The word nursing originated from the Latin *nutrire*, meaning "to nourish." The word *nurse* as a noun was first used in the English language in the thirteenth century, being spelled "norrice," then evolving to "nurice" or "nourice," and finally to the present "nurse." The word nurse as a verb meant to suckle and to nourish. The meanings of both the noun and the verb have expanded to include more and more functions related to the care of all human beings. In the sixteenth century, the meaning of the noun included "a person, but usually a woman, who waits upon or tends the sick." By the nineteenth century, the meaning of the verb included "the training of those who tend the sick and the carrying out of such duties under the supervision of a physician." With the origin of nursing as mother care came the idea that nursing was a woman's role. Suckling and nurturing were associated with maternal instincts. Ill or helpless children were also cared for by their mothers.

The image of the nurse as a loving and caring mother remains popular. The true spirit of nursing, however, has no gender barriers. History has seen both men and women respond to the needs of the sick. The role of the nurse has certainly expanded from that of the mother in the home, nourishing infants and caring for young children. Care of the sick, infirm, helpless, elderly, and handicapped and the promotion of health have become vital aspects of nursing as a whole. In history, the role of nursing developed with the culture and society of a given age. Tribal women practiced nursing as they cared for the members of their own tribes. As tribes developed into civilizations, nursing began to be practiced outside the home. As cultures developed, nursing care became more complex, and qualities other than a nurturing instinct were needed to do the work of a nurse. Members of religious orders, primarily those composed of women, responded by devoting their lives to study, service, and self-sacrifice in caring for the needs of the sick. These individuals were among the educated people of their time, and they helped set the stage for nursing to become an art and a science.

It was not until the nineteenth century that the basis of nursing as a profession was established. The beliefs and examples of Florence Nightingale laid that foundation. Nightingale was born in Italy in 1820, but she grew up in England. Unlike many of the children of her time, she was educated by governesses and by her father. Against the wishes of her family, she trained to be a nurse at the age of thirty-one. Amid enormous difficulties and prejudices, she organized and managed the nursing care for a military hospital in Turkey during the Crimean War. She returned to England after the war, where she established a school, the Nightingale Training School for Nurses, to train nurses. Again, she encountered great opposition, as nurses were considered little more than housemaids by the physicians of the time. Because of her efforts, the status of nurses was raised to a respected occupation, and the basis for professional nursing in general was established.

Nightingale's contributions are noteworthy. She recognized that nutrition is an important part of nursing care. She instituted occupational and recreational therapy for the sick and identified the personal needs of the patient and the role of the nurse in meeting those needs. Nightingale established standards for hospital management and a system of nursing education, making nursing a respected occupation for women. She recognized the two components of nursing: promoting health and treating illness. Nightingale believed that nursing is separate and distinct from medicine as a profession. Nightingale's methods and the response of nursing to American Civil War casualties in the 1860s pointed out the need for nursing education in the United States. Schools of nursing were established, based on the values of Nightingale, but they operated more like apprenticeships than educational programs. The schools were also controlled by hospital administrators and physicians.

In 1896, nurses in the United States banded together to seek standardization of educational programs, to establish laws to ensure the competency of nurses, and to promote the general welfare of nurses. The outcome of their efforts was the American Nurses Association. In 1900, the first nursing journal, the *American Journal of Nursing*, was founded. The effects of World War II also made clear the need to base schools of nursing on educational objectives. Many women had responded to the need for nurses during the war. A great expansion in medical knowledge and technology had taken place, and the roles of nurses were expanding as well. Nursing programs developed in colleges and universities and offered degrees in nursing to both women and men. While there were impressive changes in the expectations and styles with which nursing care has been delivered from ancient times into the twenty-first century, the role and function of the nurse has been and continues to be diverse. The nurse is a caregiver, providing care to patients based on knowledge and skill. Consideration is given to physical, emotional, psychological, socioeconomic, and spiritual needs. The role of the nurse-caregiver is holistic and integrated into all other roles that the nurse fulfills, thus maintaining and promoting health and well-being.

The nurse is a communicator. Using effective and therapeutic communication skills, the nurse strives to establish relationships to assist patients of all ages to manage and become responsible for their own health needs. In this way, the nurse is also a teacher who assists patients and families to meet their learning needs. Individualized teaching plans are developed and used to accomplish set goals.

The nurse is a leader. Based on the self-confidence gained from a nursing education and experience, the nurse is able to be assertive in meeting the needs of patients. The nurse facilitates change to improve care for patients, whether individually or in general. The nurse is also an advocate. Based on the belief that patients have a right to make their own decisions about health and life, the nurse strives to protect their human and legal rights in making those choices.

The nurse is a counselor. By effectively using communication skills, the nurse provides information, listens, facilitates problem-solving and decision-making abilities, and makes appropriate referrals for patients.

Finally, the nurse is a planner, a task that calls forth qualities far beyond nurturing and caring. In an age confronted with controversial topics such as abortion, organ transplants, the allocation of limited resources, and medical research, the role of nurses will continue to expand to meet these challenges in the spirit that allowed nursing to evolve and become a respected profession.

Science and Profession

While the nurse-mother of ancient times functioned within a very limited framework, the modern nurse has the choice of many careers within the nursing role. The knowledge explosion of the last century created many job specialties from which nurses can choose a career.

The *clinical nurse specialist* is a nurse with experience, education, or an advanced degree in a specialized area of nursing. Some examples are geriatrics, infection control, oncology, orthopedics, emergency room care, operating room care, intensive and coronary care, quality assurance, and community health. Nurses who function in such specialties carry out direct patient care; teach patients, families, and staff members; act as consultants; and sometimes conduct research to improve methods of care.

The *nurse practitioner* is a nurse with an advanced degree who is certified to work in a specific aspect of patient care. Nurse practitioners work in a variety of settings or in independent practice. They perform health assessments and give primary care to their patients.

The *nurse anesthetist* is a nurse who has also successfully completed a course of study in anesthesia. Nurse anesthetists make preoperative visits and assess patients prior to surgery, administer and monitor anesthesia during surgery, and evaluate the postoperative condition of patients.

The *nurse midwife* is a nurse who has successfully completed a midwifery program. The nurse midwife provides prenatal care to expectant mothers, delivers babies, and provides postnatal care after the birth.

The *nurse administrator* functions at various levels of management in the health care field. Depending on the position held, advanced education may be in business or hospital administration. The administrator is directly responsible for the operation and management of resources and is indirectly responsible for the personnel who give patient care.

The *nurse educator* is a nurse, with a master's or doctoral degree, who teaches or instructs in clinical or educational settings. This nurse can teach both theory and clinical skills.

The *nurse researcher* usually has an advanced degree and conducts special studies that involve the collection and evaluation of data in order to report on and promote the improvement of nursing care and education.

Duties and Procedures

Creativity and education are the keys to keeping pace with continued changes and progress in the nursing profession. Nurses are expected to play many roles, function in a variety of settings, and strive for excellence in the performance of their duties. A service must be provided that contributes to the health and well-being of people. The following examples of nursing-an operating room nurse and a home health nurse-provide a limited portrait of how nurses function and what roles they play in health care.

Operating room nurses function both directly and indirectly in patient care and render services in a number of ways. Operating room nurses, usually known as circulating nurses, briefly interview patients upon their arrival at the operating room. They accompany patients to specific surgery rooms and assist in preparing them for surgical procedures. They are responsible for seeing that surgeons correctly identify patients prior to anesthesia. They are also directly attentive to patients when anesthesia is first administered.

Circulating nurses perform the presurgical scrub, which is a cleansing of the skin with a specified solution for a given number of minutes. It is their overall responsibility to monitor aseptic (sterile) techniques in certain areas of the operating room and to deal with the situation immediately if aseptic techniques are broken. They count the surgical sponges with surgical technologists before the first incision is made, throughout the procedure as necessary, and again before the incision is closed. They secure needed items requested by surgical technologists, surgeons, or anesthesia personnel: medications, blood, additional sterile instruments, or more sponges. At times, they prepare and assist with the operation of equipment used for surgeries, such as lasers, insufflators (used for laparoscopic surgery), and blood saver and reinfuser machines. They arrange for the transportation of specimens to the laboratory. They may also be instrumental in sending communications to waiting family members when the surgery takes longer than anticipated. When the surgery is completed, they accompany patients to the recovery room with the anesthesia personnel.

Home health nurses, on the other hand, function in a very different manner. This type of nurse usually works for a private home health services agency, or as part of an outreach program for home services through a hospital. Referrals come to the agency or program via the physician, through the physician's office, by way of the social services department in a hospital, or by an individual requesting skilled services through the physician.

The following scenario is an example of a patient whom a home health nurse may be requested to see: a seventy-six year-old man who was hospitalized with a recent diagnosis of diabetes mellitus, for which he is now insulin-dependent. He also has an open wound on his right ankle. The number of days allowed for hospitalization for his diagnosis has expired, but he still needs help using a glucometer to take his blood sugar readings and assistance with drawing up his insulin. He still has questions about how to manage his diabetes, especially the dietary parameters. He is unable to manage the wound care on his right ankle. His wife is willing to assist him, but she has no knowledge about diabetes or wound care. The home health nurse performs the following assessments on the initial visit: general physical condition, the patient's level of knowledge and understanding and his ability to manage his diabetic condition, all medications used, and the patient's understanding of the actions, side effects, and interactions of these medications. An assessment is made of the home setting in general: the patient's safety, the support system, and any special needs, such as assistive devices. If services such as physical therapy, occupational therapy, or speech therapy are needed, the nurse makes these referrals. If the patient requires additional in-home services, a referral to a medical social worker is made. Wound care is performed, and the nurse will then set up a plan of care, with the patient's input, for follow-up visits. Guidelines requested by the physician, as well as approval needed by health insurance companies covering the cost for home health services, will be taken into consideration when planning ongoing visits. If the home health agency has a nurse who is a diabetic specialist, the nurse can either consult with that specialist about the care of this patient or have the diabetic specialist make a home visit.

Perspective and Prospects

From the beginning of time, nursing and the role of the nurse have been defined by the people and the society of a particular age. Nursing as it is known today is still influenced by what occurred over the centuries.

In primitive times, people believed that illness was supernatural, caused by evil gods. The roles of the physician and the nurse were separate and unrelated. The physician was a medicine man, sometimes called a shaman or a witch doctor, who treated disease by ritualistic chants, by fear or shock techniques, or by boring holes into a person's skull with a sharp stone to allow the evil spirit or demon an escape. The nurse, on the other hand, was usually the mother who tended to family members and provided for their physical needs, using herbal remedies when they were ill.

As tribes evolved, the centers for medical care were temples. Some tribes believed that illness was caused by sin and the displeasure of gods. The physician of this age was a priest and was held in high regard. The nurse was a woman, seen as a slave, who performed menial tasks ordered by the priest/physician. Living in the same era were Hebrew tribes who used the Ten Commandments and the Mosaic Health Code to develop standards for ethical human relationships, mental health treatment, and disease control. Nurses visited the sick in their homes, practiced as midwives, and provided for the physical and spiritual needs of family members who cared for the ill.

These nurses provided a family-centered approach to care. With the advent of Christianity, the value of the individual was emphasized, and the responsibility for recognizing the needs of each individual emerged. Nursing gained an elevated position in society. A spiritual foundation for nursing was established as well. The first organized visiting of the sick was done by deaconesses and Christian Roman matrons of the time. Members of male religious orders also cared for the sick and buried the dead.

During the time of the Crusades, there were both male and female nursing orders, and nursing at this time was a respected vocation. Men usually belonged to military nursing orders, who cared for the sick, on one hand, and defended the hospital when it was under attack, on the other. In medieval times, hospitals became a place to keep, not cure, patients. There were no methods of infection control. Nursing care was largely custodial, and the practice of accepting individuals of low character to supplement inadequate nursing staffs became common.

The worst era in nursing history was probably from 1500 to 1860. Nursing at this time was not a respected profession. Women who had committed a crime were sent into nursing as an alternative to serving a jail term. Nurses received poor wages and worked long hours under deplorable conditions. Changes in the Reformation and the Renaissance did little or nothing to improve the care of the sick. The attitude prevailed that nursing was a religious and not an intellectual occupation. Charles Dickens quite aptly portrayed the nurse and nursing conditions of the time through his caricatures of Sairey Gamp and Betsey Prig in *Martin Chuzzlewit* (1843- 1844). It was not until the middle of the nineteenth century that this situation began to change.

Through Nightingale's efforts, nursing became a respected occupation once more. The quality of nursing care improved tremendously, and the foundation was laid for modern nursing education. As innovations in health care have an impact on nursing, nurses' roles will continue to expand in the future. Nursing can also be a background from which both men and women begin to bridge gaps of service where other affiliations are needed: computer science, medical-legal issues, health insurance agencies, and bioethics, to name a few. The words of Florence Nightingale still echo as a challenge to the nursing profession:

May the methods by which every infant, every human being will have the best chance of health, the methods by which every sick person will have the best chance of recovery, be learned and practiced! Hospitals are only an intermediate state of civilization never intended, at all events, to take in the whole sick population.

Nursing will continue to meet this challenge to improve the quality of health care around the world.

—Karen A. Mattern
—Mary Dietmann, EdD, APRN, CNS
—Geraldine Marrocco

Further Reading

Berman, Audrey, Shirlee Snyder, Geralyn Frandsen, Audrey Berman, and Barbara Kozier. *Kozier and Erb's Fundamentals of Nursing: Concepts, Process and Practice.* 2018. Print.

Bureau of Labor Statistics, U.S. Department of Labor, *Occupational Outlook Handbook*, Licensed Practical and Licensed Vocational Nurses, on the Internet at https://www.bls.gov/ooh/healthcare/licensed-practical-and-licensed-vocational-nurses.htm (visited *January 13, 2019*).

———, Nurse Anesthetists, Nurse Midwives, and Nurse Practitioners, on the Internet at https://www.bls.gov/ooh/healthcare/nurse-anesthetists-nurse-midwives-and-nurse-practitioners.htm (visited *January 04, 2019*).

———, Nurse Anesthetists, Nurse Midwives, and Nurse Practitioners, on the Internet at https://www.bls.gov/ooh/healthcare/nurse-anesthetists-nurse-midwives-and-nurse-practitioners.htm (visited *January 04, 2019*).

———, Registered Nurses, on the Internet at https://www.bls.gov/ooh/healthcare/registered-nurses.htm (visited *January 21, 2019*).

Dolan, Josephine A, M L. Fitzpatrick, and Eleanor K. Herrmann. *Nursing in Society: A Historical Perspective.* Philadelphia: W.B. Saunders, 1983. Print.

Donahue, M. Patricia. *Nursing: The Finest Art.* 3d ed. Maryland Heights: Mosby Elsevier, 2011.

Potter, Patricia A, Anne G. Perry, Amy Hall, and Patricia A. Stockert. *Fundamentals of Nursing.* 2017. Print.

Vorvick, Linda J. "Types of Health Care Providers." MedlinePlus, August 14, 2018.

Education

EDUCATION FOR NURSING CAREERS

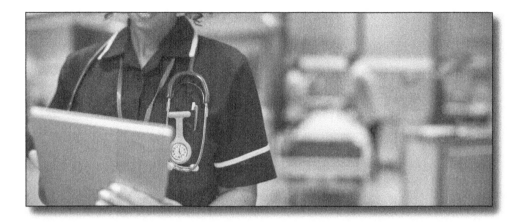

Licensed Practical Nurse/Licensed Vocational Nurse (LPN/LVN)

Associate's degrees in nursing are offered by many community colleges and some four-year institutions. An ADN program combines hands-on training with class work.

Education and Licensing

Required degree: Associate's level degree (ADN)

Licensing/certification requirement: National Council Licensure Examination (NCLEX-PN)

Although there is a continued emphasis on a bachelor's level degree as a minimum educational requirement, it remains that case that, depending the type of care (long-term or acute care) and geographic setting (urban hospital vs. rural hospital, for example, or part of the nation), the ADN may still be relevant as a starting point for a nursing career. This degree level is also often a step on the way to more advanced nursing degrees.

Courses typically include the following:

- Anatomy
- Physiology
- Biology
- Nutrition

Students also spend time in labs and clinical nursing skills clinics to prepare for common working situations.

LPN/LVN programs typically take one-to-two years to complete and are generally offered by technical schools or community colleges. Like an ADN program, an LPN/

LVN program includes a mix of instructional and hands-on courses with some or all of the following courses as part of the curriculum:

- Basic Nursing Skills
- Anatomy and Physiology
- Nutrition
- Emergency Care
- Pediatric Nursing
- Obstetric Nursing
- Medical-Surgical Nursing

Registered Nurse (RN)

The Institute of Medicine set a goal in 2010 to increase the percentage of nurses with a bachelor's level degree (BSN) to 80% by 2020. Many groups continue to work on increasing that percentage—and many more nurses than ever before are working on earning their BSNs.

Education and Licensing

Required degree: Bachelor's level degree (BSN)

Licensing/certification requirement: National Council Licensure Examination (NCLEX-RN)

Nurses with either a BSN or an ADN can practice as registered nurses (RNs). The level of licensing is the same, but while the roles do overlap, they are not the same.

There are five types of bachelor's level degrees:

- BSN: a 4-year degree and the prerequisite for applying to graduate nursing school. Years 1 and 2 cover core requirements. Years 3 and 4 focus primarily on nursing. Often the starting degree for those who aspire to become nurse practitioners in a specialty.
- LPN-to-BSN: Four additional semesters, following receiving licensing as a licensed practical nurse (LPN) or a licensed vocational nurse (LVN).
- RN-to-BSN: For RNs with an associate's degree or diploma; a way to further a career while already in the workforce.
- Second-degree BSN: For an individual with a 4-year degree in another field intent on changing careers. May be completed in 2 years or less, depending upon credit received coursework undertaken as part of the original degree.
- Accelerated Degree BSN: Students finish a degree in a shorter period of time (usually 12 to 20 months).

Examples of BSN core courses:

- Health promotion and disease prevention
- Physical examination and health assessment
- Communication and collaboration
- Critical thinking
- Genetics and genomics
- Information management

Nurse Licensing

Nursing license requirements vary by state, but according to the National Council of State Boards of Nursing, the minimum requirements for both registered nurse (RN) and licensed practical nurse (LPN) candidates are:

- Graduate, or verification of completion and eligibility for graduation, from a state-approved nursing program.
- Pass the NCLEX-RN (National Council Licensure Examination).
- Self-report any and all criminal convictions, chemical dependencies, and functional ability deficits.

Advanced Practice Registered Nurse

There are four basic certifications for APRNs

- *Nurse Practitioners (NP)* provide primary, acute, and specialty health care across the lifespan through assessment, diagnosis, and treatment of illnesses and injuries.
- *Certified Nurse-Midwives (CNM)* provide primary, gynecological, and reproductive health care.
- *Clinical Nurse Specialists (CNS)* provide diagnosis, treatment, and ongoing management of patients; provide expertise and support to nurses caring for patients; help drive practice changes throughout the organization; and ensure use of best practices and evidence-based care to achieve the best possible patient outcomes.
- *Certified Registered Nurse Anesthetists (CRNA)* provide a full range of anesthesia and pain management services.

Education and Licensing

Required degree: Master's or doctoral degree

Licensing/certification requirement: National Council Licensure Examination (NCLEX-RN) and clinical nurse specialist license or certification

A clinical nurse specialist is an advanced-practice nurse who provides patient care and consultation services for a variety of health care areas. These professionals typically practice medicine, conduct research and manage staff within a specific type of patient population, medical specialty or setting. They are licensed registered nurses (RNs) who also have a master's or doctoral degree and specialized certification in the field.

Projected Job Growth (2014-2024)*	Median Salary (2016)
16% for all RNs	$81,952**

Sources: *U.S. Bureau of Labor Statistics, **PayScale.com

Master's Degree Program (MSN)

MSN programs are generally a two-year commitment. Not only will you earn your graduate degree, but you will also be trained in a specialty of your choosing. Many MSN programs are available both online and at traditional schools.

Below is a list of sample coursework that may be covered in a MSN:
- *Health care policy*: Health care delivery system, financial and political impacts; policy issues.
- *Advanced concepts in pharmacology*: Prescription guidelines, drug interactions and side effects.
- *Health care ethics*: Patient-provider relationships, legal and ethical issues; moral judgment.
- *Theory and practice* (specialty-based): Theory and practice in a specialization area and in-depth training related to the patients treated as part of specialization.
- *Clinical practicum*: Hands-on experience. Clinical hours requirements vary by state.

Doctoral Program (DNP)

A doctor of nursing practice (DNP) provides a clinical focus, rather than a research focus.

Certification and credentialing

Nurse practitioners and clinical nurse specialists are certified through the American Nurses Credentialing Center (ANCC). Nurse anesthetists are certified through the National Board of Certification & Recertification for Nurse Anesthetists (NBCRNA). Nurse-midwives are certified through the American Midwifery Certification Board (AMCB)

Nurses with master's-level, post-graduate or doctoral degrees can apply for certification in adult, family and adult-gerontology nurse practitioner specialties by taking AANPCP's exam. To be eligible to sit for the test, applicants must have:
- NPs with an MSN, post-master's certificate or doctorate
- Active RN license
- At least 500 clinical clock hours supervised by a faculty member
- Final transcript or transcript showing work accomplished so far

Students who are within six months of graduating with an MSN or higher can begin the application process for AANPCP's certification exam. ANCC also lets students apply for their exam prior to graduation and certifies nurse practitioners in almost a dozen specialties:
- Acute Care NP
- Adult NP
- Adult-gerontology acute care NP
- Adult gerontology primary care NP

- Adult Psychiatric-mental health NP
- Family NP
- Gerontological NP
- Pediatric Primary Care NP
- Psychiatric-Mental Health NP
- School NP

The general eligibility requirements to take the ANCC exam are:
- Current RN license
- A master's degree, post-graduate or doctoral degree in a specialization area
- At minimum of 500 faculty-supervised clinical hours
- Graduate courses in physiology, pathophysiology, advanced health assessment and advanced pharmacology
- Graduate-level content in health promotion and maintenance, disease management and differential diagnosis

It's recommended that students research the exact specialization criteria before applying. For example, the Pediatric Nursing Certification Board (PNCB) and National Certification Corporation (NCC) offer exams for neonatal NPs and women's health NPs.

American Nurse Credentialing Center
https://www.nursingworld.org/ancc/

American Association of Critical Care Nurses Certification Corporation
https://www.aacn.org/

Medical-surgical (med-surg) nursing

Medical-surgical (med-surg) nursing is the single largest nursing specialty in the United States. Their practice is primarily on hospital units to provide care for acutely ill adult patients with a variety of medical issues as well as patients recovering from surgery. They provide care round-the-clock care, which means that they spend more time directly interacting with patients than any other health care professional.

Med-surg nurses coordinate not only the care for many patients but also the work of the entire unit team. They must possess high-level critical thinking skills, broad clinical knowledge, and an ability to remain calm under pressure. Although other nursing specialties require the same types of skills, the level of coordination necessary to provide excellent patient care is what sets med-surg nursing apart from other specialties.

Currently, medical-surgical nurses are the most common among all nurse specialties. Most nurses work in this field of nursing, many at the very start of their careers. Those nurses who continue on in med-surg nursing as a comprehensive specialty for their entire careers often cite the level of experience they have gained.

A certified medical-surgical registered nurse has achieved a certification granted by MSNCB (the Medical-Surgical Nursing Certification Board) - accredited by the American Nurses Credentialing Center (ANCC), the Academy of Medical-Surgical Nurses (AMSN) and American Nurses Association (ANA).

The American Nurses Credentialing Center set several eligibility criteria:

1. Hold an active, current registered nurse license within the U.S. territory
2. With a minimum of two years working experience as a RN.
3. With a minimum of 2,000 hours of clinical practice in the medical-surgical area within the last 3 years
4. Completed 30 hours of continuing education with the area of medical-surgical nursing within the last three years.

This certification lasts for 5 years - and to be re-certified, you need to meet the continuing education requirements or pass an examination given by ANCC or MSNCB.

Medical-surgical patients have complex diagnoses and correspondingly complex needs. Patients in this area vary, from ambulatory to total care and as such, medical-surgical nurses are expected to be flexible and versatile in providing holistic care. Medical-surgical nurses may care for the following types of patients:

1. Patients with acute to chronic diseases needing management
2. Patients with diverse admitting diagnosis and not limited to a single body system
3. Patients with complex and multiple co-morbidities
4. Patients and their families
5. Patients across the life span

The following are some of the functions of a medical-surgical nurse:

1. Medical-surgical (MS) nurses must be able coordinate, organize, and prioritize complex multiple client assignment.
2. Competent and knowledgeable in guiding patients and their families from the challenges that come along with the complex health care system.
3. MS nurses must integrate discharge planning into the patient's daily care.
4. Must be able to collaborate with other members of the health care team.
5. Ability to learn the use of technology, including new medical innovations.
6. Capability to integrate research in relation to a diverse care needs
7. Integrate the best practice guidelines in relation to diverse clinical situations
8. Advocate for ethical, quality, and safe work setting

Fast Fact

Nursing can be physically demanding: more than 52 percent of nurses experience chronic back pain. Moving a heavy patient requires physical fitness!

Source: usnews.com

Conversation With . . .
ROBIN HERTEL

Eds, MSN, RN, CMSRN
President, Academy of Medical-Surgical Nurses
Pitman, New Jersey

Robin Hertel has been a nurse for twenty-five years and is currently working as a Nursing Content Expert for Ascend Learning in Kansas City, Kansas.

1. What was your individual career path in terms of education/training, entry-level job, or other significant opportunity?

Originally, I wanted to become a physician and entered college with a premed focus. The more I got into it, however, the more I saw that that profession leans more toward business and less toward the patient connection. I went into nursing instead.

I was a recently divorced, single mother when I went into nursing school and needed to get into something quickly. The licensed practical nurse (LPN) route was the best way I could do that. I received my training at North Central Kansas Technical College. Following licensure, I worked for several years as a staff nurse on a medical-surgical unit before returning to the same school to obtain an associate degree and my registered nurse (RN) license. Continuing as an RN to work as a staff and charge nurse on that same unit, I decided to become certified as a medical-surgical nurse.

A med-surg nurse educates patients about what it's like to go into surgery, and what it's like in recovery. We pass medications, clean wounds, change dressings, and remove staples and sutures. You name it, we do it. What's unique in the unit is we have a wide array of patient conditions. In one room, someone has a fractured hip and is in traction, and needs to be turned in order to avoid the breakdown of skin or to avoid the risk of developing a pulmonary embolism. In another room, there might be a newly diagnosed diabetic person who has no idea how to manage self-administration of insulin.

While working in acute care, I got a call from my alma mater's dean of nursing asking if I'd be interested in teaching. I'd always loved educating my patients, and said yes right then and there. I continued to work part-time for a period, and while teaching earned my bachelor's degree via distance learning at Jacksonville University, and then my master's degree in nursing (MSN), also remotely, from Walden University. I later earned my education specialist degree from Walden.

Before becoming certified as a medical-surgical nurse, I had joined the Academy of Medical-Surgical Nurses, the specialty's only professional nursing organization. I quickly became involved at the national level, first as a member of the newsletter editorial team and legislative coordinator, and later as a board member. The decision to volunteer for that first committee changed my entire professional life. I have benefited from many more opportunities than I could have imagined or experienced otherwise.

Now, as the organization's president, I am leading such efforts as joining with other professional organizations to address common problems across specialties. These are issues such as staffing, healthy practice environments, and safety for nurses.

In addition, I am a nursing content expert for Ascend Learning, which provides education in various health care professions. I develop educational products for nursing students, such as those focused on dosage calculations or health assessments.

2. What are the most important skills and/or qualities for someone in your profession?

Managing time and keeping calm under pressure are two of the most important skills required. At any given moment, you are juggling and prioritizing care for several patients, administering medications, educating families, discharging patients and admitting new ones, all while keeping the entire health care team on the same page.

It's also important to develop high-level critical thinking skills so you can stay several steps ahead of a patient's condition and avoid potential complications.

3. What do you wish you had known going into this profession?

I wish I had known more about advanced degree opportunities and had planned for degree progression at the start of my nursing career. It would have saved time and money. For example, I obtained a master's in nursing education – which is valuable – but a degree as a clinical nurse specialist would have opened many more doors for me as a professional and provided for more avenues to pursue a doctorate.

4. Are there many job opportunities in your profession? In what specific areas?

The options in nursing are only limited by your imagination. You can find med-surg nurses in infection control, quality care services, educational services, or providing home health care. They're writing books. In the travel industry, you'll find med-surge nurses on cruise ships.

I like to tell nursing students or people considering the nursing profession to find your passion and make it a part of your nursing career. Are you interested in politics and advocacy? There are opportunities as a nurse lobbyist or for a legislator writing health policy. Do you enjoy coding and working with computers? Specialize in nursing informatics.

5. How do you see your profession changing in the next five years, how will technology impact that change, and what skills will be required?

There is an increased focus on promoting wellness and prevention instead of simply managing illness. This requires medical-surgical nurses to work with patients to determine their current status along with their personal goals and, together, develop a plan to promote wellness. An important strategy is care coordination to provide seamless services across all levels of care from preadmission throughout a patient's hospital stay, and then during discharge to the home or another care setting.

Financial strains on the health care system have also required a new approach. Nurses must increasingly be aware of outcomes that measure the effectiveness of care administered because they will be participating even more in quality improvement activities that are becoming requisites for a facility's insurance reimbursement.

Technology will include everything from equipment that monitors patient conditions such as blood pressure and activity levels to telemedicine. Artificial intelligence (AI) means robots are doing everything from interacting with dementia patients to transferring patients from bed to chair. Nurses need to get involved in the decision-making regarding such technologies to ensure that the holistic aspect of nursing care remains intact and that patient safety isn't compromised. Nurses who embrace technological change will advance further than those who are resistant. One futurist predicts that nursing will evolve into a practice in which the nurse oversees the patient's care delivery and care coordination, and directs aides and technologies in the completion of that work.

Nurses also can use gaming technology to teach health care concepts to patients and their caregivers, making the learning more interactive and fun.

6. What do you enjoy most about your job? What do you enjoy least about your job?

I love the interaction with patients and helping them to achieve their highest level of wellness. I love the detective work involved in putting together laboratory findings and patient signs/symptoms, identifying an appropriate course of nursing treatment, and anticipating the patient's needs. I love the camaraderie of the med-surg nursing team when we have a patient who has an increased need or a team member who needs lifting up. I love that my work as a nurse is not limiting at all, and that I can follow my passion and work as a nurse in so many different settings and ways. I love that my profession is respected and trusted by the general public.

My least favorite part of my job is being so busy some days that I feel like I didn't have enough time to give to each individual patient.

7. Can you suggest a valuable "try this" for students considering a career in your profession?

Unfortunately, finding a nurse to shadow will be difficult because of patient privacy issues. However, I would suggest that a student who is considering a career in nursing visit a school of nursing and ask to spend some time in the simulation lab. Here, the student can work with some of the equipment and, if the school uses high-fidelity mannequins, actually have the opportunity to participate in some of the nursing tasks. Some schools of nursing dedicate a day to working with high school students, so it's worth checking at your school to see if this is the case.

Famous First

The pinning ceremony can be traced back to the Crusades of the 12th century. The Knights of The Order of the Hospital of St. John the Baptist tended to the injured Crusaders. When new monks would be initiated, they held a ceremony where they took a vow to serve the sick soldiers. They also received a Maltese cross, this being the first badge given to those who nurse.

Source: https://peacelovenursing.com/history-and-meaning-behind-the-pinning-ceremony/

Ambulatory Care Nursing

Nurses who practice in a setting other than a traditional inpatient arena such as a hospital are called ambulatory care nurses. You may think of them as nurses who work in outpatient settings such as:

- A physician group practice or health center
- Medical office
- University, community, or private hospital
- Military clinic
- Community health centers
- Free-standing facilities, such as a surgical center
- Home health setting
- School
- Telehealth/call center
- Government institution
- Managed care payers, such as an HMO or insurance company

Source: American Academy of Ambulatory Care Nursing, www.aaacn.org

Professional ambulatory care nursing is a complex, multifaceted specialty that encompasses independent and collaborative practice, Nurses use evidence based information across a variety of outpatient health care: hospital-based clinic/centers, solo or group medical practices, ambulatory surgery & diagnostic procedure centers, telehealth service environments, university and community hospital clinics, military and veterans administration settings, nurse-managed clinics, managed care organizations, colleges and educational institutions, free standing community facilities, care coordination organizations, and patient homes. They interact with patients during face-to-face encounters or through a variety of telecommunication strategies.

During each encounter, the ambulatory care registered nurse focuses on patient safety and the quality of nursing care by applying appropriate nursing interventions, such as identifying and clarifying patient needs, performing procedures, conducting health education, promoting patient advocacy, coordinating nursing and other health services, assisting the patient to navigate the health care system, and evaluating patient outcomes.

Ambulatory care nurses help patients and families to optimally manage their health care, respecting their culture and values, individual needs, health goals and treatment preferences. They are responsible to design, administer, and evaluate nursing services within an organization so that care meets all federal requirements, state laws and nurse practice acts, regulatory standards, and institutional policies and procedures. They often are the go-between during interactions with physicians, social workers, pharmacists, and other members of the health care team, and sometimes even with family members.

They provide care when a patient is discharged to home or another health care facility by making sure that follow-up appointments, medication, and other services are arranged. These nurses provide patients with the information they need to keep them safe, as well as how to lead healthier lives through preventive and self-care measures. They also take on leadership roles in government agencies and the military to manage health care in times of crisis and conflict or to implement public health programs, such as influenza prevention.

Travel Nurses

A travel nurse is a nurse who is hired to work in a specific location for a limited amount of time. Travel nurses typically work 13 week periods in one area, and move around the country depending on where they are needed. Because the demand for nurses is so high, there are often shortages in certain areas, and a traveling nurse will be hired to come in and work in a specific position for a short amount of time.

Profiles

EMTs and Paramedics

Snapshot

2017 Median Pay: $33,380 per year, $16.05 per hour

Typical Entry-Level Education: Postsecondary nondegree award

Career Cluster: Health science

On-the-job Training: None

Number of Jobs, 2016: 248,000

Job Outlook, 2016-26: 15% (Much faster than average)

Employment Change, 2016-26: 37,400

Holland Score: RSI

CAREER OVERVIEW

Emergency medical technicians (EMTs) and paramedics care for the sick or injured in emergency medical settings. People's lives often depend on the quick reaction and competent care provided by these workers. EMTs and paramedics respond to emergency calls, performing medical services and transporting patients to medical facilities.

Most EMTs and paramedics work full time. Their work can be physically strenuous and stressful, sometimes involving life-or-death situations. Emergency medical technicians (EMTs) and paramedics typically complete a postsecondary educational program. All states require EMTs and paramedics to be licensed; requirements vary by state.

A 911 operator sends EMTs and paramedics to the scene of an emergency, where they often work with police and firefighters.

Duties

EMTs and paramedics typically do the following:
- Respond to 911 calls for emergency medical assistance, such as cardiopulmonary resuscitation (CPR) or bandaging a wound
- Assess a patient's condition and determine a course of treatment
- Provide first-aid treatment or life support care to sick or injured patients
- Transport patients safely in an ambulance
- Transfer patients to the emergency department of a hospital or other health care facility
- Report their observations and treatment to physicians, nurses, or other health care facility staff
- Document medical care given to patients
- Inventory, replace, and clean supplies and equipment after use

When transporting a patient in an ambulance, one EMT or paramedic may drive the ambulance while another monitors the patient's vital signs and gives additional care. Some paramedics work as part of a helicopter's or an airplane's flight crew to transport critically ill or injured patients to a hospital.

EMTs and paramedics also transport patients from one medical facility to another. Some patients may need to be transferred to a hospital that specializes in treating their particular injury or illness or to a facility that provides long-term care, such as a nursing home.

If a patient has a contagious disease, EMTs and paramedics decontaminate the interior of the ambulance and may need to report the case to the proper authorities.

The specific responsibilities of EMTs and paramedics depend on their level of certification and the state they work in. The National Registry of Emergency Medical Technicians (NREMT) provides national certification of EMTs and paramedics at four levels: EMR, EMT, Advanced EMT, and Paramedic. Some states, however, have their own certification programs and use similar titles

Emergency Medical Responders, or EMRs, are trained to provide basic medical care with minimal equipment. These workers may provide immediate lifesaving interventions while waiting for other emergency medical services (EMS) resources to arrive. Jobs in this category may also go by a variety of titles including Emergency Care Attendants, Certified First Responders, or similar.

An EMT, also known as an EMT-Basic, cares for patients at the scene of an incident and while taking patients by ambulance to a hospital. An EMT has the skills to assess a patient's condition and to manage respiratory, cardiac, and trauma emergencies.

An Advanced EMT, also known as an EMT-Intermediate, has completed the requirements for the EMT level, as well as instruction in more advanced medical procedures, such as administering intravenous fluids and some medications.

Paramedics provide more extensive prehospital care than do EMTs. In addition to doing the tasks of EMTs, paramedics can give medications orally and intravenously, interpret electrocardiograms (EKGs)—which monitor heart function—and use other monitors and complex equipment.

The specific tasks or procedures EMTs and paramedics are allowed to perform vary by state.

WORK ENVIRONMENT

EMTs and paramedics held about 248,000 jobs in 2016. The largest employers of EMTs and paramedics were as follows:

Ambulance services	48%
Local government, excluding education and hospitals	28
Hospitals; state, local, and private	18

The above percentages exclude volunteer EMTs and paramedics who do not receive pay.

EMTs and paramedics work both indoors and outdoors, in all types of weather. Their work is physically strenuous and can be stressful, sometimes involving life-or-death situations.

Volunteer EMTs and paramedics share many of the same duties as paid EMTs and paramedics. They volunteer for fire departments, providers of emergency medical services, or hospitals. They may respond to only a few calls per month.

Injuries and Illnesses

EMTs and paramedics have one of the highest rates of injuries and illnesses of all occupations. They are required to do considerable kneeling, bending, and lifting while caring for and moving patients. They may be exposed to contagious diseases and viruses, such as hepatitis B and HIV. Sometimes they can be injured by combative patients. These risks can be reduced by following proper safety procedures, such as waiting for police to clear an area in violent situations or wearing gloves while working with a patient.

Work Schedules

Most paid EMTs and paramedics work full time. About 1 in 3 worked more than 40 hours per week in 2016. Because EMTs and paramedics must be available to work in emergencies, they may work overnight and on weekends. Some EMTs and paramedics work shifts in 12- or 24-hour increments. Volunteer EMTs and paramedics have variable work schedules. For example, they may work only a few days per week.

HOW TO BECOME AN EMT OR PARAMEDIC

Emergency medical technicians (EMTs) and paramedics typically complete a postsecondary educational program. All states require EMTs and paramedics to be licensed; requirements vary by state.

Important Qualities

Compassion. EMTs and paramedics must be able to provide emotional support to patients in an emergency, especially patients who are in life-threatening situations or extreme mental distress.

Interpersonal skills. EMTs and paramedics usually work on teams and must be able to coordinate their activities closely with others in stressful situations.

Listening skills. EMTs and paramedics need to listen to patients to determine the extent of their injuries or illnesses.

Physical strength. EMTs and paramedics need to be physically fit. Their job requires a lot of bending, lifting, and kneeling.

Problem-solving skills. EMTs and paramedics must evaluate patients' symptoms and administer appropriate treatments.

Speaking skills. EMTs and paramedics need to clearly explain procedures to patients, give orders, and relay information to others.

Education

Both a high school diploma or equivalent and cardiopulmonary resuscitation (CPR) certification typically are required for entry into postsecondary educational programs in emergency medical technology. Most of these programs are nondegree award programs that can be completed in less than 1 year; others last up to 2 years. Paramedics, however, may need an associate's degree. Programs in emergency medical technology are offered by technical institutes, community colleges, universities, and facilities that specialize in emergency care training. Some states have EMR positions that do not require national certification. These positions typically require state certification.

The Commission on Accreditation of Allied Health Education Programs offers a list of accredited programs for EMTs and paramedics, by state.

Programs at the EMT level include instruction in assessing patients' conditions, dealing with trauma and cardiac emergencies, clearing obstructed airways, using field equipment, and handling emergencies. Formal courses include about 150 hours of specialized instruction, and some instruction may take place in a hospital or ambulance setting.

Programs at the Advanced EMT level typically require about 400 hours of instruction. At this level, candidates learn EMT-level skills as well as more advanced ones, such as using complex airway devices, intravenous fluids, and some medications.

Paramedics have the most advanced level of education. To enter specific paramedical training programs, they must already be EMT certified. Community colleges and universities may offer these programs, which require about 1,200 hours of instruction and may lead to an associate's or bachelor's degree. Paramedics' broader scope of practice may include stitching wounds or administering intravenous medications.

High school students interested in becoming EMTs or paramedics should take courses in anatomy and physiology and consider becoming certified in CPR.

Licenses, Certifications, and Registrations

The National Registry of Emergency Medical Technicians (NREMT) certifies EMTs and paramedics at the national level. All levels of NREMT certification require completing a certified education program and passing the national exam. The national exam has both written and practical parts. Some states have first-level state certifications that do not require national certification.

All states require EMTs and paramedics to be licensed; requirements vary by state. In most states, an individual who has NREMT certification qualifies for licensure; in others, passing an equivalent state exam is required. Usually, an applicant must be over the age of 18. Many states require background checks and may not give a license to an applicant who has a criminal history.

Although some emergency medical services hire separate drivers, most EMTs and paramedics take a course requiring about 8 hours of instruction before they can drive an ambulance.

ADVANCEMENT

EMTs and paramedics may advance into other related health care occupations, such as physician assistants and medical assistants, as well as administrative positions in various health care settings, such as ambulatory care companies or hospitals.

Pay

The median annual wage for EMTs and paramedics was $33,380 in May 2017. The lowest 10 percent earned less than $21,880, and the highest 10 percent earned more than $56,990.

Median annual wages, May 2017

Health technologists and technicians: $43,590

Total, all occupations: $37,690

Emergency medical technicians and paramedics: $33,380

Note: All Occupations includes all occupations in the U.S. Economy. Source: U.S. Bureau of Labor Statistics, Occupational Employment Statistics

In May 2017, the median annual wages for EMTs and paramedics in the top industries in which they worked were as follows:

Hospitals; state, local, and private	$35,990
Local government, excluding education and hospitals	35,620
Ambulance services	30,800

Most paid EMTs and paramedics work full time. About 1 in 3 worked more than 40 hours per week in 2016. Because EMTs and paramedics must be available to work in emergencies, they may work overnight and on weekends. Some EMTs and paramedics work shifts in 12- or 24-hour increments. Volunteer EMTs and paramedics have variable work schedules. For example, they may work only a few days per week.

JOB OUTLOOK

Percent change in employment, projected 2016-26

Emergency medical technicians and paramedics: 15%

Health technologists and technicians: 14%

Total, all occupations: 7%

Note: All Occupations includes all occupations in the U.S. Economy. Source: U.S. Bureau of Labor Statistics, Employment Projections program

Employment of emergency medical technicians (EMTs) and paramedics is projected to grow 15 percent from 2016 to 2026, much faster than the average for all occupations. Emergencies, such as car crashes, natural disasters, and acts of violence, will continue to require the skills of EMTs and paramedics. The need for volunteer EMTs and paramedics in rural areas and smaller metropolitan areas will also continue.

Growth in the middle-aged and older population will lead to an increase in age-related health emergencies, such as heart attacks and strokes. This increase, in turn, will create greater demand for EMT and paramedic services. An increase in the number of specialized medical facilities will require more EMTs and paramedics to transfer patients with specific conditions to these facilities for treatment.

JOB PROSPECTS

Job opportunities should be good because the growing population will require more emergency services generally. There will also be a need to replace workers who leave the occupation due to the high stress nature of the job or to seek job opportunities in other health care occupations.

Employment projections data for EMTs and paramedics, 2016-26

Occupational Title	Employment, 2016	Projected Employment, 2026	Change, 2016-26	
			Percent	Numeric
Emergency medical technicians and paramedics	248,000	285,400	15	37,400

Source: Bureau of Labor Statistics, Employment Projections program

SIMILAR OCCUPATIONS

This list shows occupations with job duties that are similar to those of EMTs and paramedics.

Emergency Management Directors: Emergency management directors prepare plans and procedures for responding to natural disasters or other emergencies. They also help lead the response during and after emergencies, often in coordination with public safety officials, elected officials, nonprofit organizations, and government agencies.

Firefighters: Firefighters control and put out fires and respond to emergencies where life, property, or the environment is at risk.

Medical Assistants: Medical assistants complete administrative and clinical tasks in the offices of physicians, hospitals, and other health care facilities. Their duties vary with the location, specialty, and size of the practice.

Police and Detectives: Police officers protect lives and property. Detectives and criminal investigators, who are sometimes called agents or special agents, gather facts and collect evidence of possible crimes.

Physician Assistants: Physician assistants, also known as PAs, practice medicine on teams with physicians, surgeons, and other health care workers. They examine, diagnose, and treat patients.

Registered Nurses: Registered nurses (RNs) provide and coordinate patient care, educate patients and the public about various health conditions, and provide advice and emotional support to patients and their family members.

Famous First

The famous poet and essayist Walt Whitman served as a volunteer nurse during the Civil War in Fredericksburg, Virginia. His poem entitled "The Wound Dresser" got its theme from his nursing experience in the battlefield.

> On, on I go, (open doors of time! open hospital doors!)
> The crush'd head I dress, (poor crazed hand tear not
>   the bandage away,)
> The neck of the cavalry-man with the bullet through
>   and through I examine,
> Hard the breathing rattles, quite glazed already the
>   eye, yet life struggles hard,
> (Come sweet death! be persuaded O beautiful death!
>   In mercy come quickly.)

Source: *The Wound Dresser* by Walt Whitman

MORE INFORMATION

For more information about emergency medical technicians and paramedics, visit

**National Association of
Emergency Medical Technicians**
http: //www.naemt.org/

**National Registry of Emergency
Medical Technicians**
https: //www.nremt.org/rwd/public

**National Association of State
EMS Officials**
https: //nasemso.org/

For information about educational programs, visit

**Commission on Accreditation
of Allied Health Education
Programs**
https: //www.caahep.org/

O*NET
Emergency Medical Technicians and
Paramedics

Source: Bureau of Labor Statistics, U.S. Department of Labor, Occupational Outlook *Handbook*, EMTs and Paramedics, on the Internet at https: //www.bls.gov/ooh/ healthcare/emts-and-paramedics.htm (visited *January 22, 2019*).

Home Health Aides and Personal Care Aides

Snapshot

2017 Median Pay: $23,130 per year, $11.12 per hour

Typical Entry-Level Education: High school diploma or equivalent

Career Cluster: Health science

On-the-Job Training: Short-term on-the-job training

Number of Jobs, 2016: 2,927,600

Job Outlook, 2016-26: 41% (Much faster than average)

Employment Change, 2016-26: 1,208,800

Holland Score: SRC, SEC

CAREER OVERVIEW

Home health aides and personal care aides help people with disabilities, chronic illnesses, or cognitive impairment by assisting in their daily living activities. They often help older adults who need assistance. In some states, home health aides may be able to give a client medication or check the client's vital signs under the direction of a nurse or other health care

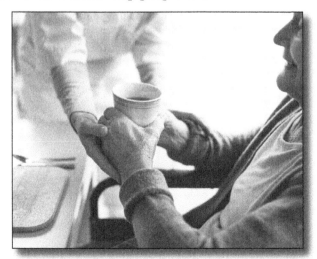

practitioner. Home health aides and personal care aides work in a variety of settings, including clients' homes, group homes, and day services programs.

Home health aides and personal care aides help people with disabilities, chronic illness, or cognitive impairment by assisting in their daily living activities. They often help older adults who need assistance. Home health aides may be able to give a client medication or check the client's vital signs under the direction of a nurse or other health care practitioner.

Duties

Home health aides and personal care aides typically do the following:

- Assist clients in their daily personal tasks, such as bathing or dressing
- Housekeeping, such as laundry, washing dishes, and vacuuming
- Help to organize a client's schedule and plan appointments
- Arrange transportation to doctors' offices or other outings
- Shop for groceries and prepare meals to meet a client's dietary specifications
- Keep clients engaged in their social networks and communities

Home health aides may provide some basic health-related services (depending on the state they work in), such as checking a client's pulse, temperature, and respiration rate. They may also help with simple prescribed exercises and or with giving medications. Occasionally, they change bandages or dressings, give massages, care for skin, or help with braces and artificial limbs. With special training, experienced home health aides also may help with medical equipment such as ventilators, which help clients breathe.

Personal care aides—sometimes called caregivers or personal attendants—are generally limited to providing non-medical services, including companionship, cleaning, cooking, and driving.

Direct support professionals work with people who have developmental or intellectual disabilities. They may help create a behavior plan and teach self-care skills, such as doing laundry or cooking meals.

Certified home health or hospice agencies often receive payments from government programs and therefore must comply with regulations regarding aides' employment. Aides work under the direct supervision of medical professionals, usually nurses. These aides keep records of services performed and of clients' conditions and progress. They report changes in clients' conditions to supervisors or case managers, and work with therapists and other medical staff.

WORK ENVIRONMENT

Home health aides held about 911,500 jobs in 2016. The largest employers of home health aides were as follows:

Home health care services	45%
Services for the elderly and persons with disabilities	23
Continuing care retirement communities and assisted living facilities for the elderly	10
Residential intellectual and developmental disability facilities	6
Nursing care facilities (skilled nursing facilities)	3

Personal care aides held about 2.0 million jobs in 2016. The largest employers of personal care aides were as follows.

Services for the elderly and persons with disabilities	46%
Home health care services	15
Residential intellectual and developmental disability facilities	9
Continuing care retirement communities and assisted living facilities for the elderly	7
Private households	7

Most home health aides and personal care aides work in clients' homes; others work in small group homes or larger care communities. Some visit four or five clients in the same day, and others only work with one client all day—in some cases staying with one client on a long-term basis. They may work with other aides in shifts so that the client always has an aide. They help people in hospices and day services programs, and may travel as they also help people with disabilities go to work and stay engaged in their communities.

Injuries and Illnesses

Personal care aides have one of the highest rates of injuries and illnesses of all occupations. Home health aides have a higher rate of injuries and illnesses than the national average.

Work as a home health or personal care aide can be physically and emotionally demanding. Aides must guard against back injury because they often move clients into and out of bed or help them to stand or walk.

In addition, aides frequently work with clients who have cognitive impairments or mental health issues and who may display difficult or violent behaviors. Aides also face hazards from minor infections and exposure to communicable diseases, but can lessen their chance of infection by following proper procedurese.

Work Schedules

Most aides work full-time, others work part-time. They may be required to work evening and weekend hours, depending on their clients' needs.

HOW TO BECOME A HOME HEALTH AIDE OR PERSONAL CARE AIDE

Home health aides and personal care aides typically need a high school diploma or equivalent, though some positions do not require it. Those working in certified home health or hospice agencies must complete formal training and pass a standardized test.

Important Qualities

Detail oriented. Home health aides and personal care aides must adhere to specific rules and protocols and carefully follow instructions to help take care of clients. Aides must carefully follow instructions from health care professionals, such as how to care for wounds or how to identify changes in a client's condition.

Integrity. Home health aides and personal care aides should make clients feel comfortable when they tend to personal activities, such as helping a client bathe. In addition, aides must be dependable and trustworthy so that clients and their families can rely on them.

Interpersonal skills. Home health aides and personal care aides must work closely with clients. Sometimes, clients are in extreme pain or distress, and aides must be sensitive to their emotions. Aides must be compassionate, and they must enjoy helping people.

Physical stamina. Home health aides and personal care aides should be comfortable performing physical tasks. They might need to lift or turn clients.

EDUCATION

Home health aides and personal care aides typically need a high school diploma or equivalent, though some positions do not require it. There are also postsecondary nondegree award programs at community colleges and vocational schools.

Training

Home health aides and personal care aides may be trained in housekeeping tasks, such as cooking for clients who have special dietary needs. Aides may learn basic safety techniques, including how to respond in an emergency. Specific training may be needed for certification if state certification is required.

Training may be done on the job or through specialized programs. Training typically includes learning about personal hygiene, reading and recording vital signs, infection control, and basic nutrition.

In addition, clients have their own preferences, and aides may need time to become comfortable working with them.

Licenses, Certifications, and Registrations

Aides who work for agencies that receive reimbursement from Medicare or Medicaid must get a minimum level of training and pass a competency evaluation to be certified. Some states allow aides to take a competency exam in order to become certified without taking any training.

Additional requirements for certification vary by state. In some states, the only requirement for employment is on-the-job training, which employers generally provide. Other states require formal training, which is available from community colleges, vocational schools, elder care programs, and home health care agencies. In addition, states may conduct background checks on prospective aides. For specific state requirements, contact the state's health board.

Aides also may be required to obtain CPR certification.

Pay

The median annual wage for home health aides was $23,210 in May 2017. The lowest 10 percent earned less than $18,450, and the highest 10 percent earned more than $31,260.

Median annual wages, May 2017

Total, all occupations: $37,690

Home health aides: $23,210

Home health aides and personal care aides: $23,130

Personal care aides: $23,100

Note: All Occupations includes all occupations in the U.S. Economy. Source: U.S. Bureau of Labor Statistics, Occupational Employment Statistics

The median annual wage for personal care aides was $23,100 in May 2017. The lowest 10 percent earned less than $18,160, and the highest 10 percent earned more than $30,750.

In May 2017, the median annual wages for home health aides in the top industries in which they worked were as follows:

Nursing care facilities (skilled nursing facilities)	$24,360
Continuing care retirement communities and assisted living facilities for the elderly	23,760
Residential intellectual and developmental disability facilities	23,310
Services for the elderly and persons with disabilities	23,200
Home health care services	22,900

In May 2017, the median annual wages for personal care aides in the top industries in which they worked were as follows:

Residential intellectual and developmental disability facilities	$23,590
Continuing care retirement communities and assisted living facilities for the elderly	23,410
Services for the elderly and persons with disabilities	23,280
Home health care services	20,750

Most aides work full-time, others work part-time. They may be required to work evening and weekend hours in order to attend to clients' needs.

JOB OUTLOOK

Percent change in employment, projected 2016-26

Home health aides: 47%

Home health aides and personal care aides: 41%

Personal care aides: 39%

Total, all occupations: 7%

Note: All Occupations includes all occupations in the U.S. Economy. Source: U.S. Bureau of Labor Statistics, Employment Projections program

Overall employment of home health aides and personal care aides is projected to grow 41 percent from 2016 to 2026, much faster than the average for all occupations. As the baby-boom generation ages and the elderly population grows, the demand for the services of home health aides and personal care aides will continue to increase.

Elderly clients and people with disabilities are increasingly relying on home care as an alternative to nursing homes or hospitals. Families may prefer to keep aging family members in their homes rather than in nursing homes or hospitals. Clients who need help with everyday tasks and household chores, rather than medical care, may be able to reduce their medical expenses by staying in or returning to their homes.

JOB PROSPECTS

Job prospects for home health aides and personal care aides are excellent. These occupations are large and are projected to add many jobs. In addition, the low pay and high emotional demands may cause many workers to leave this occupation, and they will have to be replaced.

Employment projections data for home health aides and personal care aides, 2016-26

Occupational Title	Employment, 2016	Projected Employment, 2026	Change, 2016-26	
			Percent	Numeric
Home health aides and personal care aides	2,927,600	4,136,400	41	1,208,800
Home health aides	911,500	1,342,700	47	431,200
Personal care aides	2,016,100	2,793,800	39	777,600

SIMILAR OCCUPATIONS

This list shows occupations with job duties that are similar to those of home health aides and personal care aides

Childcare Workers: Childcare workers attend to the basic needs of children, such as dressing, bathing, feeding, and overseeing play. They may help younger children prepare for kindergarten or assist older children with homework.

Licensed Practical and Licensed Vocational Nurses: Licensed practical nurses (LPNs) and licensed vocational nurses (LVNs) provide basic nursing care. They work under the direction of registered nurses and doctors.

Medical Assistants: Medical assistants complete administrative and clinical tasks in the offices of physicians, hospitals, and other health care facilities. Their duties vary with the location, specialty, and size of the practice.

Nursing Assistants and Orderlies: Nursing assistants, sometimes called nursing aides, help provide basic care for patients in hospitals and residents of long-term care facilities, such as nursing homes. Orderlies transport patients and clean treatment areas.

Occupational Therapy Assistants and Aides: Occupational therapy assistants and aides help patients develop, recover, improve, as well as maintain the skills needed for daily living and working. Occupational therapy assistants are directly involved in providing therapy to patients; occupational therapy aides typically perform support activities. Both assistants and aides work under the direction of occupational therapists.

Physical Therapist Assistants and Aides: Physical therapist assistants, sometimes called PTAs, and physical therapist aides work under the direction and supervision of physical therapists. They help patients who are recovering from injuries and illnesses regain movement and manage pain.

Psychiatric Technicians and Aides: Psychiatric technicians and aides care for people who have mental illness and developmental disabilities. Technicians typically provide therapeutic care and monitor their patients' conditions. Aides help patients in their daily activities and ensure a safe, clean environment.

Registered Nurses: Registered nurses (RNs) provide and coordinate patient care, educate patients and the public about various health conditions, and provide advice and emotional support to patients and their family members.

Social and Human Service Assistants: Social and human service assistants provide client services, including support for families, in a wide variety of fields, such as psychology, rehabilitation, and social work. They assist other workers, such as social workers, and they help clients find benefits or community services.

Fast Fact

Home health care is growing by leaps and bounds. About 12,000 home health agencies exist, up from about 10,500 only ten years ago.
Source: insynchs.com

Conversation With . . .
MARY LOCK

LPN
In-home Licensed Practical Nurse

Mary Lock has been an in-home licensed practical nurse (LPN) for thirty-eight years and has worked in pediatric private duty for the last eight years at Maxim HealthCare in Raleigh, North Carolina.

1. What was your individual career path in terms of education/training, entry-level job, or other significant opportunity?

I had an interest in nursing from the age of five. One of my younger sisters had a high fever, so my family went to the emergency room. I was fascinated with the nurse who cared for my sister, and I don't even really remember what she did to help.

As a teenager, I served as an American Red Cross volunteer one summer at Womack Army Medical Center in Fort Bragg, North Carolina. I found out about this opportunity through my father, who served in the U. S Army for twenty-six years. Volunteering on a surgical floor and seeing what the nurses did influenced my decision to pursue nursing: it was their bedside manner, personal care, and involvement with the patients.

Professionally, I started out as a nursing assistant at Cape Fear Valley Medical Center in Fayetteville, North Carolina, after completing a three-month program at Fayetteville Technical Institute, now Fayetteville Technical Community College (FTCC). Then, I decided I wanted to do more in the field of nursing.

I returned to FTCC and graduated from the twelve-month Practical Nursing Program. As a licensed practical nurse (LPN), I continued at the same hospital and on the same floor where I had worked as a nursing assistant. In nursing, you are always continuing your education with in-services, hands-on demonstrations, and workshops.

I decided to change jobs and worked at the Veteran Affairs Hospital on the Oncology/Medical floor in the same city. I chose to work there because the benefits and pay were better.

In 1990, I began working in home health because it afforded me better hours and flexibility of time. I was able to be home with my three daughters and send them to school. I didn't need a babysitter. It turned out to be a good thing.

Home health nursing allowed me to see what happens when patients are discharged from the hospital as they make the transition to home. A vast amount of teaching needed to be done in the home to allow patients to live within the means of their illness, and prevent exacerbation of their illness and further hospitalization.

Currently, I work with a health care agency providing pediatric care in a home setting. These patients require twenty-four-hour skilled nursing care involving feeding, breathing, and moving.

2. What are the most important skills and/or qualities for someone in your profession?

The most important skills for someone in nursing are a willingness to learn, patience, the ability to work with all types of people, flexibility, and readiness for the unexpected. You need a real passion for the field of nursing. It isn't always the cleanest job, patients aren't always the friendliest, and families can be rude. But a good nurse can make a difference in any situation.

3. What do you wish you had known going into this profession?

I wish I had known that nothing goes as planned, your day can change instantly, and every nurse isn't always fair and honest. I didn't expect to have to work every holiday and almost every weekend. I didn't expect that I would work longer hours and sometimes in short-staffed situations. This also holds true in home health. Some people think that because you work in home health, you don't work weekends or holidays, although sometimes you still do.

I've learned a lot along the way in in-home health. Nursing is a constant, ever-changing profession where you're learning new trends and new information.

4. Are there many job opportunities in your profession? In what specific areas?

The field has diversified in recent years. There are many job opportunities in home health care. I can speak best to my home region in North Carolina, but there are a lot of agencies in Durham and Fayetteville that employ registered nurses, certified nursing assistants, and LPNs. They cover a wide variety of nursing such as geriatric, medical surgery, and pediatric.

For pediatric nursing-private duty, many agencies exist that only do pediatric cases.

There is more need for in-home health care because the hospitals aren't keeping patients as long, sending them home early. Insurance companies do not want to pay for long hospital stays because the cost is so high. That's where in-home health comes in. Patients are still in need of care, and home health nurses can teach families how to care for the patients, and instruct them on medicines they didn't have time to learn about in their short stay in the hospital. Home health can contribute to a faster recovery for patients and prevent them from going back to the hospital.

5. How do you see your profession changing in the next five years, how will technology impact that change, and what skills will be required?

Hospital admissions and hospital stays will decrease because home health nurses are able to go to the home and perform dressing changes on wounds, monitor patients, and report findings to the doctor. Problems that arise can be handled at home with teaching, and monitoring vital signs can be done via telehealth monitoring. A face-to-face visit can be done through a device such as a tablet where you can talk through video or send doctors notes about a patient via email. Earlier in my time as a nurse, we used computers to do face-to-face monitoring, now called telehealth monitoring. Tablets can also store lab results and notes from doctors about a patient.

The skills that will be required will be continuing education and agency in-services on changing trends in home health.

6. What do you enjoy most about your job? What do you enjoy least about your job?

I enjoy being able to make a positive difference in someone's life, and to be able to inform and teach patients and families about the disease process. By "process," I mean administration of medications, recognizing the signs and symptoms of the disease, and how to live within its boundaries.

The downside of home health nursing would be that the home environment isn't always clean and never sterile. You don't always have available supplies, and sometimes family members aren't always kind.

7. Can you suggest a valuable "try this" for students considering a career in your profession?

Nursing schools can create partnerships with home health agencies. Students who may want to pursue home health could shadow a nurse for a day or two. Students may also volunteer at a nursing home or a hospital that might help them decide if they are interested in nursing.

CONTACTS FOR MORE INFORMATION

For more information about home health aides and personal care aides, including voluntary credentials for aides, visit

American Society on Aging
https: //www.asaging.org/

National Association for Home Care & Hospice
https: //www.nahc.org/

Paraprofessional Healthcare Institute
https: //phinational.org/

O*NET
Home Health Aides
Personal Care Aides

SELECTED SCHOOLS

Many technical and community colleges offer programs in professional health care or pre-nursing. Interested students are advised to consult with a school guidance counselor or research area postsecondary schools. Also advisable is contacting your state health department and/or local American Red Cross along with hospitals, nursing homes, and residential care facilities to learn first-hand about training opportunities—and CNA certification—in your area.

MORE INFORMATION

American Health Care Association
1201 L Street NW
Washington, DC 20005
202.842.4444
www.ahcancal.org

National Association for Home Care and Hospice
228 7th Street SE
Washington, DC 20003
202.547.7424
pubs@nach.org
www.nahc.org

National Association of Health Care Assistants
501 E. 15th Street
Joplin, MO 64080
417.623.6049
www.nahcacares.org

National Network of Career Nursing Assistants
3577 Easton Road
Norton, OH 44203
330.825.0342
cna-network.org

Source: Bureau of Labor Statistics, U.S. Department of Labor, Occupational Outlook *Handbook*, Home Health Aides and Personal Care Aides, on the Internet at https: // www.bls.gov/ooh/healthcare/home-health-aides-and-personal-care-aides.htm (visited *January 22, 2019*).

Licensed Practical and Licensed Vocational Nurses

Snapshot

2017 Median Pay: $45,030 per year, $21.65 per hour

Typical Entry-Level Education: Postsecondary nondegree award

Career Cluster: Health science

On-the-job Training: None

Number of Jobs, 2016: 724,500

Job Outlook, 2016-26: 12% (Faster than average)

Employment Change, 2016-26: 88,900

Holland Score: IRC, IRS

CAREER OVERVIEW

Licensed practical nurses (LPNs) and licensed vocational nurses (LVNs) provide basic nursing care. They work under the direction of registered nurses and doctors. Licensed practical and licensed vocational nurses work in many settings, including nursing homes and extended care facilities, hospitals, physicians' offices, and private homes. Most work full time. Licensed practical and licensed

vocational nurses must complete a state-approved educational program, which typically takes about 1 year to complete. They must be licensed.

Duties

Licensed practical and licensed vocational nurses typically do the following:

- Monitor patients' health—for example, by checking their blood pressure
- Administer basic patient care, including changing bandages and inserting catheters
- Provide for the basic comfort of patients, such as helping them bathe or dress
- Discuss the care they are providing with patients and listen to their concerns
- Report patients' status and concerns to registered nurses and doctors
- Keep records on patients' health

Duties of LPNs and LVNs vary, depending on their work setting and the state in which they work. For example, they may reinforce teaching done by registered nurses regarding how family members should care for a relative; help to deliver, care for, and feed infants; collect samples for testing and do routine laboratory tests; or feed patients who need help eating.

LPNs and LVNs may be limited to doing certain tasks, depending on the state where they work. For example, in some states, LPNs with proper training can give medication or start intravenous (IV) drips, but in other states LPNs cannot perform these tasks. State regulations also govern the extent to which LPNs and LVNs must be directly supervised. For example, an LPN may provide certain forms of care only with instructions from a registered nurse.

In some states, experienced licensed practical and licensed vocational nurses supervise and direct other LPNs or LVNs and unlicensed medical staff.

WORK ENVIRONMENT

Licensed practical and licensed vocational nurses held about 724,500 jobs in 2016. The largest employers of licensed practical and licensed vocational nurses were as follows:

Nursing and residential care facilities	38%
Hospitals; state, local, and private	16
Offices of physicians	13
Home health care services	12
Government	7

Nurses must often be on their feet for much of the day. They are vulnerable to back injuries, because they may have to lift patients who have trouble moving in bed, standing, or walking. These duties can be stressful, as can dealing with ill and injured people.

Work Schedules

Most licensed practical and licensed vocational nurses (LPNs and LVNs) work full time, although about 1 in 5 worked part time in 2016. Many work nights, weekends, and holidays, because medical care takes place at all hours. They may be required to work shifts of longer than 8 hours.

HOW TO BECOME A LICENSED PRACTICAL OR LICENSED VOCATIONAL NURSE

Becoming a licensed practical or licensed vocational nurse (LPN or LVN) requires completing an approved educational program. LPNs and LVNs must have a license.

Important Qualities

Compassion. Licensed practical and licensed vocational nurses must be empathetic and caring toward the people they serve.

Detail oriented. LPNs and LVNs need to be responsible and detail oriented, because they must make sure that patients get the correct care at the right time.

Interpersonal skills. Interacting with patients and other health care providers is a big part of their jobs, so LPNs and LVNs need good interpersonal skills.

Patience. Dealing with sick and injured people may be stressful. LPNs and LVNs should be patient, so they can cope with any stress that stems from providing care to these patients.

Physical stamina. LPNs and LVNs should be comfortable performing physical tasks, such as bending over patients for a long time.

Speaking skills. It is important that LPNs and LVNs communicate effectively. For example, they may need to relay information about a patient's current condition to a registered nurse.

Education

LPNs and LVNs must complete an approved educational program. These programs award a certificate or diploma and typically take about 1 year to complete, but may take longer. They are commonly found in technical schools and community colleges, although some programs may be available in high schools or hospitals.

Practical nursing programs combine classroom learning in subjects such as nursing, biology, and pharmacology. All programs also include supervised clinical experience.

Contact state boards of nursing for lists of approved programs.

Licenses, Certifications, and Registrations

After completing a state-approved educational program, prospective LPNs and LVNs can take the National Council Licensure Examination (NCLEX-PN). In all states, they must pass the exam to get a license and work as an LPN or LVN. For more information on the NCLEX-PN examination and a list of state boards of nursing, visit the National Council of State Boards of Nursing.

LPNs and LVNs may choose to become certified through professional associations in areas such as gerontology and intravenous (IV) therapy. Certifications show that an LPN or LVN has an advanced level of knowledge about a specific subject.

In addition, employers may prefer to hire candidates who are trained to provide cardiopulmonary resuscitation (CPR).

ADVANCEMENT

With experience, licensed practical and licensed vocational nurses may advance to supervisory positions. Some LPNs and LVNs advance to other health care occupations. For example, an LPN may complete a LPN to RN education program to become a registered nurse.

Pay

The median annual wage for licensed practical and licensed vocational nurses was $45,030 in May 2017. The lowest 10 percent earned less than $32,970, and the highest 10 percent earned more than $61,030.

Median annual wages, May 2017

Licensed practical and licensed vocational nurses: $45,030%

Health technologists and technicians: $43,590

Total, all occupations: $37,690

Note: All Occupations includes all occupations in the U.S. Economy. Source: U.S. Bureau of Labor Statistics, Occupational Employment Statistics

In May 2017, the median annual wages for licensed practical and licensed vocational nurses in the top industries in which they worked were as follows:

Government	$46,660
Nursing and residential care facilities	46,280
Home health care services	45,220
Hospitals; state, local, and private	43,550
Offices of physicians	41,270

Most licensed practical and licensed vocational nurses (LPNs and LVNs) work full time, although about 1 in 5 worked part time in 2016. Many work nights, weekends, and holidays, because medical care takes place at all hours. They may be required to work shifts of longer than 8 hours.

JOB OUTLOOK

Employment of licensed practical and licensed vocational nurses (LPNs and LVNs) is projected to grow 12 percent from 2016 to 2026, faster than the average for all occupations.

Percent change in employment, Projected 2016-26

Health technologists and technicians: 14%

Licensed practical and licensed vocational nurses: 12%

Total, all occupations: 7%

Note: All Occupations includes all occupations in the U.S. Economy. Source: U.S. Bureau of Labor Statistics, Employment Projections program

As the baby-boom population ages, the overall need for health care services is expected to increase. LPNs and LVNs will be needed in residential care facilities and in home health environments to care for older patients.

A number of chronic conditions, such as diabetes and obesity, have become more prevalent in recent years. LPNs and LVNs will be needed to assist and care for patients with chronic conditions in skilled nursing and other extended care facilities. In addition, many procedures that once could be done only in hospitals are now being done outside of hospitals, creating demand in other settings, such as outpatient care centers.

JOB PROSPECTS

Job prospects should be favorable for LPNs and LVNs who are willing to work in rural and medically underserved areas. Employers also may prefer candidates who have certification in a specialty area such as gerontology or intravenous (IV) therapy.

Employment projections data for
licensed practical and licensed vocational nurses, 2016-26

Occupational Title	Employment, 2016	Projected Employment, 2026	Change, 2016-26	
			Percent	Numeric
Licensed practical and licensed vocational nurses	724,500	813,400	12	88,900

Note: U.S. Bureau of Labor Statistics, Employment Projections program

Fast Fact

The United States saw its first school of nursing established in 1862. The first nurse to earn a nursing diploma in the United States did so in 1873.

Source: monster.com

Famous First

Notes on Nursing: What it is and What it is Not is a book first published by Florence Nightingale in 1859. A 76-page volume with 3-page appendix published by Harrison of Pall Mall, it was intended to give hints on nursing to those entrusted with the health of others. Florence Nightingale stressed that it was not meant to be a comprehensive guide from which to teach one's self to be a nurse but to help in the practice of treating others.

Nightingale wrote about many of the essential beliefs of the natural hygiene movement. She referred to these hygienic beliefs as the "*laws of life*" that would give mothers knowledge of "*how to give their children healthy existences.*" Further, she clearly placed the comfort and needs of the patient ahead of the thoughtless pursuit of science; a trait which is more commonly associated today with alternative medicine than it is with conventional medicine.

Source: http://naturalhealthperspective.com/tutorials/notes-on-nursing.html

SIMILAR OCCUPATIONS

This list shows occupations with job duties that are similar to those of licensed practical and licensed vocational nurses.

Nursing Assistants and Orderlies: Nursing assistants, sometimes called *nursing aides*, help provide basic care for patients in hospitals and residents of long-term care facilities, such as nursing homes. Orderlies transport patients and clean treatment areas.

Occupational Therapy Assistants and Aides: Occupational therapy assistants and aides help patients develop, recover, improve, as well as maintain the skills needed for daily living and working. Occupational therapy assistants are directly involved in providing therapy to patients; occupational therapy aides typically perform support activities. Both assistants and aides work under the direction of occupational therapists.

Physical Therapist Assistants and Aides: Physical therapist assistants, sometimes called *PTAs*, and physical therapist aides work under the direction and supervision of physical therapists. They help patients who are recovering from injuries and illnesses regain movement and manage pain.

Psychiatric Technicians and Aides: Psychiatric technicians and aides care for people who have mental illness and developmental disabilities. Technicians typically provide therapeutic care and monitor their patients' conditions. Aides help patients in their daily activities and ensure a safe, clean environment.

Registered Nurses: Registered nurses (RNs) provide and coordinate patient care, educate patients and the public about various health conditions, and provide advice and emotional support to patients and their family members.

Surgical Technologists: Surgical technologists, also called *operating room technicians*, assist in surgical operations. They prepare operating rooms, arrange equipment, and help doctors during surgeries.

Medical Assistants: Medical assistants complete administrative and clinical tasks in the offices of physicians, hospitals, and other health care facilities. Their duties vary with the location, specialty, and size of the practice.

CONTACTS FOR MORE INFORMATION

For more information about licensed practical or licensed vocational nurses, visit

National Association of Licensed Practical Nurses
https://nalpn.org/

For more information about the National Council Licensure Examination (NCLEX-PN) and a list of individual state boards of nursing, visit

National Council of State Boards of Nursing
https://www.ncsbn.org/

Medical and Health Services Managers

Snapshot

2017 Median Pay: $98,350 per year, $47.29 per hour

Typical Entry-Level Education: Bachelor's degree

Career Cluster: Health science

On-the-job Training: None

Number of Jobs, 2016: 352,200

Job Outlook, 2016-26: 20% (Much faster than average)

Employment Change, 2016-26: 72,100

Holland Score: ESA, ESI

CAREER OVERVIEW

Medical and health services managers, also called *health care executives or health care administrators*, plan, direct, and coordinate medical and health services. They may manage an entire facility, a specific clinical area or department, or a medical practice for a group of physicians. Medical and health services managers must adapt to changes in health care laws, regulations, and technology.

Duties

Medical and health services managers typically do the following:

- Improve efficiency and quality in delivering health care services
- Develop departmental goals and objectives
- Ensure that the facility in which they work is up to date on and compliant with laws and regulations
- Recruit, train, and supervise staff members
- Manage the finances of the facility, such as patient fees and billing
- Create work schedules
- Prepare and monitor budgets and spending to ensure departments operate within funding limits
- Represent the facility at investor meetings or on governing boards
- Keep and organize records of the facility's services, such as the number of inpatient beds used
- Communicate with members of the medical staff and department heads

Medical and health services managers work closely with physicians and surgeons, registered nurses, medical and clinical laboratory technologists and technicians, and other health care workers. Others may interact with patients or insurance agents.

Medical and health services managers' titles depend on the facility or area of expertise in which they work.

The following are examples of types of medical and health services managers:

Nursing home administrators manage staff, admissions, finances, and care of the building, as well as care of the residents in nursing homes. All states require licensure for nursing home administrators; licensing requirements vary by state.

Clinical managers oversee a specific department, such as nursing, surgery, or physical therapy, and have responsibilities based on that specialty. Clinical managers set and carry out policies, goals, and procedures for their departments; evaluate the quality of the staff's work; and develop reports and budgets.

Health information managers are responsible for the maintenance and security of all patient records and data. They must stay up to date with evolving information technology, current or proposed laws about health information systems, and trends in managing large amounts of complex data. Health information managers must ensure that databases are complete, accurate, and accessible only to authorized personnel. They also may supervise the work of medical records and health information technicians.

WORK ENVIRONMENT

Medical and health services managers held about 352,200 jobs in 2016. The largest employers of medical and health services managers were as follows:

Hospitals; state, local, and private	36%
Offices of physicians	11
Nursing and residential care facilities	10
Government	8
Outpatient care centers	7

Most medical and health services managers work in offices.

Work Schedules

Most medical and health services managers work full time. About 3 in 10 managers worked more than 40 hours per week in 2016. Work during evenings or weekends may be required in health care settings that are open at all hours, such as hospitals and nursing homes. Medical and health services managers may need to be on call in case of emergencies.

HOW TO BECOME A MEDICAL OR HEALTH SERVICES MANAGER

Most medical and health services managers have at least a bachelor's degree before entering the field. However, master's degrees are common and sometimes preferred by employers. Educational requirements vary by facility and specific function.

Important Qualities

Analytical skills. Medical and health services managers must understand and follow current regulations and adapt to new laws.

Communication skills. These managers must effectively communicate policies and procedures to other health professionals and ensure their staff's compliance with new laws and regulations.

Detail oriented. Medical and health services managers must pay attention to detail. They might be required to organize and maintain scheduling and billing information for very large facilities, such as hospitals.

Interpersonal skills. Medical and health services managers discuss staffing problems and patient information with other professionals, such as physicians and health insurance representatives.

Leadership skills. These managers are often responsible for finding creative solutions to staffing or other administrative problems. They must hire, train, motivate, and lead staff.

Technical skills. Medical and health services managers must stay up to date with advances in health care technology and data analytics. For example, they may need to use coding and classification software and electronic health record (EHR) systems as their facility adopts these technologies.

EDUCATION

Medical and health services managers typically need at least a bachelor's degree to enter the occupation. However, master's degrees are common and sometimes preferred by employers. Graduate programs often last between 2 and 3 years and may include up to 1 year of supervised administrative experience in a hospital or health care consulting setting.

Prospective medical and health services managers typically have a degree in health administration, health management, nursing, public health administration, or business administration. Degrees that focus on both management and health care combine business-related courses with courses in medical terminology, hospital organization, and health information systems. For example, a degree in health administration or health information management often includes courses in health services management, accounting and budgeting, human resources administration, strategic planning, law and ethics, health economics, and health information systems.

Work Experience in a Related Occupation

Many employers require prospective medical and health services managers to have some work experience in either an administrative or a clinical role in a hospital or other health care facility. For example, nursing home administrators usually have years of experience working as a registered nurse.

Others may begin their careers as medical records and health information technicians, administrative assistants, or financial clerks within a health care office.

Licenses, Certifications, and Registrations

All states require licensure for nursing home administrators; requirements vary by state. In most states, these administrators must have a bachelor's degree, complete a state-approved training program, and pass a national licensing exam. Some states also require applicants to pass a state-specific exam; others may require applicants to have previous work experience in a health care facility. Some states also require licensure for administrators in assisted-living facilities. For information on specific state-by-state licensure requirements, visit the National Association of Long Term Care Administrator Boards.

A license is typically not required in other areas of medical and health services management. However, some positions may require applicants to have a registered nurse or social worker license.

Although certification is not required, some managers choose to become certified. Certification is available in many areas of practice. For example, the Professional Association of Health Care Office Management offers certification in medical management, the American Health Information Management Association offers health information management certification, and the American College of Health Care Administrators offers the Certified Nursing Home Administrator and Certified Assisted Living Administrator distinctions.

ADVANCEMENT

Advancement

Medical and health services managers advance by moving into higher paying positions with more responsibility. Some health information managers, for example, can advance to become responsible for the entire hospital's information systems. Other managers may advance to top executive positions within the organization. Advancement to top level executive positions usually requires a master's degree.

Pay

The median annual wage for medical and health services managers was $98,350 in May 2017. The lowest 10 percent earned less than $58,350, and the highest 10 percent earned more than $176,130.

Median annual wages, May 2017

Medical and health services managers: $98,350

Other management occupations: $88,720

Total, all occupations: $37,690

Note: All Occupations includes all occupations in the U.S. Economy. Source: U.S. Bureau of Labor Statistics, Occupational Employment Statistics

In May 2017, the median annual wages for medical and health services managers in the top industries in which they worked were as follows:

Hospitals; state, local, and private	$107,230
Government	106,230
Outpatient care centers	89,910
Offices of physicians	89,760
Nursing and residential care facilities	82,950

Most medical and health services managers work full time. About 3 in 10 managers worked more than 40 hours per week in 2016. Work during evenings or weekends may be required in health care settings such as hospitals and nursing homes, which are open at all hours. Medical and health services managers may need to be on call in case of emergencies

JOB OUTLOOK

Employment of medical and health services managers is projected to grow 20 percent from 2016 to 2026, much faster than the average for all occupations. As the large baby-boom population ages and people remain active later in life, there should be increased demand for health care services.

Percent change in employment, projected 2016-26

Medical and health services managers: 20%

Other management occupations: 8%

Total, all occupations: 7%

Note: All Occupations includes all occupations in the U.S. Economy. Source: U.S. Bureau of Labor Statistics, Employment Projections program

This means greater needs for physicians and other health care workers, medical procedures, and health care facilities, and therefore greater needs for managers who organize and manage medical information and health care staff. There should also be increased demand for nursing care facility administrators as the population grows older.

Employment is projected to grow in offices of health practitioners. Many services previously provided in hospitals will shift to these settings, especially as medical technologies improve. Demand in medical group practice management is projected to grow as medical group practices become larger and more complex.

In addition, widespread use of electronic health records (EHRs) will continue to create demand for managers with knowledge of health information technology (IT) and informatics systems. Medical and health services managers will be needed to organize, manage, and integrate these records across areas of the health care industry

Fast Fact

The number of men going into nursing has risen, and is now almost ten percent of the RN workforce. That's triple the number in 1970.

Source: usnews.com

JOB PROSPECTS

Job prospects for medical and health services managers are likely to be favorable. In addition to rising employment demand, the need to replace managers who retire over the next decade will result in some openings. Candidates with a master's degree in health administration or a related field, as well as knowledge of health care IT systems, will likely have the best prospects.

Employment projections data for medical and health services managers, 2016-26

Occupational Title	Employment, 2016	Projected Employment, 2026	Change, 2016-26	
			Percent	Numeric
Medical and health services managers	352,200	424,300	20	72,100

Source: U.S. Bureau of Labor Statistics, Employment Projections program

Famous First

Lenah H. Sutcliffe Higbee (May 18, 1874 – January 10, 1941) was a pioneering Canadian-born United States Navy chief nurse. She was one of the first nurses to join the U.S. Navy Nurse Corps when it was established in 1908. Lenah Higbee was quickly appointed Chief Nurse and, a few years later, was promoted to Superintendent of the Nurse Corps, the second woman to hold the position.

Higbee was the first female to be awarded the Navy Cross, for her unusual and conspicuous devotion to duty during WWI. And after her death, a naval combat ship was named USS *Higbee* in her honor. It was the first time a naval vessel had been named after a female service member.

Source: https://en.wikipedia.org/wiki/Lenah_Higbee

SIMILAR OCCUPATIONS

This list shows occupations with job duties that are similar to those of medical and health services managers.

Administrative Services Managers: Administrative services managers plan, direct, and coordinate supportive services of an organization. Their specific responsibilities vary, but administrative service managers typically maintain facilities and supervise activities that include recordkeeping, mail distribution, and office upkeep.

Computer and Information Systems Managers: Computer and information systems managers, often called information technology (IT) managers or IT project managers, plan, coordinate, and direct computer-related activities in an organization. They help determine the information technology goals of an organization and are responsible for implementing computer systems to meet those goals.

Financial Managers: Financial managers are responsible for the financial health of an organization. They produce financial reports, direct investment activities, and develop strategies and plans for the long-term financial goals of their organization.

Human Resources Managers: Human resources managers plan, direct, and coordinate the administrative functions of an organization. They oversee the recruiting, interviewing, and hiring of new staff; consult with top executives on strategic planning; and serve as a link between an organization's management and its employees.

Insurance Underwriters: Insurance underwriters decide whether to provide insurance, and under what terms. They evaluate insurance applications and determine coverage amounts and premiums.

Medical Records and Health Information Technicians: Medical records and *health information technicians*, commonly referred to as health information technicians, organize and manage health information data. They ensure that the information maintains its quality, accuracy, accessibility, and security in both paper files and electronic systems. They use various classification systems to code and categorize patient information for insurance reimbursement purposes, for databases and registries, and to maintain patients' medical and treatment histories.

Social and Community Service Managers: Social and community service managers coordinate and supervise social service programs and community organizations. They manage workers who provide social services to the public.

Top Executives: Top executives devise strategies and policies to ensure that an organization meets its goals. They plan, direct, and coordinate operational activities of companies and organizations.

Purchasing Managers, Buyers, and Purchasing Agents: Buyers and purchasing agents buy products and services for organizations to use or resell. Purchasing managers oversee the work of buyers and purchasing agents.

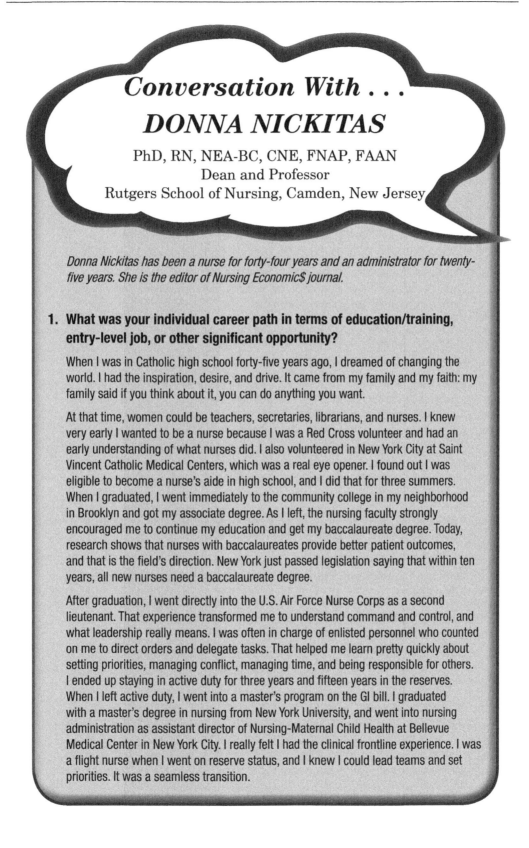

Conversation With . . .
DONNA NICKITAS

PhD, RN, NEA-BC, CNE, FNAP, FAAN
Dean and Professor
Rutgers School of Nursing, Camden, New Jersey

Donna Nickitas has been a nurse for forty-four years and an administrator for twenty-five years. She is the editor of Nursing Economic$ journal.

1. What was your individual career path in terms of education/training, entry-level job, or other significant opportunity?

When I was in Catholic high school forty-five years ago, I dreamed of changing the world. I had the inspiration, desire, and drive. It came from my family and my faith: my family said if you think about it, you can do anything you want.

At that time, women could be teachers, secretaries, librarians, and nurses. I knew very early I wanted to be a nurse because I was a Red Cross volunteer and had an early understanding of what nurses did. I also volunteered in New York City at Saint Vincent Catholic Medical Centers, which was a real eye opener. I found out I was eligible to become a nurse's aide in high school, and I did that for three summers. When I graduated, I went immediately to the community college in my neighborhood in Brooklyn and got my associate degree. As I left, the nursing faculty strongly encouraged me to continue my education and get my baccalaureate degree. Today, research shows that nurses with baccalaureates provide better patient outcomes, and that is the field's direction. New York just passed legislation saying that within ten years, all new nurses need a baccalaureate degree.

After graduation, I went directly into the U.S. Air Force Nurse Corps as a second lieutenant. That experience transformed me to understand command and control, and what leadership really means. I was often in charge of enlisted personnel who counted on me to direct orders and delegate tasks. That helped me learn pretty quickly about setting priorities, managing conflict, managing time, and being responsible for others. I ended up staying in active duty for three years and fifteen years in the reserves. When I left active duty, I went into a master's program on the GI bill. I graduated with a master's degree in nursing from New York University, and went into nursing administration as assistant director of Nursing-Maternal Child Health at Bellevue Medical Center in New York City. I really felt I had the clinical frontline experience. I was a flight nurse when I went on reserve status, and I knew I could lead teams and set priorities. It was a seamless transition.

Even though my master's degree was in nursing education, I had the opportunity to do clinical leadership in acute care, as well be a preceptor for graduate students doing leadership at Hunter-Bellevue School of Nursing at the City University of New York (CUNY). A faculty member who wrote a grant to create a curriculum for middle managers asked me to teach full time. I was at Hunter for thirty years. I loved teaching and the opportunity to build the next generation of nurse clinicians, and not only to prepare them for clinical work, but to be registered nurses governed by policy. States grant nursing licenses, and there are rules, regulations, and standards of care we are obligated to fulfill to advance the health of the nation.

One of the essential skills of being an academic is that you're a scholar and you disseminate scholarship. Starting with being asked to review manuscripts for a journal, I have expanded in this area and now am the editor of *Nursing Economic$*.

The driving force of being the editor is that it gives me legitimacy to use my words, voice, and values to change the world in perpetuity. My words are printed and systematically put into databases such as PubMed. I take my editorials very seriously because I know they are going to be impactful.

In my role as *Nursing Economic$* editor, I clearly see the business case for caring. That's what nurses do, right? The journal tries to measure the impact of quality on the patient's side in terms of the services we provide.

For ten years prior to coming to Rutgers, I was the executive officer for doctoral education for the nursing program at CUNY. It was the same work a dean does: allocating resources, providing student services, and managing a budget, curriculum, and faculty. I was recruited for the position of dean and professor of Rutgers, which I began about six months ago. I had been in a large public urban institution in New York, and that is the case here in Camden. We have many first-generation college students, and I understand the dynamics of being in a large, diverse city. I was very comfortable transitioning and feel I can make a difference.

Where you think you're going to start is not always where you think you're going to end up, and that is one of the beautiful things about being an RN.

2. What are the most important skills and/or qualities for someone in your profession?

If you are in leadership, you need to be an astute listener, effective communicator, and know how to make your case. Sometimes you think you have the answer, but you'd better make sure you have your facts. If not, the best option is to say, "I don't have what you're asking but I'll get back to you." Also, accept you're going to make mistakes.

All undergraduate nursing programs offer leadership in their curriculum. Regardless of whether you are a formal leader or an informal leader, there's a set of skills you need as a nurse on the front line as part of a team, or as a working supervisor: you have to manage time, conflicts, understand priorities, oversee emergencies, and make spot decisions with good clinical judgment and critical thinking skills. Most important, you need to have strong relational skills. Can you work with others?

3. What do you wish you had known going into this profession?

I wish as a young nurse I had known the level of influence policy and politics have in health care. Circumstances may include scarce resources or staff shortages, and your patients' care and safety must be your utmost priority. It's the same in academics: for my faculty, my staff, or my students, I always keep their best interests at heart and make the right decisions at the right time given the resources I have.

4. Are there many job opportunities in your profession? In what specific areas?

There is no better time to be a nurse than right now. It affords you a living wage where you can sustain yourself and your family, and, in many cases, it lifts people out of poverty. There are lots of opportunities, especially as Baby Boomers age.

In nurse administration, broadly speaking, I think there's room for everyone at the top, but not everybody wants to go to the top. You can be an informal leader or a designated leader; the skillsets are complementary. Those who decide to be a formal leader need advanced degrees, either a master's or doctorate.

5. How do you see your profession changing in the next five years, how will technology impact that change, and what skills will be required?

The biggest change is the increase in telemedicine. Patients will not always receive care in a doctor's office or hospital. We will be able to take care of patients where they live, work, and play. Using the telephone, Skype, or some other mechanism, patients will share their weight, blood pressure, glucose, or other results via machines in their homes. We're using clinical simulation in our classrooms and labs.

6. What do you enjoy most about your job? What do you enjoy least about your job?

The most important thing is our human dynamics: to be able to change a student's life, one at a time, and to train the next generation of nurse clinicians or researchers. What job is better?

However, there's never enough time. The thing that gets in the way is technology, such as email.

7. Can you suggest a valuable "try this" for students considering a career in your profession?

If you don't know a nurse, find one you can talk to. A lot of people think they get what nurses do, but what they don't understand is the sheer depth of what nurses know and the high-level skills they have. My nursing students will come in and say, "I didn't think it was going to be this hard." I say, "Remove that word from your vocabulary." Being in college is hard, being in nursing is vigorous.

Volunteer where you have the opportunity to work with individuals, whether it's the American Red Cross, a health literacy program, a local food bank, or a homeless shelter. Work where people are most vulnerable and need service. Ask yourself, "Can I help?"

CONTACTS FOR MORE INFORMATION

For more information about medical and health care management, visit

Professional Association of Health Care Office Management
www.cms.gov

American College of Health Care Administrators
https: //achca.memberclicks.net/

American Health Information Management Association
http: //www.ahima.org/

For more information about academic programs in this field, visit

Association of University Programs in Health Administration
www.aupha.org/

Commission on Accreditation of Healthcare Management Education
www.cahme.org

For information about career opportunities in health care management, visit

American College of Healthcare Executives
https: //www.ache.org/

For information about career opportunities in medical group practices and ambulatory care management, visit

Medical Group Management Association
https: //www.mgma.com/

For more information about licensure and training requirements for nursing home and assisted-living facility administrators, visit

National Association of Long Term Care Administrator Boards
https: //www.nabweb.org/

Medical Assistants

Snapshot

2017 Median Pay: $32,480 per year , $15.61 per hour

Typical Entry-Level Education: Postsecondary nondegree award

Career Cluster: Health science

On-the-job Training: None

Number of Jobs, 2016: 634,400

Job Outlook, 2016-26: 29% (Much faster than average)

Employment Change, 2016-26: 183,900

Holland Score: ESI, ERI

CAREER OVERVIEW

Medical assistants complete administrative and clinical tasks in the offices of physicians, hospitals, and other health care facilities. Their duties vary with the location, specialty, and size of the practice. Most medical assistants work in physicians' offices, hospitals, outpatient clinics, and other health care facilities. Most medical assistants have postsecondary education such as a certificate. Others enter the occupation with a high school diploma and learn through on-the-job training.

Duties

Medical assistants typically do the following:

- Record patient history and personal information
- Measure vital signs, such as blood pressure
- Help physicians with patient examinations
- Give patients injections or medications as directed by physicians and as permitted by state law
- Schedule patient appointments
- Prepare blood samples for laboratory tests
- Enter patient information into medical records

Medical assistants take and record patients' personal information. They must be able to keep that information confidential and discuss it only with other medical personnel who are involved in treating the patient.

Electronic health records (EHRs) are changing some medical assistants' jobs. More and more physicians are adopting EHRs, moving all their patient information from paper to electronic records. Assistants need to learn the EHR software that their office uses.

Medical assistants should not be confused with physician assistants, who examine, diagnose, and treat patients under a physician's supervision.

In larger practices or hospitals, medical assistants may specialize in either administrative or clinical work.

Administrative medical assistants often fill out insurance forms or code patients' medical information. They often answer telephones and schedule patient appointments.

Clinical medical assistants have different duties, depending on the state where they work. They may do basic laboratory tests, dispose of contaminated supplies, and sterilize medical instruments. They may have additional responsibilities, such as instructing patients about medication or special diets, preparing patients for x rays, removing stitches, drawing blood, or changing dressings.

Some medical assistants specialize according to the type of medical office where they work. The following are examples of *specialized medical assistants*:

- *Ophthalmic medical assistants and optometric assistants* help ophthalmologists and optometrists provide eye care. They show patients how to insert, remove, and care for contact lenses. Ophthalmic medical assistants also may help an ophthalmologist in surgery.
- *Podiatric medical assistants* work closely with podiatrists (foot doctors). They may make castings of feet, expose and develop x rays, and help podiatrists in surgery.

WORK ENVIRONMENT

Medical assistants held about 634,400 jobs in 2016. The largest employers of medical assistants were as follows:

Offices of physicians	57%
Hospitals; state, local, and private	15
Outpatient care centers	9
Offices of chiropractors	4

Work Schedules

Most medical assistants work full time. Some work evenings, weekends, or holidays to cover shifts in medical facilities that are always open.

Fast Fact

First Lady Mary Todd Lincoln was a volunteer nurse at Union hospitals during the Civil War.

Source: nursebuff.com

HOW TO BECOME A MEDICAL ASSISTANT

Most medical assistants have a postsecondary education award such as a certificate. Others enter the occupation with a high school diploma and learn through on-the-job training.

Important Qualities

Analytical skills. Medical assistants must be able to understand and follow medical charts and diagnoses. They may be required to code a patient's medical records for billing purposes.

Detail oriented. Medical assistants need to be precise when taking vital signs or recording patient information. Physicians and insurance companies rely on accurate records.

Interpersonal skills. Medical assistants need to be able to discuss patient information with other medical personnel, such as physicians. They often interact with patients who may be in pain or in distress, so they need to be able to act in a calm and professional manner.

Technical skills. Medical assistants should be able to use basic clinical instruments so they can take a patient's vital signs, such as heart rate and blood pressure.

EDUCATION

Medical assistants typically graduate from postsecondary education programs. Although there are no formal educational requirements for becoming a medical assistant in most states, employers may prefer to hire assistants who have completed these programs.

Programs for medical assisting are available from community colleges, vocational schools, technical schools, and universities and take about 1 year to complete. These programs usually lead to a certificate or

diploma. Some community colleges offer 2-year programs that lead
to an associate's degree. All programs have classroom and laboratory
portions that include lessons in anatomy and medical terminology.

Some medical assistants have a high school diploma or equivalent
and learn their duties on the job. High school students interested
in a career as a medical assistant should take courses in biology,
chemistry, and anatomy, and possibly business and computers.

Training

Medical assistants who do not have postsecondary education
certificates learn their skills through on-the-job training. Physicians
or other medical assistants may teach a new assistant medical
terminology, the names of the instruments, how to do daily tasks,
how to interact with patients, and other tasks that help keep an office
running smoothly. Medical assistants also learn how to code both
paper and electronic health records (EHRs) and how to record patient
information. It can take several months for an assistant to complete
training, depending on the facility.

Licenses, Certifications, and Registrations

Medical assistants are not required to be certified in most states.
However, employers may prefer to hire certified assistants.

Several organizations offer certification. An applicant must pass an
exam and have taken one of several routes to be eligible for each
certification. These routes include graduation from an accredited
program and work experience, among others. In most cases,
an applicant must be at least 18 years old before applying for
certification.

The National Commission for Certifying Agencies, part of the Institute
for Credentialing Excellence, accredits five certifications for medical
assistants:

- Certified Medical Assistant (CMA) from the American Association
  of Medical Assistants
- Registered Medical Assistant (RMA) from American Medical
  Technologists
- National Certified Medical Assistant (NCMA) from the National
  Center for Competency Testing

- Certified Clinical Medical Assistant (CCMA) from the National Healthcareer Association
- Certified Medical Administrative Assistant (CMAA) from the National Healthcareer Association

Some states may require assistants to graduate from an accredited program, pass an exam, or both, in order to practice. Contact the state board of medicine for more information.

ADVANCEMENT

With experience, medical assistants can specialize and move into leadership roles. With more education they may advance into other health care occupations such as registered nurse, physician assistant, or nurse practitioner.

Pay

The median annual wage for medical assistants was $32,480 in May 2017. The lowest 10 percent earned less than $23,830, and the highest 10 percent earned more than $45,900.

Median annual wages, May 2017

Total, all occupations: $37,690

Other health care support occupations: $33,920

Medical assistants: $32,480

Note: All Occupations includes all occupations in the U.S. Economy. Source: U.S. Bureau of Labor Statistics, Occupational Employment Statistics

In May 2017, the median annual wages for medical assistants in the top industries in which they worked were as follows:

Outpatient care centers	$33,820
Hospitals; state, local, and private	33,590
Offices of physicians	32,710
Offices of chiropractors	29,010

Most medical assistants work full time. Some work evenings, weekends, or holidays to cover shifts in medical facilities that are always open.

JOB OUTLOOK

Employment of medical assistants is projected to grow 29 percent from 2016 to 2026, much faster than the average for all occupations. The growth of the aging baby-boom population will continue to increase demand for preventive medical services, which are often provided by physicians. As a result, physicians will hire more assistants to perform routine administrative and clinical duties, allowing the physicians to see more patients.

Percent change in employment, projected 2016-26

Medical assistants: 29%

Other health care support occupations: 22%

Total, all occupations: 7%

Note: All Occupations includes all occupations in the U.S. Economy. Source: U.S. Bureau of Labor Statistics, Employment Projections program

An increasing number of group practices, clinics, and other health care facilities will also need support workers, particularly medical assistants, to complete both administrative and clinical duties. Medical assistants work mostly in primary care, a steadily growing sector of the health care industry.

JOB PROSPECTS

Medical assistants are expected to have good job prospects; however, those who earn certification and have familiarity with electronic health records (EHRs) may have better job prospects.

Employment projections data for medical assistants, 2016-26

Occupational Title	Employment, 2016	Projected Employment, 2026	Change, 2016-26	
			Percent	Numeric
Medical assistants	634,400	818,400	29	183,900

Source: U.S. Bureau of Labor Statistics, Employment Projections program

SIMILAR OCCUPATIONS

This list shows occupations with job duties that are similar to those of medical assistants.

Dental Assistants: Dental assistants perform many tasks, ranging from providing patient care and taking x rays to recordkeeping and scheduling appointments. Their duties vary by state and by the dentists' offices where they work.

Dental Hygienists: Dental hygienists clean teeth, examine patients for signs of oral diseases such as gingivitis, and provide other preventive dental care. They also educate patients on ways to improve and maintain good oral health.

Licensed Practical and Licensed Vocational Nurses: Licensed practical nurses (LPNs) and licensed vocational nurses (LVNs) provide basic nursing care. They work under the direction of registered nurses and doctors.

Medical Records and Health Information Technicians: Medical records and health information technicians, commonly referred to as *health information technicians*, organize and manage health information data. They ensure that the information maintains its quality, accuracy, accessibility, and security in both paper files and electronic systems. They use various classification systems to code and categorize patient information for insurance reimbursement purposes, for databases and registries, and to maintain patients' medical and treatment histories.

Nursing Assistants and Orderlies: Nursing assistants, sometimes called nursing aides, help provide basic care for patients in hospitals and residents of long-term care facilities, such as nursing homes. Orderlies transport patients and clean treatment areas.

Occupational Therapy Assistants and Aides: Occupational therapy assistants and aides help patients develop, recover, improve, as well as maintain the skills needed for daily living and working. Occupational therapy assistants are directly involved in providing therapy to patients; occupational therapy aides typically perform support activities. Both assistants and aides work under the direction of occupational therapists.

Pharmacy Technicians: Pharmacy technicians help pharmacists dispense prescription medication to customers or health professionals.

Phlebotomists: Phlebotomists draw blood for tests, transfusions, research, or blood donations. Some explain their work to patients and provide assistance when patients have adverse reactions after their blood is drawn.

Physical Therapist Assistants and Aides: Physical therapist assistants, sometimes called PTAs, and physical therapist aides work under the direction and supervision of physical therapists. They help patients who are recovering from injuries and illnesses regain movement and manage pain.

Psychiatric Technicians and Aides: Psychiatric technicians and aides care for people who have mental illness and developmental disabilities. Technicians typically provide therapeutic care and monitor their patients' conditions. Aides help patients in their daily activities and ensure a safe, clean environment.

Conversation With . . .
KIMBERLEE P. FLANNERY

MSN, BSN, RN
Lt. Commander, Nurse Corps, United States Navy

Kimberlee P. Flannery has been a nurse for sixteen years and is the Clinic Manager for the Internal Medicine Clinic at Naval Medical Center in Portsmouth, Virginia.

1. What was your individual career path in terms of education/training, entry-level job, or other significant opportunity?

Shortly after graduating with my bachelor's degree in nursing from the University of Cincinnati, I joined the Navy Nurse Corps via the Nurse Candidate Program. Students typically join in their junior year of college. The program offers a sign-on bonus and a monthly stipend until graduation.

My first job assignment was at the National Naval Medical Center, now known as Walter Reed National Military Medical Center in Bethesda, Maryland. After completing the nurse residency program, I was assigned to work on the hematology and oncology unit. While stationed there, I deployed on the United States Naval Ship (USNS) *Comfort* during the Iraq War when it first began, in support of Operation Iraqi Freedom. After Bethesda, I moved to Pensacola, Florida, where I worked as a medical-surgical and critical care nurse. During my tour in Pensacola, I deployed to Guantanamo Bay, Cuba. Next, I moved to Yokosuka, Japan, and worked as an emergency medicine nurse. This by far was my favorite duty station. Growing up, I never really imagined traveling to Japan, but now I feel as if it's the Navy's best-kept secret. The local Japanese are the friendliest people you will ever meet. Being immersed in a different culture was fascinating.

As far as significant opportunities, the Nurse Corps offers "Duty under Instruction," which pays for your master's or doctorate degree while paying your regular salary. I was lucky enough to attend the University of California, San Francisco, to obtain my master's degree in critical care and trauma nursing. After finishing graduate school, I moved to San Diego, where I worked in the emergency department as a clinical nurse specialist before my next assignment on the USNS *Mercy* for Pacific Partnership. We provided humanitarian support to the Philippines, Cambodia, Vietnam, and Indonesia. After returning from deployment, I worked as the Nurse of the Day, where I oversaw the daily staffing and bed management for the Naval Medical Center San Diego. From there, I moved slightly north to Camp Pendleton and worked as the division officer of the Emergency Management Department for Naval Hospital Camp Pendleton. After that, I deployed to Kandahar, Afghanistan, for seven months – boots on the ground. After returning from deployment, I worked as the clinical nurse specialist for the Emergency Medicine Department at Naval Hospital Camp Pendleton. My current duty station is at the medical center in Portsmouth, Virginia. Shortly after arriving, I deployed on the USNS Comfort to Puerto Rico for Hurricane Maria relief. For a little more than a year, I have worked as the clinic manager in an internal medicine clinic at Naval Medical Center Portsmouth in Virginia. Serving in the Navy has given me the opportunity to live and work in different areas. While moving from duty station to duty station can be difficult at times, the Navy has given me the opportunity to meet so many people and develop a professional network across the nation and other countries. Sometimes I get bored easily, so moving every three years is actually exciting for me. I get to live in and travel to places that most people only dream about. The Nurse Corps has developed me into a strong leader and mentor to other sailors.

2. What are the most important skills and/or qualities for someone in your profession?

One of the main jobs for Navy Nurse Corps officers is not only to take care of patients but also train the enlisted corpsman. Think of the corpsmen as licensed practical nurses or medical assistants. They receive initial basic medical training after boot camp, but it is up to the Nurse Corps to carry on that training because they will eventually treat the Marines and/or be stationed on ships to take care of fellow shipmates. Navy Medicine goes wherever the Marines go. You also need to be able to work well with others and have the ability to lead. In addition, you need to be flexible, as you may find yourself assigned to roles you may have not chosen.

3. What do you wish you had known going into this profession?

As you earn promotion through the ranks, you will more than likely do less bedside nursing. As I mentioned above, currently I am a clinic manager of an internal medicine clinic, but I have a master's degree in critical care and trauma nursing. Your role as a nurse may not coincide with your clinical background.

4. Are there many job opportunities in your profession? In what specific areas?

There are countless opportunities in the Nurse Corps. You can be a nurse in a hospital or clinic setting. You can work on a carrier out at sea or be a flight nurse responsible for transporting critical patients. You have the opportunity to live abroad and deploy around the world. You can work as a nurse in manpower or informatics. After obtaining your master's or doctorate degree, you can work as a clinical nurse specialist, nurse anesthetist, or nurse practitioner.

5. How do you see your profession changing in the next five years, how will technology impact that change, and what skills will be required?

I can see technology changing how we document patient care while out to sea and on "forward deployment," meaning a military unit is positioned where it could be the first unit to make contact with the enemy or be a lead in a battle. Currently, patient care documentation can be on paper charts or on multiple electronic systems, depending on where someone is in the world. As far as the profession changing in the next few years, I can see a push for increasing the number of critical care and emergency/trauma nurses. Deployability is what sets us apart from the civilian nursing staff. Critical care and emergency/trauma nurses are highly deployable due to their experience and the nature of combat injuries we encounter.

6. What do you enjoy most about your job? What do you enjoy least about your job?

I enjoy moving to a different area every three years. Some may see this as a negative, but I see it as an opportunity.

As far as what I enjoy the least, some days I wish I could be a "worker bee" instead of managing people.

7. Can you suggest a valuable "try this" for students considering a career in your profession?

I suggest talking to a recruiter and then speaking directly with a current Nurse Corps officer. Everyone will have helpful information for you.

CONTACTS FOR MORE INFORMATION

For more information about medical and health care management, visit

American Association of Medical Assistants
http: //www.aama-ntl.org/

American Medical Technologists
https: //www.americanmedtech.org/

National Center for Competency Testing
https: //www.ncctinc.com/

National Healthcareer Association
https: //www.nhanow.com/

Institute for Credentialing Excellence
http: //www.credentialingexcellence. org/

American Optometric Association
https: //www.aoa.org/

American Society of Podiatric Medical Assistants
https: //aspma.org/

Joint Commission on Allied Health Personnel in Ophthalmology
http: //www.jcahpo.org/

American Medical Certification Association
https: //www.amcaexams.com/

For lists of accredited educational programs in medical assisting, visit

Commission on Accreditation of Allied Health Education Programs
https: //www.caahep.org/

Accrediting Bureau of Health Education Schools
https: //www.abhes.org/

Source: Bureau of Labor Statistics, U.S. Department of Labor, *Occupational Outlook Handbook*, Medical Assistants, on the Internet at https: //www.bls.gov/ooh/healthcare/ medical-assistants.htm (visited *January 22, 2019*).

Nurse Anesthetists, Nurse Midwives, and Nurse Practitioners

Snapshot

2017 Median Pay: $110,930 per year, $53.33 per hour

Typical Entry-Level Education: Master's degree

Career Cluster: Health science

On-the-Job Training: None

Number of Jobs, 2016: 203,800

Job Outlook, 2016-26: 31% (Much faster than average)

Employment Change, 2016-26: 64,200

Holland Score: IRS, IRE

CAREER OVERVIEW

Nurse anesthetists, nurse midwives, and nurse practitioners, also referred to as *advanced practice registered nurses (APRNs)*, coordinate patient care and may provide primary and specialty health care. The scope of practice varies from state to state.

Duties

Advanced practice registered nurses typically do the following:

- Take and record patients' medical histories and symptoms
- Perform physical exams and observe patients
- Create patient care plans or contribute to existing plans
- Perform and order diagnostic tests
- Operate and monitor medical equipment
- Diagnose various health problems
- Analyze test results or changes in a patient's condition, and alter treatment plans, as needed
- Give patients medicines and treatments
- Evaluate a patient's response to medicines and treatments
- Consult with doctors and other health care professionals, as needed
- Counsel and teach patients and their families how to stay healthy or manage their illnesses or injuries
- Conduct research

APRNs work independently or in collaboration with physicians. In most states, they can prescribe medications, order medical tests, and diagnose health problems. APRNs may provide primary and preventive care and may specialize in care for certain groups of people, such as children, pregnant women, or patients with mental health disorders.

Some APRN duties are the same as those for registered nurses, including gathering information about a patient's condition and taking action to treat or manage the patient's health. However, APRNs are trained to perform many additional functions, including ordering and evaluating test results, referring patients to specialists, and diagnosing and treating ailments. APRNs focus on patient-centered care, which means understanding a patient's concerns and lifestyle before choosing a course of action.

APRNs also may conduct research or teach staff about new policies or procedures. Others may provide consultation services based on a specific field of knowledge, such as oncology, which is the study of cancer.

The following are types of APRNs:

Nurse anesthetists (CRNAs) provide anesthesia and related care before, during, and after surgical, therapeutic, diagnostic, and obstetrical procedures. They also provide pain management and some emergency services. Before a procedure begins, nurse anesthetists discuss with a patient any medications the patient is taking as well as any allergies or illnesses the patient may have, so that anesthesia can be safely administered. Nurse anesthetists then give a patient general anesthesia to put the patient to sleep so they feel no pain during surgery or administer a regional or local anesthesia to numb an area of the body. They remain with the patient throughout a procedure to monitor vital signs and adjust the anesthesia as necessary.

Nurse midwives (CNMs) provide care to women, including gynecological exams, family planning services, and prenatal care. They deliver babies; manage emergency situations during labor, such as hemorrhaging; repair lacerations; and may provide surgical assistance to physicians during cesarean births. Nurse midwives may act as primary care providers for women and newborns. They also provide wellness care, educating their patients on how to lead healthy lives by discussing topics such as nutrition and disease prevention. Nurse midwives also provide care to their patients' partners for sexual or reproductive health issues.

Nurse practitioners (NPs) serve as primary and specialty care providers, delivering advanced nursing services to patients and their families. They assess patients, determine the best way to improve or manage a patient's health, and discuss ways to integrate health promotion strategies into a patient's life. Nurse practitioners typically care for a certain population of people. For instance, NPs may work in adult and geriatric health, pediatric health, or psychiatric and mental health.

Although the scope of their duties varies some by state, many nurse practitioners work independently, prescribe medications, and order laboratory tests. All nurse practitioners consult with physicians and other health professionals when needed.

See the profile on registered nurses for more information on ***Clinical Nurse Specialists (CNSs)***, also considered to be a type of APRN.

WORK ENVIRONMENT

Nurse anesthetists, nurse midwives, and nurse practitioners held about 203,800 jobs in 2016. Employment in the detailed occupations that make up nurse anesthetists, nurse midwives, and nurse practitioners was distributed as follows:

Nurse practitioners	155,500
Nurse anesthetists	41,800
Nurse midwives	6,500

The largest employers of nurse anesthetists, nurse midwives, and nurse practitioners were as follows:

Offices of physicians	46%
Hospitals; state, local, and private	28
Outpatient care centers	8
Educational services; state, local, and private	4
Offices of other health practitioners	3

Some advanced practice registered nurses (APRNs) may treat patients in their patients' homes. Some nurse midwives work in birthing centers, which are a type of outpatient care center.

APRNs may travel long distances to help care for patients in places where there are not enough health care workers.

Injuries and Illnesses

APRN work can be both physically and emotionally demanding. Some APRNs spend much of their day on their feet. They are vulnerable to back injuries because they must lift and move patients. APRN work can also be stressful because they make critical decisions that affect a patient's health.

Because of the environments in which they work, APRNs may come in close contact with infectious diseases. Therefore, they must follow strict, standardized guidelines to guard against diseases and other dangers, such as accidental needle sticks or patient outbursts

Work Schedules

Most APRNs work full time. APRNs working in physicians' offices typically work during normal business hours. Those working in hospitals and various other health care facilities may work in shifts to provide round-the-clock patient care. They may work nights, weekends, and holidays. Some APRNs, especially those who work in critical care or those who deliver babies, also may be required to be on call.

Fast Fact

Nurse anesthetists, who are highly educated, are among the highest-paid nursing specialty, earning average salaries from $144,000-$165,000.

Source: besthealthdegrees.com

HOW TO BECOME A NURSE ANESTHETIST, NURSE MIDWIFE, OR NURSE PRACTITIONER

Nurse anesthetists, nurse midwives, and nurse practitioners, also referred to as *advanced practice registered nurses (APRNs)*, must earn at least a master's degree in one of the specialty roles. APRNs must also be licensed registered nurses in their state and pass a national certification exam.

Important Qualities

Communication skills. Advanced practice registered nurses must be able to communicate with patients and other health care professionals to ensure that the appropriate course of action is understood.

Critical-thinking skills. APRNs must be able to assess changes in a patient's health, quickly determine the most appropriate course of action, and decide if a consultation with another health care professional is needed.

Compassion. APRNs should be caring and sympathetic when treating patients who are in pain or who are experiencing emotional distress.

Detail oriented. APRNs must be responsible and detail oriented because they provide various treatments and medications that affect the health of their patients. During an evaluation, they must pick up on even the smallest changes in a patient's condition.

Interpersonal skills. APRNs must work with patients and families as well as with other health care providers and staff within the organizations where they provide care. They should work as part of a team to determine and execute the best possible health care options for the patients they treat.

Leadership skills. APRNs often work in positions of seniority. They must effectively lead and sometimes manage other nurses on staff when providing patient care.

Resourcefulness. APRNs must know where to find the answers that they need in a timely fashion.

EDUCATION

Nurse anesthetists, nurse midwives, and nurse practitioners must earn a master's degree from an accredited program. These programs include both classroom education and clinical experience. Courses in anatomy, physiology, and pharmacology are common as well as coursework specific to the chosen APRN role.

An APRN must have a registered nursing (RN) license before pursuing education in one of the advanced practice roles, and a strong background in science is helpful.

Most APRN programs prefer candidates who have a bachelor's degree in nursing. However, some schools offer bridge programs for registered nurses with an associate's degree or diploma in nursing. Graduate-level programs are also available for individuals who did not obtain a bachelor's degree in nursing but in a related health science field. These programs prepare the student for the RN licensure exam in addition to the APRN curriculum.

Although a master's degree is the most common form of entry-level education, APRNs may choose to earn a Doctor of Nursing Practice (DNP) or a Ph.D. The specific educational requirements and qualifications for each of the roles are available on professional organizations' websites.

Prospective nurse anesthetists must have 1 year of clinical experience as a prerequisite for admission to an accredited nurse anesthetist program. Candidates typically have experience working as a registered nurse in an acute care or critical care setting

Licenses, Certifications, and Registrations

Most states recognize all of the APRN roles. In states that recognize some or all of the roles, APRNs must have a registered nursing license, complete an accredited graduate-level program, and pass a national certification exam. Each state's board of nursing can provide details.

The *Consensus Model for APRN Regulation*, a document developed by a wide variety of professional nursing organizations, including the National Council of State Boards of Nursing, aims to standardize APRN requirements. The model recommends all APRNs to complete a graduate degree from an accredited program, be a licensed registered nurse, pass a national certification exam, and earn a second license specific to one of the APRN roles and to a certain group of patients.

Certification is required in the vast majority of states to use an APRN title. Certification is used to show proficiency in an APRN role and is often a requirement for state licensure.

The National Board of Certification and Recertification for Nurse Anesthetists (NBCRNA) offers the National Certification Examination

(NCE). Certified registered nurse anesthetists (CRNAs) must recertify via the Continued Professional Certification (CPC) Program every 4 years.

The American Midwifery Certification Board offers the Certified Nurse-Midwife (CNM). Individuals with this designation must recertify via the Certificate Maintenance Program every 5 years.

There are a number of certification exams for nurse practitioners because of the large number of populations NPs may work with and the number of specialty areas in which they may practice. Certifications are available from a number of professional organizations, including the American Nurses Credentialing Center and the Pediatric Nursing Certification Board.

In addition, APRN positions may require certification in cardiopulmonary resuscitation (CPR), basic life support (BLS) certification, and/or advanced cardiac life support (ACLS).

ADVANCEMENT

Some APRNs may take on managerial or administrative roles, while others go into academia. APRNs who earn a doctoral degree may conduct independent research or work in an interprofessional research team.

Pay

The median annual wage for nurse anesthetists, nurse midwives, and nurse practitioners was $110,930 in May 2017. The lowest 10 percent earned less than $76,830, and the highest 10 percent earned more than $180,460.

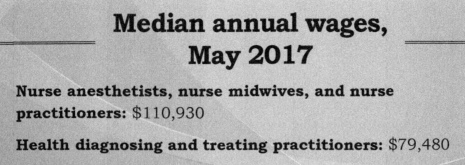

Median annual wages, May 2017

Nurse anesthetists, nurse midwives, and nurse practitioners: $110,930

Health diagnosing and treating practitioners: $79,480

Total, all occupations: $37,690

Note: All Occupations includes all occupations in the U.S. Economy. Source: U.S. Bureau of Labor Statistics, Occupational Employment Statistics

Median annual wages for nurse anesthetists, nurse midwives, and nurse practitioners in May 2017 were as follows:

Nurse anesthetists	$165,120
Nurse practitioners	103,880
Nurse midwives	100,590

In May 2017, the median annual wages for nurse anesthetists, nurse midwives, and nurse practitioners in the top industries in which they worked were as follows.

Hospitals; state, local, and private	$117,850
Outpatient care centers	112,940
Offices of physicians	108,300
Offices of other health practitioners	107,700
Educational services; state, local, and private	101,600

Most advanced practice registered nurses (APRNs) work full time. APRNs working in physicians' offices typically work during normal business hours. Those working in hospitals and various other health care facilities may work in shifts to provide round-the-clock patient care. They may work nights, weekends, and holidays. Some APRNs, especially those who work in critical care or those who deliver babies, also may be required to be on call.

JOB OUTLOOK

Overall employment of nurse anesthetists, nurse midwives, and nurse practitioners is projected to grow 31 percent from 2016 to 2026, much faster than the average for all occupations. Growth will occur because of an increase in the demand for health care services. Several factors will contribute to this demand, including an increased emphasis on preventive care and demand for health care services from the aging population.

Percent change in employment, projected 2016-26

Nurse anesthetists, nurse midwives, and nurse practitioners: 31%

Health diagnosing and treating practitioners: 16%

Total, all occupations: 7%

Note: All Occupations includes all occupations in the U.S. Economy. Source: U.S. Bureau of Labor Statistics, Employment Projections program

Advanced practice registered nurses (APRNs) can perform many of the same services as physicians. APRNs will be increasingly utilized in team-based models of care, particularly in hospitals, offices of physicians, clinics, and other ambulatory care settings, where they will be needed to provide preventive and primary care.

APRNs will also be needed to care for the large, aging baby-boom population. As baby boomers age, they will experience ailments and complex conditions that require medical care. APRNs will be needed to keep these patients healthy and to treat the growing number of patients with chronic and acute conditions.

As states change their laws governing APRN practice authority, APRNs are being allowed to perform more services. They are also becoming more widely recognized by the public as a source for primary health care.

JOB PROSPECTS

Overall, job opportunities for advanced practice registered nurses are likely to be excellent. APRNs will be in high demand, particularly in medically underserved areas such as inner cities and rural areas.

Employment projections data for nurse anesthetists, nurse midwives, and nurse practitioners, 2016-26

Occupational Title	Employment, 2016	Projected Employment, 2026	Change, 2016-26	
			Percent	Numeric
Nurse anesthetists, nurse midwives, and nurse practitioners	203,800	268,000	31	64,200
Nurse anesthetists	41,800	48,600	16	6,800
Nurse midwives	6,500	7,800	21	1,300
Nurse practitioners	155,500	211,600	36	56,100

Source: U.S. Bureau of Labor Statistics, Employment Projections program

SIMILAR OCCUPATIONS

This list shows occupations with job duties that are similar to those of nurse anesthetists, nurse midwives, and nurse practitioners.

Audiologists: Audiologists diagnose, manage, and treat a patient's hearing, balance, or ear problems.

Occupational Therapists: Occupational therapists treat injured, ill, or disabled patients through the therapeutic use of everyday activities. They help these patients develop, recover, improve, as well as maintain the skills needed for daily living and working.

Physical Therapists: Physical therapists, sometimes called *PTs*, help injured or ill people improve their movement and manage their pain. These therapists are often an important part of the rehabilitation, treatment, and prevention of patients with chronic conditions, illnesses, or injuries.

Physician Assistants: Physician assistants, also known as *PAs*, practice medicine on teams with physicians, surgeons, and other health care workers. They examine, diagnose, and treat patients.

Physicians and Surgeons: Physicians and surgeons diagnose and treat injuries or illnesses. Physicians examine patients; take medical histories; prescribe medications; and order, perform, and interpret diagnostic tests. They counsel patients on diet, hygiene, and preventive health care. Surgeons operate on patients to treat injuries, such as broken bones; diseases, such as cancerous tumors; and deformities, such as cleft palates.

Registered Nurses: Registered nurses (RNs) provide and coordinate patient care, educate patients and the public about various health conditions, and provide advice and emotional support to patients and their family members.

Speech-Language Pathologists: Speech-language pathologists (sometimes called *speech therapists*) assess, diagnose, treat, and help to prevent communication and swallowing disorders in children and adults. Speech, language, and swallowing disorders result from a variety of causes, such as a stroke, brain injury, hearing loss, developmental delay, Parkinson's disease, a cleft palate, or autism.

Conversation With . . .
CASSANDRA RAMM

MSN, RN, AGNP-C
Cardiology Nurse Practitioner

Cassandra Ramm has been a nurse for thirteen years and a nurse practitioner for three years. She currently works at UNC Hospitals in Chapel Hill and Hillsborough, North Carolina.

1. What was your individual career path in terms of education/training, entry-level job, or other significant opportunity?

I grew up on a cattle ranch in rural Nebraska. My father did a lot of his own veterinary work including doing caesarean sections and starting jugular vein IVs on sick calves. My earliest exposure to medicine was assisting him with these tasks. My grandmother was a nurse in the 1940s, and I grew up listening to her stories about the field.

I attended the University of Nebraska—Lincoln studying the premed track. I switched to nursing my sophomore year because it closely aligned with my goals. After I completed my bachelor's degree in nursing (BSN) in 2005, my first job was at Duke University Hospital in Durham, North Carolina. It was one of my best decisions in terms of my career and personal growth, as it forced me out of my comfort zone.

My first nursing position at Duke was in the cardiothoracic surgery step-down unit. It was extremely challenging, and the patient population was very sick and complex compared what I had seen in my training. I had great preceptors, and some I still work with today. After six months, I felt somewhat competent as an independent registered nurse (RN). You really hone your skills and abilities during your first job. In medicine, it's critical you never stop learning because things are constantly changing.

Working for a few years as a bedside nurse at Duke burned me out. Instead of providing the joy and self-fulfillment I had originally felt, the position depleted me. I questioned whether I wanted to continue doing shift work longterm, which has been linked to negative health outcomes. While attending nursing school, I worked in a Phase I clinical research facility—where new medications are tested on people—doing phlebotomy, electrocardiograms (EKGs), and other assessments. This experience led to a job offer as a clinical research monitor at a contract research organization (CRO) in North Carolina's Research Triangle Park. CROs are contracted by pharmaceutical companies to manage their drug trials with hopes of U.S. Food and Drug Administration

(FDA) approval. This was a change. I traveled the country visiting clinics and hospitals, monitoring clinical trial data and hospital charts for quality and accuracy, and verifying that research was completed ethically. My travel schedule was usually leaving on a Sunday afternoon or early Monday morning and returning Thursday or Friday. The job meant working more with research nurses and physicians, not patients. The position introduced me to a more corporate atmosphere and offered a good salary. I earned a promotion after three years, but I could see that further advancement into management would mean more stress and even less interaction with patients and health care providers, which I missed.

In 2010, I was offered an opportunity to manage the cardiology clinical trials group and work as a research nurse at The University of North Carolina at Chapel Hill (UNC). I greatly enjoyed the change and sleeping in my own bed every night. I worked closely with different cardiologists and patients. The position allowed me to make many changes, institute financial tracking systems, and put together a team that went from losing money to profitable.

After several years, I returned to graduate school at UNC and pursued a master's degree in nursing (MSN) to become a nurse practitioner (NP). I worked 75 percent of a full-time workweek and attended school full-time. Trying to manage both work and school was very challenging. Halfway through the graduate program, I switched positions to be a nurse coordinator for UNC's new structural heart program offering minimally invasive valve procedures. I spent nearly two years helping to build a successful structural heart program, graduated, and passed my NP boards.

During the past three years, I've worked at various UNC satellite sites such as a rural hospital. Still, I've wanted to get as much experience as I can and practice to the fullest extent of my training. I've volunteered for different opportunities and now am working in a different location every day, something I really enjoy. I mostly practice in the outpatient setting while spending half a day a week doing inpatient work. Being a nurse practitioner allows me to see patients independently with tasks such as examinations, diagnoses, prescribing, and ordering testing. North Carolina requires NPs to have a supervising physician available for consult as needed.

I'm also more involved in conducting independent research projects, writing academic papers, and giving presentations at educational conferences. I recently began a new role at the UNC School of Nursing as an adjunct faculty member, assisting students with their graduate projects and giving lectures.

2. What are the most important skills and/or qualities for someone in your profession?

Personal integrity, resilience, humility, patience, empathy, doing the right thing when no one is looking, time management, ability to speak up against people in leadership positions or with more power. Nurses are often the eyes and ears for patients and family members. It's our job to advocate on their behalf. We are often the first to notice something is wrong such as decreased urine output, low blood pressure, or we simply listen to our gut instinct. It's imperative that nurses develop effective interpersonal communication skills and become comfortable raising concerns with people who have more authority. Many new nurses feel intimidated at calling a physician to discuss concerns. Nevertheless, we are all on the same team: ensuring the best outcome for our patients.

Also, nurses should have strong interpersonal communication skills, experience interacting/working with people of different socioeconomic and cultural backgrounds, and the desire to understand complex socioeconomic factors contributing to health. And of course, a love of learning.

3. What do you wish you had known going into this profession?

Studying and getting good grades are important, but to this day, not a single patient or family member has asked me what my GPA was. It is much more important to be able to think critically and know how and when to access your resources. By "resources," I mean there is too much information to know by memory with medicine always changing. Nurses constantly consult reference books, online material, and even apps providing information about medications, diagnoses, lab interpretation, and society guidelines for management of different conditions. Working in health care also requires your ability to tap into the expertise of other team members, such as pharmacists, physical therapists, and others. You also must be able to work effectively on a team and know when to ask for help. Also, always be open to different opportunities and networking. Lastly, a good mentor can make or break a career.

4. Are there many job opportunities in your profession? In what specific areas?

There are opportunities for nurses to work in cardiology: bedside in either critical care or the floor (more stable patients), in a clinic setting, a cardiac catheterization or electrophysiology lab assisting with heart procedures, nurse managers, quality improvement, nurse coordinators who manage complex patients in different settings such as structural heart disease. There are opportunities to work in clinical research and for drug/device companies as sales reps.

Additionally, opportunities increase by earning advanced degrees to become a clinical nurse specialist, nurse practitioner (such as in women's health, pediatric, family, geriatric, critical care specialties), to teach, work in a leadership role, and/or conduct research.

5. How do you see your profession changing in the next five years, how will technology impact that change, and what skills will be required?

Electronic medical record systems require a lot of time. I spend more time in front of a computer dictating/typing a note about what I did than seeing a patient. Being tech savvy and the willingness to learn new things are helpful.

6. What do you enjoy most about your job? What do you enjoy least about your job?

I consider it a true privilege to provide health care to a variety of patients—all of whom trust in your training, knowledge, and promise to try to give them the best care. I take that trust seriously, and provide the level of care I would expect for my family or loved ones. Nursing is hard work and often not a "40-hour workweek." Still, it's rewarding to be involved in some of people's most vulnerable—and joyous—moments. I also love working in a collaborative, team-based environment. Patients get the best care when different disciplines work together (medicine, nursing, pharmacy, nutrition, and social work, physical therapy) to care for them.

I least enjoy the amount of paperwork, documentation, and charting required.

7. Can you suggest a valuable "try this" for students considering a career in your profession?

I would recommend shadowing people working in health care. It is easy to become a certified nursing assistant in high school or college—this provides invaluable experience

CONTACTS FOR MORE INFORMATION

For more information about nurse anesthetists, including a list of accredited programs, visit

American Association of Nurse Anesthetists
https: //www.aana.com/

For more information about nurse midwives, including a list of accredited programs, visit

American College of Nurse-Midwives
http: //www.midwife.org/

For more information about nurse practitioners, including a list of accredited programs, visit

American Association of Nurse Practitioners
https: //www.aanp.org/

For more information about registered nurses, including credentialing, visit

American Nurses Association
https: //www.nursingworld.org/

For more information about nursing education and being a registered nurse, visit

National League for Nursing
http: //www.nln.org/

For more information about undergraduate and graduate nursing education, nursing career options, and financial aid, visit

American Association of Colleges of Nursing
https: //www.aacnnursing.org/

For more information about the Consensus Model and for a list of the states' Boards of Nursing, visit

National Council of State Boards of Nursing
https: //www.ncsbn.org/

For more information about certification, visit

National Board of Certification and Recertification for Nurse Anesthetists
https: //www.nbcrna.com/

American Midwifery Certification Board
https: //www.amcbmidwife.org/

American Nurses Credentialing Center
https: //www.nursingworld.org/ancc/

Pediatric Nursing Certification Board
https: //www.pncb.org/

Nursing Assistants and Orderlies

Snapshot

2017 Median Pay: $27,510 per year, $13.23 per hour

Typical Entry-Level Education: Postsecondary nondegree award

Career Cluster: Health science

On-the-job Training: Short-term on-the-job training

Number of Jobs, 2016: 1,564,300

Job Outlook, 2016-26: 11% (Faster than average)

Employment Change, 2016-26: 177,700

Holland Score: SEC, SRI

CAREER OVERVIEW

Nursing assistants, sometimes called nursing aides, help provide basic care for patients in hospitals and residents of long-term care facilities, such as nursing homes. Orderlies transport patients and clean treatment areas.

Duties

Nursing assistants provide basic care and help with activities of daily living. They typically do the following:

- Clean and bathe patients or residents
- Help patients use the toilet and dress
- Turn, reposition, and transfer patients between beds and wheelchairs
- Listen to and record patients' health concerns and report that information to nurses

- Measure patients' vital signs, such as blood pressure and temperature
- Serve meals and help patients eat

Some nursing assistants also may dispense medication, depending on their training level and the state in which they work.

In nursing homes and residential care facilities, nursing assistants are often the principal caregivers. They have more contact with residents than other members of the staff. Nursing assistants often develop close relationships with their patients because some residents stay in a nursing home for months or years.

Orderlies typically do the following:
- Help patients to move around the facility, by doing such tasks as pushing wheelchairs
- Clean equipment and facilities
- Change linens
- Stock supplies

Nursing assistants and orderlies work as part of a health care team under the supervision of licensed practical or licensed vocational nurses and registered nurses.

WORK ENVIRONMENT

Nursing assistants held about 1.5 million jobs in 2016. The largest employers of nursing assistants were as follows:

Nursing care facilities (skilled nursing facilities)	40%
Hospitals; state, local, and private	26
Continuing care retirement communities and assisted living facilities for the elderly	11
Home health care services	5
Government	4

Orderlies held about 54,000 jobs in 2016. The largest employers of orderlies were as follows:

Hospitals; state, local, and private	74%
Nursing care facilities (skilled nursing facilities)	9
Ambulatory health care services	6
Government	3
Continuing care retirement communities and assisted living facilities for the elderly	3

The work of nursing assistants and orderlies can be strenuous. They spend much of their time on their feet as they take care of many patients or residents

Injuries and Illnesses

Because they frequently lift people and do other physically demanding tasks, nursing assistants and orderlies have a higher rate of injuries and illnesses than the national average. They are typically trained in how to properly lift and move patients, which can reduce the risk of injuries.

Work Schedules

Most nursing assistants and orderlies work full time. Because nursing homes and hospitals provide care at all hours, nursing assistants and orderlies may need to work nights, weekends, and holidays.

HOW TO BECOME A NURSING ASSISTANT OR ORDERLY

Nursing assistants must complete a state-approved education program and must pass their state's competency exam. Orderlies generally have at least a high school diploma.

Important Qualities

Communication skills. Nursing assistants and orderlies must communicate effectively to address patients' or residents' concerns. They also need to relay important information to other health care workers.

Compassion. Nursing assistants and orderlies assist and care for the sick, injured, and elderly. Doing so requires a compassionate and empathetic attitude.

Patience. The routine tasks of cleaning, feeding, and bathing patients or residents can be stressful. Nursing assistants and orderlies must have patience to complete these tasks.

Physical stamina. Nursing assistants and orderlies spend much of their time on their feet. They should be comfortable performing physical tasks, such as lifting or moving patients.

EDUCATION AND TRAINING

Nursing assistants must complete a state-approved education program in which they learn the basic principles of nursing and complete supervised clinical work. These programs are found in high schools, community colleges, vocational and technical schools, hospitals, and nursing homes.

In addition, nursing assistants typically complete a brief period of on-the-job training to learn about their specific employer's policies and procedures.

Orderlies typically have at least a high school diploma and receive a short period of on-the-job training.

Licenses, Certifications, and Registrations

After completing a state-approved education program, nursing assistants take a competency exam. Passing this exam allows them to use state-specific titles. In some states, a nursing assistant or aide is called a Certified Nursing Assistant (CNA), but titles vary from state to state.

Nursing assistants who have passed the competency exam are placed on a state registry. They must be on the state registry to work in a nursing home.

Some states have other requirements as well, such as continuing education and a criminal background check. Check with state boards of nursing or health for more information.

In some states, nursing assistants can earn additional credentials, such as becoming a Certified Medication Assistant (CMA). As a CMA, they can give medications.

Orderlies do not need a license, however, many jobs require a basic life support (BLS) certification, which shows they are trained to provide cardiopulmonary resuscitation (CPR).

Fast Fact

Nurses have been viewed as the most honest and ethical of American professionals for 19 of the last 20 years. In 2018, 84 percent of Americans took that view of the nursing profession.

Source: www.gallup.com

Pay

The median annual wage for nursing assistants was $27,520 in May 2017. The lowest 10 percent earned less than $20,680, and the highest 10 percent earned more than $38,630.

Median annual wages, May 2017

Total, all occupations: $37,690

Nursing assistants: $27,520

Nursing assistants and orderlies: $27,510

Orderlies: $27,180

Nursing, psychiatric, and home health aides: $25,610

Note: All Occupations includes all occupations in the U.S. Economy. Source: U.S. Bureau of Labor Statistics, Occupational Employment Statistics

The median annual wage for orderlies was $27,180 in May 2017. The lowest 10 percent earned less than $20,240, and the highest 10 percent earned more than $40,610.

In May 2017, the median annual wages for nursing assistants in the top industries in which they worked were as follows:

Government	$32,860
Hospitals; state, local, and private	29,260
Nursing care facilities (skilled nursing facilities)	26,700
Home health care services	25,940
Continuing care retirement communities and assisted living facilities for the elderly	25,880

In May 2017, the median annual wages for orderlies in the top industries in which they worked were as follows:

Government	$29,030
Ambulatory health care services	28,540
Hospitals; state, local, and private	27,630
Nursing care facilities (skilled nursing facilities)	23,380
Continuing care retirement communities and assisted living facilities for the elderly	23,110

Most nursing assistants and orderlies work full time. Because nursing homes and hospitals provide care at all hours, nursing aides and orderlies may need to work nights, weekends, and holidays.

JOB OUTLOOK

Employment of nursing assistants is projected to grow 11 percent from 2016 to 2026, faster than the average for all occupations. Employment of orderlies is projected to grow 8 percent from 2016 to 2026, about as fast as the average for all occupations.

Percent change in employment, projected 2016-26

Nursing, psychiatric, and home health aides: 24%

Nursing assistants: 11%

Nursing assistants and orderlies: 11%

Orderlies: 8%

Total, all occupations: 7%

Note: All Occupations includes all occupations in the U.S. Economy. Source: U.S. Bureau of Labor Statistics, Employment Projections program

As the baby-boom population ages, nursing assistants and orderlies will be needed to assist and care for elderly patients in long-term care facilities, such as nursing homes. Older people are more likely than younger people to have disorders such as dementia, or to live with chronic diseases, such as heart disease and diabetes. More nursing assistants will be needed to care for patients with these conditions.

Demand for nursing assistants may be constrained by the fact that many nursing homes rely on government funding. Cuts to programs, such as Medicare and Medicaid, may affect patients' ability to pay for nursing home care. In addition, patient preferences and shifts in federal and state funding are increasing the demand for home and community-based long-term care, which should lead to increased opportunities for nursing assistants working in home health and community rehabilitation services.

JOB PROSPECTS

The low pay and high emotional and physical demands cause many workers to leave the occupation, and they will have to be replaced. This creates opportunities for jobseekers.

Employment projections data for nursing assistants and orderlies, 2016-26

Occupational Title	Employment, 2016	Projected Employment, 2026	Change, 2016-26	
			Percent	Numeric
Nursing assistants and orderlies	1,564,300	1,742,100	11	177,700
Nursing assistants	1,510,300	1,683,700	11	173,400
Orderlies	54,000	58,400	8	4,400

Source: U.S. Bureau of Labor Statistics, Employment Projections program

SIMILAR OCCUPATIONS

This list shows occupations with job duties that are similar to those of nursing assistants and orderlies.

Home Health Aides and Personal Care Aides: Home health aides and personal care aides help people with disabilities, chronic illnesses, or cognitive impairment by assisting in their daily living activities. They often help older adults who need assistance. In some states, home health aides may be able to give a client medication or check the client's vital signs under the direction of a nurse or other health care practitioner.

Licensed Practical and Licensed Vocational Nurses: Licensed practical nurses (LPNs) and licensed vocational nurses (LVNs) provide basic nursing care. They work under the direction of registered nurses and doctors.

Medical Assistants: Medical assistants complete administrative and clinical tasks in the offices of physicians, hospitals, and other health care facilities. Their duties vary with the location, specialty, and size of the practice.

Occupational Therapy Assistants and Aides: Occupational therapy assistants and aides help patients develop, recover, improve, as well as maintain the skills needed for daily living and working. Occupational therapy assistants are directly involved in providing therapy to patients; occupational therapy aides typically perform support activities. Both assistants and aides work under the direction of occupational therapists.

Psychiatric Technicians and Aides: Psychiatric technicians and aides care for people who have mental illness and developmental disabilities. Technicians typically provide therapeutic care and monitor their patients' conditions. Aides help patients in their daily activities and ensure a safe, clean environment.

Physical Therapist Assistants and Aides: Physical therapist assistants, sometimes called *PTAs*, and physical therapist aides work under the direction and supervision of physical therapists. They help patients who are recovering from injuries and illnesses regain movement and manage pain.

Registered Nurses: Registered nurses (RNs) provide and coordinate patient care, educate patients and the public about various health conditions, and provide advice and emotional support to patients and their family members.

Dental Assistants: Dental assistants perform many tasks, ranging from providing patient care and taking x rays to recordkeeping and scheduling appointments. Their duties vary by state and by the dentists' offices where they work.

Veterinary Assistants and Laboratory Animal Caretakers: Veterinary assistants and laboratory animal caretakers care for animals by performing routine tasks under the supervision of scientists, veterinarians, and veterinary technologists and technicians.

CONTACTS FOR MORE INFORMATION

For more information about nursing assistants and orderlies, visit

National Association of Health Care Assistants
https: //www.nahcacna.org/

National Network of Career Nursing Assistants
http: //cna-network.org/

Registered Nurses

Snapshot

2017 Median Pay: $70,000 per year, $33.65 per hour
Typical Entry-Level Education: Bachelor's degree
Career Cluster: Health science
On-the-job Training: None
Number of Jobs, 2016: 2,955,200
Job Outlook, 2016-26: 15% (Much faster than average)
Employment Change, 2016-26: 438,100
Holland Score: IRS, IRE

CAREER OVERVIEW

Registered nurses (RNs) provide and coordinate patient care, educate patients and the public about various health conditions, and provide advice and emotional support to patients and their family members.

Duties

Registered nurses typically do the following:

- Assess patients' conditions
- Record patients' medical histories and symptoms
- Observe patients and record the observations
- Administer patients' medicines and treatments

- Set up plans for patients' care or contribute information to existing plans
- Consult and collaborate with doctors and other health care professionals
- Operate and monitor medical equipment
- Help perform diagnostic tests and analyze the results
- Teach patients and their families how to manage illnesses or injuries
- Explain what to do at home after treatment

Most registered nurses work as part of a team with physicians and other health care specialists. Some registered nurses oversee licensed practical nurses, nursing assistants, and home health aides.

Registered nurses' duties and titles often depend on where they work and the patients they work with. For example, an oncology nurse may work with cancer patients or a geriatric nurse may work with elderly patients. Some registered nurses combine one or more areas of practice. For example, a pediatric oncology nurse works with children and teens who have cancer.

Many possibilities for working with specific patient groups exist. The following list includes just a few examples:

Addiction nurses care for patients who need help to overcome addictions to alcohol, drugs, and other substances.

Cardiovascular nurses care for patients with heart disease and people who have had heart surgery.

Critical care nurses work in intensive-care units in hospitals, providing care to patients with serious, complex, and acute illnesses and injuries that need very close monitoring and treatment.

Genetics nurses provide screening, counseling, and treatment for patients with genetic disorders, such as cystic fibrosis.

Neonatology nurses take care of newborn babies.

Nephrology nurses care for patients who have kidney-related health issues stemming from diabetes, high blood pressure, substance abuse, or other causes.

Public health nurses promote public health by educating people on warning signs and symptoms of disease or managing chronic health conditions. They may also run health screenings, immunization clinics, blood drives, or other community outreach programs.

Rehabilitation nurses care for patients with temporary or permanent disabilities. Some nurses do not work directly with patients, but they must still have an active registered nurse license. For example, they may work as nurse educators, health care consultants, public policy advisors, researchers, hospital administrators, salespeople for pharmaceutical and medical supply companies, or as medical writers and editors.

Clinical nurse specialists (CNSs) are a type of advanced practice registered nurse (APRN). They provide direct patient care in one of many nursing specialties, such as psychiatric-mental health or pediatrics. CNSs also provide indirect care, by working with other nurses and various other staff to improve the quality of care that patients receive. They often serve in leadership roles and may educate and advise other nursing staff. CNSs also may conduct research and may advocate for certain policies.

Famous First

Did you know that Linda Richards was the first nurse to earn a Nursing diploma in the United States? She earned it in 1873 and the proof of her graduation is now displayed in the Smithsonian Institution in Washington.

Linda describes her nursing training: "We rose at 5.30 a.m. and left the wards at 9 p.m. to go to our beds, which were in little rooms between the wards. Each nurse took care of her ward of six patients both day and night. Many a time I got up nine times in the night; often I did not get to sleep before the next call came. We had no evenings out, and no hours for study or recreation. Every second week we were off duty one afternoon from two to five o'clock. No monthly allowance was given for three months.".

Source: Reminiscences of Linda Richards, *Whitcomb & Barrows*

WORK ENVIRONMENT

Registered nurses held about 3.0 million jobs in 2016. The largest employers of registered nurses were as follows:

Hospitals; state, local, and private	61%
Ambulatory health care services	18
Nursing and residential care facilities	7
Government	5
Educational services; state, local, and private	3

Ambulatory health care services includes industries such as physicians' offices, home health care, and outpatient care centers. In addition, some nurses serve in the military. Nurses who work in home health travel to patients' homes, while public health nurses may travel to community centers, schools, and other sites.

Some nurses move frequently, traveling in the United States and throughout the world to help care for patients in places where there are not enough health care workers.

Injuries and Illnesses

Registered nurses may spend a lot of time walking, bending, stretching, and standing. They are vulnerable to back injuries because they often must lift and move patients.

The work of registered nurses may put them in close contact with people who have infectious diseases, and they frequently come in contact with potentially harmful and hazardous drugs and other substances. Therefore, registered nurses must follow strict, standardized guidelines to guard against diseases and other dangers, such as radiation, accidental needle sticks, or the chemicals used to create a sterile and clean environment.

Work Schedules

Because patients in hospitals and nursing care facilities need round-the-clock care, nurses in these settings usually work in shifts, covering all 24 hours. They may work nights, weekends, and holidays. They may be on call, which means that they are on duty and must be available to work on short notice. Nurses who work in offices, schools, and other places that do not provide 24-hour care are more likely to work regular business hours.

HOW TO BECOME A REGISTERED NURSE

Registered nurses usually take one of three education paths: a Bachelor of Science degree in nursing (BSN), an associate's degree in nursing (ADN), or a diploma from an approved nursing program. Registered nurses must be licensed

Important Qualities

Critical-thinking skills. Registered nurses must assess changes in the health status of patients, such as determining when to take corrective action and when to make referrals.

Communication skills. Registered nurses must be able to communicate effectively with patients in order to understand their concerns and assess their health conditions. Nurses need to clearly explain instructions, such as how to take medication. They must work in teams with other health professionals and communicate the patients' needs.

Compassion. Registered nurses should be caring and empathetic when looking after patients.

Detail oriented. Registered nurses must be responsible and detail oriented because they must make sure that patients get the correct treatments and medicines at the right time.

Emotional stability. Registered nurses need emotional resilience and the ability to manage their emotions to cope with human suffering, emergencies, and other stresses.

Organizational skills. Nurses often work with multiple patients with various health needs. Organizational skills are critical to ensure that each patient is given appropriate care.

Physical stamina. Nurses should be comfortable performing physical tasks, such as moving patients. They may be on their feet for most of their shift.

EDUCATION

In all nursing education programs, students take courses in anatomy, physiology, microbiology, chemistry, nutrition, psychology, and other social and behavioral sciences, as well as in liberal arts. BSN programs typically take 4 years to complete; ADN and diploma programs usually take 2 to 3 years to complete. Diploma programs are typically offered by hospitals or medical centers, and there are far fewer diploma programs than there are BSN and ADN programs. All programs include supervised clinical experience.

Bachelor's degree programs usually include additional education in the physical and social sciences, communication, leadership, and critical thinking. These programs also offer more clinical experience in nonhospital settings. A bachelor's degree or higher is often necessary for administrative positions, research, consulting, and teaching.

Generally, licensed graduates of any of the three types of education programs (bachelor's, associate's, or diploma) qualify for entry-level positions as a staff nurse. However, employers—particularly those in hospitals—may require a bachelor's degree.

Registered nurses with an ADN or diploma may go back to school to earn a bachelor's degree through an RN-to-BSN program. There are also master's degree programs in nursing, combined bachelor's and master's programs, and accelerated programs for those who wish to enter the nursing profession and already hold a bachelor's degree in another field. Some employers offer tuition reimbursement.

Clinical nurse specialists (CNSs) must earn a master's degree in nursing and typically already have 1 or more years of work experience as an RN or in a related field. CNSs who conduct research typically need a doctoral degree.

Licenses, Certifications, and Registrations

In all states, the District of Columbia, and U.S. territories, registered nurses must have a nursing license. To become licensed, nurses must graduate from an approved nursing program and pass the National Council Licensure Examination (NCLEX-RN).

Other requirements for licensing, such as passing a criminal background check, vary by state. Each state's board of nursing provides specific requirements. For more information on the NCLEX-RN and a list of state boards of nursing, visit the National Council of State Boards of Nursing.

Nurses may become certified through professional associations in specific areas, such as ambulatory care, gerontology, and pediatrics, among others. Although certification is usually voluntary, it demonstrates adherence to a higher standard, and some employers require it.

In addition, registered nursing positions may require certification in cardiopulmonary resuscitation (CPR), basic life support (BLS) certification, and/or advanced cardiac life support (ACLS).

CNSs must satisfy additional state licensing requirements, such as earning specialty certifications. Contact state boards of nursing for specific requirements.

ADVANCEMENT

Most registered nurses begin as staff nurses in hospitals or community health settings. With experience, good performance, and continuous education, they can move to other settings or be promoted to positions with more responsibility.

In management, nurses can advance from assistant clinical nurse manager, charge nurse, or head nurse to more senior-level administrative roles, such as assistant director or director of nursing, vice president of nursing, or chief nursing officer. Increasingly, management-level nursing positions require a graduate degree in nursing or health services administration. Administrative positions require leadership, communication skills, negotiation skills, and good judgment.

Some nurses move into the business side of health care. Their nursing expertise and experience on a health care team equip them to manage ambulatory, acute, home-based, and chronic care businesses. Employers—including hospitals, insurance companies, pharmaceutical manufacturers, and managed care organizations, among others—need registered nurses for jobs in health planning and development, marketing, consulting, policy development, and quality assurance.

Some RNs may become nurse anesthetists, nurse midwives, or nurse practitioners, which, along with clinical nurse specialists, are types of advanced practice registered nurses (APRNs). APRN positions require a master's degree, and many have a doctoral degree. APRNs may provide primary and specialty care, and in many states they may prescribe medications.

Other nurses work as postsecondary teachers or researchers in colleges and universities, which typically requires a Ph.D.

Pay

The median annual wage for registered nurses was $70,000 in May 2017. The lowest 10 percent earned less than $48,690, and the highest 10 percent earned more than $104,100.

Median annual wages, May 2017

Health diagnosing and treating practitioners: $79,480

Registered nurses: $70,000

Total, all occupations: $37,690

Note: All Occupations includes all occupations in the U.S. Economy. Source: U.S. Bureau of Labor Statistics, Occupational Employment Statistics

In May 2017, the median annual wages for registered nurses in the top industries in which they worked were as follows:

Government	$75,900
Hospitals; state, local, and private	72,070
Ambulatory health care services	66,300
Nursing and residential care facilities	62,320
Educational services; state, local, and private	60,300

Because patients in hospitals and nursing care facilities need round-the-clock care, nurses in these settings usually work in shifts, covering all 24 hours. They may work nights, weekends, and holidays. They may be on call, which means that they are on duty and must be available to work on short notice. Nurses who work in offices, schools, and other places that do not provide 24-hour care are more likely to work regular business hours.

JOB OUTLOOK

Employment of registered nurses is projected to grow 15 percent from 2016 to 2026, much faster than the average for all occupations. Growth will occur for a number of reasons.

Percent change in employment, projected 2016-26

Health diagnosing and treating practitioners: 16%

Registered nurses: 15%

Total, all occupations: 7%

Note: All Occupations includes all occupations in the U.S. Economy. Source: U.S. Bureau of Labor Statistics, Employment Projections program

Demand for health care services will increase because of the aging population, given that older people typically have more medical problems than younger people. Nurses also will be needed to educate and care for patients with various chronic conditions, such as arthritis, dementia, diabetes, and obesity.

The financial pressure on hospitals to discharge patients as soon as possible may result in more people being admitted to long-term care facilities and outpatient care centers, and greater need for health care at home. Job growth is expected in facilities that provide long-term rehabilitation for stroke and head injury patients, and in facilities that treat people with Alzheimer's disease. In addition, because many older people prefer to be treated at home or in residential care facilities, registered nurses will be in demand in those settings.

Growth is also expected to be faster than average in outpatient care centers, where patients do not stay overnight, such as those which provide same-day chemotherapy, rehabilitation, and surgery. In addition, an increased number of procedures, as well as more sophisticated procedures previously done only in hospitals, are being performed in ambulatory care settings and physicians' offices.

JOB PROSPECTS

Overall, job opportunities for registered nurses are expected to be good because of employment growth and the need to replace workers who retire over the coming decade. However, the supply of new nurses entering the labor market has increased in recent years. This increase has resulted in competition for jobs in some areas of the country. Generally, registered nurses with a Bachelor of Science degree in nursing (BSN) will have better job prospects than those without one. Employers also may prefer candidates who have some related work experience or certification in a specialty area, such as gerontology.

Employment projections data for registered nurses, 2016-26

Occupational Title	Employment, 2016	Projected Employment, 2026	Change, 2016-26	
			Percent	Numeric
Registered nurses	2,955,200	3,393,200	15	438,100

Source: U.S. Bureau of Labor Statistics, Employment Projections program

SIMILAR OCCUPATIONS

This list shows occupations with job duties that are similar to those of registered nurses.

Dental Hygienists: Dental hygienists clean teeth, examine patients for signs of oral diseases such as gingivitis, and provide other preventive dental care. They also educate patients on ways to improve and maintain good oral health.

Diagnostic Medical Sonographers and Cardiovascular Technologists and Technicians, Including Vascular Technologists: Diagnostic medical sonographers and cardiovascular technologists and technicians, including vascular technologists, also called *diagnostic imaging workers*, operate special imaging equipment to create images or to conduct tests. The images and test results help physicians assess and diagnose medical conditions.

EMTs and Paramedics: Emergency medical technicians (EMTs) and paramedics care for the sick or injured in emergency medical settings. People's lives often depend on the quick reaction and competent care provided by these workers. EMTs and paramedics respond to emergency calls, performing medical services and transporting patients to medical facilities.

Licensed Practical and Licensed Vocational Nurses: Licensed practical nurses (LPNs) and licensed vocational nurses (LVNs) provide basic nursing care. They work under the direction of registered nurses and doctors.

Nurse Anesthetists, Nurse Midwives, and Nurse Practitioners: Nurse anesthetists, nurse midwives, and nurse practitioners, also referred to as *advanced practice registered nurses (APRNs)*, coordinate patient care and may provide primary and specialty health care. The scope of practice varies from state to state.

Physician Assistants: Physician assistants, also known as *PAs*, practice medicine on teams with physicians, surgeons, and other health care workers. They examine, diagnose, and treat patients.

Social Workers: Social workers help people solve and cope with problems in their everyday lives. Clinical social workers also diagnose and treat mental, behavioral, and emotional issues.

Respiratory Therapists: Respiratory therapists care for patients who have trouble breathing—for example, from a chronic respiratory disease, such as asthma or emphysema. Their patients range from premature infants with undeveloped lungs to elderly patients who have diseased lungs. They also provide emergency care to patients suffering from heart attacks, drowning, or shock.

Conversation With . . .
ERIN DICKMAN

MS, RN, OCN
Oncology Clinical Specialist
Oncology Nursing Society, Pittsburgh, Pennsylvania

Erin Dickman has been an oncology nurse for nine years and is currently working as a clinical expert on a variety of multidisciplinary projects, and as an advocate for oncology nurses.

1. What was your individual career path in terms of education/training, entry-level jobs, or other significant opportunity?

As a high schooler, I volunteered in a hospital as a candy striper. This was my first interaction with patients, and it was a joy to help them get to a test, or brighten their day by helping them pack up to be discharged. Seeing that I could impact someone's day with small actions made me look into becoming a nurse, a field I was familiar with because my mom's a nurse. In college, my mentors always said it's a good idea to work your way up and do the role that you will one day be counting on someone else to fulfill. So in college, I took opportunities to be a patient transporter at a hospital, a patient care associate, a research assistant, and a home health care aide. Not all at once, mind you, but those opportunities gave me great perspective on the responsibilities of all the members of a health care team, and how all of those roles can be challenging. They helped me find my passion.

I was drawn to oncology because of the relationships I cultivated with my patients: the opportunity to work with them to fight their cancer, and the chance to help them lead the life they wanted despite their cancer. I earned my bachelor's degree in nursing (BSN) from Ohio State University and soon began work as a staff nurse in the Acute Leukemia Progressive Care Unit at the James Cancer Hospital and Solove Research Institute in Columbus, Ohio.

A lot of people think cancer and they think death, but many therapies and options allow people to live a long life with a higher quality, or be cured. In addition, there's always that hope aspect of a cancer journey, because it is a journey. Patients don't simply come in one day, have surgery, and they're gone. You are able to have the longevity of seeing every step of the journey and have a positive impact on another human being. You can help them live life to the fullest.

Every patient has different needs, and they need to make decisions with their provider. Say there's a treatment that might make a patient feel crappy for a couple of months, but that leads to a month of feeling great. Is it worth it to that person? These conversations are difficult, but they are built into the patient's plan of care—and there is always a plan, whether it is disease management or treatment.

Oncology nursing brings difficult days because patients are scared, and they are going through what's probably the most difficult time in their lives. One of the best parts about being on this scary journey with them is not about giving that person a shot or a pill. You listen to music together, you laugh with them, and you talk about their family. These patients are people, and they still have passions and dreams they want to share. Sometimes they want to forget about having cancer. As an oncology nurse, I can help them forget sometimes, which in small ways helps them heal.

Leukemia (hematology/oncology) remains my specialty, and I have had the privilege to support oncology nurses through my roles in education, program development, and leadership. My road to administration started one day when I was a patient care associate talking someone through how to take a blood draw. I realized I had helped someone learn this lifelong skill, and that influenced me. I went back to my alma mater and earned a master's degree in health systems administration with a focus in public health. James was opening a 1.1-million-square-foot, state-of-the-art cancer center that I knew would be an amazing upgrade for our patients, with more technology, lots of natural light, and private rooms. I wanted to help our staff prepare to move by learning the new work environment and workflows. I was hired onto the project team that helped to build the training and educational curriculum for nurses to work in the new space, along with the new technology they would be using day to day.

My last role at the hospital was as the nurse manager for the James Clinical Resource Unit. A year ago, I took a position as an oncology clinical specialist with the Oncology Nursing Society, which allows me to update courses, review books, write, act as the clinical expert on a variety of multidisciplinary projects, and advocate for oncology nurses.

2. What are the most important skills and/or qualities for someone in your profession?

You need to have great communication skills and be a strong team member. It takes a village to care for patients, and sometimes they are very sick and their treatment is complicated. It's important to communicate with both your patient and your coworkers so you have trust, and you all are on the same page and can work together. In addition, you need to be flexible because circumstances change. A good science background and critical thinking skills are also important.

3. What do you wish you had known going into this profession?

It's nice that most nurses work a three-day-a-week, twelve-hour shift schedule, but it can be challenging to work a twelve-hour shift, especially a night shift. You need to create healthy routines and make lifestyle modifications. For instance, I worked a night shift for a time and made the mistake of not getting blackout curtains so I could sleep during the day. And you need to eat the right foods so you're energized. Also, I wish I had learned more about end-of-life care. I learned a lot from more experienced nurses, who shared some of the words they use to talk to patients—and those conversations do take practice. Sometimes you need to know you don't need to say anything.

4. Are there many job opportunities in your profession? In what specific areas?

Oncology is a fast-growing field with new developments in cancer prevention, screening, and treatment that have led to different roles and job opportunities. Oncology nurses care for medical, surgical, or radiation therapy patients. Some work in research, some help patients navigate care, some are focused on managing patients' symptoms, and some are supporting cancer survivors.

5. How do you see your profession changing in the next five years, how will technology impact that change, and what skills will be required?

Immunotherapy and targeted therapies have changed the way we are treating patients. Precision medicine, also known as individualized medicine, is the present and future of treating cancer not by the tumor's location in the body but by its genetic makeup. We will continue to see many new anticancer drugs come to market, and many oral medications that patients can take at home. Thousands of clinical trials currently are testing new cancer drugs and combination treatments. We currently have more than 15.5 million cancer survivors, a number that will increase to more than twenty million by 2026. We will probably see telemedicine increase and genetic testing become part of all diagnostic work-ups.

6. What do you enjoy most about your job? What do you enjoy least about your job?

My favorite part about my job might sound clichéd, but it's helping people. It feeds my soul to know that I am working toward a bigger mission and helping people through a very difficult and vulnerable time in their lives. The people I work with have the biggest hearts and feel the same, which keeps me motivated. Throughout my career, all the teams I have been part of share a strong sense of pride and dedication to oncology care.

This can be a double-edged sword because, even with the advances, there is still much to be researched and figured out. Staying up-to-date can feel overwhelming. That's where I find the Oncology Nursing Society—my professional home and the place I go for information—to be so helpful.

7. Can you suggest a valuable "try this" for students considering a career in your profession?

Reach out to your local hospital and see if they will let you shadow or volunteer on their oncology unit. (Whether they will or not depends on the hospital.) If that isn't an option, see if they can put you in touch with an oncology nurse who can talk to you about what the job entails. Or reach out to your local Oncology Nursing Society chapter, which would be happy to connect you with a nurse or a shadowing opportunity. The website is www.ons.org.

Conversation With . . .
JOAN FULCHER
MS, BA, BSN, RN-BC
Psychiatric/Mental Health Nurse

Joan Fulcher has been a psychiatric/mental health nurse for nine years and currently works at a Veterans Affairs Hospital in California.

1. What was your individual career path in terms of education/training, entry-level job, or other significant opportunity?

I started out studying sociology in college and earned my degree in the field from the University of California, Irvine. I chose sociology because I found it interesting, but career-wise, I didn't know what to do with that degree. I give credit to my brother for my interest in wanting to become a school psychologist. At the time, he became disabled and worked closely with a school psychologist; that relationship inspired me. I earned my master's degree in counseling with a specialization in school psychology from California State University, Northridge, and became a school psychologist. Although I was helping others, I was working a lot in the office by myself. Still, I enjoyed helping others, especially individuals who felt misunderstood. During this time, I married my husband, who was in the military. I wanted a career that could easily fit with the military lifestyle of moving around, so I chose to go back to school for nursing and earned my nursing degree from National University. Now, I'm doing what I love while being surrounded by supportive co-workers. I come from a family of nurses, so I can also look to them as well as my colleagues for advice or as a sounding board.

Currently—and as at my previous jobs—I work with the patients in therapeutic groups such as recovery, cognitive-behavioral therapy (CBT), and many more. Knowing the various psychotropic medications is a very important part of my job. What's also important is knowing the patients, talking to them, and monitoring their physical and emotional responses to medications and their side effects.

Right now, I work with veterans. My patients have experienced various traumas; some suffer from substance abuse while tackling mental health issues. For me, that has been the most rewarding population to serve so far in my career. I enjoy hearing their stories. They have so much life experience to share with us.

2. What are the most important skills and/or qualities for someone in your profession?

Being able to multitask and stay organized. Often, you have to think quickly and act, so having a consideration for the safety of yourself and others around you is very important.

As with other careers in the health care field, being genuinely caring and empathetic is very important. Other important communication skills are being able to actively listen and take direction when needed. Being in tune with yourself and recognizing your own strengths and weaknesses—as well as what may trigger you emotionally—is important, too.

3. What do you wish you had known going into this profession?

I wish I had known I don't have to do everything all by myself. When I first went into this field, I had difficulty juggling the many tasks I had to do to care for all of my patients. However, I learned that there were trained staff to whom I could delegate certain tasks such as giving showers and baths to patients unable to bathe themselves. Most of the tasks were related to grooming and ADLs (activities of daily living). It was still my responsibility to make sure the tasks were completed. In addition, I find that I see the same patients through the years. Mental health/psychiatric nursing is about the recovery process. It never follows a straight line. No one is ever really "cured." If these duties and responsibilities frustrate you, this field of nursing may not be for you.

4. Are there many job opportunities in your profession? In what specific areas?

Yes! There are many job opportunities in my profession. There are also growing opportunities for nurse practitioners in psychiatry/mental health. This requires additional education and training, but the people I know who have pursued this path enjoy it very much.

5. How do you see your profession changing in the next five years, how will technology impact that change, and what skills will be required?

In the future, telehealth will have a big impact on the health care field, especially in mental health. Sometimes people are not able to receive mental health services due to a lack of transportation, or their mental illness itself is preventing them from coming in to receive help. Technology allows us to meet the patients where they are and provide them with services that might have been inaccessible.

6. What do you enjoy most about your job? What do you enjoy least about your job?

What I enjoy most is helping people. I find it fulfilling to serve veterans because so many of them have sacrificed so much for us. I feel like there is still a stigma around mental illness and working to help educate others about mental illness is very rewarding. I pride myself on being a strong advocate for my patients and treating them with kindness and respect. I'm proud I can help my patients navigate through all of this to find their path.

What I enjoy least about my job is the violence I may encounter from time to time. Sometimes I realize every time I go to work, I am risking my life. It's always in the back of my mind. If a patient becomes violent, that possibility becomes more real, although it doesn't happen often. We have many opportunities to meet the patients' needs and recognize frustrations before they escalate emotionally. At times, substance abuse can play into the violent behavior.

7. Can you suggest a valuable "try this" for students considering a career in your profession?

I suggest going into the community and volunteering or working with advocacy groups like National Alliance on Mental Illness (NAMI). Talking to other psychiatric nurses or those who work in the mental health field can be very eye-opening and give you an idea about what it is like to work in this field.

CONTACTS FOR MORE INFORMATION

For more information about registered nurses, including credentialing, visit

American Nurses Association
https: //www.nursingworld.org/

For more information about nursing education and being a registered nurse, visit

American Society of Registered Nurses
https: //www.asrn.org/

Johnson & Johnson, Nurses change lives
https: //nursing.jnj.com/home

National League for Nursing
http: //www.nln.org/

National Student Nurses' Association
https: //www.nsna.org/

For more information about undergraduate and graduate nursing education, nursing career options, and financial aid, visit

American Association of Colleges of Nursing
https: //www.aacnnursing.org/

For more information about the National Council Licensure Examination (NCLEX-RN) and a list of individual state boards of nursing, visit

National Council of State Boards of Nursing
https: //www.ncsbn.org/

For more information about clinical nurse specialists, including a list of accredited programs, visit

National Association of Clinical Nurse Specialists
https: //nacns.org/

O*NET
Acute Care Nurses
Advanced Practice Psychiatric Nurses
Clinical Nurse Specialists
Critical Care Nurses
Registered Nurses

Source: Bureau of Labor Statistics, U.S. Department of Labor, *Occupational Outlook Handbook*, Registered Nurses, on the Internet at https: //www.bls.gov/ooh/healthcare/registered-nurses.htm (visited *January 20, 2019*).

Surgical Technologists

Snapshot

2017 Median Pay: $46,310 per year, $22.26 per hour

Typical Entry-Level Education: Postsecondary nondegree award

Career Cluster: Health science

On-the-job Training: None

Number of Jobs, 2016: 107,700

Job Outlook, 2016-26: 12% (Faster than average)

Employment Change, 2016-26: 12,600

Holland Score: RSI

CAREER OVERVIEW

Surgical technologists, also called *operating room technicians*, assist in surgical operations. They prepare operating rooms, arrange equipment, and help doctors during surgeries. Most surgical technologists work in hospitals. They spend much of their time on their feet. Surgical technologists typically need a postsecondary nondegree award or an associate's degree. Certification can be beneficial in finding a job. A small number of states regulate surgical technologists.

As a member of the surgical team, a surgical technologist anticipates the needs of the surgeon, prepares the instruments to be used for surgery, hands instruments to the surgeon, promotes efficiency, and at the same time helps prevent infection by maintaining the sterile field. A surgical technologist may also be referred to as a scrub nurse, a surgical assistant, a private scrub, or simply a scrub

Duties

Surgical technologists typically do the following:

- Prepare operating rooms for surgery
- Sterilize equipment and make sure that there are adequate supplies for surgery
- Ready patients for surgery, such as by washing and disinfecting incision sites
- Help surgeons during surgery by passing them instruments and other sterile supplies
- Count supplies, such as sponges and instruments
- Maintain a sterile environment

Surgical technologists work as members of a health care team alongside physicians and surgeons, registered nurses, and other health care workers.

Before an operation, surgical technologists prepare the operating room by setting up surgical instruments and equipment. They also prepare patients for surgery by washing and disinfecting incision sites, positioning the patients on the operating table, covering them with sterile drapes, and taking them to and from the operating room. Surgical technologists prepare sterile solutions and medications used in surgery and check that all surgical equipment is working properly. They help the surgical team put on sterile gowns and gloves.

During an operation, surgical technologists pass instruments and supplies to surgeons and first assistants. They also hold retractors, hold internal organs in place during the procedure, or set up robotic surgical equipment. Technologists also may handle specimens taken for laboratory analysis.

Once the operation is complete, surgical technologists may apply bandages and other dressings to the incision site. They may also help transfer patients to recovery rooms and restock operating rooms after a procedure.

Surgical first assistants have a hands-on role, directly assisting surgeons during a procedure. For instance, they may help to suction the incision site or suture a wound.

WORK ENVIRONMENT

Surgical technologists held about 107,700 jobs in 2016. The largest employers of surgical technologists were as follows:

Hospitals; state, local, and private	71%
Offices of physicians	11
Outpatient care centers	11
Offices of dentists	4

Ambulatory surgical centers are included in outpatient care centers.

Surgical technologists wear scrubs (special sterile clothing) while they are in the operating room. Their work may be physically demanding, requiring them to be on their feet for long periods. Surgical technologists also may need to help move patients or lift heavy trays of medical supplies. At times, they may be exposed to communicable diseases and unpleasant sights, odors, and materials.

Work Schedules

Most surgical technologists work full time. Surgical technologists employed in hospitals may work or be on call during nights, weekends, and holidays. They may also be required to work shifts lasting longer than 8 hours.

HOW TO BECOME A SURGICAL TECHNOLOGIST

Surgical technologists work as members of a health care team alongside physicians and surgeons, registered nurses, and other health care workers.

Surgical technologists typically need a postsecondary nondegree award or an associate's degree. Certification can be beneficial in finding a job. A small number of states regulate surgical technologists.

Important Qualities

Detail oriented. Surgical technologists must pay close attention to their work at all times. For example, they need to provide the correct sterile equipment for surgeons during an operation.

Dexterity. Surgical technologists should be comfortable working with their hands. They must provide needed equipment quickly.

Integrity. Because they are trusted to provide sterile supplies and quality patient care during surgical procedures, surgical technologists must be ethical and honest.

Physical stamina. Surgical technologists should be comfortable standing for extended periods.

Stress-management skills. Working in an operating room can be stressful. Surgical technologists should work well under pressure while providing a high level of care.

EDUCATION

Surgical technologists typically need postsecondary education. Many community colleges and vocational schools, as well as some universities and hospitals, have accredited programs in surgical technology. Programs range in length from several months to 2 years, and they grant a diploma, certificate, or associate's degree upon completion. Admission typically requires a high school diploma or the equivalent.

Surgical technology education includes courses in anatomy, physiology, biology, medical terminology, pharmacology, and other topics. Surgical technologists are trained in the care and safety of patients, sterilization techniques, how to set up technical or robotic equipment, and preventing and controlling infections. In addition to classroom study, students also work in supervised clinical settings to gain hands-on experience.

Surgical first assistants may complete a formal education program in surgical assisting. Others may work as surgical technologists and receive additional on-the-job training before becoming first assistants.

In 2016, there were about 500 surgical technologist programs accredited by the Commission on Accreditation of Allied Health Education Programs (CAAHEP).

Licenses, Certifications, and Registrations

Certification can be beneficial in finding a job. Surgical technologists may earn certification through credentialing organizations.

Certification through the National Board of Surgical Technology and Surgical Assisting allows the use of the title "Certified Surgical Technologist (CST)." Certification typically requires completing an accredited formal education program or military training program and passing an exam.

Certification through the National Center for Competency Testing allows the use of the title "Tech in Surgery – Certified or TS-C (NCCT)." Applicants may qualify through formal education, military training, or work experience. All require documenting critical skills and passing an exam.

Both certifications require surgical technologists to complete continuing education to maintain their certification.

In addition, many jobs require technologists to become certified in CPR or basic life support (BLS), or both.

A small number of states have regulations governing the work of surgical technologists or surgical first assistants, or both.

The National Board of Surgical Technology and Surgical Assisting, the National Commission for the Certification of Surgical Assistants, and the American Board of Surgical Assistants offer certification for surgical first assistants.

ADVANCEMENT

A surgical technologist who has gained some experience may gain a specific area of interest within a broader field and decide to become a specialist. Common areas in which to specialize include eye surgery, neurosurgery, orthopedics, and plastic surgery. If this is the case, the technologist might be invited to work for a certain doctor or may find a number of (perhaps unaffiliated) doctors with whom to work. Working as a private scrub offers a different way to practice in the field. The surgical technologist works directly for the surgeon, instead of working for the hospital or surgical facility, and can usually expect to charge and earn more. There is also the possibility of greater camaraderie with the physician and more trust of the surgical technologist by the physician. Concentrating in a specific area may offer greater remuneration to the surgical technologist, greater rapport with a familiar surgeon, and a more regular schedule, with no requirement for working on the weekends.

Surgical technologists may choose to advance to other health care occupations, such as registered nurse. Advancement to other health care occupations would usually require additional education, training, and/or certifications or licenses. A technologist may also choose to become a postsecondary teacher of health specialties.

Pay

The median annual wage for surgical technologists was $46,310 in May 2017. The lowest 10 percent earned less than $32,470, and the highest 10 percent earned more than $67,000.

Median annual wages, May 2017

Surgical technologists: $46,310

Health technologists and technicians: $43,590

Total, all occupations: $37,690

Note: All Occupations includes all occupations in the U.S. Economy. Source: U.S. Bureau of Labor Statistics, Occupational Employment Statistics

In May 2017, the median annual wages for surgical technologists in the top industries in which they worked were as follows:

Outpatient care centers	$48,900
Offices of physicians	45,980
Hospitals; state, local, and private	45,930
Offices of dentists	44,760

Most surgical technologists work full time. Surgical technologists employed in hospitals may work or be on call during nights, weekends, and holidays. They may also be required to work shifts lasting longer than 8 hours.

JOB OUTLOOK

Employment of surgical technologists is projected to grow 12 percent from 2016 to 2026, faster than the average for all occupations. Advances in medical technology have made surgery safer, and more operations are being done to treat a variety of illnesses and injuries.

Percent change in employment, projected 2016-26

Health technologists and technicians: 14%

Surgical technologists: 12%

Total, all occupations: 7%

Note: All Occupations includes all occupations in the U.S. Economy. Source: U.S. Bureau of Labor Statistics, Employment Projections program

In addition, the aging of the large baby-boom generation is expected to increase the need for surgical technologists because older people usually require more operations. Moreover, as these individuals age, they may be more willing than those in previous generations to seek medical treatment to improve their quality of life. For example, an individual may decide to have a knee replacement operation in order to maintain an active lifestyle or to have cataracts removed to improve vision.

JOB PROSPECTS

Job prospects should be best for surgical technologists who have completed an accredited education program and hold a certification.

Employment projections data for surgical technologists, 2016-26

Occupational Title	Employment, 2016	Projected Employment, 2026	Change, 2016-26	
			Percent	Numeric
Surgical technologists	107,700	120,300	12	12,600

Source: U.S. Bureau of Labor Statistics, Employment Projections program

SIMILAR OCCUPATIONS

This list shows occupations with job duties that are similar to those of surgical technologists.

Dental Assistants: Dental assistants perform many tasks, ranging from providing patient care and taking x rays to recordkeeping and scheduling appointments. Their duties vary by state and by the dentists' offices where they work.

Licensed Practical and Licensed Vocational Nurses: Licensed practical nurses (LPNs) and licensed vocational nurses (LVNs) provide basic nursing care. They work under the direction of registered nurses and doctors.

Medical and Clinical Laboratory Technologists and Technicians: Medical laboratory technologists (commonly known as *medical laboratory scientists*) and medical laboratory technicians collect samples and perform tests to analyze body fluids, tissue, and other substances.

Medical Assistants: Medical assistants complete administrative and clinical tasks in the offices of physicians, hospitals, and other health care facilities. Their duties vary with the location, specialty, and size of the practice.

CONTACTS FOR MORE INFORMATION

For more information about surgical technologists, visit

Association of Surgical Technologists
https: //www.ast.org/

For a list of accredited programs for surgical technologists, visit

Commission on Accreditation of Allied Health Education Programs
https: //www.caahep.org/

For information about certification, visit

The National Board of Surgical Technology and Surgical Assisting
https: //www.nbstsa.org/

National Commission for the Certification of Surgical Assistants
https: //www.csaexam.com/

National Center for Competency Testing
https: //www.ncctinc.com/

American Board of Surgical Assistants
https: //www.absa.net/

O*NET
Surgical Technologists

Source: Bureau of Labor Statistics, U.S. Department of Labor, *Occupational Outlook Handbook*, Surgical Technologists, on the Internet at https: //www.bls.gov/ooh/healthcare/surgical-technologists.htm (visited *January 22, 2019*).

Setting

ASSISTED LIVING FACILITIES

Background

Assisted living care is a form of long-term care. Although assisted living facilities (ALFs) cater to populations other than senior citizens (for example, individuals with disabilities), most facilities provide services for retired senior citizens. Those individuals who require assistance with general activities of daily living such as housekeeping and cooking but do not need significant medical care can often avoid an unnecessarily early entry into a nursing home by first living in an assisted living facility. Therefore, these facilities provide varying degrees of daily assistance for otherwise healthy and independent seniors.

Although assisted living as a practice is regulated throughout the United States, not all states use the same terminology, making comparisons difficult. States use various terminology-senior housing, board and care, adult foster care-that may or may not espouse the principles of ALFs. Accordingly, state regulation of a particular facility may be minimal to nonexistent. For example, some states regulate the type of services while others regulate the building itself. Many of the states with a high percentage of seniors, such as Florida, have adopted an inclusive umbrella model that regulates the entire ALF. However, this lack of consistent federal oversight throughout all states proves confusing for many individuals-especially those searching for long-term care. However, "assisted living facility" is the most common term for longterm care that provides some, but not all, assistance in activities of daily living for its residents.

The ongoing cost of long-term care often consumes the retirement savings of many seniors. The combined expenses of medications, visits to the primary care provider and personal assistance often outweigh simple housing costs, and elderly individuals are often at risk for injury when performing household chores at home. However, seniors now have the option of an ALF, which often provides individual treatment plans that maintain privacy and dignity by permitting broad independence at a fraction of what nursing homes charge. To contain costs, assisted living facilities have replaced comprehensive in-house medical services, such as those available at traditional nursing homes, with individual treatment plans that provide their residents with the optimal amount of help for their particular situations.

Assisted living facilities are fundamentally different from other senior-oriented care options. Similar to child-care facilities, adult day-care facilities provide daytime care for seniors who live with their children. Often, adult day-care facilities cater to individuals who have cognitive dysfunction (for example, memory loss or Alzheimer's disease). Adult daycare facilities typically operate during the weekday work hours, providing caregivers respite either during the day or during their work commitments. In contrast to ALFs, residents leave the facility at the end of the day. Another senior-oriented care option is a nursing home. Nursing homes are similar to ALFs in that the resident lives full time at the facility; however, nursing homes manage medical routines, provide intensive medical and nursing care, and all of daily care-often including dressing, bathing, and additional self-care activities.

Types of Assisted Living Facilities

Although differences abound in ALFs, there are basic similarities. Assisted living facilities typically require residents to be generally in control of the majority of their activities of daily living. Residents are expected to perform their own bathing, dressing, and personal care, including medication routines. Although some residents might have minor memory impairments, most are generally in good physical and psychological health, and ALFs strive to create an environment to foster the continued good health of their residents. Strong social connections can often form between residents at cohesive ALFs, an important element of the aging process. Research suggests maintaining strong social interactions is key to maintaining health and well-being as one ages.

There are as many living arrangements as there are ALFs. Some ALFs resemble hostels with eight or more beds in one room, several rooms to a floor, and a separate communal bathroom. Because of the high volume of residents, these ALFs often do not offer individualized treatment plans and, in a situation reminiscent of nursing homes, independence and autonomy are often replaced by resident infantilization. Although these ALFs lack privacy and the staff-to-resident ratio, by necessity, is high, these are generally the least expensive among all the ALFs. General health and well-being often decline rapidly after admittance, forcing relocation to a more care-intensive facility. Accordingly, these ALFs have the quickest resident turnover of all the long-term care facilities.

On the opposite end of the ALF spectrum is the assisted living retirement community. These facilities mimic in-home care as precisely as possible. Whereas retirement communities are generally populated by completely healthy and independent older adults, assisted living retirement communities offer all the amenities and privacy of retirement communities as well as daily in-home care. Often these communities have extensive amenities, including recreation facilities, swimming pools, and other outside sport facilities. In addition, they frequently have numerous staff members dedicated to organizing and maintaining these amenities. Accordingly, these facilities are generally the most expensive but offer the greatest privacy and most closely resemble the aging-at-home experience.

Between crowded communal living and luxurious retirement- style living is the most common form of ALFs, the apartment-style assisted living facility. Constructed as typical apartments, these facilities provide each resident with a complete and separate living facility. Each unit generally has a complete bathroom, bedroom, and living room-full kitchens are often not included. Each resident lives independently but eats in a communal dining room with other residents. Communal social rooms and twenty-four-hour security and staff presence are standard amenities. High-end facilities may provide shuttle services, hairdressers, comprehensive exercise facilities-often with a full-time activity director- and monthly visits from nurse practitioners or medical doctors. Regardless of their size, most ALFs often look and feel like home for the residents and their visitors.

Safety Concerns

The expansion of assisted living facilities benefits the long term care industry writ large. Prior to the large numbers of ALFs, nursing homes bore the brunt of aging seniors. Seniors experiencing even the smallest impediment in independence were forced into nursing homes. Because nursing homes are designed to cater to the most dependent seniors, even the most functional seniors often experience precipitous drops in functioning from early entry. The same health impediments that nursing homes cater to are, conversely, also a struggle for ALFs.

The line between whether someone should remain in his or her home versus residing in an ALF can be difficult to determine for a spouse and other family members. Often safety concerns become the final determinant. An inability to cook for themselves or minor memory concerns (for example, forgetfulness with the stove) are often used to rationalize a difficult decision. This decision may be easier in the future, however, as research suggests that ALFs prolong independence compared to remaining in one's residential setting. Often removing one's responsibility for a few activities of daily living relieves stress and mental reserves, allowing the senior to focus on other personal care routines. The independent orientation of ALFs stands in contrast to nursing homes, which often contribute to dependency rather than facilitate independence. Just as safety concerns may lead to the move to an ALF, the decision to discharge a resident from an ALF is also often driven by safety concerns. Because ALFs do not provide twenty-four-hour intensive service, residents are free to come and go from the facility and use the bathroom or other accident-prone areas. Residents who are either cognitively impaired or whose health has declined dramatically are often asked to leave the ALF, and for many seniors the next move is into a nursing home.

Regardless of the size, philosophical orientation, or services provided, ALFs provide a much-needed option in longterm care. Seniors with minor impairments can extend their functional independence for many years, and seniors in ALFs actually experience prolonged independence over remaining in home. In tandem with the rapidly aging population, ALFs are evolving even as they struggle with their own identity nationally and within each state.

Perspective and Prospects

Assisted living facilities burgeoned as the aging baby boomers approached retirement. Baby boomers, the generation born between 1946 and 1964, are healthier and more independent than retirees of the past, and the long-term care industry responded to this demographic shift with the expansion of ALFs. Prior to the broad expansion of ALFs, seniors in need of even the smallest amount of assistance were forced into nursing homes unless they could afford costly in-home care. More recent developments in long-term care involve graduated levels of care in one facility to accommodate residents' needs as they age. In contrast to assisted living-only facilities, where residents must move out after they become unable to bathe, dress, or manage their general health successfully, facilities that offer an increased level of care as needed permit residents to move through their retirement years in a single location. Providing flexible services is especially important to a senior's quality of life, as familiarity and daily routines often can mask advancing stages of mental confusion. These facilities, sometimes referred to as continuing-care retirement communities, have residence fees that are typically higher-most facilities require an entrance fee of more than $60,000-thus limiting this option to the most wealthy of seniors. Nevertheless, these facilities are an important part of the ongoing redefinition of independent living. Where pure ALFs provide a designated set of services, continuing care communities can adapt to the particular needs of each resident throughout the aging process.

This revolution in long-term care has also carried over to nursing homes and has led to the creation of green nursing homes. These nursing homes house approximately ten residents in a large house like structure and provide a full range of personal care and medical services. As in ALFs, the focus in these green homes is on independent thriving. Whereas nursing homes were historically viewed as the last option for seniors, these new green nursing homes are often abundant with plants, domestic animals, homelike furnishings, and daily visitors and volunteers who try to keep the residents and staff cheerful and healthy.

Irrespective of any particular facility or philosophy of care, assisted living facilities are the favored choice of aging seniors. No spouse or family member wants to watch a loved one lose control of daily functioning. Overworked and economically strapped children of aging parents often find themselves faced with a difficult decision. By focusing on dignity, independence, and freedom, assisted living facilities make these choices easier for many.

Dana K. Bagwell
Ophelia Empleo-Frazier, MSN, GNP-BC, WCC, DCP

CASE MANAGEMENT

In general terms, case management is a process that brings together the resources of disparate people and agencies to evaluate a person's health needs and put together, implement, coordinate, and monitor a plan to address them. The process combines, as needed, the resources of patients and their families, health care professionals, social service agencies, community groups, employers, and insurance carriers to meet its goals.

Goals of case management

The principal goal of case management is to help patients and their families navigate the complex and fragmented health care system by coordinating efforts among service providers to deliver timely, appropriate, and cost-effective care according to each individual's needs. Health care has been increasingly moving toward a patient-centered model, in which the values, preferences, cultural traditions, family situations, and lifestyles of patients and their families are taken into consideration. Therefore, case management typically tries to involve patients and their families in prevention plans, treatment options, and financial decisions. It also aims to reduce health care costs for patients and service providers. By coordinating all the various functions of treating people for serious diseases such as cancer, efficiency is increased and cost is decreased. Case management also tries to improve the standards of care for patients.

Many medical and government organizations along with individual hospitals, clinics, and medical centers (including cancer centers) have established case management guidelines. These guidelines, based on empirical research and numerous trials and observations, provide a system to help patients across what is known as the continuum of care. Clinical and ethical standards apply in all areas of care, from prevention of disease to end-of-life issues, and to all the components of case management.

Case management components

Case management has developed a set of core components: screening and assessment, treatment, community involvement, arranging for nonmedical services, monitoring, and reassessment. These core components, along with sets of subcomponents, come together to create a specific care plan for each patient. For example, the case management components and subcomponents for the care plan of a seventy-five-year-old man with prostate cancer might include the following:

- Screening and assessment: examinations by the patient's primary care provider, referrals to an oncologist or urologist, testing to determine the nature of the disease, establishing a treatment plan based on the stage of the cancer, evaluating the patient's financial status, creating the cancer care plan

- Treatment: aggressive radiation therapy, five days a week for seven weeks at a cancer center

- Community involvement: scheduling rides for the patient to and from the cancer center with volunteers from the local chapter of the American Cancer Society, introducing the patient and the patient's family to a local support group, referring the patient to an oncology social worker

- Arranging for nonmedical services: working with Medicare or Medicaid to pay for treatment

- Monitoring: periodic checking to see that all components of the cancer care plan are functioning, and adjusting the plan if necessary

- Reassessment: scheduled follow-up visits with doctors, the oncology social worker, and Medicare or Medicaid

Managing all these components to create the cancer care plan is the job of the medical case manager.

Fast Fact

Occupational nurses can always use additional training outside the usual medical realm. For instance, a course in Occupational Safety and Ergonomics teaches principals that affect the design of the workplace in terms of lifting and posture—issues that could impact workers.

Source: careersinpublichealth.net

The medical case manager

Most medical case managers (MCMs) are registered nurses. The medical case manager may also be a staff member of a hospital or cancer center and is often hired by an employer or insurance carrier. The role of the medical case manager includes, but is not limited to, the following:

- Overseeing patients' cancer care throughout diagnosis, treatment, and follow-up
- Assessing patients' health, nutrition, psychological, and care needs
- Assessing patients' financial needs
- Educating patients on different cancer types, treatments and side effects, and possible outcomes to allow them to make informed decisions about their care
- Helping patients communicate more effectively with their doctors
- Linking patients with the appropriate community resources
- Coordinating the efforts of the cancer care team

Famous First

Dorothea Lynde Dix (April 4, 1802 – July 17, 1887) was an American advocate on behalf of the indigent mentally ill who, through a vigorous and sustained program of lobbying state legislatures and the United States Congress, created the first generation of American mental asylums. During the Civil War, she served as a Superintendent of Army Nurses beating out Dr. Elizabeth Blackwell.

Source: https://en.wikipedia.org/wiki/Dorothea_Dix

The cancer care team

Each cancer patient's needs are different. Meeting those needs requires a team of professionals with different expertise. Depending on the patient, the cancer care team may consist of the following individuals, all under the watchful eye of the medical case manager:

- Oncology social worker: a professional trained in counseling and providing practical assistance in navigating the health care system
- Psychiatrist or psychologist: to help the patient who has trouble coping psychologically with cancer
- Nurses: providers of a wide range of help, from implementing the care plan to answering questions for the patient and family
- Home health aide: a worker who helps cancer patients at home with daily living tasks

- Rehabilitation specialists: physical, occupational, and speech therapists who help patients recover from the physical changes caused by cancer or cancer treatment
- Oncology nutritionist: a specialist who advises on diet to help the patient cope with the consequences of cancer and side effects of treatment
- Hospice workers: caregivers who focus on the special needs of patients with terminal cancer

---

Wendell Anderson, B.A.

CLINICS

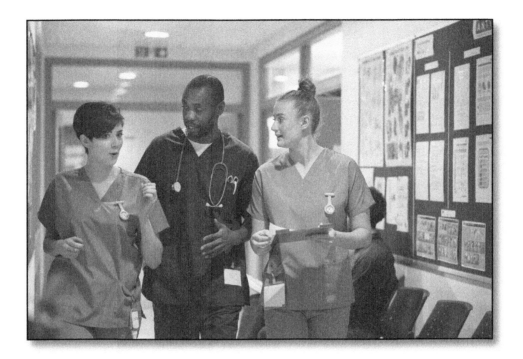

Organizations that provide outpatient care to specific types of patients; they can be in-hospital or out of hospital, usually consist of a physical space with reception and examination rooms, and are staffed by doctors, nurses, and other health care professionals.

Organization and Functions

There are three main types of patient care facilities in North America: hospitals, ambulatory surgery centers, and clinics. Hospitals care for patients who require overnight care, emergency care, or intensive care treatment. Hospital emergency rooms are not usually considered a clinic due to the highly specialized equipment needed and the fact that many patients who are treated in the emergency room are then admitted for overnight stay at a hospital. Ambulatory surgery centers provide outpatient surgery. Clinics provide outpatient nonsurgical care. In some cases, minor procedures are performed in clinics; however, a clinic does not provide outpatient surgery.

A clinic will usually consist of at least a waiting room and patient exam rooms. The number of examination rooms and size of the clinic will depend on the number of providers and the clinic type. Clinics can range in size from a solo practice with a very small office to very large multispecialty outpatient clinics such as the Mayo

Clinic or Cleveland Clinic. Specialized equipment may be part of a clinic, such as in a dental clinic. Clinics may be located within a hospital, in a private building, or in a public building. Clinics can be owned and operated by a single practitioner, a group of practitioners, a private group, a public or nonprofit group, a hospital, or a government agency.

Clinics will most often have regular business hours and are not usually open overnight. Some urgent care walk-in clinics may have extended hours. Most clinics will be closed on major holidays. Some smaller solo practitioner clinics may close for one or more weeks per year when the provider is on vacation. Some clinics will have an answering service or after-hours coverage for emergency calls.

Clinic administration will depend on the ownership of the clinic. A solo private practitioner may do administration as well as provision of care. Hospital-based clinics will generally have a clinic manager who works within the administrative system of the hospital. Some clinics may be part of a publicly held company and will have an office manager who reports to a board. Most clinics will have a clinic manager and a medical director. Larger clinics will have more administrative staff, including human resource staff and marketing staff.

Each clinic serves a specific patient population that will be determined by the primary provider or providers within the clinic. For example, a solo family practice physician will serve children and adults for treatment of common illnesses and conditions. In contrast, a pediatric clinic will see only children, and some public health clinics may provide only immunization services. There are as many clinics as there are health care specialties. Some providers will work in groups, such as a multidiscipline group that may contain internal medicine, pediatrics, and dermatology.

Clinics may accept direct fee-for-service payment, insurance, or government funding such as Medicare, Veterans Administration, or Indian Health Service. In Canada, most clinics will accept fee-for-service payment, provincial health insurance payment, or both.

A large number of combinations are possible in terms of specific services offered, number of providers, payment types accepted, clinic size, and clinic location. No matter what the combination of these features, all clinics have in common the provision of nonsurgical outpatient health care services.

Staff and Services

A health care clinic will generally be staffed by a primary provider and support staff. The primary provider will often be a medical doctor but can be another type of provider such as physical therapist, chiropractor, optometrist, dentist, or naturopath. Support staff will include nurses, physician assistants, technicians, office staff, and, in some cases, specialized paraprofessionals. Providers and other specialized staff who provide direct patient care will have licensing requirements that are specific to the state or province and that will vary depending on the field. For example, physicians and dentists will have different licensing requirements.

Depending on the clinic, patients may require referral from a physician. Other clinics such as urgent care clinics will accept walk-ins without referral. Walk-in clinics may refer patients to family practice clinics or other clinics for ongoing care of chronic disease.

Services will depend on the clinic providers. For example, a family practice clinic will provide physical examination, diagnosis, and treatment recommendations for people of all ages for general nonsurgical outpatient medical care. Diagnosis might include giving a patient requisitions to have laboratory or radiology (X-ray) or other specialized tests done at a laboratory or radiology facility. Some family practice clinics may have the capacity to do some simple laboratory tests such as a dip urinalysis or electrocardiography (ECG or EKG). Treatment may include advice, prescription for medications, or treatment of minor injuries.

Another example of a clinic would be a physical therapy clinic. This type of clinic would have one or more physical therapists as providers. These providers would provide limited physical examination, usually of the musculoskeletal system. Diagnosis would be based on the physical examination. Physical therapists would not usually order specialized testing such as X rays or magnetic resonance imaging (MRI) but might comanage a patient with a physician provider if these additional diagnostic tests were needed. Treatment within a physical therapy clinic will usually consist of specialized exercises, massage therapy, heat or cold treatment, specialized physical therapy maneuvers, and, in some cases, acupuncture.

Specialized clinics will treat only specific groups of patients. For example, an obstetrics clinic will provide care only to pregnant women. Pediatrics clinics will treat only children. Ophthalmology clinics will treat both children and adults but will care only for vision and other eye-related problems. Similarly, an orthopedic clinic will be focused on musculoskeletal disorders, and sports medicine clinics will treat sports-related injuries.

Urgent care clinics are designed to treat minor illnesses and minor injuries. More significant illness or injury would be treated in a hospital emergency room. Most urgent care clinics will operate on a walk-in basis due to the nature of the clinic focus. Some hospitals have both an urgent care clinic and an emergency room to keep the emergency room available for the more seriously ill or injured.

The Mayo Clinic and the Cleveland Clinic are examples of clinics that have grown to become very large multidisciplinary clinics that provide outpatient care. These large clinics are affiliated with hospitals that provide inpatient and surgical care.

Some clinics receive public funding to serve low-income populations. This type of clinic may operate on a sliding scale for fee payment. Often this type of clinic will be located in an urban area and may serve homeless populations as well. These clinics are sometimes staffed by volunteers, including volunteer providers.

Regardless of the clinic type, the usual practice is to have the patient check in at a desk in the reception area. Patients may have to wait in the reception area until the appropriate staff is ready and until an exam or treatment room is available. Each patient will have a paper or computerized chart that will record the examinations, diagnosis, and treatment recommendations. The patient will then be taken to the exam room, where a nurse or other specialized staff will often do some preliminary testing such as blood pressure and a preliminary history to determine what services are needed. If the chart is a paper chart, then it will be taken along with the patient to the exam room. The provider will often go from one exam room to the next to examine and treat patients. The support staff will clean each exam room as it is vacated and then room the next patient. This system allows for more efficiency for the provider. Once the provider is done with examination, diagnosis, and treatment, the patient is directed back to the reception area to book additional appointments or testing, if necessary, and is then dismissed from the clinic.

A patient who comes to a clinic with a life-threatening condition or serious injury will be directed to the nearest emergency room. In some cases, an ambulance will be called to transport a patient who is in need of inpatient care, emergency treatment, or immediate surgery.

Fast Fact

When school is out, emergency room visits from children under 14 rise by 18 percent.
Source: monster.com

Perspective and Prospects

The word "clinic" is derived from the Greek word for bed, *kline*. Evidence exists for the use of herbs and other natural substances for the treatment of medical conditions even in prehistoric times. The provision of health care has been historically linked with religious and spiritual beliefs. In some cases, religious leaders such as shamans or monks were the providers of health care, and illness was attributed to demons or witchcraft.

Ancient Egypt has been credited with having organized houses of medicine, and Herophilos (335-280 BCE) is considered the founder of the medical school in Alexandria, Egypt. The knowledge of human anatomy was very limited, there was no understanding of sterile technique, no understanding of germ theory, and few treatment options were available; however, these early institutions served to further medical knowledge. In the Middle Ages, medical care was provided in monasteries, which in some cases had hospitals attached.

Licensing standards vary across the world, and in some places the provision of health care is still largely unregulated. There are some areas in which the only clinics in existence are provided by volunteer organizations, and in some areas these clinics are in the form of mobile trailers.

The Mayo Clinic is one of the best known multidisciplinary clinics. It was established in the aftermath of a destructive tornado in Rochester, Minnesota, in 1883. William

Mayo and his sons Charles and William joined the Sisters of St. Francis to establish a hospital and clinic to care for tornado victims. It grew to be the first and largest nonprofit multispecialty clinic serving more than one-half million patients annually at its three locations.

E. E. Anderson Penno, M.D., M.S., FRCSC

Conversation With . . .
DEBARATH HADDAD
RN
Health Services Nurse

Deborah Haddad has been a nurse for thirty years and a health services nurse for ten years at Cumberland County Schools in Fayetteville, North Carolina.

1. What was your individual career path in terms of education/training, entry-level job, or other significant opportunity?

I earned my associate degree in nursing (ADN) in 1988 and my bachelor's degree in nursing (BSN) in 1990 from Armstrong State College in Savannah, Georgia. After graduation, I worked at a local hospital. Initially, I was unsure of what area of nursing I wanted to pursue. The hospital offered a critical care residency program for new graduates, so I began there. The new nurse is paired with an experienced nurse in each of the critical care units to learn the skills necessary to function effectively in these areas. At some point, I realized this type of nursing was not the best fit for me. Around the same time, the hospital started a pediatric unit, so I switched to pediatrics and worked in that unit for three-and-a-half years. I had always wanted to work with children, and this is the area in which I excelled. It was the best choice in my career, a perfect match.

Sometimes I assumed the responsibility of charge nurse who oversees the function of the unit. I also served as preceptor for nursing students from local colleges.

Now, as a health services nurse in Cumberland County Schools, I provide care to children who may require gastrostomy tube feedings, urinary catheterizations, tracheostomy care, diabetes management, and other special health care needs a child may require. Health Services consists of nineteen staff members: registered nurses, licensed practical nurses, and certified nursing assistants who visit schools and provide care to special needs children. We are different from "school nurses" who are usually employed by a county's health department.

Our student populations can range from a typically developing child to a child with children with autism, cerebral palsy, and even severe neurological impairment. I absolutely love seeing my students every day and caring for them. Some of our students are nonverbal, and this poses a bit of a challenge to providing care. This is where you have to rely on your assessment skills and getting to know the children—individually—because they cannot tell you they do not feel well or that something is wrong. It is the best feeling in the world when you do connect with these children, and they smile and squeal when you walk into the classroom or they attempt to sing along with you in their own way by making sounds.

2. What are the most important skills and/or qualities for someone in your profession?

First, you should genuinely enjoy working with and caring for people. Good communication skills are needed in general. You'll be interacting with not only the patients and families but also physicians and others from many disciplines, especially in a hospital setting. In addition, your assessment skills are very important. With all of the advances in technology, I feel the nurse must not forget to always assess the patient and not only focus on all the machines. Lastly, you need to have excellent organizational skills.

3. What do you wish you had known going into this profession?

The best wages are in the hospital setting. Working in a hospital is also the most physically demanding type of nursing, in my opinion. Personally, this was not ideal when I started my family and wanted to be home with my children. Being an employee of a school system allows you to work a similar schedule to your children. This was always a priority for me. When I began working for Cumberland County Schools ten years ago, my children were of school age.

4. Are there many job opportunities in your profession? In what specific areas?

There are various opportunities for a nurse who wants to work in a school setting. Health services nurses work in all grades, from elementary to high school. In higher education, colleges and universities have nurses on campus who have a range of duties such as caring for sick students, overseeing immunization requirements, and monitoring infection control concerns.

5. How do you see your profession changing in the next five years, how will technology impact that change, and what skills will be required?

The nursing profession is constantly evolving and advancing. With new technology and the development of more sophisticated equipment, nurses have to show they are proficient and competent to perform the skills required within their scope of practice. Health Services nurses usually do their charting on a school computer. The main change I've noticed within the last few years is more children attending school who require more complex care. For example, some children not only have a tracheostomy (breathing) tube but also a portable ventilator. A nurse must have a basic understanding of the equipment a child uses for his/her condition(s). I expect to see more of this trend in the coming years.

6. What do you enjoy most about your job? What do you enjoy least about your job?

It's working and interacting with special needs children—all children, really.

What I enjoy least is, at times, not knowing the complete health history of a child. I formerly worked in a hospital setting where you usually have an understanding of the patients, the tests they have had, and the results. As a nurse, I think you are constantly asking yourself questions, trying to connect the dots to make sense of what is going on with a patient. The school setting is different in that regard. A child may be out for a test or even surgery, and I may or may not receive a very limited explanation. Although I work with these children on a daily basis, at times I don't get a full explanation of what is going on. I have to rely on whatever the parent chooses to share.

7. Can you suggest a valuable "try this" for students considering a career in your profession?

Look for any volunteer opportunities, or even consider working as a nurse's aide. I worked as an aide when I was in nursing school. You may be able to become a certified nursing assistant (CNA), which allows you to perform some basic procedures once you are competent in the job.

CRITICAL CARE

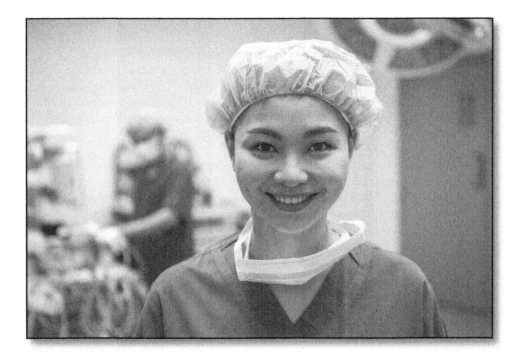

The care of patients who are experiencing severe health crises-short-lived or prolonged, accidental or anticipated-that require continuous monitoring.

Science and Profession

Critical care is the branch of medicine that provides immediate services, usually on an emergency basis. It also encompasses some forms of ongoing care provided in a hospital setting for patients who are so sick that they are medically unstable and must be monitored constantly. Such patients are at an ongoing high risk for disastrous complications.

Critical care personnel must be specially trained, and standards for training and evaluation in this field have been prepared for physicians, nurses, and other hospital personnel. Approximately 90 percent of hospitals in the United States with fewer than two hundred beds have a single critical care unit, usually called an intensive care unit (ICU). Only 9 percent of these hospitals have a second intensive care facility, typically dedicated solely to the care of heart attack victims. In total, 7 to 8 percent of all hospital beds in the United States are used for intensive care. Because ICU facilities are at a premium and are expensive to operate, patients are transferred to a regular hospital bed as quickly as possible, given the severity of their specific medical condition. Of the physicians who are certified in critical care, most are anesthesiologists, followed by internists.

Critical care facilities are available in several varieties, providing specialized care to particular patients. The most common type of ICU is for individuals who require care for medical crises. These patients frequently have a short-term condition or disease that can be treated successfully. Others are admitted to a medical ICU for multiple organ system failure. These people are often very sick with conditions that overwhelm even the best available care and equipment. Heart attack victims are often admitted to a coronary ICU, which has specialized equipment for support and resuscitation if needed. Once medically stable, coronary ICU patients are transferred to a regular hospital bed.

Larger hospitals may have an ICU for surgical patients. Typically, these individuals are admitted to the surgical ICU from the operating room after a procedure. In the ICU, they are stabilized while the effects of anesthesia wear off. They, too, are transferred to a normal hospital room as soon as is medically safe. Neonatal ICUs exist in some larger hospitals to provide care for premature and very sick infants. Such infants may stay in neonatal ICUs for extended periods of time (weeks to months) depending on their specific condition. There may also be a pediatric ICU specially designed for very sick children.

Diagnostic and Treatment Techniques

Critical care is synonymous with immediate care: Swift action is required on an emergency basis to sustain or save a life. The most immediate of critical care needs are to establish and maintain a patent airway for ventilation and to maintain sufficient cardiac functioning to provide minimal perfusion or blood supply to critical organs of the body.

Resuscitation is the support of life by external means when the body is unable to maintain itself. Basic life support is for emergency situations and consists of delivering oxygen to the lungs, maintaining an airway, inflating the lungs if necessary, and assisting with circulation. These methods are collectively known as cardiopulmonary resuscitation (CPR). Oxygen can be transferred from one mouth to another by forceful breathing or by the means of pumps and pure oxygen from a container. The airway is commonly maintained by positioning the head and neck so as to extend the chin and open the trachea. It is also possible to make an incision in the trachea, insert a tube, and provide oxygen through the tube. The lungs may be inflated by using the force of exhaled air from one person breathing into another's mouth or by utilizing a machine that inflates the lungs to a precise level and delivers oxygen in accurate, predetermined amounts. When a victim's heart is not working, the circulation of blood is provided by external compression of the chest. This action squeezes the heart between the sternum and the spine, forcing blood into the circulatory system.

Advanced life support includes attempts to restart a nonfunctioning heart. This goal is commonly accomplished by electrical means (defibrillation). The heart is given a brief shock that is sufficient to start it beating on its own. Drugs can also be used to restore spontaneous circulation in cardiac arrest. Epinephrine (adrenaline) is the most commonly used drug, although sodium bicarbonate is used for some conditions. A heart can be restarted by manual compression. This technique requires direct access to the heart and is limited to situations in which the heart stops beating during a surgical procedure involving the thorax, when the heart is directly accessible.

Prolonged life support is administered after the heart has been restarted and is concerned chiefly with the brain and other organs such as the kidneys that are sensitive to oxygen levels in the blood. Drugs and mechanical ventilation are used to supply oxygen to the lungs. Prolonged life support uses sophisticated technology to deliver oxygenated blood to the organs continuously. The body can be maintained in this manner for long periods of time. Once begun, prolonged life support is continued until the patient regains consciousness or until brain death has been certified by a physician. A patient's state of underlying disease may be determined to be so severe that continuing prolonged life support becomes senseless. The factors entering into a decision to terminate life support are complex and involve a patient's family, the physician, and other professionals.

Individuals who are critically ill must be closely monitored. Many of the advancements in the care of these patients have been attributable to improvements in monitoring. While physiologic measurements cannot replace the clinical impressions of trained professionals, monitoring data often provide objective information that reinforces clinical opinions. More people die from the failure of vital organs than from the direct effects of injury or disease. The most commonly monitored events are vital signs: heart rate, blood pressure, breathing rate, and temperature. These are frequently augmented by electrocardiograms (ECGs or EKGs). Other, more sophisticated electronic methods are available for individuals in intensive care units.

Vital signs are still frequently assessed manually, although machinery is available to accomplish the task. Modern intensive care units are able to store large amounts of data that can be analyzed by computer programs. Data can be transmitted to distant consoles, thus enabling a small number of individuals to monitor several patients simultaneously. Monitoring data can also be displayed on computer screens, allowing more rapid evaluation. Automatic alarms can be used to indicate when bodily functions fall outside predetermined parameters, thus rapidly alerting staff to critical or emergency situations.

Breathing-or, more correctly, ventilation-can be monitored extensively. The volume of inspired air can be adjusted to accommodate different conditions. The amount of oxygen can be changed to compensate for emphysema or other loss of oxygen exchange capacity. The rate of breathing can also be regulated to work in concert with the heart in order to provide maximum benefit to the patient. The effectiveness of pulmonary monitoring is itself monitored by measuring the amount of oxygen in arterial blood. This, too, can be accomplished automatically, with adjustments made by instruments.

Common situations that require critical care are choking, drowning, poisoning, physical trauma, psychological trauma, and environmental disasters.

Choking. Difficulty in either breathing or swallowing is termed choking. The source of the obstruction may be either internal or external. Internal obstructions can result from a foreign body becoming stuck in the mouth (pharynx), throat (esophagus or trachea), or lungs (bronchi). The blockage may be partial or total. A foreign body that is caught in the esophagus will create difficulty in swallowing; one that is caught in the trachea will obstruct breathing. Any foreign body may become lodged and create a blockage. Objects that commonly cause obstructions include teeth (both natural and false), food (especially meat and fish bones), and liquids such as water and blood.

Obstructions can occur externally. Examples of external causes of choking include compression of the larynx or trachea as a result of blunt trauma (a physical blow or other injury sustained in an accident), a penetrating projectile such as a bullet or stick, and toys or small items of food that are swallowed accidentally. An object that becomes stuck in the lungs frequently does not cause an acute shortage of breath, but this situation can lead to aspiration pneumonia, which is extremely difficult to treat.

The symptoms of choking are well known: gagging, coughing, and difficulty in breathing. Pain may or may not be present. Frequently, there is a short episode of difficulty in breathing followed by a period when no symptoms are experienced. The foreign body may be moved aside or pushed deeper into
he body by the victim's initial frantic movements. A foreign body lodged in the esophagus will not interfere with breathing but may cause food or liquids to spill into the trachea and become aspirated; as with an object in the lungs, this usually leads to pneumonia or other serious respiratory conditions.

Drowning. Drowning is defined as the outcome (usually death) of unanticipated immersion into a liquid (usually water). Consciousness is an important determinant of how an individual reacts to immersion in water. A person who is conscious will attempt to escape from the fluid environment, which involves attempts to regain orientation and not to aspirate additional liquids. An unconscious person has none of these defenses and usually dies when the lungs fill rapidly with water. Normal persons can hold their breath for thirty seconds or more. Frequently, this is sufficient time for a victim to escape from immersion in a fluid environment. When a victim exhales just prior to entering water, this time period is not available; indeed, panic frequently develops, and the victim aspirates water.

Most but not all victims of drowning die from aspirating water. Approximately 10 percent of drowning victims die from asphyxia while underwater, possibly because they hold their breath or because the larynx goes into spasms. The brain of the average person can survive without oxygen for about four minutes. After that time, irreversible damage starts to occur; death follows in a matter of minutes. After four minutes, survival is possible but unlikely to be without the permanent impairment of mental functions.

The physical condition of the victim exerts a profound influence on the outcome of a drowning situation. Physically fit persons have a far greater chance of escaping from a drowning environment. Individuals who are in poor condition, who are very weak, or who have disabilities must overcome these conditions when attempting to escape from a drowning situation; frequently, they are unable to remove themselves and die in the process.

Another physical condition such as exhaustion or a heart attack may also be present. An exhausted person is weak and may not have the physical strength or endurance to escape. A person who experiences a heart attack at the moment of immersion is at a severe disadvantage. If the heart is unable to deliver blood and nutrients to muscles, even a physically fit person is weakened and may be less likely to escape a drowning situation.

The temperature of the water is critical. Immersing the face in cold water (below 20 degrees Celsius or 56 degrees Fahrenheit) initiates a reflex that slows the person's heart rate and shunts blood to the heart and brain, thus delaying irreversible cerebral damage. Immersion in water even colder leads to hypothermia (subnormal body temperature). In the short term, hypothermia reduces the body's consumption of oxygen and allows submersion in water for slightly longer periods of time. There have been reports of survival after immersion of ten minutes in warm water and forty minutes in extremely cold water. Age is also a factor: Younger persons are more likely to tolerate such conditions than older persons.

Poisoning. Whether intentional or accidental, poisoning demands immediate medical care. Intoxication can also initiate a crisis that requires critical care. Alcohol is the most common intoxicant, but a wide range of other substances are accidentally ingested. When an individual is poisoned, the toxic substance must be removed from the body. This removal may be accomplished in a variety of ways and is usually done in a hospital. Supportive care may be needed during the period of acute crisis. The brain, liver, and kidneys are usually at great risk during a toxic crisis; steps must be taken to protect these organs.

Physical trauma. Trauma is the leading cause of death in persons under the age of forty. Motor vehicle accidents alone account for nearly 2 percent of all deaths worldwide. Globally, nearly six million people die each year from accidental or violence-related injury, accounting for nearly 9 percent of total global mortality. The three leading causes of trauma-related deaths are motor vehicle accidents, suicide, and homicide. Trauma is commonly characterized as either blunt or penetrating.

Blunt trauma occurs when an external force is applied to tissue, causing compression or crushing injuries as well as fractures. This force can be applied directly from being hit with an object or indirectly through the forces generated by sudden deceleration. In the latter event, relatively mobile organs or structures continue moving until stopped by adjacent, relatively fixed organs or structures. Any of these injuries can result in extensive internal bleeding. Damage may also cause fluids to be lost from tissues and lead to shock, circulatory collapse, and ultimately death.

The most frequent sources for penetrating wounds are knives and firearms. A knife blade produces a smaller wound; fewer organs are likely to be involved, and adjacent structures are less likely to sustain damage. In contrast, gunshot wounds are more likely to involve multiple tissues and to damage adjacent structures. More energy is released by a bullet than by a knife. This energy is sufficient to fracture a bone and usually leads to a greater amount of tissue damage.

The wound must be repaired, typically through surgical exploration and suturing. Extensively damaged tissue is removed in a process called debridement. Any visible sources of secondary contamination must also be removed. With both knife and firearm wounds often comes contamination by dirt, clothing, and other debris; this contamination presents a serious threat of infection to the victim and is also a problem for critical care workers. The wound is then covered appropriately, and the victim is given antibiotics to counteract bacteria that may have been introduced with the primary injury.

Psychological trauma. Critical care is often required in situations that lead to psychological stress. Individuals taking drug overdoses require critical supportive care until the drug has been metabolized by or removed from the body. Respiratory support is needed when the drug depresses the portion of the brain that controls breathing. Some drugs cause extreme agitation, which must be controlled by sedation.

Severe trauma to a loved one can initiate a psychological crisis. Psychological support must be provided to the victim; frequently, this is done in a hospital setting. An entire family may require critical care support for brief periods of time in the aftermath of a catastrophe. Severe trauma, disease, or the death of a child may require support by outsiders. Most hospitals have professionals who are trained to provide such support. In addition, people with psychiatric problems sometimes fail to take the medications that control mental illness. Critical care support in a hospital is often needed until these people are restabilized on their medications.

Environmental disasters. The need for psychological support, as well as urgent medical care, is magnified with natural or environmental disasters such as earthquakes, hurricanes, floods, or tornadoes. Environmental disasters seriously disrupt lives and normal services; they can arise with little or no warning. The key to providing critical care in a disaster situation is adequate prior planning.

Responses to disasters occur at three levels: institutional (hospital), local (police, fire, and rescue), and regional (county and state). The plan must be simple and evolve from normal operations; individuals respond best when they are asked to perform tasks with which they are familiar and for which they are trained. The response must integrate all existing sources of emergency medical and supportive services. Those who assume responsibilities for overall management must be well trained and able to adapt to different and rapidly changing conditions that may be encountered. Because no two disasters are ever alike, such flexibility is essential. Summaries of individual duties and responsibilities should be available for all involved individuals. Finally, the disaster plan should be practiced and rehearsed using specific scenarios. Experience is the single best method to ensure competency when a disaster strikes.

Environmental disasters such as earthquakes, hurricanes, floods, or tornadoes cause loss of life and extensive property damage. Essential services such as water, gas, electricity, and telephone communication are often lost. Victims must be provided food, shelter, and medical care on an immediate basis. Critical care is usually required at the time of the disaster, and the need for support may continue long after the immediate effects of the disaster have been resolved.

Fast Fact

Your heart is about the size of your two hands clasped together. The earth's largest mammal—the blue whale—has a heart that weighs more than 1,500 pounds.

Source: Clevelandclinic.com

Perspective and Prospects

One of the most important issues with regard to critical care is sometimes controversial: when to discontinue life support. Life-support equipment is usually withdrawn as soon as patients are able to function independent of the machinery. These patients continue to recover, are discharged from the hospital, and complete their recovery at home. For some, however, the outcome is not as positive. Machines may be used to assist breathing. For a patient who does not improve, or who deteriorates, there comes a point in time when a decision to stop life support must be made. This is not an easy decision, nor should it be made by a single individual.

The patient's own wishes must be paramount. These wishes, however, must have been clearly communicated while the individual was in good health and had unimpaired thought processes. A patient's family is entitled to provide input in the decision to terminate care, but others are also entitled to provide input: the patient's physician, representatives of the hospital or institution, a representative of the patient's religious faith, and the state.

Medical science has developed criteria for death. The application of these criteria, however, is not uniform. The final decision to terminate life support is frequently a consensus of all the parties mentioned above. When there is a dispute, the courts are often asked to intervene. Extensive disagreements exist concerning the ethics of terminating critical care. It is beyond the scope of this discussion to provide definitive guidelines. This logical extension of critical care may not have a uniform resolution; the values and beliefs of each individual determine the outcome of each situation.

L. Fleming Fallon Jr., M.D., Ph.D., M.P.H.

EMERGENCY ROOMS

Sites that provides twenty-four-hour emergency medical care. Metropolitan trauma centers often have more than fifty patient care areas and treat hundreds of patients daily. Rural or community hospital ERs may be as small as several rooms but usually have many treatment areas available.

Background

Emergency medicine is one of twenty-four medical specialties recognized by the American Board of Medical Specialties (ABMS). Aboard-certified specialist in emergency medicine meets training and certification requirements established by the American Board of Emergency Medicine (ABEM). Emergency medicine became a medical specialty in 1979 and is well established as a recognized body of medical specialists and knowledge.

After World War II, emergency rooms became primary health care access points for an increasing number of people. Many factors contributed to this change, including increasing specialization among physicians along with decreasing numbers of primary care and general practitioners. The resultant decrease in hospital on-call physicians available to treat ER patients fostered the concept of full-time ER specialists, whose primary duties involve treating patients coming to ERs.

The first plans for full-time emergency room physician coverage originated in the 1960s. A model featuring dedicated ER doctors proved to be the most attractive among hospitals and patients. Emergency physicians limit their practice to the emergency department while providing 24-7 coverage. Emergency physicians treat all patients, regardless of ability to pay, while establishing contractual relationships with hospitals. This model for emergency care fostered the development of emergency medicine, setting standards of care for the new specialty. (Michael T. Rapp and George Podgorny provide a detailed consideration of the many factors in the developmental history of emergency medicine in their 2005 article "Reflections on Becoming a Specialist and Its Impact on Global Emergency Medical Care: Our Challenge for the Future" in *Emergency Medicine Clinics of North America*.)

The National Academy of Sciences and the National Research Council raised concern with a 1966 report titled *Accidental Death and Disability: The Neglected Disease of Modern Society*. More rapid prehospital response along with better emergency care standards were needed to improve emergency care in the United States. Emergency physicians from Michigan, including John Wiegenstein, founded an organization fostering the national development of Emergency Medicine, the American College of Emergency Physicians (ACEP), in 1968.

Emergency room personnel integrate medical care in a variety of settings, including military, disaster, community, and academic settings. Emergency physicians are experts in emergent cardiovascular care, including resuscitative medicine and the various highly specialized procedures that accompany that care. Accident and trauma stabilization is another area of ER expertise.

Traumatic injuries, such as stabbings, shootings, industrial accidents, and automobile accidents, are also treated and stabilized in the emergency department, which is the major care location for disaster care. Emergency departments treat all age groups and all conditions, at all hours of the day, simultaneously.

Features and Procedures

Emergency rooms vary in size, but most share uniform characteristics. The first ER assessment is triage, a term with French roots meaning "to pick or cull." In triage, health care personnel, usually nurses, determine the severity of a patient's injury or illness and record the patient's chief complaint or medical problem. They measure and record vital signs, including pulse, temperature, respiratory rate, and blood pressure. If the patient's condition is stable, then triage personnel obtain other important information, such as medications taken, a brief medical history, and any patient allergies.

The most important triage duty determines the severity of an illness. Usually, there are three main categories: critical and immediately life threatening, such as a myocardial infarction; urgent but not immediately life threatening, such as most abdominal pain; and less urgent, such as a minor leg laceration, known as the "walking wounded" in military triage. ER personnel often refer to these categories as Cat I, Cat II, or Cat III. After assessing the patient's condition, triage personnel advance patients to appropriate care areas. A new category I patient may be wheeled on a gurney directly to the critical area, with the nurse announcing to any doctors on the way, "new Cat I patient in 101." These patients need immediate emergency care.

A stable patient is registered by front-desk personnel. Registration clerks obtain insurance and contact information. New medical charts are generated for new patients, or old records are requested if they already exist at that hospital. Patients arriving by ambulance or critically ill category I patients bypass this step until after treatment or stabilization in the critical care area of the emergency room.

Most emergency departments have many patient care areas, reflecting the wide variety of patients seen in the ER. These areas include resuscitation rooms for patients needing cardiopulmonary resuscitation; trauma care areas for patients with severe injuries like gunshot wounds or accident victims; critical care areas for patients needing cardiac monitoring along with ongoing critical care; pediatric ERs for the care of children; chest-pain evaluation areas; and suture rooms for the repairs of lacerations (cuts). Rooms for the examination of women with gynecological problems are available. ERs usually have a fast track or urgent care area for minor illness (such as sore throats) and an observation unit for patients waiting for hospital admission or diagnostic tests.

Many personnel contribute to the wide variety of care provided in emergency departments. Emergency physicians, nurses, physician assistants, medical technologists, and medical assistants have specified health care roles. Unit clerks help with the paperwork, and laboratory personnel assist with radiological and laboratory procedures. Administrative people help with staffing issues, equipment purchasing, facility maintenance, and scheduling of workers. These are some of the important roles necessary to deliver emergency care. To a varying degree, ERs will also have social workers, psychological care providers, and patient advocates available as full-time ER personnel.

Fast Fact

Technically, it's called the Emergency Department—and that's because the days when the Emergency Room was a single room are long gone. Back then, staff was not specialized. Today, as anyone who has ever rushed off to the "ER" well knows, emergencies are treated in a department that includes many rooms. And they're staffed by emergency-trained nurses and doctors.

Perspective and Prospects

Many agencies promote effective, more standardized emergency and trauma care. In addition to the American Board of Emergency Medicine and the American College of Emergency Physicians, many other agencies promote effective emergency care, such as the American Academy of Emergency Medicine. The American Heart Association takes a lead in cardiopulmonary resuscitation (CPR) guidelines. The American College of Surgeons (ACS) develops standards for trauma care. Nursing organizations, emergency medical technician (EMT) agencies, and other professional organizations develop standards for improving emergency care.

The American College of Surgeons provides trauma center designation guidelines. Trauma center designation requires various important resources and characteristics. Although the ACS provides consultants and guidelines for this process, other agencies designate trauma centers, such as local or state governments. Three main trauma center levels exist in ACS guidelines.

In level I, comprehensive 24-7 trauma care specialists are available in the hospital, including emergency medicine, general surgery, and anesthesiology. Various surgical specialists are available, including neurosurgery, orthopedic surgery, and plastic surgery. Level I designation requires intensive care units (ICUs) along with operating rooms staffed and ready to go twenty-four hours daily all year round. These are major referral centers, often known as tertiary care facilities.

Level II offers comprehensive trauma and critical care, but the full array of specialists may not be as readily available as those found in a level I trauma center. Trauma volume levels are usually lower than the level I trauma centers.

In level III, resources are available for critical care and stabilization of trauma victims. Patient volume, array of specialists, and 24-7 availability vary. Transfer protocols with level II and I trauma centers allow comprehensive care after stabilization. Community or rural hospitals may have this designation.

The efforts of all these groups enhance emergency care, in all of its various forms. Emergency medicine is at the front lines of medical care. Like any forward-moving group, backup and support improve the ultimate goal-available and effective emergency care delivered when needed the most.

Richard P. Capriccioso, M.D.

Conversation With . . .
JEFF SOLHEIM

MSN, RN, CEN, TCRN, CFRN, FAEN, FAAN
Emergency Nurses Association President, 2018

Jeff Solheim has been a nurse for thirty years and is the founder of Solheim Enterprises in Portland, Oregon.

1. What was your individual career path in terms of education/training, entry-level job, or other significant opportunity?

I always had a desire to do this work, and three paths intersected. My father had a friend who was the administrator of a nursing home, so my high school job was working in a nursing home caring for older patients. Also, I was diagnosed with cancer at fifteen. I successfully battled it for a year but, unfortunately, due to treatments back in the day, I developed a secondary cancer that I continue to deal with. Finally, it just happened there was a nursing program near the town where I lived. So, being a patient and watching what nurses did, it all came together. That's how I chose nursing.

I graduated with an associate degree in nursing from Medicine Hat College in Alberta, Canada, and immediately got a job as a staff nurse taking care of patients directly in the intensive care unit. After a few years, an opportunity arose in the emergency department (ED), and I transferred to that area. During that time, I knew I had an interest in leadership, so I earned a certificate in health care. After three years in the ED, I accepted a leadership position in south Texas and relocated. There, I managed a telemetry unit and shortly thereafter was given responsibility to manage the ICU and ED.

During this time, I picked up a job as a flight nurse on weekends. There are two types of flight nursing: one is on a helicopter. In Texas, a large and rural state, say a farmer is injured in the field. It's much quicker to dispatch a helicopter than to try to get a ground ambulance out there. The helicopter lands right at the scene, and we stabilize the patient. I did this on the side for many, many years. More recently, I do the second type, international flight nursing. If somebody is overseas on vacation or working and needs to be repatriated back to the United States, a flying intensive care unit is deployed. It's a very specialized subset of emergency nursing and difficult to enter. I also am a cruise ship nurse several weeks a year. That's the great thing about emergency nursing: you can work in a prison, the ED, flights, and many other places. It's a great, versatile career.

Cases can be very difficult. I'll never forget the family who ran out of gas and was pushing their car along the side of the road, the father standing in the door steering and the wife and two teens in back pushing. A stolen, speeding vehicle hit the back of the car, and the three family members in back were pinned at high speed and suffered traumatic amputations. The father was not injured. Imagine trying to be comforter-in-chief while we two flight nurses triaged quickly and administered care.

I was in hospital administration for quite a few years. During this time, I was invited to the governor's office to help write legislation for trauma care in the state of Texas. This provided an opportunity to be a nurse in the governor's office and work on health care policy. Once that was over, I started my own consulting firm to assist states in setting up trauma systems, became a speaker and educator, and grew my company, which helps people become better nurses.

I worked with an associate degree for much of my career but felt the need to continue my education. Several years ago, I returned to school and earned my bachelor's and master's degrees in nursing at Western Governors University in Utah.

During 2018, I served as president of the Emergency Nurses Association. My job entailed representing and guiding our profession around the world. I've traveled almost a half-million miles. My other responsibility was to guide and lead the changes that impact the profession when we set standards for care.

My term recently ended, and I'm considering my options for what's next.

2. What are the most important skills and/or qualities for someone in your profession?

One of the greatest skills you must possess for emergency nursing is flexibility. Say I'm working at bedside with a child with a laceration, next to someone with severe abdominal pain who may have appendicitis, and I stop to give CPR to somebody who passed away from a heart attack. I might have started the hour thinking about discharging the child but now need to reprioritize to care for the cardiac patient.

Emergency nursing requires a good mixture of being organized and liking chaos. I know that sounds odd. If I have six patients and a really sick person is thrown into the mix, I have to figure out how to take care of everybody. In other words, you need to thrive on chaos while keeping organized.

3. What do you wish you had known going into this profession?

I was prepared because I had the advantage of working in a nursing home in high school. I do notice a lot of other nurses are surprised that this is a twenty-four-hour-a-day, 365-day-per-year job. New nurses graduate, hear they have to work Christmas Eve and Christmas, and say, "Wait, that's my family time." Well, no. Now you're a nurse, and that requires personal sacrifice.

4. Are there many job opportunities in your profession? In what specific areas?

Nursing, and especially emergency nursing, can't be taken over by automation. The population is growing. There will always be jobs in this field. Sometimes when you graduate as a nurse, you have to work in different areas and wait for an opening in the ED, which might be a few years down the road.

5. How do you see your profession changing in the next five years, how will technology impact that change, and what skills will be required?

One of the biggest changes nursing is experiencing is the rise of advanced practice. Nurse practitioner is a new educational level, and a lot of young nurses want to go right into it. That's going to be an issue for us. We may find advanced practice is more desirable than bedside nursing and have a re-engineering of our field on the horizon.

New technology is constantly being introduced, which means as a nurse you will constantly be on a learning curve. You are going to have to learn new skills and integrate the technology into your practice.

6. What do you enjoy most about your job? What do you enjoy least about your job?

I most like the camaraderie with my coworkers. Emergency nursing is a team sport. A bad trauma comes in, and we go in and do the impossible. It feels really good when a very difficult case comes through, and as a team you save a life and overcome a challenge.

The challenging aspects are the intense social needs emergency nurses are forced to see at work. I will care for celebrities and politicians, but I will also care for the homeless person, the person with a life sentence injured in prison, children beaten by parents, women beaten by husbands, or innocent people shot in a robbery attempt who then die in front of you. This is hard. A mentally ill patient comes in, and there's no hospital bed; what do I do with that person? It can wear on you.

7. Can you suggest a valuable "try this" for students considering a career in your profession?

Can I start with what they should not do? Do not base your decision to go into emergency nursing on TV dramas. That will give you a false sense of what we do. If you really, really want to see this work up close, the best way is to join a volunteer group. Every hospital has one, and many love to have high school students. You might work out front, you might work back in the ER passing out water.

EXTENDED CARE

Definition: The management of the health, personal care, and social needs of elderly people as they experience decreases in physical, mental, and/or emotional abilities.

The Problems Associated with Aging

The process of aging is inevitable. In the earlier stages of life, aging involves the acquisition and development of new skills and abilities, facilitated by the guidance and assistance of others. Later, the middle stages involve the challenges of maintaining and applying those skills and abilities in a manner that is primarily self-sufficient. Finally, in the end stages of life, aging involves the deterioration and loss of skills and abilities, with adequate functioning again being somewhat dependent on the assistance of others.

For many individuals, the final stages are brief, allowing them to live independently right up to their time of death. Thus, many experience little loss of their abilities to function independently. Others, however, endure more extended stages of later life and require greater care. For these individuals, losses in physical, emotional, and/or cognitive functioning frequently result in a need for specialized care. Such care involves whatever is necessary so that these individuals may live as comfortably, productively, and independently as possible.

The conditions leading to a need for long-term care are as varied as the elderly themselves are. Special needs for elders requiring extended care often include the management of physical, health, emotional, and cognitive problems. Physical problems dictating lifestyle adjustments include decreased speed, dexterity, and strength, as well as increased fragility. Changes to the five senses are also common. Visual changes include the development of hyperopia (farsightedness) and sometimes decreased visual acuity. Hearing loss is also common, such that softer sounds cannot be heard when background noise is present or sounds need to be louder in order to be perceived. Particularly noteworthy is that paranoia, depression, and social isolation often result as side effects of visual and hearing impairments in elders; they are not always signs of mental deterioration. Similarly, one's sense of touch may also be affected, such that the nerves are either more or less sensitive to changes in temperatures or textures. Consequently, injuries attributable to a lack of awareness of potential hazards or supersensitivities to temperature or texture may result. One example would be an elderly woman overdressing or underdressing for the weather because of an inability to judge the outside temperature properly. Another would be an elderly man cutting or wounding himself out of a lack of awareness of the sharpness of an object. Finally, both taste and smell may change, creating a situation in which subtle tastes and odors become imperceptible or in which tastes and smells that were once pleasant become either bland or unpleasant.

Health problems among the aged often demand increased management as well. Coordination of drug therapies and other medical interventions by a case manager is critical, as a result of increasing sensitivities in elders to physical interventions. Typical health conditions bringing elderly people into long-term care settings may include heart disease and stroke, hypertension, diabetes mellitus, arthritis, osteoporosis, chronic pain, prostate disease, and cancers of the digestive tract and other vital organs. Estimates are that approximately 86 percent of the aged are affected by chronic illnesses. Long-term care addresses both the medical management of these chronic illnesses and their impact on the individual.

An issue related to health and physical problems in the aged is malnutrition. For a variety of reasons, elders often fall victim to malnutrition, which can contribute to additional health problems. For example, calcium deficiency can increase both the severity of heart disease and the likelihood of osteoporosis and tooth loss. Thus, a vicious cycle of medical problems can be put into motion. Factors contributing to malnutrition are multifaceted. Poverty, social isolation, decreased taste sensitivity, and tooth loss combine with lifelong dietary habits that can sometimes predispose certain elders to malnutrition. As such, attention to the maintenance of healthy dietary habits in the elderly is critical to successful long-term care, regardless of the type of setting in which the care is being given.

Along with these physical aspects of aging come emotional and cognitive changes. Depression, anxiety, and paranoia over health concerns, for example, are not uncommon. Additionally, concerns about the threat of losing one's independence, friends, and former lifestyle may contribute to acute or chronic mood disorders. Suicide is a particular danger with the elderly when mood disorders such as depression are present. Elderly people are one of the fastest growing groups among those who commit suicide. The stresses accompanying losing a spouse or enduring a chronic health problem can often be triggers to suicide for depressed elders. One should note, however, that elders are not particularly prone to depression or suicide because of their age but that they are more likely to experience significant stressors that lead to depression.

Remote Monitoring at Home

Remote monitoring provides real-time health care data while patients are away from their health care providers. Conceivably, a patient could be anywhere in the world while providing his or her doctor with general monitoring data such as blood pressure or feedback from a newly installed pacemaker. Historically, remote monitoring devices have been stand-alone contraptions that involve extensive training to utilize; however, more recent advances include data reporting using the Internet, wireless local area networks, and cell phones.

At least as early as 2002, the Food and Drug Administration (FDA) granted approval for remote monitoring of patients with cardiovascular complications. In November, 2009, the FDA approved a more general health data reporting device that can work in tandem with a cell phone. This streamlining of health care could potentially save hospitals the unnecessary expense of emergency room visits while simultaneously alerting a patient that a hospital visit is needed.

Remote monitoring shows particular promise for the aging population, as it can help maintain general health while monitoring chronic conditions. Cell phones and other wireless devices can provide the patient with reminders, alerts, and motivational encouragement to engage in healthy behaviors throughout the day. This daily feedback can alert the patient of small changes in health status, such as informing the patient of high blood pressure, and then provide strategies to compensate. Catching and changing lifestyle factors early could save an untold number of unnecessary procedures yearly.

Noncompliance with doctor's orders is an estimated $100 billion yearly tax on the health care system. Daily feedback would permit doctors to track patients who do not adhere to medical regimes. Cell phones with global positioning systems (GPS) could easily monitor a patient's daily activity level. Remote monitoring holds the possibility of improving patient's quality of life, reducing health care costs and enhancing early detection of health changes in those individuals most at risk.

More common, less lethal problems associated with conditions such as depression, anxiety, and paranoia are weight change, insomnia, and other sleep problems. Distractibility, decreased ability to maintain attention and concentration, and rumination over distressing concerns are also common. Finally, some elders may be observed as socially isolated and prone to avoidance behavior. As a result, some become functionally incapacitated because of distressing emotions.

What is critical to remember, in addition to these signs, is that some elders may not describe their problems as emotional at all, even though that is the primary cause of their discomfort. Individual differences in how people express themselves must be taken into account. Thus, while some elders may report being depressed or anxious, others may instead report feeling tired. Reports of low-level health problems that are vague in nature, such as aches and pains, are also common in elders who are depressed. It is not uncommon for emotional problems to be expressed or described indirectly as physical complaints.

Decreased cognitive functioning may result from more serious problems than depression, such as organic brain syndromes. These typically include problems such as dementias from Alzheimer's disease, Pick's disease, Huntington's disease, alcohol-related deterioration, or stroke-related problems. Other causes may be brain tumors or thyroid dysfunction. With all dementias, however, the hallmark signs are a deterioration of intellectual function and emotional response. Memory, judgment, understanding, and the experience and control of emotional responses are affected. Functionally, these conditions reveal themselves as a combination of symptoms, including increased forgetfulness, decreased ability to plan and complete tasks, difficulties finding names or words, decreased abilities for abstract thinking, impaired judgment, inappropriate sexual behavior, and sometimes severe personality changes. In some cases, affected individuals are aware of these difficulties, usually in the earlier stages of the disease processes. Later, however, even though their behavior and abilities may be quite disturbed, they may be completely unaware of the severity of their problems. In these cases, long-term care often begins as a result of outside intervention by concerned friends and family members.

Options for Long-Term Care

Extended care for the aged requires an interdisciplinary effort that usually involves a team of physicians, psychologists, nurses, social workers, and other rehabilitative specialists. Depending on the nature of the problems requiring care and management, any of these professionals may take part in the care process. Additionally, the involvement of concerned individuals who are close to the elder needing care is critical. Family members (including the spouse, children, and extended family) and close friends are invaluable sources of information and of emotional and instrumental support. Their ability to assist an elder with instrumental tasks such as cooking, housecleaning, shopping, and money and medication management is crucial to the successful implementation of a long-term care plan.

In all cases, long-term care for the aged involves the design of a comprehensive plan to address the multifaceted needs of the elder. Just as younger persons have psychological, social, intellectual, and physical needs, so do elders. As such, thorough assessment of an elder's abilities, goals, expectations, and functioning in each of these areas is required. A mental status exam and a thorough physical exam are usually the primary methods of evaluation. Once needs are identified, a plan can then be designed by the team of health care professionals, family and friends assisting with care, and, whenever possible, the elder. In general, the overarching goal is to design a case management plan that maximizes the independent functioning of the aged person, given certain physical, psychiatric, social, and other needs.

Specific management strategies are designed for the problems that need to be addressed. Physical, health, nutritional, emotional, and cognitive problems all demand different management settings and strategies. Additionally, care settings may vary depending on the severity of the problems that are identified. In general, the more severe the problems, the more structured the long-term care setting and the more intense the psychosocial interventions.

For less severe problems, adequate management settings may include the elder's own home, the home of a family member or friend, a shared housing setting, or a seniors" apartment complex. Shared housing is sometimes called group-shared, supportive, or matched housing. Typically, it refers to residences organized by agencies where up to twenty people share a house and its expenses, chores, and management. Ideal candidates for this type of setting include elders who want some daily assistance or companionship but who are still basically independent. Senior apartments, also called retirement housing, are usually "elderly-only" complexes that range from garden-style apartments to high-rises. Ideal candidates for this type of setting include nearly independent elders who want privacy, but who no longer desire or can manage a single-family home. In either of these types of settings, the use of periodic or regular at-home nursing assistance for medical problems, or "home-helpers" for more instrumental tasks, might be a successful adjunct to regular consultation with a case manager or physician.

Problems of moderate severity may demand a more structured setting or a setting in which help is more readily available. Such settings might include continuing care retirement communities or assisted-living facilities. Continuing care retirement communities, also called life-care communities, are large complexes offering lifelong care. Residents are healthy, live independently in apartments, and are able to use cafeteria services as necessary. Additionally, residents have the option of being moved to an assisted-living unit or an infirmary as health needs dictate. Assisted-living facilities—also called board-and-care, institutional living, adult foster care, and personal care settings—offer care that is less intense than that received in a medical setting or nursing home. These facilities may be as small as a home where one person cares for a small group of elders or as large as a converted hotel with several caregivers, a nurse, and shared dining facilities. Such settings are ideal for persons needing instrumental care but not round-the-clock skilled medical or nursing care.

When more severe conditions such as incontinence, dementia, or an inability to move independently are present, nursing, convalescent, or extended care homes are more appropriate settings. Intense attention is delivered in a hospital-like setting where all medical and instrumental needs are addressed. Typical nursing homes serve a hundred clients at a time, utilizing semiprivate rooms for personal living space and providing community areas for social, community, and family activities. Often, the decision to place an elder in this type of facility is difficult to make. The decision, however, is frequently based on the knowledge that these types of facilities provide the best possible setting for the overall care of the elder's medical, health, and social needs. In fact, appropriate use of these facilities discourages the overtaxing of the elder's emotional and familial resources, allowing the elder to gain maximum benefit. An elder's placement into this type of facility does not mean that the family's job is over; rather, it simply changes shape. Incorporation of family resources into long-term care in a nursing home setting is critical to the adjustment of the elder and family members to the elder's increased need for care and attention. Visits and other family involvement in the elder's daily activities remain quite valuable.

Regardless of the management setting, some basic caveats exist with regard to determining management strategies. First and foremost is that the aged individuals should, whenever possible, be encouraged to maintain independent functioning. For example, even though physical deterioration such as decreased visual or hearing abilities may be present, there is no need to take decision-making authority away from the elder. Decreased abilities to hear or see do not necessarily mean a decreased ability to make decisions or think. Second, it is crucial to ask elders to identify their needs and how they might desire assistance. Some elders may wish for help with acquiring basic living supplies from outside the home, such as foods and toiletries, but desire privacy and no assistance within the home. In contrast, others may desire independence outside the home with regard to social matters but need more instrumental assistance within the home. Finally, it is important to recognize that even the smallest amount of assistance can make a significant difference in the lifestyle of the elder. A prime example is availability of transportation. The loss of a driver's license or independent transportation signifies a major loss of independence for any elder. Similarly, the challenges posed by public transit may seem insurmountable because of a lack of familiarity or experience. As such, simple and small interventions such as a ride to a store or a doctor's office may provide great relief for elders by assisting their efforts to meet their own needs.

Special management strategies may be required for specific problem areas. For physical deterioration, adequate assessment of strengths and weaknesses is important, as are referrals to medical, rehabilitative, and home-help professionals. Hearing and visual or other devices to make lifting, mobility, and day-to-day tasks easier are helpful. Similarly, assisting the aged with developing alternative strategies for dealing with diminished sensory abilities can be valuable. Examples would be checking a thermometer for outdoor temperature to determine proper dress, rather than relying purely on sensory information, or having a phone that lights up when it rings. Health conditions also demand particular management strategies, varying greatly with the type of problem experienced. In all cases, however, medical intervention, drug therapies, and behavior modification therapies are commonly employed. Dietary problems (such as malnutrition or diabetes), cardiovascular problems (such as heart attacks), and emotional problems (such as depression) often require all three approaches. Finally, cognitive problems, particularly those related to depression, are sometimes alleviated with drug therapies. Others related to organic brain syndromes or organic mental disorders require both medical interventions and significant behavior modification therapies and/or psychosocial interventions for elders and their families.

Perspective and Prospects

Advances in modern medicine are continually extending the human life span. Cures for dread diseases, improved management of chronic health problems, and new technologies to replace diseased organs are facilitating this evolution. For many, these advances translate into greater longevity, the maintenance of a high quality of life, and fewer obstacles related to ageism. For others, however, the trade-off for longevity is some loss of independence and a need for extended care and management. Thus, the medical field is also affected by the trade-off of extending life, while experiencing an increasing need to improve strategies for long-term care for those who are able to live longer and longer despite health conditions.

As a result of this evolution, long-term care for the aged presents special challenges to the medical field. Over time, medicine has been a field specializing in the understanding of particular organ systems and the treatment of related diseases. While an understanding of how each system affects the functioning of the whole body is necessary, health care providers must struggle to understand the complexities in the case management required for high-quality long-term care for the aged. Care must be interdisciplinary, addressing the physical, mental, emotional, social, and familial needs of the aged individual. Failure to address any of these areas may ultimately sabotage the successful long-term management of elderly individuals and of their problems. In this way, medical, psychiatric, social work, and rehabilitative specialists need to work together with elders and their families for the best possible results.

Integrated case management with a team leader is increasingly the trend so that a variety of services can be provided in an orchestrated manner. While specialty providers still play a role, managers (usually primary care physicians) ensure that complementary drug therapies as well as psychiatric and other medical treatments are administered. Additionally, they are key in bringing forth family resources for emotional and instrumental support whenever possible, as well as community and social services when needed.

What was once viewed as helping a person to die with dignity is now viewed as helping a person to live as long and as productive a life as possible. Increasing awareness that old age is not simply a dying time has facilitated an integrated approach to long-term care. The news that elders can be as social, physical, sexual, intellectual, and productive as their younger counterparts has greatly stimulated improved long-term care strategies. No longer is old age seen as a time for casting elders aside or as a time when a nursing home is an inescapable solution in the face of health problems affecting the aged. Alternatives to care exist and are proliferating, with improved outcomes for both patients and care providers.

Nancy A. Piotrowski, Ph.D.

HOME CARE

Skilled health and nonskilled support care services provided in the home.

Home Care Option

Many health care and support services can be delivered outside the traditional acute care environment, such as a hospital, rehabilitation center, or skilled nursing facility. Home care services allow people to live at home and still receive necessary health and support care. Examples of persons who can benefit from home care include those discharged from a hospital, rehabilitation center, or skilled nursing unit; older adults with limited caregivers or support systems; chronically ill or disabled persons; postsurgical patients; and at-risk newborns or children. Home care makes staying in one's residence while ill or injured a reality. Anurse or medical social worker can help people assess their needs and access appropriate agencies for home care services. Urban areas usually have more home care agencies offering a wider variety of home care services than rural areas.

Skilled and Nonskilled Home Care

Just as people have different care needs, varied types of home care organizations offer diverse services to meet those needs. For example, some people need nonskilled services to remain in their home. Communities and private companies offer continuous care services such as sitters/attendants who can stay with the person for eight- to twelve-hour shifts. These attendants may provide personal care such as bathing or hair washing. Some agencies connect live-in companions that are available twenty-four hours a day with people needing home care help. Homemaker services are offered through community programs for light house cleaning, clothes washing, grocery shopping, and preparing of simple meals. Home care agencies may align with volunteer groups who have visitation programs and assist with light yard work or transportation to the grocery store or doctor's office. These types of services are important, as they provide help with activities of daily living (ADL) necessary for a dependent person to stay in his or her residence. Most nonskilled home care services are selfpay unless covered by a grant, long-term care insurance, or government-sponsored program such as Medicaid.

Many patients are discharged from hospitals earlier than they once were, to recuperate from illness or surgery at home. Home health care is a less costly alternative to institutional care. Medically necessary skilled home care services are often covered by full or partial reimbursement through private insurance or by government-sponsored programs like Medicare or Medicaid; others may access home care services through self-pay. The home care team is usually an interdisciplinary team of professionals and support staff that work together to maintain a person in his or her home and out of the hospital or other institutional care. The interdisciplinary team may include the registered nurse, licensed practical nurse, home health aid/assistant/attendant, physical therapist, occupational therapist, speech therapist, and medical social worker. Chaplains and volunteers may be part of the home care team. The group works under the direction of the agency administrator, providing care with a medical plan and orders from the attending physician.

Services delivered are based on the patient's condition, individual needs, home location, and sources of reimbursement. Home health care services are provided on an intermittent basis, with care delivered several times each week for an average of thirty minutes to an hour per visit. The patient, along with his or her caregiver, remains responsible for daily care. Intermittent care means the nurse or physical therapist will come to the home to teach or provide specific care but will not stay in the home. The skilled provider will teach the caregiver how to perform necessary tasks. Skilled home health care services are not designed to provide home care for extended periods of time but to assist the person to regain independence or optimal functioning.

Skilled nursing services are provided in the home by a registered nurse (RN). Examples of nursing care include monitoring of vital signs such as blood pressure and pulse; teaching the patient and other caregivers medication indications, dosage, and side effects; encouraging medication and treatment compliance; changing dressings; and providing infusion or intravenous (IV) therapy. Patients who need IV antibiotics, chemotherapy, or home parenteral nutritional can receive these safely at home. The RN performs a physical assessment of the patient and a safety assessment of the home, making recommendations to keep the patient safe while recovering at home. The RN is responsible for teaching necessary care to both the patient and the family or significant support person in the home. The RN might teach the patient and family how to manage pain or give medications safely, watching for any untoward side effects. The RN also supervises the licensed practical nurse (LPN) and home health aides (HHA) who may provide home care services.

Physical therapists provide in-home skilled services that strengthen and restore movement of bones, muscles, and joints. Physical therapists set reasonable goals with the patient and family and monitor progress toward those goals. The physical therapist helps the patient regain strength and function to minimize decline and further injury. Sometimes the patient needs special equipment. The physical therapist can recommend what equipment is best for the individual patient and teach the patient how to use the equipment to maintain or increase function and to gain independence.

Another home care team member is the occupational therapist. This professional teaches the critical skills needed to accomplish daily living activities at home. The occupational therapist helps the patient compensate for loss of function. For example, the occupational therapist may assess the layout of the kitchen in the patient's home and reorganize the placement of dishes and cooking pans for patient accessibility. Occupational therapists show patients how to utilize adaptive equipment such as prostheses or eating utensils and garden tools designed for those with arthritis. The goal is to attain and maintain the highest level of patient functioning to live a productive life.

Speech therapists work in-home with patients who have experienced strokes or accidents, have difficulty swallowing or communicating, or have some form of neurological health problem. The goal is to get the patient to the optimal level of receptive and expressive communication possible for normal life at home.

The medical social worker can be one of the most useful members of the home care team. This professional knows the community resources and helps the patient and family access additional care services. The medical social worker serves as a facilitator and liaison, making referrals to community agencies for the patient and family. Trained to provide support and counseling, the medical social worker is an advocate for the patient now living at home.

Home health aides are a vital part of the home care team. In fact, many patients and families consider the home health aide the most valuable care provider in their homes. Supervised by the RN, home health aides provide personal care and hygiene services such as bathing, hair washing, feeding, and dressing. They can assist in ambulation of the patient and provide light housekeeping or a simple meal if covered by the patient's reimbursement source. Home health aides can be critical to positive home care outcomes.

Other professionals may be available for in-home consultation at some home care agencies. Registered dietitians or nutritionists may offer home visits to discuss diet compliance and special cooking considerations. Nutrition and proper diet are important for achieving healthy outcomes at home. When a patient has a prescribed diet that represents a significant lifestyle change, such as a low-salt or low-fat diet, the registered dietitian can support the patient to success.

Hospice is a special type of care often provided within the home. Hospice home care is for patients diagnosed with end-stage or life-threatening disease with a prognosis of six months or less. Like home health care, hospice home care is coordinated by a multidisciplinary team of providers. Many are the same types of professionals and support staff as with home health care, but the purpose of hospice care is different. The goal in hospice home care is quality of life, not restoration of function and wellness. Additional members of the hospice home care team will include spiritual or pastoral counselors or chaplains, bereavement and grief counselors, and volunteers. All hospice home care services are designed to support and maintain the patient and family at home during the illness and death. Hospice home care is usually reimbursed by private insurance, Medicare, and Medicaid. Most hospice programs accept donations and raise funds to cover nonreimbursed care, so that patients are not denied care due to inability to pay.

Famous First

Founded in 1893 by nursing pioneer Lillian D. Wald and Mary M. Brewster, the Visiting Nurse Service of New York (VNSNY) is one the largest not-for-profit home- and community-based health care organization in the United States, serving the five boroughs of New York City; Nassau, Suffolk, and Westchester Counties; and parts of upstate New York. Lillian Wald briefly attended medical school and began to teach community health classes. After founding the Henry Street Settlement, she became an activist for the rights of women and minorities. She campaigned for suffrage and was a supporter of racial integration. She was involved in the founding of the National Association for the Advancement of Colored People (NAACP).

Source: https://en.wikipedia.org/wiki/Lillian_Wald

Perspective and Prospects

The roots of home care in the United States can be traced to the Charleston Ladies Benevolent Society in 1813. These female volunteers are credited with the early efforts that led to public health nursing in South Carolina. After the Civil War, home care evolved into the British visiting nurse or district nursing model. Home care nurses worked six days a week for eight to twelve hours each day providing bedside care for the patient while holistically supporting the family as well. In 1877, trained home care nurses were sent by the New York Mission to care for the sick poor in their homes. By 1890, the

United States boasted twenty-one visiting nurse associations. Lillian Wald, a nurse from New York, established and directed the Henry Street Settlement. In 1911, her organization consisted of fifty-five home care nurses, who made over 175,000 home visits. She is credited with defining the term "public health nursing." The year 1919 brought the first reimbursement for home care nursing services through the Metropolitan Life Insurance Company. However, when the economy crashed in the late 1920s, many home care agencies closed. Home care was then provided primarily by charities. Change came when Medicare laws, established in 1966, included coverage for home care services. By 1988, home care agencies had increased their numbers by 48 percent. Medicare-certified home care agencies expanded their services but became subject to more regulation.

Home care is a significant part of the health care delivery system in the United States. In 2007, more than 7.6 million people in the United States received some form of home care. That same year, the projected expenditures on home care services were $57.6 billion. Home care, along with nurses and other service providers, can boast almost two centuries of history in the United States.

Marylane Wade Koch, R.N., M.S.N..

HOSPICE

A hospice is a facility or program that provides physical and emotional comfort to dying individuals and their family and friends. Hospice services emphasize pain management rather than curative measures, involve a multidisciplinary team, and often allow the dying individual to stay at home with family.

Introduction

Hospice programs are designed for those who are dying or who have no reasonable hope of benefit from cure-oriented interventions. Hospice care typically starts when life expectancy is six months or less if the illness runs its normal course, but this type of care can continue longer than six months with physician certification. Hospice services can include home care, inpatient care, consultation, and bereavement follow-up. With a mission of palliative rather than curative care, hospice programs neither prolong life nor hasten death. The goal is to prolong the quality of life.

Hospice programs deal with whole individual, including the physical, emotional, social, and spiritual impact of the disease on the patient and the patient's friends and family. Hospice staff and volunteers offer specialized knowledge of medical care, including pain management. Most hospice care, about 75 percent, takes place within the dying person's home, the home or a friend or relative, a nursing home, or an assisted living facility. Other locations include residential hospice facilities or hospice units within hospitals.

Hospice care involves a multidisciplinary team, including physicians, nurses, pharmacists, social workers, physical and occupational therapists, and clergy. The team also includes family members and trained volunteers, who help with household chores and give family caregivers respite time. The team approach provides state-of-the-art care for pain and other distressing symptoms and emotional and spiritual support for the patient and family.

Before providing care, hospice staff members meet with the patient's personal physician and a hospice physician to discuss the patient's history, current physical symptoms, and life expectancy. Alternatively, families or patients can self-refer if the patient's physician is unavailable or unable to discuss the hospice program. After this initial meeting, hospice staff members meet with both the patient and family to discuss pain and comfort levels, support systems, financial and insurance resources, medications and equipment needs, and the hospice philosophy. Together, they develop an individualized care plan for the patient, and regularly review and revise this plan according to the patient's condition.

Hospice provides services to the family and friends of the dying individual. On average, about two family members per hospice death receive bereavement services, and they typically receive seven contacts (visits, phone calls, and mailings) in the year after the death.

Fast Fact

Just over one-third of hospice patients—36.6 percent-- have cancer. People with numerous other diseases also take advantage of hospice services: heart disease, debility (frailty or weakness), dementia (including Alzheimer's disease), lung disease, and stroke.

Source: hospiceactionnetwork.com.

History and Status

Hospice programs trace their roots to age-old customs of hospitality and medieval religious institutions offering rest and support for weary travelers. In England, the modern hospice movement began in 1967 when Dame Cicely Saunders founded St. Christopher's Hospice in southeast London. In the United States, hospice care began in 1974 with a community-based home care program in New Haven, Connecticut.

From these roots, the hospice movement has grown tremendously. In 2006, the National Hospice and Palliative Care Organization (NHPCO) estimated that the United States had more than forty-five hundred hospices, including ones in all states and territories. These hospices served 1.3 million people in 2006, approximately

36 percent of all Americans who died that year. Of these patients, 56 percent were women, 64 percent were over the age of seventy-five, and 81 percent were white. The three diseases with the highest utilization rates were malignancies, nephritis or kidney disease, and Alzheimer's disease.

In 2006, the average length of hospice service was fifty-nine days; the median, which represents what the most people actually experienced, was twenty-one days.

Funding for hospice services is strong. The U.S. Congress enacted the Medicare Hospice Benefit in 1982, so most hospice programs are covered under Medicare. In addition, most states offer Medicaid coverage, and many private health insurance policies and health maintenance organizations (HMOs) cover hospice services. Unlike hospital funding, which is retrospective and fee-for-service, hospice funding is prospective and flat-rate. Hospice coverage includes physicians, nurses, and home health aides; medicine, medical appliances, and supplies; spiritual, dietary, and other counseling services; continuous home-care or inpatient care during crises; and around-the-clock on-call support.

Lillian M. Range

Conversation With . . .
BETH MARTIN
RN, MSN, ACNP-BC, ACHPN
President, Hospice and Palliative Nurses Association

Beth Martin has been a registered nurse (RN) for forty-two years and a hospice and palliative care nurse practitioner for fourteen years. She is the Senior Director, Medical Services, for Palliative Medicine Consultants, Charlotte, North Carolina.

1. What was your individual career path in terms of education/training, entry-level job, or other significant opportunity?

Years ago, women had very limited career choices, and nursing was one of them. I was not only interested in helping people, but I was also interested in the science, knowing it would be challenging and a lot to learn in terms of health, health care, and the human body. After high school, I earned my bachelor's degree in nursing (BSN) at Spalding University in Louisville, Kentucky. I started as a charge nurse in intensive care, and my primary clinical focus for the next two decades was the care of the most critically ill adults in the hospital.

I always planned to further my education with the goal of teaching. Nine years into my career I earned a master's degree in nursing (MSN) from the University of South Florida in Tampa and went on to teach in hospitals and academic settings for about twenty years. I taught a range of classes, from the introduction to nursing at the baccalaureate level to classes on legal-ethical aspects of nursing.

I was working in a hospital as a clinical specialist and teaching in academia when I increasingly felt I wanted to be more of a direct caregiver to the patient, so I went back to school and earned a post-master's certificate as an acute care nurse practitioner at the University of South Carolina. I honestly thought I would stay in a hospital setting and work with critical patients in an advanced practice nursing role. However, I worked with a palliative nurse practitioner as I went through the program and decided that would be my focus.

My evolution toward hospice and palliative care came over a long period of time. For the first ten to fifteen years of my career, health care was all about technology and artificial support or advanced cardiac techniques to treat illnesses to save people or correct their physiologic abnormalities. Over time, and with more data on outcomes, a lot of people in health care started to realize: we have lots of technology and interventions we can do to people, but *should* we be using them?

People come to the hospital because they want to get fixed or cured. They think they'll have surgery or get medication, go home, and life will return to normal. That's not always the reality, especially for people with chronic diseases. I spent years supporting families in crisis who were trying to make decisions for a loved one who had had a stroke or another sudden, serious condition.

I realized I could be the person who could take this family aside and tell them about technologies, medicines, and procedures that are available to try to help a person get better. Modern medicine is amazing! There are so many advancements, and many patients survive who would not have in years past. However, it might be the case that in your loved one's situation, these advancements may not provide the outcome we would all hope for. Decisions need to be made based on what is an acceptable quality of life for the patient. I found families are often not knowledgeable and may have unrealistic expectations because of what's on medical dramas on TV.

I wanted to focus my teaching on individual patients and families having all the information needed to make the decisions that were right for them or their loved one. The opportunity to marry someone's quality of life with the best outcome is what really spoke to me.

I started working in palliative care for the same company I work for now. I worked in the hospital for about five years. Now, I'm the senior director for Medical Services for Palliative Medicine Consultants, an administrative role leading our palliative medicine program in the community. We have the same conversations with families and patients, but we're not in that crisis situation. Instead, we're a little further upstream, so to speak, so we can talk to families and patients about their diseases and what to expect. Many chronic diseases, such as coronary artery disease and diabetes, cannot be cured. We discuss what the future may hold, what treatment options are available, and what to expect regarding their quality of life. My goal is to help them make informed decisions about their health care.

2. What are the most important skills and/or qualities for someone in your profession?

Today, advances in science, medicine, available technology, and nursing knowledge mean you have to be really smart and know how to critically think about how to use all of that to improve the outcomes of your patients. Nursing is an art. When you are working with families and patients who are at their most vulnerable, they are dependent on you. You have to have compassion and the conscience to advocate for them. You also need to be a team player; health care is provided by teams of people with various skills and expertise.

I think in our society, people don't want to talk about death. In hospice and palliative medicine, people are faced with the reality of their mortality. Nurses need to have insight and good listening skills to help them sort through what is important to them and how that blends with what modern health care can provide. People might be afraid of dying, aging, or losing their quality of life. You need to hear what they are saying and understand their emotions and perspectives.

3. What do you wish you had known going into this profession?

If I had known about the specialty of palliative nursing, I would have integrated it into my practice sooner. Twenty years ago, I really didn't know about it, except for a general awareness of hospice in the community.

4. Are there many job opportunities in your profession? In what specific areas?

Nursing is a wide-open field with innumerable opportunities. As a specialty, hospice and palliative care is growing, although typically a nurse with more experience goes into this specialty. They often come to this specialty after having had experience in adult or geriatric care.

5. How do you see your profession changing in the next five years, how will technology impact that change, and what skills will be required?

Social media and immediate access to information are changing how people manage their health. Unfortunately, the information may not be valid, safe, or based on medical evidence. Nurses increasingly need to be very tech savvy to help patients and their families be smart consumers of information; they need to be able to direct them to legitimate websites and provide the best evidence-based information available.

The specialty of hospice and palliative nursing is growing. End-of-life training is being integrated into nursing curricula as well as within the education for other health care disciplines. The Hospice & Palliative Nursing Association offers education and professional resources, while the Hospice & Palliative Credentialing Center offers certification in this area.

6. What do you enjoy most about your job? What do you enjoy least about your job?

I enjoy meeting people of all ages and from all walks of life. I am always amazed by how open patients and their families are, and the continued trust they have in nurses. I never take that for granted and know nursing is the most trusted profession due to how each one of us works and represents nursing.

What I struggle with most in the hospice and palliative specialty is that not enough people understand it—even other health care providers. They often have a preconceived notion that hospice means we are giving up on patients. It doesn't mean giving up; it's a redirection of focus. It's helping people have the best quality of life possible.

7. Can you suggest a valuable "try this" for students considering a career in your profession?

Consider being a volunteer in a hospital or with a health care agency. Also, practice being a good and compassionate listener. Ask friends or family members what brings quality to their lives. Listen to their story and then summarize the meaning for them. See if you are able to discern the values and beliefs they communicate.

INTENSIVE CARE UNIT (ICU)

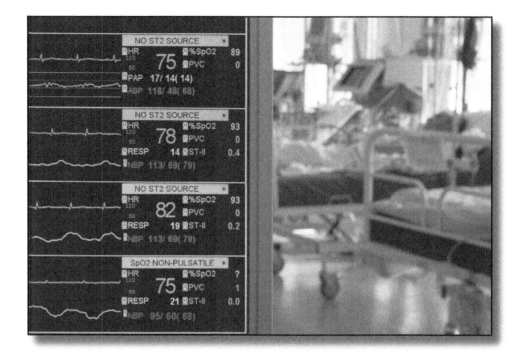

Critical care is a field of medicine that supports patients with complex and critical medical conditions. This essay provides a description of the structure and staffing of intensive care units (ICUs), and some of the important devices and methods they use to support patients. It is not a comprehensive description of every treatment and therapy used in the ICU.

ICUs are organized in various ways depending on the size, resources, and community needs for a given hospital. Large academic medical centers or teaching hospitals most often have multiple units and cluster specific patient populations on a unit. For example, adult patients undergoing a surgical procedure are admitted to the same unit, while adult patients suffering severe trauma are admitted to a different unit. Large hospitals with multiple ICUs are usually located in densely populated areas, such as an urban or metropolitan area. The other extreme is the small community hospital in a rural area that has multiple beds on a clinical unit that are dedicated for intensive care use.

Intensive care units are organized by clinical specialty and the type of services and treatments needed for that population of patients. The most common type is a combined medical, surgical, and respiratory ICU. Surgical ICUs (SICU) care for postoperative patients, medical ICUs manage patients requiring medical care for one or multiple critical illnesses (for example, pneumonia or a poisoning), and respiratory

ICUs manage patients with severe breathing problems. Cardiac ICUs, sometimes called coronary care units (CCUs), provide intensive heart monitoring and treatments for patients with heart problems. Some hospitals will have a cardiac-surgical ICU that is separate from the CCU and SICU, where patients are admitted following a cardiac operation, such as coronary artery bypass graft surgery. Trauma ICUs manage patients who were severely injured from a gunshot or stabbing wound, a car accident, a fall, or burns. Neurologic ICUs help patients recover from a stroke or spinal cord or brain injury. Most of these ICUs treat adult patients. Children who require critical care are usually admitted to a pediatric ICU or a neonatal ICU (NICU). The pediatric ICU cares for patients from birth until eighteen or nineteen years of age, and neonatal units care for newborns in their first twenty-eight days of life.

Most ICUs have a nurse manager to oversee the nursing staff and a physician director who sets policies, develops protocols, and communicates with patients, their primary care physicians and family members, and other specialists. An ICU either has full-time intensivist physicians who act as the primary care physicians and fully manage each patient (sometimes called a closed ICU) or brings in intensivists to consult on a patient's care (sometimes called an open ICU). The physician in charge (often called the attending) manages the patients and coordinates their medical care with other health care professionals on and off the unit and outside the hospital. Patients are admitted from the emergency room or other inpatient unit in the hospital or from another facility such as a nursing home.

One activity performed to deliver the best care possible is daily patient rounds, in which a critical care team visits each patient. Rounds are usually done early in the morning, and in some units teams may revisit patients in the evening. During rounds, the team discusses each patient's current medical condition and decides what treatments or therapies are needed for the day. The health care professionals performing rounds will vary but always include the attending physician. In teaching hospitals, fellows training to be critical care physicians, residents assigned for a one- or several-month ICU rotation, and medical students from the affiliated medical school will perform rounds with the attending. In some cases, the team is interdisciplinary (multiple clinical disciplines working together), and nurses, pharmacists, respiratory therapists, and others providing medical care to the patients will join rounds.

Staff

Intensive care units are staffed by professionals who are highly trained in a certain clinical discipline (type of job). These individuals work together on the unit as a critical care team to provide total and continuous care to patients. The critical care team on a unit includes intensivists, critical care nurses, a pharmacist, a registered dietitian, a social worker, a respiratory therapist, a physical or occupational therapist, physician assistants, nurse practitioners, a hospital chaplain, and child-life specialists.

Intensivists are board-certified or board-eligible in a medical specialty (for example, surgery or pediatrics). They have additional training, education, and certification to know every organ system in the body and how treatments, procedures, and medications may affect critically ill patients.

Critical care nurses are trained to monitor and manage the needs of acutely and critically ill patients. For example, they clean and monitor open wounds and ventilators to prevent patients from developing infections. Moreover, a nurse can receive additional education and training to become certified as a critical care registered nurse (CCRN).

Pharmacists are trained and board-certified or board-eligible in the appropriate and safe use of medications. They also can choose to undertake additional training to understand the specific problems and needs of critical care patients.

Respiratory therapists monitor and manage a patient's breathing using a variety of methods and devices, such as oxygen therapy or mechanical ventilation. Physical therapists work with patients to restore or improve mobility, relieve pain, and limit or prevent physical disability. Occupational therapists assess the impact of the disease or injury on the patients' ability to function at home, at work, and during physical activity after hospital discharge.

Physician assistants and nurse practitioners are licensed with advanced critical care training and work directly under the intensivist. They assist the intensivist, for example, by performing physical exams and procedures, diagnosing and treating illnesses, writing orders, and talking with patients and families. Child-life specialists are licensed professionals who provide play therapy to help children recover from an illness and therapies to distract them during painful procedures. The hospital chaplain offers pastoral support to patients, family members, and staff.

Supportive Care

A wide array of devices, equipment, and medications are used in the ICU to provide supportive care to patients recovering from life-threatening illnesses or injuries. Thus, it is one of the most complex clinical areas in the hospital. In an ICU, lines, tubes, drains, and other devices are attached to or inserted into patients. Any one patient may have as many as fourteen of these different-sized tubes attached in some way to the body. All patients will have heart monitor leads attached to the chest area to monitor the electrical activity of the heart and a pulse oximeter that typically clasps onto a finger to monitor oxygen levels in the blood and pulse rate. Patients may also have a cuff on the arm for periodic blood pressure monitoring and a peripheral IV inserted in a vein on the top of the hand to give fluids or medications. A patient may need a Foley catheter inserted up to the bladder to collect urine or a dialysis catheter inserted in the groin area and attached to a machine to assist the kidneys in cleaning the blood. Other small, tube-like catheters include central line/pulmonary artery (PA) catheters inserted in the neck to monitor blood flow or give medications or life-sustaining nutrition, an arterial line inserted in an artery at the wrist to monitor blood pressure, or an intracranial pressure catheter inserted in the brain to monitor its swelling.

A patient may need assistance breathing. In this case, either an endotracheal tube is inserted in the mouth or a tracheostomy tube is inserted in the neck and attached to a machine (a process called mechanical ventilation) to regulate the patient's breathing and provide the appropriate mix of oxygen and gas. A tracheostomy tube is used only if the patient will need mechanical ventilation for a prolonged period. Chest tubes are inserted under the skin around the rib cage area to remove escaped air or drain blood from the space around the lungs. This type of drainage tube is also used in other areas of the body to remove fluids or blood from a wound. A nasogastric tube inserted through the nose and down into the stomach can remove acid or other unwanted fluids or can supply nutrition. An intra-aortic balloon pump inserted into the groin helps the heart pump blood through the body.

Several emergency procedures can be performed in the ICU to revive a patient who has stopped breathing or is experiencing cardiac arrest. Cardiopulmonary resuscitation (CPR) is a series of things done to open the patient's airway (tilting the chin up, opening the mouth, holding down the tongue), help with breathing (blowing air into the mouth), and help pump blood from the heart into the body (chest compressions). Sometimes manual resuscitation will be done. In this case, a face mask is placed over the patient's mouth or a breathing tube inserted down the throat, and a plastic bag is attached and manually squeezed by the doctor, nurse, or respiratory therapist to fill the lungs with oxygen. Manual resuscitation is a short-term solution for a breathing problem. A patient who continues to require breathing support will be placed on a mechanical ventilator. A patient experiencing cardiac arrest will be defibrillated by placing two paddles attached to a defibrillator on the chest to send an electrical shock through the heart in an attempt to restart the heart's natural rhythm. This procedure may have to be done more than once to convert the heart back to its natural rhythm.

Perspective and Prospects

Intensive care units are relatively new considering the practice of medicine dates to about 4000 BCE, during ancient Egyptian times. The history of intensive care began in the late 1920s when W. E. Dandy opened a three-bed unit for patients following neurosurgery at Johns Hopkins Hospital in Baltimore. About the same time, in 1927, Sarah Morris Hospital in Chicago opened the first center to care for infants born prematurely. The devastation of World War II prompted the creation of wards to resuscitate and care for severely injured soldiers, and afterward, recovery rooms were opened to group postoperative patients together to compensate for a nursing shortage. By 1960, postoperative recovery rooms were in every hospital. Another catastrophic event that contributed to intensive care was the polio epidemic in 1947-48. To compensate for the development of respiratory paralysis and death from polio, doctors in Denmark developed mechanical ventilation therapy to keep patients breathing during this illness. The benefits of this therapy prompted the opening of respiratory ICUs in the 1950s. Then, in 1958, Baltimore City Hospital (now Johns Hopkins Bayview Medical Center) opened the first multidisciplinary ICU in the United States. By the late 1960s, most US hospitals had at least one ICU, and in the late 1990s there were about six thousand ICUs.

Christine G. Holzmueller

Conversation With . . .
CAROL CONGER

RN, BSN
Intensive Care Unit Nurse

Carol Conger has been in nursing for thirty-two years and an Intensive Care Unit (ICU) nurse for twenty-eight years. She works at a Level 1 Trauma Center in Georgia.

1. What was your individual career path in terms of education/training, entry-level job, or other significant opportunity?

Two things made me interested in a health care career: my older brother became a doctor, and I wanted to combine my interest in science with my love for working with people.

If you're going to pursue a four-year degree in nursing, you have to know you want to do that upon entering college. So, I made my decision freshman year. I graduated with a bachelor's degree in nursing (BSN) from the University of Maryland and started working at the George Washington University Hospital in Washington, D.C., on the medical-surgical unit. At that time, I did a lot of AIDS care, and peritoneal dialysis, which is the type of dialysis people on home dialysis need when they get infections. I was there three years but got to a point where I needed a break from all the death and dying. So I went to the Columbia Hospital for Women for eight months, working with mothers and babies. It was very happy but very dull. I left and went to the medical ICU unit at Washington Hospital Center for four years.

Then I moved to Georgia and started working in a hospital's float pool. That means the central nursing office sends you to whatever area of critical care has a staffing need. I've been working in their ICU for twenty-three years.

Typically, I work with one or two patients. In ICU, the nurse basically runs the situation. My job is to carefully monitor these patients, who are in a delicate situation. If you are in critical care, I'm monitoring your vital signs, doing bedside dialysis and monitoring your urinary intake and output, and your drips. If I'm not watching you in person by your bedside, I probably have an eye on you on a monitor.

Particularly in surgery and trauma patients, if you're watching your patient you usually have a heads-up before things go south. It's not that our patients don't code and die. But carefully monitoring them is the whole point of a patient being in the ICU.

Sometimes the situation is so intense that I must rely on my coworkers. We had a car accident victim who died the other night and five nurses took turns doing CPR—because CPR is exhausting—prior to his passing.

2. What are the most important skills and/or qualities for someone in your profession?

Important skills are organization, ability to multi-task, stress tolerance, application of knowledge. Important qualities include honesty, integrity, approachability, confidence, resiliency, grit, and being open to cultural diversity.

3. What do you wish you had known going into this profession?

I wish I had known how demanding the work hours are, and the subsequent burden on family life. Most inpatient hospitals have 12-hour shifts—often committed to either straight day or night shifts—and include a requirement for weekends and holidays. While many people are settling in for family birthdays or Thanksgiving dinner, the hospital life requires that nurses be there. I have four children and many family events happen on Sunday afternoon. On Sunday afternoon, I'm taking a nap because I have to go to work.

4. Are there many job opportunities in your profession? In what specific areas?

There are lots of job opportunities, probably in most areas. Healthcare is quickly evolving to include a more substantial role for nurses. Many doctor's offices have a nurse practitioner on staff. In intensive care, where traditionally we've just had residents, you will see more nurse practitioners.

Applications for nursing school and some of the advanced practice areas such as nurse practitioners or CRNA are highly competitive. My daughter considered nursing when she was in college, and you had to have a 3.7 GPA to even think about applying at her school. The prerequisite classes, such as chemistry and biology, are difficult and peers in those classes are also pursuing competitive fields like engineering or becoming an MD. So, there's no slacking along the way.

5. How do you see your profession changing in the next five years, how will technology impact that change, and what skills will be required?

In addition to the evolving role of nurse practitioners, technology will continue to drive care. In the ICU, my bedside monitors now even include an EKG function. We are also able to retrieve information in less invasive ways. Ten years ago, if you wanted information about a patient's volume status, you'd insert a fancy intravenous catheter that lies in center of the heart. Now we can gather some of that same information from an IV that's put in the artery in the wrist. I expect to see this evolution continue.

6. What do you enjoy most about your job? What do you enjoy least about your job?

I love being able to work hard—sometimes to the point of exhaustion—and see a patient do well. Good nursing care has a huge impact on patient outcome and I definitely see that in trauma. When someone who was near death goes back to living a real life (sometimes after months of hospital care and then rehab) it is so rewarding! There's a lot of scut work—think unpleasant tasks or odors—along the way. I also like working in a teaching facility, which provides lots of opportunity to broaden my knowledge and understanding of what I'm doing, and I can still stay at the bedside and not in a classroom. I really like working with the medical and surgical residents as they learn their specialty. The culture is such that I can teach them too—some are more willing to learn than others, but experience is a very good teacher.

I least like when patients in intensive care become chronic and don't get well enough to leave and they just linger. Say someone is in a wreck and becomes quadriplegic. They're needy because they can't do anything for themselves and if they are ventilated and can't talk, they get so frustrated. It's frustrating for me because I can't take any palliative measures to improve their situation.

I also dislike when families come in and tell me they looked something up on the internet.

7. Can you suggest a valuable "try this" for students considering a career in your profession?

HIPPA (Health Insurance Portability and Accountability Act) requirements and health care issues (like that you have to have a TB test before you can be with patients) make it harder to shadow a nurse in the clinical setting, at least where I work. A good bet would be to talk with a nurse and see what they do or ask them to describe what a usual work day is like. You can also pursue volunteer opportunities within a hospital.

INTERNET MEDICINE

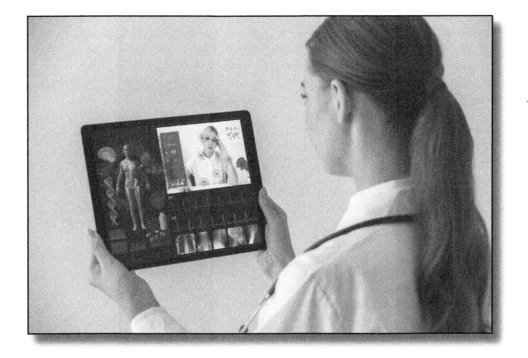

The use of Web-based and other electronic long-distance communication technologies for health information, assessment, service delivery, training, and public health administration.

Science and Profession

The Internet is a computer-based tool that is facilitating communication among vast numbers of individuals, groups, businesses, and governments. In addition to facilitating purely social and business-related ventures, the Internet is proving to be a valuable tool for improving the state of public health. This is because a new type of medical care and medical services has developed. These services, typically called telehealth, telemedicine, and e-medicine, use the Internet as a key tool in their dispensation, organization, and evaluation of health care services. Such services have taken the form of a variety of health care-related websites that provide services once available only through a face-to-face visit with a doctor or other health or social services professional. The websites are valuable in that they provide almost instantaneous information and other communications assistance to patients, their families, treatment professionals, trainers, trainees in the health care and social service professions, and medical researchers.

In terms of assisting patients, Internet-based medical approaches provide a variety of services to individual Internet users. First, they provide a wealth of information on different symptoms and medical conditions. They also allow for screening of such conditions to see if they warrant further attention from medical professionals and advice on how to handle minor health ailments and medical emergencies. They also help consumers to find medical advice, health care providers, self-help or support groups, and therapy over the Internet, all of which may or may not be supervised by medical professionals. Finally, they can give patients and their families information on different treatment options, including common procedures, the latest in alternative medicine, and even current clinical trials information.

Internet medicine can also be very helpful for family members of individuals having medical problems. Often, family members do not know how best to help their significant others in times of medical need. To meet this need, websites may post a wide variety of information that can help people understand the conditions, the requirements of treatment, the limits of treatment, and things they can do to be helpful to the ill family member. Additionally, websites sometimes offer lists of resources for family members.

Health care and social service providers also find the Internet beneficial for their work. For some, it might be as simple as using the Internet to schedule appointments, or to communicate test results, reminder information about treatment procedures, or appointment reminders via e-mail with clients. For others, it might involve using special websites to conduct assessments of clients for the purpose of tracking their treatment success or progress. Professionals may also use telemedicine in order to learn about new treatments and procedures, or to learn about new drugs and other pharmaceutical products. In addition, health care and social service providers may benefit their general practice by using the Internet to keep abreast of new clinical trials to test state-of-the-art treatments, changes in licensing laws affecting their practice, and the development of new health care databases for tracking, triage, and communication with insurance companies. Finally, some providers are actually using the Internet for health services delivery.

Health care providers in training and their trainers also benefit greatly from telemedicine. To trainees living in remote areas or those who might be highly mobile, such as those in the armed forces, the Internet provides immediate access to large online libraries, knowledgeable online teachers, and databases full of important medical information. Both long-established and new institutions interested in telemedicine increasingly are translating typical face-to-face training approaches into distance-based training programs utilizing the Internet. Encyclopedias, descriptions of techniques, pictures of what different conditions might look like both inside and outside the body, and even video of actual procedures are available online. Similarly, instruction in the use of such material is available online through training programs that lead to certificates of training and actual accredited degrees, ranging from bachelor's to doctoral degrees and postdoctoral training. In addition to helping individuals who are at remote locations, such material also can be used to reach a larger number of trainees than might typically be able to observe or attend such training. The increased ability to teach, show procedures, or give supervision at a distance using pictorial, written, oral, and video information greatly facilitates continuing education and improvement of general health care practice. It also helps to facilitate the evaluation of those practices and training sessions. Since all of the work takes place over the Internet, different aspects of the work can be monitored and evaluated electronically.

Much of the evaluation of this kind of information is done by researchers who are studying client, trainer, provider, or even health care system behavior and organization. This is done by evaluating information, also known as data, in individual sessions or visits to websites, as well as by examining data that are collected over time, across multiple visits. For instance, a person might first go to a website for information on a specific medical condition and then, at a later time or times, come back and look up different treatment approaches, or visit online discussion groups. What they do from time to time would be evaluated by researchers to see how individuals use the site, how long they stay on it, or what things they try searching for that may not yet be on the site. The process of watching behavior over time is called tracking. Tracking allows researchers to profile the users of websites to learn more about their behavior, usually for the purpose of predicting their behavior and response to treatment. The information gathered by creating tracking databases of what happens with Web site users can be used to improve services and to decrease long-term health care service, training, and administration costs on a continuing basis.

Because of all the data being collected on how individuals are using different websites or other Internet-based services, there has been some concern over the individual's right to privacy and the protection of the information collected. For instance, some people have been concerned that if they are searching for information related to the human immunodeficiency virus (HIV) or substance use, they might be identified as being at risk for having that condition whether they do or not. Furthermore, many individuals do not want that information linked to their identities or medical records. On one hand, they may be wishing to avoid solicitation of business from sellers of medical services or products because of their association with the condition; they do not want their personal information sold for that purpose to the providers of such products or services. On the other hand, they may also wish to maintain privacy and keep their information confidential so as to avoid having any threat to their future insurability or their ability to get health care coverage. As an example, if a health care provider such as a health maintenance organization (HMO) tracked users' information on a website and discovered, through the database, that someone who was now applying for coverage had certain medical conditions, that person might have a greater risk of being refused coverage if his or her time on the website was not completely anonymous. In sum, given these concerns, users of Internet medicine need to understand that there are differences between the terms privacy, confidentiality, and anonymity, as well as in the legal issues and protections one can exercise when using this type of medicine. Each website may be operating under different constraints, and so it is always important for users of these services to be sure they understand how the websites handle privacy. Finding out how a website protects or does not protect the privacy of its users is the only way users can determine how safe it is to reveal confidential information when they use a specific website.

Diagnostic and Treatment Techniques

One of the biggest opportunities offered by Internet medicine is that of increasing the ability of individuals to do selfscreening for medical conditions to see if they need medical assistance. Likewise, the ability of service providers to do screening and assessment for a larger number of people is increased relative to what can be done in person. This is because the assessments can be administered via the computer, saving valuable provider time. Additionally, assessments can be completed online and sent to providers in advance for immediate evaluation. While it may be some time before conclusive diagnoses can be offered via online technology, such advances are not far off; the differences between online and in-person assessments are being studied.

Intervention via the Internet is also much improved because large quantities of information can be dispensed electronically, printed out by clients or their families, or distributed to large numbers of individuals. Such informational interventions can be important for facilitating proper compliance with medical prescription regimens, helping clients to avoid bad drug interactions, or providing reminders about other things needed to facilitate wellness. Informational interventions can also be used for primary prevention, or preventing problems from happening in the first place. By providing suggestions for problem prevention, much suffering could be spared and many health care dollars can be saved. This is especially true for teenagers and college-age populations, who are often savvy web users.

Treatment also takes place on the Internet via simultaneous online interactions such as in chat rooms, communicating via videoconferencing as in a normal conversation but using video cameras, and simple asynchronous e-mail between the client and the provider. Generally this type of treatment is a complement to face-to-face treatment. For instance, some HMOs use online support groups as additional treatment for persons already receiving therapy. Others are using programs such as self-guided online courses that clients can work through to benefit their health. In general, practitioners are permitted to do this so long as they are properly licensed. This usually requires being licensed by the state in which they are practicing and/or where the client is receiving the services.

Perspective and Prospects

The Internet continues to grow on a daily basis, with an increasing number of computer owners and websites taking advantage of its capabilities. Communications technologies are also improving constantly, allowing for almost instant individual communication of written, oral, and visual information at distances and speeds that were inconceivable in the past. As a result of these developments, as well as increases in health care costs and the potential economic and health benefits provided by Internet medicine, this specialty area is here to stay. Commitments by governments to examine such developments in health care underscore this likelihood. In 1998, for example, the Health Resources and Service Administration of the United States Department of Health and Human Services established the Office for the Advancement of Telehealth. This office is devoted to advancing the use of telehealth and Internet-based medicine to facilitate improvement in the state of public health and research on public health. The ability of such approaches to provide more services with streamlined administrative procedures and decreased costs holds much promise for improving the state of public health.

For Further Information

Barrett, David. "Should Nurses Be at the Forefront of Telehealth?" *The Guardian*, 20 Jan. 2014, www.theguardian.com/healthcare-network/2012/jan/20/nurses-needed-at-telehealth-forefront. Accessed 20 Dec. 2016.

Bunn, Jennifer. "Telehealth-the Future of Healthcare?" *Ausmed*, 26 Oct. 2016, www.ausmed.com/articles/telehealth/. Accessed 20 Dec. 2016.

Edmunds, Marilyn W., et al. "Telehealth, Telenursing, and Advanced Practice Nurses." *Journal of Nursing Practices*, Apr. 2010, www.medscape.com/viewarticle/719335. Accessed 20 Dec. 2016.

Llewellyn, Anne. "Beyond the Bedside: The Role of Telehealth Nursing." *Nursetogether.com*, 23 June 2014, www.nursetogether.com/beyond-bedside-role-telehealth-nursing. Accessed 20 Dec. 2016.

Taylor, Goldie. "The Evolution of Telehealth Nursing." *Minority Nurse*, 8 Apr. 2016, minoritynurse.com/the-evolution-of-tele health-nursing/. Accessed 20 Dec. 2016.

Telehealth Nursing Practice Scope and Standards of Practice, 5th Ed.. American Academy of Ambulatory Care Nursing. Downloaded August 14, 2017 from https://www.aaacn.org/tnp-scope-standards-practice.

"Telehealth Nursing Practice." *American Academy of Ambulatory Care Nursing*, www.aaacn.org/telehealth. Accessed 20 Dec. 2016. Weselby, Cathy. "Is Telenursing for You?" *Wilkes University,* 28 Jan. 2015, onlinenursing.wilkes.edu/telenursing/. Accessed 20 Dec. 2016.

Westra, Bonnie. "Telenursing and Remote Access Telehealth." *American Association of Colleges of Nursing*, Oct. 2012, www.aacn.nche.edu/qsen-informatics/2012-workshop/presentations/westra/Telehealth.pdf. Accessed 20 Dec. 2016.

Nancy A. Piotrowski, Ph.D.

TELEHEALTH NURSING

Telehealth nursing, or telenursing, is the use of audio and video technology and advanced digital and optical communications by specially trained nurses to deliver nursing care. This type of nursing care is usually in the form of care management for emergent or chronic conditions, coordination of care, and health maintenance services within the scope of nursing practice. The American Academy of Ambulatory Care Nursing wrote *Telehealth Nursing Scope and Standards of Practice* that delineates clinical, managerial and administrative approaches to the complex nursing roles required in Telehealth Nursing interventions.

Telenursing benefits both the patient and the nurse; the patient benefits from increased access to services, while the nurse benefits from a more flexible and less physically stressful work environment. It is predicted that telehealth nursing will become more widespread in the future.

Background

Telehealth nursing is a subfield of a medical practice area known as telehealth or telemedicine. This refers to any health care delivered through some form of communication other than personal contact. The field is as old as the telephone. Within a few years of the first telephone patent being issued in 1876, at least one medical journal, *The Lancet,* was advocating the use of the telephone for physician-patient consultations to eliminate the need for some in-person appointments. Since that time, physicians and nurses have frequently used the telephone to assess basic health issues, answer questions about medications and side effects, and reassure anxious patients. Twenty-four-hour access to nurse-staffed helplines have been a staple of health insurance benefits for many years.

What has brought the concept to the forefront is the increased availability and capability of new technology that can be used in the twenty-first century. Instead of merely listening to a parent describe his or her child's rash, for instance, a telehealth nurse, or telenurse, can use a video link to see the child. . This virtual link allows the nurse to use a wider range of education and experience to determine whether a situation is serious enough to require the in-person attention of a medical practitioner or whether another remedy can be recommended within practice guidelines.

Telenurses can use technology to have virtual consultations with patients who need assistance with health improvement programs such as smoking cessation or weight loss. The connection can help patients stay on track with their efforts, provide encouragement and support, and help the nurse identify any potential issues that are emerging. Prenatal patients and new mothers also benefit from these consultations.

Technology exists that allows a patient to connect in-home monitoring equipment, such as blood pressure devices, scales and blood glucose monitors, to a computer that can communicate with the nurse's computer. The nurse has direct access to the readings and can determine whether a patient's condition is under control or is in need of adjustment or care. Telenurses can provide guidance and assurance to patients managing complex and chronic conditions, helping to improve their health outcomes, while also reducing the number of in-person office or hospital visits these patients need. Telenurses are valuable in helping senior patients with multiple health issues and patients with illnesses such as multiple sclerosis, hepatitis, AIDS, and other serious conditions to better manage their condition and coordinate their care.

Improved technology allows telehealth nurses to access far more patient records than any single nurse in a physician's office could. Records from several associated offices or from many offices within an insurance network can be accessed from a single call center. This allows the nurse to provide more personalized care, maintain better records of the care administered, and often, decrease duplication of care and medication interactions. The result is an improved patient experience that can often yield better outcomes. Fewer nurses are able to provide better care to more patients than would be possible if each office had to staff its own call center or if patients had to come in for in-person visits.

Fast Fact

Moving fast out of the gate is the relatively new specialty of Telehealth—which includes telenursing. The District of Columbia and 29 states mandate that health plans cover these services.
Source: waldenuniversity.com

Overview

Telehealth nursing is evolving from simply answering questions about medications or the possible causes of symptoms to being an integrated part of health care management for many patients. Nurses working in this capacity can develop ongoing connections with patients that allow them to develop a better perspective on how a patient's treatment is progressing, what problems the patient is experiencing with his or her treatment, and other information that can help the physician and the patient's entire health care team to provide better care. The technology-based consultations can provide more frequent interactions with patients who live in remote areas or who have barriers to coming to the physician's office, such as mobility or transportation issues.

Telenurses can serve as health coaches for people endeavoring to improve their health or for people recovering from life-altering medical situations, such as heart attacks or strokes. They often help to coordinate care for patients who see several physicians for multiple conditions, such as a patient with diabetes who needs to see a cardiologist for heart concerns, an ophthalmologist to monitor potential vision problems, and a podiatrist for proper foot care. Telenurses can serve as educators for people learning to cope with new illnesses or recovering from surgical procedures. In most cases, all of these efforts can be done with fewer staff and at a lower cost than in-person care would require.

The practice of telehealth nursing provides some benefits for nurses, too. For many telehealth nurses, the job provides shorter, more regular work hours. Telenursing can allow for more focused specialization if the nurse so desires. It can allow the nurse to develop better relationships with patients in his or her caseload. Telenursing can also provide a way for nurses who have problems with the physical aspects of nursing such as long hours of standing and lifting patients, to continue practicing their profession.

While telenursing has many advantages, it also raises some concerns. Nurses sometimes worry that telenursing will eliminate jobs in the future. Others fear that the trend will lead to less personal health care, where in-person visits with nurses or physicians are the exception instead of the norm. Other concerns include the possibility of increased medical errors, the potential for medical problems to be missed by the lack of personal contact, and the greater possibility of electronic records theft and resulting medical fraud. It is also imperative that the telenurse practice within the scope of practice defined by state laws and the practice standards defined by the employer.

Janine Ungvarsky,
Patricia Stanfill Edens, PhD, RN, LFACHE

Specialties

ANESTHESIOLOGY

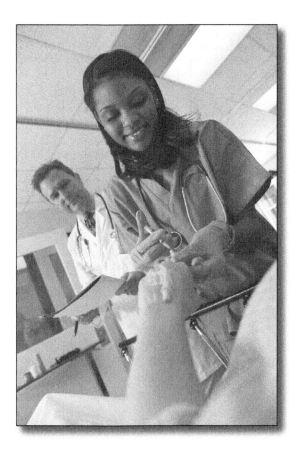

The History of Anesthesiology

In a modern hospital, the surgical operating room normally is a very quiet place. The anesthesiologist, surgeon, assisting doctors, and nurses perform their duties with little conversation while the patient sleeps. Family members sit quietly in a nearby waiting room until the operation is over. Before the advent of anesthesiology in the 1840s, however, surgery was a thoroughly gruesome experience. Patients might drink some whiskey to numb their senses, and several strong men were recruited to hold them down. Surgeons cut the flesh with a sharp knife and sawed quickly through the bone while patients screamed in agony. The operating room in the hospital was located as far as possible from other patients awaiting surgery so that they would not hear the cries so plainly.

Many kinds of operations were performed before anesthetics were discovered. Among these were the removal of tumors, the opening of abscesses, amputations, the treatment of head wounds, the removal of kidney stones, and cesarean sections and other surgeries during childbirth. The frightful ordeal of "going under the knife," however, often caused patients to delay surgery until it was almost too late. Also, for the surgeon it was nerve-racking to work without anesthetics, trying to operate while the patient screamed and struggled.

Sir Humphry Davy (1778-1829) was a distinguished British chemist who studied the intoxicating effect of a gas called nitrous oxide. While suffering from the pain of an erupting wisdom tooth, he sought relief by inhaling some of the gas. In 1800, he published a paper suggesting the use of nitrous oxide to relieve pain during surgery. There was no follow-up on his idea, however, and it was forgotten until after anesthesia had been discovered independently in the United States.

The next episode in the history of anesthesiology was the work of Crawford W. Long (1815-78), a small-town doctor in Georgia. In the early nineteenth century, "ether frolics" had become popular, in which young people at a party would inhale ether vapor to give them a "high" such as from drinking alcohol. One young man was to have surgery on his neck for a tumor. Long was the town druggist as well as the doctor, so he knew that this fellow had purchased ether and enjoyed its effects. Long suggested that he inhale some ether to ready himself for surgery. On March 30, 1842, the tumor was removed with little pain for the patient. It was the first successful surgery under anesthesia.

Unfortunately, Long did not recognize the great significance of what he had done. He did not report the etherization experiment to his colleagues, and it remained relatively unknown. He used ether a few more times in his own surgical practice, one time while amputating the toe of a young slave. Long finally wrote an article for a medical journal in 1849 telling about his pioneering work, three years after anesthesia had been publicly demonstrated and widely adopted by others.

The story of anesthesiology then moved to Hartford, Connecticut, where a young dentist named Horace Wells (1815-48) played a major role. P. T. Barnum, of show business and circus fame, was advertising an entertaining "GRAND EXHIBITION of the effects produced by inhaling NITROUS OXIDE or LAUGHING GAS!" Wells decided to attend. He was one of the volunteers from the audience and "made a spectacle of himself," according to his wife.

Another volunteer who had inhaled the gas began to shout and stagger around; finally he ran into a bench, banging his shins against it. The audience laughed, but the observant Wells noticed that the man showed no pain, even though his leg was bleeding. This demonstration gave Wells a sudden insight that a person might have a tooth pulled or even a leg amputated and feel no pain while under the influence of the gas.

Wells became so excited by the idea of eliminating pain that he arranged to have some nitrous oxide gas brought to his office on the next day. Then he had a long talk with a young dentist colleague, John Riggs, about the potential risks of trying it out on a patient. Finally, Wells decided to make himself the first test case, if Riggs would be willing to extract one of his wisdom teeth.

On the morning of December 11, 1844, a bag of nitrous oxide gas was delivered by the man who had been in charge of the previous evening's exhibition. Wells sat in the dental chair and breathed deeply from the gas bag until he seemed to be asleep. Riggs went to work with his long-handled forceps to loosen and finally pull out the tooth, with no outcry from the patient. After a short time, Wells regained consciousness, spit out some blood, and said that he had felt "no more pain than the prick of a pin."

After this success, Wells immediately set to work on further experiments. He acquired the apparatus and chemicals to make his own nitrous oxide. Within the next month, he used the gas on more than a dozen patients. Other dentists in Hartford heard about the procedure and started using it. By the middle of January 1845, Wells was confident enough to propose a demonstration to a wider audience.

Wells was able to arrange for a demonstration at Massachusetts General Hospital in Boston. While the audience watched, he anesthetized a volunteer patient with gas and extracted his tooth. Unfortunately, the patient groaned at that moment, causing laughter and scornful comments from the onlookers. Wells was viewed as another quack making grandiose claims without evidence. His demonstration had failed, and he returned to Hartford in discouragement. He later commented that he had probably removed the gas bag too soon, before the patient was fully asleep.

It was another dentist, William T. G. Morton (1819-68), who finally provided a convincing demonstration of anesthesia. Morton tried to obtain some nitrous oxide from a druggist, who did not have any on hand and suggested that ether fumes could be substituted. Morton then used ether on several dental patients, with excellent results. In 1846, he obtained permission for a demonstration at the same hospital where Wells had failed two years earlier. Famous Boston surgeon John Warren and a skeptical audience watched as Morton instructed a patient to breathe the ether. When the patient was fully asleep, Warren removed a tumor from his neck. To everyone's amazement, there was no outcry of pain during the surgery. After the patient awoke, he said that he felt only a slight scratch on his neck. Warren's words have been recorded for posterity: "Gentlemen, this is no humbug!" Another doctor said, "What we have seen here today will go around the world."

The result of this dramatic demonstration of October 16, 1846, spread quickly to other hospitals in the United States and Europe. Several hundred surgeries were performed under anesthesia in the next year. In England, John Snow experimented with a different anesthetic, chloroform, and began to use it for women in childbirth. In 1853, Queen Victoria took chloroform from Snow during the delivery of her eighth child. Acceptance of anesthesia, and the science of anesthesiology, by the medical profession and the general public grew rapidly.

Science and Profession

Nitrous oxide, ether, and chloroform were the big three anesthetics for general surgery and dentistry for nearly a hundred years after their discovery. All three were administered by inhalation, but there were differences in safety, reliability, and side effects for the patient.

Wells, the dentist who had unsuccessfully tried to demonstrate nitrous oxide anesthesia in 1844, came to a tragic end in 1848 because of chloroform. He was testing the gas on himself to find out what an appropriate dosage should be. Unfortunately, he became addicted to the feeling of intoxication that it gave him. While under the influence of a chloroform binge, he accosted a woman on the street and was arrested. He committed suicide while in prison.

Nitrous oxide is a nearly odorless gas that must be mixed with oxygen to prevent asphyxiation. Storing the gases in large, leakproof bags was awkward. By comparison, ether and chloroform were much more convenient to use because they are liquids that can be stored in small bottles. The liquid was dripped onto a cloth and held over the patient's nose. Ether is hazardous, however, because it is flammable, and it also has a disagreeable odor. Chloroform is not flammable but is more difficult to administer because of the danger of heart stoppage.

Anesthesiology was practiced primarily by dentists, eye doctors, chemists, and all types of surgeons for many years. The Mayo Clinic in Rochester, Minnesota, was one of the first hospitals to recognize the need for specialists to administer anesthesia. In 1904, a nurse from Mayo named Alice Magaw gave a talk on what she had learned from eleven thousand procedures performed under anesthesia. Her concluding comment was that "ether kills slowly, giving plenty of warning, but with chloroform there is not even time to say good-by." Ether takes more time to induce anesthesia, but Magaw asserted that the patient's life was in less danger than from chloroform.

A Scottish physician, James Y. Simpson, was one of the early advocates of using chloroform for partial anesthesia during childbirth. The woman could breathe the vapor intermittently for several hours as needed without the disagreeable odor of ether. She would remain conscious, but the anesthetic apparently produced a kind of amnesia so that the pain was not fully remembered. Simpson received much public acclaim for his help to women in labor, including a title of nobility. (One humorist of the day suggested a coat-of-arms for Sir Simpson, showing a newborn baby with the inscription, "Does your mother know you're out?")

In the 1920s, several new anesthetic gases were created by chemists working closely with medical doctors. The advantages and drawbacks of each new synthesized compound were tested first on animals, then on human volunteers, and finally during surgery. One of the most successful ones was cyclopropane: it was quick acting and nontoxic and could be mixed with oxygen for prolonged operations. Like other organic gases, however, it was explosive under certain conditions and had to be used with appropriate caution.

A major development in 1928 was the invention of the endotracheal tube by Arthur Guedel. A rubber tube was inserted into the mouth and down the trachea (windpipe) to carry the anesthetic gas and oxygen mixture directly to the lungs. The space around the rubber tube had to be sealed in some way in order to prevent blood or other fluid from going down the windpipe. Guedel's ingenious idea was to surround the tube with a small balloon. When inflated, it effectively closed off the gap between the tube and the trachea wall. He gave a memorable demonstration at a medical meeting using an anesthetized dog with a breathing tube in its throat. After inflating the seal, the dog was submerged under water for several hours and then revived, showing that no water had entered its lungs.

The first local anesthetic was discovered in 1884 by Carl Koller, a young eye doctor in Vienna. He was a colleague of the famous psychoanalyst Sigmund Freud, and together they had investigated the psychic effects of cocaine. Koller noticed that his tongue became numb from the drug. He had the sudden insight that a drop of cocaine solution might be usable as an anesthetic for eye surgery. He tried it on a frog's eye, with much success. Following the tradition of other medical pioneers, he then tried it on himself. The cocaine made his eye numb. Koller published a short article, and the news spread quickly. Within three months, other doctors reported successful local anesthesia, using cocaine for dentistry, obstetrics, and many kinds of general surgery.

Chemists investigated the molecular structure of cocaine and were able to develop synthetic substitutes such as novocaine, which was faster and less toxic. Another improvement was to inject local anesthetic under the skin with a hypodermic needle. With this technique, it was possible to block off pain from a whole region of the body by deadening the nerve fibers. A spinal or epidural block is often used to relieve the pain of childbirth or for various abdominal surgeries.

There is another class of anesthetic drugs called barbiturates, which were originally developed for sleeping pills. Any medication that induces sleep automatically becomes a candidate for use as an anesthetic. The most successful barbiturate anesthetic has been sodium pentothal. It is normally administered by injection into a vein in the arm and puts the patient to sleep in a matter of seconds. When the surgery is over, the needle is withdrawn and consciousness returns, with few aftereffects for most people. The anesthesiologist may use sodium pentothal in combination with an inhaled anesthetic if the surgery is expected to be lengthy.

Diagnostic and Treatment Techniques

Suppose that a man is scheduled to have some kind of abdominal surgery, such as the repair of a hernia or hemorrhoids or the removal of the appendix, an intestinal blockage, or a cancerous growth. The anesthesiologist would select a sequence of anesthetics that depends primarily on the expected length of the operation and the physical condition of the patient.

About an hour before surgery, the patient receives a shot of morphine to produce relaxation and drowsiness. After he is wheeled into the operating room, the anesthesiologist inserts a needle into a vein in the patient's arm and injects a barbiturate such as sodium pentothal. This drug puts him to sleep very quickly because it is rapidly distributed through the body, but it is not suitable for maintaining anesthesia.

A muscle-paralyzing agent such as curare is now injected, which allows the anesthesiologist to insert an endotracheal tube into the lungs. The tube delivers a mixture of nitrous oxide and oxygen, supplemented with a small amount of other organic additives or of a more potent gas such as ether. The seal around the tube must be inflated to prevent fluids from entering the windpipe. The patient is now in a state of surgical anesthesia.

For a difficult surgery, additional curare may be injected to paralyze the abdominal muscles completely. In this case, the breathing muscles would also become paralyzed, which means that a mechanical respirator would be needed to inflate and deflate the lungs.

The anesthesiologist monitors the patient's condition with various instruments, such as a stethoscope, blood pressure and temperature sensors, and an electrocardiograph (EKG or ECG) with a continuous display. A catheter may be inserted into a vein to inject drugs or to give a blood transfusion if necessary. When the surgery is completed, the anesthesiologist is responsible for overseeing procedures undertaken in the recovery room as the patient slowly regains consciousness.

Perspective and Prospects

Many modern surgeries would be impossible without anesthesia. Kidney or other organ transplants, skin grafts for a burn victim, or microsurgery for a severed finger all require that the patient remain still for an extended period of time. Anesthesiologists choose from a variety of local and general anesthetics as the individual situations require.

In the emergency room of a hospital, patients are brought in with injuries from industrial, farm, or car accidents. Gunshot and knife wounds, the ingestion of toxic chemicals, or sports injuries often require immediate action to reduce pain and preserve life. Soldiers who are wounded or burned in battle can be given relief from pain because of the available anesthetics. Beyond operating room patients, another category of people who benefit greatly from anesthesia are those who suffer from chronic pain, including that from arthritis, back pain, asthma, brain damage, cancer, and other serious ailments.

A more recent innovation is electric anesthesia, which employs an electric current. It is widely used for animals and is gaining acceptance for humans. A marine biologist can submerge two electrodes into water and cause nearby fish to become rigid and unable to swim. After being netted and tagged, the fish are released with no harmful aftereffects. Veterinarians can use a commercially available device with two electrodes that attach to the nose and tail of a farm animal. Pulses of electricity are applied, causing the animal to remain immobilized until surgery is completed.

The most common human application of electric anesthesia is in dentistry. The metal drill itself can act as an electrode, sending pulses of electric current into the nerve to deaden the sensation of pain. The discomfort of novocaine injections and the possible aftereffects of the drug are avoided. Another application is to provide relief for people with chronic back pain, using a small, battery-powered unit attached to the person's waist.

Experiments have been done using electricity for total anesthesia, both on animals and on human volunteers. Electrodes are strapped to the front and back of the head. When an appropriate voltage is applied, the subject falls into deep sleep in a short time. When the electricity is turned off, consciousness is regained almost immediately. In one experiment, two dogs underwent "electrosleep" for thirty days with no apparent ill effects. Long-term studies with more subjects are needed to establish this new technology.

Hans G. Graetzer, Ph.D.

Conversation With . . .
GARRY BRYDGES

DNP, MBA, CRNA, ACNP-BC, FAAN
Chief Nurse Anesthetist

Garry Brydges is Chief Nurse Anesthetist at the M. D. Anderson Cancer Center in Houston, Texas. He has been a nurse for 24 years, a Certified Registered Nurse Anesthetist for 18 years, and is the president of the American Association of Nurse Anesthetists (AANA).

1. What was your individual career path in terms of education/training, entry-level job, or other significant opportunity?

I knew I wanted to go into some form of health care delivery, so I earned my bachelor's degree in organic chemistry-biochemistry at the University of Alberta. At the same time, I was competing in world championship-level weight lifting, trying to get to the Olympics. Ten months before the Olympics, I was in a car accident. I had to redirect my life.

Although I considered med school, I returned to the University of Alberta and earned a bachelor's degree in nursing (BSN). In retrospect, I'm glad I did because going through med school and a residency is a lifelong commitment. I think it's important to live a little first. Nursing got my feet wet and didn't mean I couldn't go later.

After graduating, I worked briefly in Vancouver. It was atrociously expensive, and cold. I ended up moving to the Rio Grande Valley in South Texas, and worked at Valley Baptist Hospital, fifteen minutes from the Mexican border. I started out doing the night shift. It was an underserved area with a high incidence of diabetes, and associated renal problems and cardiac issues. I came in as a critical care nurse, was quickly promoted to a charge nurse, and became passionate about work in the intensive care unit (ICU). I became an ICU educator and was promoted to manager of the ICU.

In areas where access to care is limited, all the physicians rely heavily on nurses. There are trust, communication, and educational opportunities. In a short period of time, I became basically the parallel of a resident or fellow in the ICU.

After three years, I came to a pivotal point where I could go into med school or pursue avenues that were starting to open up. I decided to go to the University of Texas at Houston and earned a master's in nursing (MSN) Advanced Practice specialty as an acute care nurse practitioner. For two years, I'd work the night shift, drive five-and-a-half hours from my home to Houston, study Sunday afternoon, go to classes Monday and Tuesday, and drive back Tuesday evening and go back to work. Fortunately, I was able to choose most of my clinical sites at my workplace. I picked cardiovascular, pulmonology, and other surgeons who would challenge me the most.

It was fun but grueling. Thinking longterm, I started to seek out other opportunities. I knew nurse anesthetist training was an academic challenge, applied at the UT Health Sciences Center in Houston, and ended up getting in. It's an extremely intense, full-time, three-year program. The market was opening up for anesthesia providers, so I didn't have to worry if I was going to be employed when I graduated with my master's degree in nursing (MSN) in nurse anesthesia. At the same time, my wife went back to school and became a nurse practitioner. I started working at MD Anderson Cancer Center, and so did she.

The knowledge and experience we both garnered in the Rio Grande Valley more than prepared us for the future. We managed high-acuity patients with severe heart failure. When people go into heart failure, a key measurement is ejection fraction. Normal is 60 percent or better. In the Rio Grande, 15 or 16 percent was a norm. So, I knew what to do in my advanced training due to my experience.

By 2005, I was director of Anesthesia Services, or chief nurse anesthetist. I also moved into professional leadership roles and set up mentorship programs to push my peers to go back to school.

I became a director, then vice president and president of the Texas Association of Nurse Anesthetists. To supplement my leadership development skills, I earned a doctorate of nursing practice at Texas Christian University. My PhD research looked at financial literacy in leadership in the nursing discipline. I became increasingly involved in health care policy development and moved into the national professional association as a director, participating in a number of national committees. I also went back for my master's in business administration at Texas Woman's University.

All of this work spilled right back to the institution where I worked. I went from being the only leader to having six managers on my leadership team with staff that report up to them. Some are doing administrative degrees, and we all do clinical work. Some weeks clinical takes up 50 to 60 percent of my time, and some weeks, 10 percent of my time.

My first attempt to become president-elect of the American Association of Nurse Anesthetists was unsuccessful, but I ended up doing a fair amount of speaking across the country. When you're interacting with people, you talk about important things concerning our practice and profession. Working with professional members in their states, we launched a program on opioid-sparing techniques in anesthesia, which has transformed patient outcomes by controlling pain without opioids.

I ran a second time and won. Being the association's president has been a tremendous experience, not only in serving members and opening up access to care across the US, but interfacing with federal agencies to make health care delivery better for every citizen in the country.

2. What are the most important skills and/or qualities for someone in your profession?

Attention to detail is paramount in this role; check three times to make sure before you execute. You need to exercise organization. You need to have compassion and care for human beings. Communication is critical.

3. What do you wish you had known going into this profession?

If I had known earlier how to leverage new study techniques, I could have been more proactive and gained more knowledge rather than sitting in the library for hours. The current information technology and Internet provide an incredible opportunity to excel faster than in the days of typewriters and library Dewey decimal systems. Now, at the click of the button, I can get targeted information and, more importantly, information I can interact with in realtime.

4. Are there many job opportunities in your profession? In what specific areas?

The market in nursing is wide open, whether you want to be in an academic setting, rural America, or a subspecialty. There are rich, rich opportunities.

5. How do you see your profession changing in the next five years, how will technology impact that change, and what skills will be required?

There's going to be a movement to achieve quality patient outcomes, which enforces vigilance on the nurse's part. If you're not engaged in reevaluating your practice every day, you're going to be left behind.

Numerous technologies clinically allow us to be more precise practitioners, such as bedside ultrasonography. We have probes that allow us to do a rapid assessment on the spot instead of a chest X-ray or CT scan. Pharmacological agents are revolutionizing how we practice due to pharmacogenetics, which tells me exactly what drugs I need to pick based on a person's genetic makeup. Genomics is going to be another field we'll need to better understand; it's not yet fully integrated with pharmacology. All the chemistry, biochemistry, genetics, physiology, and pharmacology we learn in school is used in this area of health care delivery.

6. What do you enjoy most about your job? What do you enjoy least about your job?

It's a privilege to take care of people. They put their lives in your hands at their most vulnerable moments, and you're their eyes and ears. I never take that for granted. I also enjoy following up with patients, making sure I did a good job, and getting feedback. Also, watching my peers grow and develop over the years has been extremely gratifying.

I least like the cultural movement I see now as new practitioners emerge: a sense that work-life balance is so paramount that if you schedule me for eight hours, I should work only eight hours. Not eight hours and fifteen minutes, or nine or ten hours. That's just not a reality of this profession. When you're doing a procedure, sometimes it ends early. Sometimes it takes longer. You're taking care of a human life. Surgeons do not stop surgery because it is 3 p. m. They stop surgery when the surgery is finished and the patient is safe in recovery.

Instant gratification, driven by social media platforms and text messaging, is also creating unrealistic expectations. Immediate delivery for a medical emergency is great, but the expectation that everything should function at that speed is a setup for failure. I watch people when they can't get an instant reaction or result, and they don't do well. It's a concern.

7. Can you suggest a valuable "try this" for students considering a career in your profession?

Reach out to a professional organization. There's always a national or state meeting, and that's probably one of the best places to network and pick the brains of CRNAs (certified registered nurse anesthetists) or NAs (nurse anesthetists). Organizations like the American Association of Nurse Anesthetists (AANA) run programs such as diversity programs intended to bring out people who have an interest. You can go in and do a skills lab, see some of the basic skillsets we have, handle the equipment such as a fiberoptic scope. Start at www.aana.com.

There's a lot of rigor in a nurse's education process, so whether you are in high school or the initial stages of college, know that every piece of coursework—such as math, biochemistry, or organic chemistry—is applicable to being a nurse anesthetist. Take those courses.

FAMILY MEDICINE

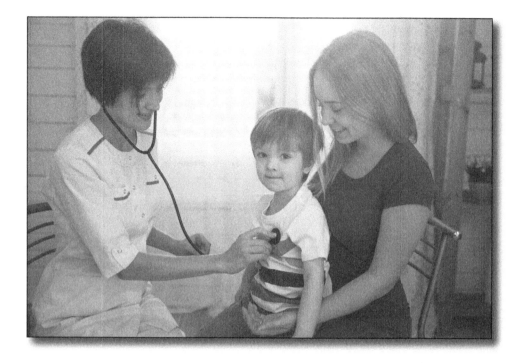

Science and Profession

From cradle to grave, family physicians have the ability to take care of patients from all age groups and manage a great variety of medical problems on a daily basis. As the primary care provider, they are central to a patient's care, either by providing it directly (85 percent of all medical problems) or by consulting specialists and following their management recommendations. They act as the patient's advocate even when healthy by providing preventive care services to find disease earlier in an attempt to eliminate it or slow its progression.

In the United States, there are approximately 80,000 practicing family physicians, accounting for more than 240 million annual office visits. More than a third of all US counties have access to only family physicians to provide medical care to their communities.

Family medicine is the direct descendant of general practice. For many years, most physicians were general practitioners. In the mid-to-late twentieth century, however, the explosion of medical knowledge led to the specialization of medicine. For example, increased knowledge of the function and diseases of the heart seemed to demand creation of the specialty of cardiology. The model of the country doctor or jack-of-all-trades physician taking care of a wide range of medical problems seemed doomed to sink in the sea of subspecialization in medicine. The general practitioner, the venerable physician who hung out his or her shingle after medical school and one or more years of internship or residency training, appeared to be headed for extinction. Indeed, in their then-existent forms, the general practitioner and general practice would not have survived. Several forces came into play which did result in the passing of general practice but which also changed general practice into family medicine.

The primary force pushing for general practice to survive and improve was the desire of the general public to retain the family doctor. The services that these physicians rendered and the relationships developed between physician and patients were held in high esteem. Through such voices as the Citizen Commission on Graduate Medical Education appointed by the American Medical Association (AMA), the public requested the rescue of the family doctor.

Other major players in the movement to revive and reshape general practice included the AMA itself and the American Academy of General Practice. On February 8, 1969, approval was granted for the creation of family medicine as medicine's twentieth official specialty. The American Academy of General Practice became the American Academy of Family Physicians (AAFP), and a certifying board, the American Board of Family Practice (ABFP), was established. The name has since been changed to the American Board of Family Medicine (ABFM). After these steps were completed, three-year training programs (residencies) in family medicine were established in medical universities and larger community hospitals to provide the necessary training for family physicians.

Family physicians are trained to provide comprehensive ongoing medical care and health maintenance for their patients. Those people who choose to become family physicians tend to value relationships over technology and service over high financial rewards. Many family physicians find themselves providing service to underserved populations and in mission work both inside and outside the United States. Family physicians often become advocates, providing counseling and advice to patients who are trying to sort out medical treatment options. They generally enjoy close relationships with their patients, who often hold them in high esteem.

Following graduation from medical school, students interested in a career in family medicine begin a three-year residency in the specialty. During the residency, these physicians train in actual practice settings under the supervision of faculty physicians. Family medicine residency training consists of three years of rotations with other medical specialties, such as internal medicine, pediatrics, surgery, and psychiatry. The unifying thread in family medicine residency training is the continuity clinic. Throughout their training, the residents see their own patients several days a week under the supervision of family medicine faculty physicians. Every effort is made to make this training as close as possible to experiences in the real world. Family medicine residents will deliver their patients' babies, hospitalize their patients, and deal with the emotional issues of death and dying, chronic illness, and disability.

Family medicine residents receive intensive training in behavioral and psychosocial issues, as well as "bedside manner" training. Scientific research has shown that many patients who seek care from family physicians have problems that require the physician to be a good listener and a skilled counselor. Family medicine residency training emphasizes these skills. It also emphasizes the functioning (or malfunctioning) of the family as a system and the effect of major changes (such as the birth of a child or retirement) on the health and functioning of the family members.

The length of training (three years versus one year) and the emphasis on psychosocial and family systems training are two of the major differences in the training of a family physician and the training of a general practitioner. Moreover, family physicians spend up to 30 percent of their training time outside the hospital in a clinic. Family medicine was the first medical specialty to emphasize this type of training, and family physicians spend more time in ambulatory (clinic) training than virtually any other specialist.

Following the successful completion of a residency program, a family physician may take a competency examination devised and administered by the ABFM. Passing this examination allows the physician to assume the title of Diplomate of the American Board of Family Medicine and makes him or her eligible to join the American Academy of Family Physicians, the advocacy and educational organization of family medicine.

There are about 330 fellowships now available to graduating family medicine residents: faculty development, geriatrics, obstetrics, preventive medicine, research, rural medicine, sports medicine, and others such as occupational medicine.

If family physicians wish to retain their diplomate status, they must take at least fifty hours per year of medical education. After a family physician fulfills all educational and other requirements of the ABFM, that physician must then retake the certifying examination every seven years or the certification will lapse. This periodic retesting is required by the ABFM to make sure that family physicians keep up their medical education and maintain their knowledge level and clinical skills. Family medicine was the first specialty to require periodic reexamination of its physicians. In fact, since family medicine has mandated reexaminations, many other medical specialty organizations now require periodic reexamination of their members or are considering such a move. Many former general practitioners who did not have a chance to do a three-year family medicine residency took the ABFM certifying examination and became diplomates based on their years of practice experience and successful completion of the certifying examination. This option was closed to general practitioners in 1988.

A new recertification program, called the Maintenance of Certification Program for Family Physicians (MC-FP), is being required by the ABFM starting with diplomates who recertified in 2003 and all diplomates phased in by 2010. To maintain certification, candidates must perform the following every seven years: submit an online application, maintain a valid medical license, verify completion of three hundred credits of accepted CME credits, and pass the cognitive exam.

Currently, the American Academy of Family Physicians requires new active physician members to be residency-trained in family medicine. Diplomate status reflects only an educational effort by the physician and does not directly affect medical licensure. Medical licensure is based on a different testing mechanism, and license requirements vary from state to state. According to a 2012 report published by the Association of American Medical Colleges, there are more than one-hundred thousand family physicians providing health care in the United States. Family medicine residency programs are approximately 460 in number and usually have about three thousand residents in training.

Diagnostic and Treatment Techniques

Service to patients is the primary concern of family medicine and all those who practice, teach, administer, or foster the specialty. Of all the family physicians in practice, more than 80 percent are involved in direct patient care. While family physicians by no means constitute a majority of physicians, they are among the busiest when measured in terms of ambulatory patient visits. Family physicians see 30 percent of all ambulatory patients in the United States, which is more than the number of ambulatory visits to the next two specialty groups combined. Because of their training, family physicians can successfully care for more than 85 percent of all patient problems they encounter. Consultation with other specialty physicians is sought for the problems that are outside the scope of the family physician's knowledge or abilities. This level of consultation is not unique to family physicians, as other specialty physicians find it necessary to seek consultation for 10 to 15 percent of their patients as well.

Family physicians can be found in all areas of the United States and in virtually all types of practice situations, providing a wide range of medical services. Family physicians can successfully practice in metropolitan areas or rural communities of one thousand people (or less), and they can be found teaching or doing research in medical colleges. Because of their training and the fact that they see a truly undifferentiated patient population, family physicians deliver a wide range of medical services. Besides seeing many patients in their offices, family physicians care for patients in nursing homes, make house calls, and admit patients to the hospital. Within the hospital, many family physicians care for patients in intensive care and other special care units and assist in surgery when their patients have operations. A small number perform extensive surgical procedures in the hospital setting. A sizable minority of family physicians take care of pregnant women and deliver their children; some of these physicians also perform cesarean sections. Because family physicians see anyone that walks through the door, it is not unheard of for a family physician to deliver a child in the morning, see the siblings in the office in the afternoon, and make a house call to the grandparents in the evening. Over 80 percent of family physicians perform dermatologic procedures, musculoskeletal injections, and electrocardiograms (EKGs) in their own offices.

The thing that makes family physicians different from other physicians is their attention to the physician-patient relationship. The family physician has first contact with the patient and is in a position to bond with the patient. The family physician evaluates the patient's complete health needs and provides personal care in one or more areas of medicine. Such care is not limited to any particular type of problem, be it biological, behavioral, or social, and the patients seen are not screened according to age, sex, or illness. The family physician utilizes knowledge of the patient's functioning in the family and community and maintains continuity of care for the patient in a hospital, clinic, or nursing home or in the patient's own home. Thus, in family medicine, the patient-physician relationship is initiated, established, and nurtured for both sexes, for all ages, and across time for many types of problems.

Because of their training, family physicians are highly sought-after care providers. Small rural communities, insurance companies, and government agencies at all levels actively seek family physicians to care for patients in a wide variety of settings. In this respect, family medicine is the most versatile medical specialty. Family physicians are able to practice and live in communities that are too small to support any other types of physician.

In two reports released by Merritt Hawkins, a national recruiting company, requests for family physicians surged by 55 percent, more than all other specialties. According to data from the Massachussetts Medical Society, community hospitals reported family physicians constituted their "most critical shortage."

While the vast majority of family physicians find themselves providing care for patients, there is a minority of family physicians who serve in other, equally important roles. Roughly 1.5 percent of family physicians serve as administrators and educators. They can be found working in state, federal, and local governments; in the insurance industry; and in residency programs and medical schools. Family physicians in residency programs provide instruction and role modeling for family medicine residents in community-based and university-based residency programs. Family physicians in medical colleges design, implement, administer, and evaluate educational programs for medical students during the four years of medical school. The Society of Teachers of Family Medicine (STFM) is the organization that supports family physicians in their teaching role.

One problem facing the specialty of family medicine is the very small percentage who are dedicated to research: only 0.2 percent of all family physicians. There is a large need for research in family medicine to determine the natural course of illnesses, how best to treat them, and the effects of illness on the functioning of the family unit. The need for research in the ambulatory setting is especially acute because, while most medical research is done in the hospital setting, most medical care in the United States is provided in clinics and offices. This problem will not be easily solved because of the service focus of family medicine training and the small number of family physicians dedicated to research.

Fast Fact

Nurse practitioners can write prescriptions, including for controlled substances, in all 50 states and Washington, DC.

Source: aanp.org American Association of Nurse Practitioners

Perspective and Prospects

Family medicine developed as a medical specialty because of the demands of the citizens of the United States; it is the only medical specialty with that claim. The ancestor of family medicine was general practice, and there is a direct link from the family physician to the general practitioner. Family medicine has grown and evolved into the specialty best suited to provide for the primary health care needs of most patients. Because of their broad scope of practice, cost-effective methods, and versatility, family physicians are found in virtually every type of medical and administrative setting. Family physicians provide a large portion of all ambulatory health care in the United States, and in some settings they are the sole providers of health care. General practice has been around as long as there have been physicians-Hippocrates was a general practitioner-but family medicine has a definite point of origin. It was created from general practice on February 8, 1969.

In January, 2000, a leadership team consisting of seven national family medicine organizations began the Future of Family Medicine (FMM) Project with its goal being "to develop a strategy to transform and renew the specialty of family medicine to meet the needs of patients in a changing health care environment." Six task forces were created as a result, with each one formed to address specific issues that aid in meeting the core needs of the people receiving care, the family physicians delivering that care, and shaping a quality health care delivery system. The FFM Leadership Committee has focused on improving the American health care system by implementing the following strategies:

> *taking steps to ensure that every American has a personal medical home, has health care coverage for basic services and protection against extraordinary health care costs, promoting the use and reporting of quality measures to improve performance and service, advancing research that supports the clinical decision making of family physicians, developing reimbursement models to sustain family medicine and primary care offices, and asserting family medicine's leadership to help transform the US health care system.*

The present role of the family physician is and will continue to be to seek to improve the health of the people of the United States at all levels. Major problems exist for family medicine, including attrition as older family physicians retire or die, lack of medical student interest in family medicine as a career choice, and the lack of a solid cadre of researchers to advance medical knowledge in family medicine. The major strengths supporting family medicine are its service ethic, attention to the physician-patient relationship, and cost-effectiveness.

After their near demise as a recognizable group in the mid-twentieth century, family physicians have a number of reasons to expect that they will have expanded opportunities to provide for the health care needs of their patients in the future. As the United States, for example, examines its system of health care, which is the most costly and the least effective of any health care system in the developed world, many medical and political leaders look to generalism, and particularly family medicine, to provide answers. Research has shown that, for many medical problems, family physicians can provide outcomes very similar to those provided by specialists. When one couples that fact with the versatility and cost-effectiveness of generalist physicians, it can be argued that to save health care dollars the nation must reverse the 30 percent to 70 percent ratio of generalist to specialist physicians. A ratio of 50 percent to 50 percent generalist to specialist physicians has been proposed at many levels in medicine and government.

As the population ages due to improved mortality statistics and the addition of baby boomers to the geriatric age group, a further shortage of general practitioners such as family physicians is inevitable. This situation will force the United States to deal with its health care issues in order to provide its citizens with cost-effective and adequate coverage. The shortage of family physicians specifically in rural areas has led to approximately 65 million Americans living in federally designated health professions shortage areas (HPSAs), defined as less than 1 primary care physician per 3,500 people. A growing challenge exists for those physicians living in rural areas as a lack of training and preparation for practice in their medical education and residency training has led to a steady decline in their choosing to practice there.

Paul M. Paulman, M.D.,
Kenneth Dill, M.D.

Conversation With . . .
JENNA HERMAN

DNP, APRN, FNP-BC
Family Nurse Practitioner

Jenna Herman has been a nurse practitioner for seven years and is the Family Nurse Practitioner Program Coordinator for the University of Mary in Bismarck, North Dakota.

1. What was your individual career path in terms of education/training, entry-level job, or other significant opportunity?

When I was ten years old, I was in a serious bike accident, and spent the first week in intensive care and the second week at a rehabilitation center. Many wonderful health care professionals were part of my recovery, and by observing the compassion and fortitude of the nurses who took care of me day after day, I knew nursing was the career for me.

After graduating with my bachelor's degree from Augustana University in Sioux Falls, South Dakota, my first job as a registered nurse was at a large medical center in Minneapolis, Minnesota. I enjoyed taking care of cancer patients and seeing them fight a critical disease. I saw a lot of patients pass away, and I wanted to try to help people before they got to a disease state, to try to make more of a difference and maybe prevent some of these diseases.

While volunteering as a nurse at a free clinic that provided services to uninsured individuals, I met a family nurse practitioner (FNP). She examined patients, diagnosed illness, and provided treatment, often prescribing medication that made a difference in patients' lives. She also helped them to make healthier choices and have a better quality of life. I wanted to do the same, so I went back to graduate school to become an FNP. I earned my master's degree in nursing (MSN) at the College of St. Scholastica in Duluth, Minnesota, while continuing to work as a nurse.

Currently, I teach FNP students at the University of Mary in courses ranging from physical assessment to acute and emergent care. In addition, I continue to practice part-time at several nurse practitioner-run urgent care clinics. In addition, I am fortunate to be part of medical mission and service learning trips to Ayaviri, Peru, through the university, which established a partnership with the local medical community. We take week-long service learning trips to provide care and model continuity of care so people will keep coming back.

2. What are the most important skills and/or qualities for someone in your profession?

Nursing has been the number one trusted profession for many years, according to Gallup polls. Trust is established because nurses, including FNPs, display skills and qualities including empathy, commitment, and determination. Obtaining nursing experience before becoming an FNP is highly recommended because it provides a foundation of knowledge, cultivates patient interaction skills, and develops critical thinking. FNPs are often at the center of a patient's care and require collaboration skills. It is essential to be an advocate to ensure that patients receive the best care possible.

3. What do you wish you had known going into this profession?

Being an FNP is a great career, but you will face many demands. The hours can be long, and a patient's care and treatment have become more complex because we're living longer than previous generations and are therefore faced with increasing disease. FNPs are often expected to be ready to go on their first day. I recall many days struggling to complete all of my required tasks: seeing patients, charting, answering questions, making referrals, and contacting patients with results. It was challenging to find time to eat or even take a bathroom break. To overcome these difficulties, identify a mentor of whom you can ask questions, and get help identifying priorities for each day and improving time management. You will often be challenged to do more with less with increased pressure to see more patients as health care costs continue to rise.

4. Are there many job opportunities in your profession? In what specific areas?

The job market is bright for FNPs in general as the population continues to age and the shortage of primary care professionals increases. There are nearly 250,000 NPs in the United States, almost double the number practicing in 2008. In particular, jobs are more plentiful in rural areas compared to urban because people tend to want to live in larger cities. As a consequence, some larger cities are starting to become saturated, so FNPs—particularly new graduates—are having a harder time finding a job in these areas.

5. How do you see your profession changing in the next five years, how will technology impact that change, and what skills will be required?

NPs, including FNPs, are fighting to practice at the full scope of their education and training. When I first met the FNP at the free clinic, I was in awe of her confidence and abilities, but later learned she needed a physician to sign off on her charts and treatment plans.

NPs have reduced or restricted practice in more than half of the states in the United States. I respect and value physicians as important members of the health care team, but with the provider shortage, NPs need to practice at the highest levels of their education and training to help combat this issue. I do hope these barriers will continue to fall over the next five years.

I see patients, especially younger ones, who have grown up with the Internet and cell phones, want quick and easy access to care through technology. Many FNPs are part of practices that incorporate technology such as patients being able to report symptoms, chat with an FNP, and receive a prescription if needed without having to leave home. I believe this is the future of health care, and FNPs need to continue to adapt to these changes.

6. What do you enjoy most about your job? What do you enjoy least about your job?

I greatly enjoy the difference I make in my students' and patients' lives. Seeing patients get better from an acute illness or make better choices to become healthier is very rewarding. The best part of teaching is when students become colleagues.

A well-known adage in health care is, "If it wasn't documented it wasn't done." Therefore, I dislike all of the required documentation, as it takes away time from interacting with patients.

7. Can you suggest a valuable "try this" for students considering a career in your profession?

Shadow or interview an FNP to get an idea of what the day-to-day job may involve. Also, training to become a nursing assistant, paramedic, or EMT will give you firsthand experience and skills that are valuable if you choose to pursue more education. Be realistic regarding your reactions and tolerance toward handling things like bodily fluids or blood, because that is an integral part of an FNP's job.

GERIATRICS AND GERONTOLOGY

The Study of Aging

The field of geriatrics deals with the care of the elderly. The U.S. government's definition of elderly includes persons sixty-five years of age or older. Geriatricians are physicians with specialized training in geriatric medicine who restrict their practices to caring for persons seventy-five years of age or older. These patients are most likely to suffer from specific geriatric syndromes, including dementia, delirium, urinary incontinence, malnutrition, osteoporosis, falls and immobility, decubitus ulcers, polypharmacy, and sleep disorders.

The majority of older persons in the United States live in family settings with their spouses or children. Approximately 30 percent of older persons live alone, the majority of them being women. According to the U.S. Census Bureau, in 2000 the proportion of older persons (those over sixty-five) who lived in nursing homes was about 4.5 percent. Those aged eighty-five and over had a higher proportion, at 18.2 percent, thus indicating that the number of elderly people residing in nursing homes increases strikingly with age. However, the overall percentage of the elderly living in nursing homes is declining. While one may attribute this change to improvements in health care, it may also be attributable to the use of home health aides who provide assisted living services to seniors.

The focus of geriatric medicine is on improving functional disability and treating chronic disease conditions that impair a person's ability to perform such activities of daily living as bathing and dressing, maintaining urinary and bowel continence, and eating. A more objective measure of an older person's ability to live independently is the instrumental activities of daily living scale. This scale measures an individual's ability to use the telephone, obtain transportation, go shopping, prepare meals, do housework and laundry, self-administer medicines, and manage money.

The maximum life span of an organism is the theoretical longest duration of that organism's life, excluding premature, unnatural death. The maximum life span of humans is unknown, although most experts believe it to be approximately 120 years. Most people will die of disease or accident, however, before they reach this biological limit. Attempts to understand why this occurs have led to the development of several theories of aging. The aging process is controlled, in large part, by genetic mechanisms. Aging is a biologic process characterized by a progressive development and maturation leading to senescence and death. There are profound changes in cells, tissues, and organs as well as in physiological, cognitive, and psychological processes. Aging is not the acquisition of disease, although aging and disease can be related. In the absence of disease, normal aging is a slow process. It involves the steady decline of organ reserves and homeostatic control mechanisms, which is often not apparent unless there is maximal exertion or stress on an individual system or on the total organism.

Numerous changes in the body occur as people age. For example, one can expect to lose two inches in height from age forty to age eighty. This shrinkage results from a decrease in vertebral bone mass and in the thickness of intervertebral disks, as well as from postural alterations with increased flexion or bending at the hips and knees. Total body fat increases as one ages, accompanied by decreases in muscle mass and total body water. Such changes in body composition have important implications for drug treatments and nutritional plans. For example, fat-soluble medications exhibit a longer duration of action in the elderly. Older persons also experience a thinning of the dermal layer of the skin, with thinner blood vessels, decreased collagen, and less skin elasticity. Sun damage can accelerate these changes. Graying of the hair reflects a progressive loss of functional melanocytes from the hair bulbs. The number of hair follicles of the scalp decreases, as does the growth rate of remaining follicles. The brain also alters with age: The weight of the brain declines, blood flow to the brain decreases, and there is a loss of neurons in specific areas of the brain. These changes in brain structure are highly variable and do not necessarily affect thinking and behavior.

Many changes occur in the vision of the older person. Loss of elasticity in the lens leads to presbyopia, the most common visual problem associated with aging. Presbyopia is a condition in which the distance that is needed to focus on near objects increases. Cataracts increase in prevalence with age, although unprotected exposure of the eyes to ultraviolet rays has been implicated in the pathogenesis as well. Glaucoma also occurs more often in the elderly.

Older persons often experience hearing loss from degenerative processes, including atrophy of the external auditory canal and thickening of the tympanic membrane. The result is presbycusis, a bilateral hearing loss for pure tones. Higher frequencies are more affected than lower ones, and the condition is more severe in men than in women. Pitch discrimination also declines with age, which may account for an increased difficulty in speech discrimination.

The heart alters with age, although the significance of these changes is unclear in the absence of disease. There are declines in intrinsic contractile function and electrical activity. The resting heart rate and cardiac output do not change, but the maximum heart rate decreases in a linear fashion and may be estimated by subtracting a person's age from 220. There are also modest increases in systolic blood pressure.

Minor changes occur in the gastrointestinal system. The liver and pancreas maintain adequate function throughout life, although the metabolism of specific drugs is prolonged in older people. Kidney function declines with age, with a 30 percent loss in renal mass and a decrease in renal blood flow. A linear decline in the ability of the kidneys to filter blood after the age of forty can lead to a decrease in the clearance of some drugs from the body.

In the endocrine system, the blood glucose level before meals changes minimally after the age of forty, although the level of blood glucose after meals increases. These changes may be related to decreases in muscle mass and a decreased insulin secretion rate. Glucose intolerance with aging must be distinguished from the hyperglycemia that can accompany diabetes mellitus; the latter requires treatment. No clinically significant alterations in the levels of the thyroid hormone occur, although the end organ response to thyroid hormones may be decreased. The hypothalamic-pituitary-adrenal axis remains intact. Plasma basal and stimulated norepinephrine levels are higher in healthy elderly individuals than in the young. The secretion of hormones such as androgens and estrogens falls sharply as a result of the loss of endocrine cells.

Diseases Affecting the Elderly

One of the chronic diseases frequently seen in elderly people is osteoporosis. Osteoporosis is defined as a decreased amount of bone per unit of volume; mineralization of the bone remains normal. Many studies have shown that bone mass decreases with age. Vertebral fractures resulting from osteoporosis cause deformity of the spine, loss in height, and pain. The absolute number of vertebral fractures that occur in older persons has been difficult to estimate, as some of these fractures go undiagnosed. The approximately 300,000 hip fractures that the elderly in the United States suffer annually have much more serious consequences. The lifetime risk of hip fracture by the age of eighty is approximately 15 percent for white women and 7 percent for white men. The risk of hip fracture by this age is significantly less in African Americans, with a 6 percent risk for women and a 3 percent risk for men.

One approach to preventing osteoporosis is to maximize the amount of bone that is formed during adolescence. Under normal circumstances, people begin to experience a net bone loss after the age of thirty-five. In women, the onset of menopause accelerates bone loss because of the decline in estrogen levels. Relative calcium deficiency has also been implicated in age-related osteoporosis. By definition, age-related osteoporosis is a diagnosis of exclusion. An older patient who has suffered a fracture first should be evaluated for other causes of osteoporosis, including hyperparathyroidism, hyperthyroidism, diabetes, glucocorticoid excess, or, in men, hypogonadism. Other secondary causes of osteoporosis include malignancy, such as multiple myeloma, leukemia, or lymphoma, and the drug-related effects of alcohol or steroids. Any identifiable causes should be corrected.

People at increased risk for age-related osteoporosis include those with a family history of the disease; light hair, skin, and eyes; and a small body frame. Bone densitometry or quantitative computed tomography (CT) scanning can be performed to provide the most accurate estimates of the risk of an initial fracture. There are a number of prevention and treatment strategies for patients. One should ensure an adequate calcium intake; the current recommendation is a daily intake of 1,200 milligrams of calcium for postmenopausal women. Weight-bearing exercise should be performed throughout the life span. After menopause when estrogen levels decrease, the bone breakdown process accelerates. In postmenopausal women, two types of treatment options are available, estrogen treatment and bisphosphonates. Bisphosphonates are the most common medications prescribed. Bisphosphonates slow the bone breakdown process. While estrogen has not been shown conclusively to increase bone density, it does prevent further bone loss. However, estrogen replacement therapy may increase the risk of heart attacks and some types of cancer. In patients who cannot take estrogen, an alternative treatment is the hormone calcitonin. Calcitonin works by inhibiting osteoclast function, thereby halting the otherwise normal breakdown of bone.

A disorder that is commonly seen in elderly men is benign prostatic hyperplasia (BPH), or prostate enlargement. The incidence of this disease increases in a progressive fashion, with approximately 90 percent of men aged eighty affected by this condition. The pathogenesis of BPH is hormonal, caused by increased levels of dihydrotestosterone formed from the testosterone within the gland itself. The usual symptoms are those of urinary obstruction, which include hesitancy, straining, and decreased force and dimension of the urinary stream. Screening for benign prostatic hypertrophy includes two parts. The first is a blood test for prostate-specific antigens. The second is a digital rectal exam to inspect the prostate gland. Patients with positive findings will require further evaluation. A significant increase in prostatic tissue may need to be removed surgically. In patients with minimal disease, drug treatment may be used. Finesteride is an inhibitor of the enzyme 5-alpha reductase that is responsible for the conversion of testosterone to dihydrotestosterone. It slows the rate of increase in prostate tissue mass.

Depression is a common problem in both men and women as they get older. The elderly can experience transient mood changes that are the result of an identifiable stress or loss. In older persons, however, depression may be related to some medical condition, particularly dementia, which is associated with multiple strokes or Parkinson's disease. Major depression is more common in hospital and long-term care settings, where the prevalence is about 13 percent. The symptoms of depression include significant weight change, insomnia or hypersomnia, psychomotor agitation or retardation, decreased energy and easy fatigability, feelings of worthlessness or excessive guilt, decreased ability to think or concentrate, and recurrent thoughts of death or suicide. The diagnosis of major depression can be made if at least five of these symptoms are present for at least two weeks. Depressive symptoms must be taken seriously in the elderly. The rate of suicide in older persons is higher than for other groups, with older white males having the highest rates of any age, racial, or ethnic group.

Another depressive disorder experienced by the elderly is dysthymia. Dysthymic disorders are characterized by less severe symptoms than those associated with major depression and by a duration of at least two years. The symptoms generally include at least two of the following: poor appetite or overeating, insomnia or hypersomnia, low energy and fatigue, low self-esteem, poor concentration or difficulty in making decisions, and feelings of hopelessness. Dysthymia may be primary or secondary to a preexisting chronic psychiatric or medical illness, with accompanying loss of function and debilitation.

Adjustment disorders with depressed mood are also seen in older persons. Such disorders occur within three months of a stressful situation and last up to six months. The prototypical situation is the depressive reaction that follows an acute medical illness. In the elderly, the four most common stressors are physical illness, reactions to the death of family and friends, retirement, and moving to an institutional setting. In dealing with depressive symptoms, however, it is important to consider other diagnoses, such as underlying medical illnesses, drug reactions to prescribed or over-the-counter medicines, hypochondriasis, alcohol abuse, and dementias. In older patients, the disorder most often associated with depression is dementia.

Incontinence affects a vast number of elders yet is often unaddressed during a clinic visit because of either lack of the patient's knowledge about potential treatments or embarrassment regarding the issue. Incontinence has a major impact on an elder's quality of life, and, as it is often a treatable condition, it should be discussed by patients with their physicians.

Another topic frequently not discussed involves the issue of remaining sexually active as an elder. Over half of married elders continue to have sex, although sometimes this activity is complicated by fears such as having a heart attack or stroke as a result of the exertion. In addition, medical problems and medication side effects can affect the elder's sexual abilities. Some potential treatments for sexual dysfunction include phosphodiesterase inhibitors and, in the case of low testosterone or low estrogen, hormone therapies, which can aid in increasing the sexual satisfaction of elders.

A thorough diagnostic evaluation can help in the diagnosis of a depressive disorder and can rule out other complicating problems. A careful history is elicited from the patient and from a family member or caretaker. A formal mental status examination is conducted to uncover abnormalities in concentration, speech, psychomotor skills, cognitive ability, and memory. Laboratory blood tests often include a complete blood count, chemical analysis, and thyroid function tests. Abbreviated neuropsychological tests can differentiate between patients with dementia and those with depression alone. The treatment of depression includes psychotherapy and pharmacotherapy. Behavioral interventions, such as special weekly activities and assignments, can be helpful. Most often, some kind of antidepressant medication is effective.

Fast Fact

Eighty percent of the population aged 65 and over has a chronic illness, a population whose numbers will reach 72.1 million by 2030. That's almost twice their number in 2008.
Source: www.vanderbilt.edu

Perspective and Prospects

In the United States, there has been increasing interest in the fields of geriatrics and gerontology because of the country's changing demographics. In 2000, 35 million Americans were sixty-five years of age or older. Because of the very large numbers in the baby-boom age group-that is, people born between 1946 and 1964-it was expected that the number of elderly people would increase dramatically by the year 2030 to 71.5 million, more than doubling the amount of elderly people in 2000. By 2050, it is expected that this number will reach 86.7 million. Those individuals aged sixty-five and over made up approximately 12.5 percent of the U.S. population in 2000. In 2030, this percentage could increase to 19.5 percent.

Another reason for the increase in the size of the older population in the United States is an increase in life expectancy. Life expectancy is defined as the average number of years a person is expected to live, given population mortality rates. It can be calculated for any age category but is usually given as life expectancy from birth. The life expectancy in the United States is much higher than in undeveloped countries and in most other developed countries as well. This figure rose steadily throughout the twentieth century. A child born in 2000 could expect to live seventy-five years, while someone born in 1900 could expect to live only fifty years. Most of this increase in life expectancy is attributable to a decreased death rate for infants and children resulting from improvements in sanitation, active immunization against childhood diseases, and advances in medical treatments. For persons aged sixty-five, there was an increase in life expectancy over that same time period of only five years, probably the result of improved medical therapies. While the geriatric population is dramatically increasing, the availability of geriatricians is not. As the population continues to grow, the shortage will increase.

Making healthy lifestyle modifications, receiving appropriate medical screening exams, and partaking in numerous prevention strategies may improve the quality of life of the elderly. These actions may also lead to preventing serious accidents and disabling conditions. Lifestyle modifications that should be attempted include alcohol and smoking cessation, as well as diet and exercise programs. With the increasing awareness of obesity as a major problem in society, it is important to keep the geriatric population at a healthy weight that will not lead to adverse health effects.

With the decline in vision and hearing that may be experienced by the older population, audio/visual screening should be performed and proper corrective measures taken. This may help avoid accidents around the home and while driving. Vaccinations should be up to date to help prevent disease. Unless contraindicated, the elderly should consider obtaining the annual flu vaccine. The pneumococcal vaccine should also be considered. In addition, screening tests are available to assess some of the common conditions affecting the elderly. Those preventive services covered by Medicare as of 2006 include a "Welcome to Medicare Physical Exam" once during the first six months of enrollment, serum cholesterol levels every five years, annual mammograms in women aged forty and over, biannual Pap tests and pelvic exams, fecal occult blood tests starting at age fifty and then annually, a flexible sigmoidoscopy at age fifty and then every four years, a colonoscopy at age fifty and then every ten years, serum prostate specific antigen levels and digital rectal exams starting at age fifty and then annually, glaucoma screening if over fifty and then annually, and bone densitometry testing in women over fifty or at high risk and then biannually. Medicare will also cover the following vaccines: pneumococcal one time, hepatitis B vaccine series one time, and influenza vaccines annually.

Because elders may be taking multiple medications, it is important that they occasionally review these medications with their doctors. By doing so, side effects can be discussed and any drug interactions may be avoided. All dosages and correct use should be reviewed to make sure that the appropriate medications are taken daily and that accidental overdose may be avoided. Pillboxes are an excellent tool to make sure that medications are taken correctly. In addition, it is advisable that elders keep a list of all medications and allergies on their person should an emergency arise.

With the popularity of herbal supplements, it is essential that the elderly discuss their use with a physician. Some of these regimens may have adverse effects of which patients are unaware. In addition, herbal supplements may interact with some of the medications that their physicians have prescribed.

As Americans live longer, the length of time that older persons will rely on society for their care increases as well. This situation places a greater burden on those persons who are working, as they must support greater numbers of people receiving Social Security and Medicare benefits, and requires a rethinking of the age requirements to be eligible for these programs. In 1997, while older persons represented 13 percent of the population, they accounted for 38 percent of the total costs for health care. Other factors adding to the cost of health care include such new technologies as specialized imaging equipment, complex laboratory procedures, and new therapeutic drugs. The goal of much research in geriatric medicine is to prevent or slow down the effects of aging so that the elderly may live in good health. Further research to understand better the mechanisms involved in human aging will help to design preventive and treatment strategies.

RoseMarie Pasmantier, M.D.,
L. Fleming Fallon Jr., M.D., Ph.D., M.P.H.,
Christie Leal, D.O.

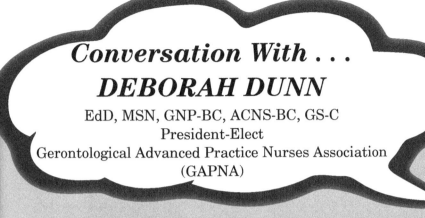

Conversation With . . .
DEBORAH DUNN
EdD, MSN, GNP-BC, ACNS-BC, GS-C
President-Elect
Gerontological Advanced Practice Nurses Association
(GAPNA)

Deborah Dunn has been a registered nurse (RN) for forty years; a nurse practitioner for twenty-three years; and in nursing education for twenty-nine years. She is the Dean at The Graduate School and Director of the Center for Research at Madonna University in Livonia, Michigan.

1. What was your individual career path in terms of education/training, entry-level job or other significant opportunity?

I was drawn to nursing by my interest in science and a desire to understand more about health and illness, as well as a deep desire to help others. I felt I should get as much education as I could in order to do my very best, so I pursued a bachelor's degree in nursing (BSN) at Eastern Michigan University. My BSN program provided both a great education and leadership opportunities because I was able to become involved in our National Student Nurses' Association (NSNA), organize activities, and attend the NSNA's state and regional meetings as our school representative.

After graduation, I was offered a job at the first hospital to which I applied, St. Mary Mercy Hospital in Livonia. New nurses were encouraged to work in medical-surgical nursing for the first years of their careers to obtain broad-based training and to have time to think about an area in which they might like to specialize. I initially worked the night shift on a surgical unit before moving a year later to the day shift for a med-surg unit with a rotating assignment to pediatrics.

I became increasingly interested in learning about cardiac care. The hospital offered continuing education for nurses, so I signed up and started working my way through each training class. I also transferred to a position in the critical care unit.

In intensive care, I worked mainly in the cardiac care unit, caring for patients who had heart attacks, heart failure, cardiac arrest, acute cardiac arrhythmia, and pacemaker insertions. I also rotated to the medical intensive care unit. While working in the ICU, I read in a nursing journal about a certification examination for critical care nurses. I sat for and passed the Critical Care Registered Nurse (CCRN) examination offered by the American Association of Critical Care Nurses (AACN), a proud achievement early in my career.

At that point, I felt I needed to earn an advanced degree. The clinical nurse specialist (CNS) role was emerging, which called for nurses with master's degrees to provide specialized clinical care to patients, provide continuing education to nurses, and the opportunity to work as nurse managers. I worked part-time while earning my MSN in this specialty at Wayne State University. I also was recommended for a job in the hospital's nursing education department, and I jumped at the opportunity. Later, I was promoted through the hospital's educational administration ranks.

Another transition occurred during this time: I became a mother. Following maternity leave, I returned to the hospital as a contingent critical care nurse and part-time nurse educator. My thesis advisor recommended me for an adjunct teaching position, so I began to teach at Wayne State University. One day at work at the hospital, a former nursing supervisor told me Madonna University's School of Nursing was looking for a full-time nursing instructor. After applying for the position, I was accepted, and for the past twenty-seven years have enjoyed a very proud and fulfilling career in nursing academia. I have taught undergraduate, master's, and doctoral students. I also have constructed numerous nursing programs including nurse practitioner programs, hospice, and palliative care programs, and contribute as a founding faculty of a doctor of nursing practice (DNP) program.

Near the start of my teaching career—because of the growing need for nurse practitioners—I earned a post-master's certificate as a gerontological nurse practitioner. I had developed a love of older adults while working in critical care. They always had a constellation of many illnesses that made their care complex, and you really had to learn to fine-tune how you treated them. When not in the hospital, they depended on their family and their environment.

Concurrent with my teaching career, I entered private practice with two physicians to take care of patients in assisted and independent living, and nursing homes.

I think sometimes when health care professionals don't have the training, experience, and thoughtfulness needed for geriatrics, they may think, "There's not much more I can do here for these people: they are old and sick." That is so far from the truth. It's all about the life in your years, and it's an incredible privilege to help these patients be better in the moment. They appreciate the respect. I had a 101-year-old patient I was friends with who recovered and moved to South Carolina to be closer to a great-granddaughter. I cried when she left. I also was involved in end-of-life care. It's so rewarding to work with people at these terrible times.

My career in education has expanded over the years. I earned a doctorate in education and moved through Madonna University's administrative ranks from the College of Nursing and Health to become dean of the university's Graduate School and Center for Research. I continued my private practice up until the past year, when my mother was dying and in hospice. I plan to go back to it as soon as I can.

2. What are the most important skills and/or qualities for someone in your profession?

You need to have a desire to help people, and enjoy interacting with all types of people. You should value advocating for others, because you will need to be a patient advocate. You should be able to suspend your own needs for those of others. You must value truth and honesty because you must perform your work with integrity, accuracy, and, at all times, honesty.

3. What do you wish you had known going into this profession?

Probably that you don't have to know it all. Nurses place a lot of pressure on themselves to have all the answers and feel guilty when they don't. Also, that being part of a highly functioning health care team is extremely rewarding. It provides the best patient care and the best environment for personal professional growth.

Also, being part of a professional organization can be career sustaining. Stay as involved as you can. Those professional connections can be supportive when on-the-job life becomes difficult. Getting involved with the Gerontological Advanced Practice Nurses Association (GAPNA) led to my involvement at the state and national levels.

4. Are there many job opportunities in your profession? In what specific areas?

Hospitals are creating acute care units, known as ACE units, for elders, and implementing a lot of interventions across medical-surgical, ambulatory, and pre- and post-operative units to provide additional safety. This presents a lot of opportunities for geriatric nurses. Senior emergency rooms employ nurses specially trained in elder care. Transition care nurses help with seniors discharged from the hospital and follow that patient home or into rehabilitation. There are dementia care clinics.

5. How do you see your profession changing in the next five years, how will technology impact that change, and what skills will be required?

Hospitalized patients have become more intensely ill. They are sicker and their length of stay in the hospital has become shorter. As a result, all nurses working in hospitals become intensive care specialists. We are going to need home care nurses who have critical care nursing skills because this level of care will be delivered in the home in the future. You need that trained nurse to come out and lay eyes on people because families don't know how to deliver that care and have no recourse but to take the person back to the ER.

6. What do you enjoy most about your job? What do you enjoy least about your job?

Nursing is the most amazing profession. It provides so many opportunities to positively affect people's lives and truly make a difference. I think that's the most wonderful part of being a nurse.

The time demands can be overwhelming. You can end up feeling too rushed because you have a heavy workload or that you don't have enough time to give to your patients and their families.

7. Can you suggest a valuable "try this" for students considering a career in your profession?

Find a program through your high school or community college that allows you to shadow several health care professionals to see what they do. Ask them about what they like best about their job and what they like least about it. Don't limit yourself to just one practice. Compare occupations: nurse, doctor, nurse practitioner, physician assistant, physical therapist, occupational therapist, social worker, radiology technician, laboratory technician.

Keep a journal of your observations and reflections on what you experienced. Research the occupations in which you are interested. Use this information to hone in on your area(s) of interest.

GYNECOLOGY AND OBSTETRICS

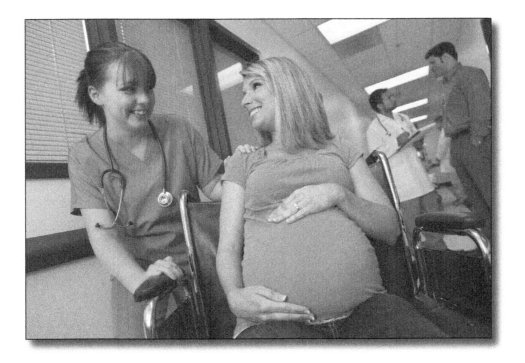

Gynecology

Gynecology is the branch of medical science that treats the functions and diseases unique to women, particularly in the nonpregnant state. A gynecologist is a licensed medical doctor who has obtained specialty training. Unlike many fields in medicine that are clearly defined by surgical or nonsurgical practice, gynecology involves both. In the early nineteenth century, gynecology was closely tied to general surgery. In fact, one of the first reported cases of abdominal surgery in which the patient survived and was cured of a condition occurred in 1809, with the successful removal of a massive ovarian tumor by Ephraim McDowell (without the benefit of anesthesia or antibiotics).

Gynecology is much more than just a surgical field. With the tremendous progress made in the basic sciences and medical sciences by the twenty-first century, gynecology now involves a broad spectrum of medical fields, including developmental and congenital disorders relating to puberty and adolescence, sexually transmitted infections (STIs) and other infectious diseases, contraception, menstrual disturbances, endocrinology, early pregnancy issues, infertility, preventive health, problems related to menopause, incontinence, and oncology, specifically dealing with cancers of the reproductive system (such as the ovaries, uterus, and breasts). Although much gynecologic care is provided by medical doctors, routine gynecologic care is also often provided by nurse practitioners (especially those with specialty certification in women's health) and certified nurse midwives.

Many of the medical problems dealt with in gynecology have far-reaching social, ethical, and legal consequences. Among the most controversial issues in medicine today involve abortion and STDs (such as human immunodeficiency virus, or HIV), both of which are conditions commonly managed by gynecologists. Another example of a common problem managed by gynecologists with important social implications is contraception. Female steroid hormones were among the first biological substances to be purified in the laboratory in the twentieth century. These hormones were then intentionally fed to animals for their contraceptive effect and eventually given to human beings as well in the form of the birth control pill. The birth control pill is an invention that has been widely credited with providing women with a relatively easy means to control their own fertility. Many social scholars would argue that women's ability to harness their own fertility was key in enabling women to delay childbearing, pursue education and careers, and take roles in society that were formerly occupied almost exclusively by men.

Diagnostic and Treatment Techniques

Many gynecologic visits are done for routine screening of healthy women. When a patient presents with a problem or complaint, a good history from the patient regarding the nature of the problem is crucial for diagnosis. The history is almost always followed by a physical examination. Probably the best known diagnostic technique in gynecology is the pelvic examination. Women should have routine screening examinations beginning at age twenty-one, or three years after onset of sexual activity, whichever age is first. The purpose of the examination is to confirm normal anatomy, rule out pathological conditions, and prevent the development of cancers through early screening tests such as the Pap test.

The pelvic examination is typically performed with the woman on her back, knees apart, with feet and legs supported by stirrups. Visual inspection of the external genitalia is performed; this involves inspecting the pubic region to ensure normal secondary sexual development as well as to look for abnormalities such as unusual lesions on the labia, which may indicate infections (by fungi, bacteria, viruses, or parasites), skin conditions (such as eczema), or cancer. The next portion is a bimanual examination. The examiner places one hand on the patient's abdomen and gently inserts two fingers of the other hand into the patient's vagina; gloves are worn at all times. The examiner proceeds to feel the uterus and ovaries by gently pushing them toward the anterior abdomen. The external hand on the abdomen serves as a counterforce to enable the examiner to feel the contours of the uterus and ovaries and hence to assess their size.

The last portion of the examination is a visual inspection of the interior of the vagina and the surface of the cervix. Because the vagina is normally closed, a device called a speculum is carefully placed in the vaginal canal. The speculum has two "blades"-each blade is analogous to a tongue depressor, which pushes the tongue out of the way to enable inspection of the throat. The blades are then slowly opened to part the vaginal tissues and enable visualization of the vaginal canal and cervix. The vaginal walls and cervix are inspected for abnormalities, and the consistency of vaginal fluid is noted. If any abnormalities are noted, cultures or biopsies may taken to facilitate diagnosis. When indicated, a Pap test is performed by swabbing the exterior of the cervix as well as the cervical canal. The cells that are obtained from the swab can then be sent to the pathology laboratory for analysis to screen for precancer or cancer of the cervix.

Although the bimanual examination is the mainstay of office practice, this examination is but a small fraction of diagnostic modalities commonly employed by gynecologists. A complete physical examination, including breast examination, is often performed for a comprehensive survey to aid in diagnosis. When abnormalities are suspected, imaging techniques and laboratory tests can be invaluable in diagnosis. For instance, when a pelvic mass is felt on bimanual examination, the gynecologist may order an ultrasound to better characterize the mass. Laboratory tests such as CA-125 levels may be indicated to help differentiate the pelvic mass from a benign growth versus a malignancy, such as of the ovary.

Other diagnostic tests commonly employed in gynecological office practices are blood and urine tests for pregnancy, blood or culture tests (for STIs such as HIV, syphilis, gonorrhea, chlamydia, and herpes), and biopsies of the external genitalia, which may assist in diagnosing skin conditions such as lichen sclerosis or precancers. If an endocrinologic abnormality is suspected, then blood tests to check the levels of various hormones (such as thyroid hormone, follicle-stimulating hormone, or prolactin) can help pinpoint the problem. In a patient with urinary incontinence, urodynamic testing, which records the pressures of the bladder and abdomen under different conditions, may help diagnose and characterize the type of incontinence.

A number of diagnostic tests commonly employed by gynecologists require going to an operating room, most often because of the need for patient sedation or anesthesia. One example is hysteroscopy, whereby a small camera mounted on a cannula is introduced through the cervix to visualize the cervical canal and uterine lining. Hysteroscopy can be useful in the diagnosis of polyps or fibroids (benign tumors of the uterus) which may be causing abnormal vaginal bleeding. Another example is diagnostic laparoscopy, whereby a small camera mounted on a cannula is introduced into the abdominal and pelvic cavity to inspect for abnormalities such as pelvic scarring, masses, or endometriosis, a condition in which cells resembling the uterine lining are found in the pelvic or abdominal cavities.

Gynecologic providers have a vast array of treatment options available to them. In the office setting, common treatment modalities include the use of antibiotics for uncomplicated cervical infections, such as chlamydia and gonorrhea, or for vaginal infections, such as trichomoniasis. Another problem commonly treated in the office setting is undesired fertility. A number of contraceptive modalities exist, including the prescription of birth control pills, the placement of an intrauterine device (IUD), or the injection of sustained-release hormones. In women experiencing menopausal symptoms such as hot flashes, hormonal pills or other medications may be prescribed. Women with chronic pelvic pain may be treated with medications such as antidepressants. Urinary incontinence may respond to bladder training, pessaries, or medications.

In the operating room, procedures may be carried out in a controlled setting to treat disease. A woman with abnormal vaginal bleeding caused by fibroids who no longer desires childbearing may receive a hysterectomy, with or without removal of the ovaries. If a woman is interested in retaining her uterus, the fibroids can be isolated and removed surgically through a common surgical procedure called a myomectomy. In women who desire permanent sterilization, a common surgical procedure performed by gynecologists is tubal ligation. Another common surgical procedure is the removal of pelvic masses such as ovarian cysts. Endometriosis or pelvic scars can be removed or destroyed through laparotomy (also known as abdominal surgery) or laparoscopy (minimally invasive abdominal surgery). When a Pap test or biopsy indicates noninvasive cancer of the cervix, treatment is possible through excision of the part of the cervix surrounding the cancer. In women with urinary incontinence not helped by medical management, surgery may be indicated to treat the problem. Women who are infertile as a result of blocked Fallopian tubes can be treated with in vitro fertilization. In this procedure, eggs are harvested from the woman in the operating room, and fertilization is performed in the laboratory. When the embryos are sufficiently developed, they are placed in the uterine cavity through an office procedure.

Perspective and Prospects

The formation of a medical field specific to women's diseases largely began in the nineteenth century. At the time, the treatment of women's diseases was inextricably linked with the role of women in society. In the nineteenth century, women were often viewed as frail and limited by their cyclical physiology and childbearing role. Consequently, they were excluded from the male-dominated spheres of politics, professional careers, and education. For instance, influential psychiatrist Henry Maudsley (1835-1918) wrote about the harm that higher education would cause to the physiologic development of postpubescent girls. Edward Clarke (1820-1877), a Harvard Medical School professor, wrote in 1873 that higher education might develop the intellect, but at the expense of the reproductive organs, leading to painful menstrual periods and abnormal uterine function.

The field has evolved dramatically since then, with much of the evolution tied to changes in the role of women in society as well as to technological and scientific advances. Today, one of the major forces changing gynecological practice (as well as many other fields of medicine) is the concept of evidence-based medicine. This movement is based on the idea that medical practice must be guided by scientific evidence as well as good intentions. Without objective evidence that a treatment is effective, even the best of intentions can result in patient harm. Although a physician may practice evidence-based medicine, this does not mean that clinical judgment and the tailoring of treatments to fit individual patients should be ignored. In fact, applying scientific evidence in an automatic way to all patients is not endorsed. Gynecologists today most often practice evidence-based medicine either by examining the available literature themselves, by using evidence-based medical summaries developed by others, or by using evidence-based protocols developed by others.

One example of evidence-based medicine guiding clinical practice involves Pap testing. Although the classical teaching had been that Pap tests were recommended on a yearly basis, this frequency was not based on any direct evidence that this protocol would lead to better outcomes than screening less frequently. Consequently, both the US Preventive Services Task Force and the American Cancer Society have suggested lengthening the period between successive Pap tests in women thirty years of age or older who have had negative results on three or more consecutive Pap tests. In fact, the Preventive Services Task Force recommends Pap tests be performed "at least every three years" rather than every year. The optimum use of limited resources is of concern to patients, physicians, health maintenance organizations (HMOs), and insurance companies alike; the careful application of evidence-based medicine to appropriate situations in medical practice can result in the best overall benefit for all parties involved.

Obstetrics

Obstetrics is the branch of medical science dealing with pregnancy and childbirth in women. Once conception has occurred and a woman is pregnant, major physiological changes occur within her body as well as within the body of the developing embryo or fetus. Obstetrics deals with these changes leading up to and including childbirth. As such, obstetrics is a critical branch of medicine, for it involves the complex physiological events by which every person comes into existence.

The professional obstetrician is a licensed medical doctor whose area of expertise is pregnancy and childbirth. Often, the obstetrician is also a specialist in the closely related science of gynecology, the study of diseases and conditions that specifically affect women, particularly nonpregnant women. The obstetrician is especially knowledgeable in female anatomy and physiology, including the major bodily changes that occur during and following pregnancies. Obstetricians also have a detailed understanding of the necessary diagnostic procedures for monitoring fetal and maternal health, and they are educated in the latest technologies for facilitating a successful pregnancy and childbirth with minimal complications. Obstetrical care is also provided by certified nurse midwives (CNMs) and by nurse practitioners, particularly those with certification in women's health (women's health care nurse practitioners).

Broadly, the diseases and conditions managed by the clinicians in this field include preconception counseling, normal prenatal care, and the management of pregnancy-specific problems such as preeclampsia, gestational diabetes, premature labor, premature rupture of membranes, multiple gestations, fetal growth problems, and isoimmunization. In addition, obstetricians manage medical problems that can occur in any woman but that take on special importance in pregnancy, such as thyroid disorders or infections. Obstetricians make assessments and decisions regarding when a baby is best delivered, particularly if there are in utero conditions that make it safer for the baby to be born immediately, even if prematurely. Obstetricians manage both normal and abnormal labors. They are able to assess the progress and position of the infant as it makes its way down the birth canal. They are knowledgeable about pain control options during labor and make decisions regarding when a cesarean section is indicated. Obstetricians assist with normal vaginal deliveries, either spontaneous or induced, and sometimes use special instruments such as forceps or vacuum-suction devices. They also perform cesarean sections. Obstetricians are trained in appropriate postpartum care for the mother and infant.

In natural, spontaneous fertilization, pregnancy begins with the fertilization of a woman's egg by a man's sperm following sexual intercourse, the chances of which are highest if intercourse takes place during a two-day period following ovulation. Ovulation is the release of an unfertilized egg from the woman's ovarian follicle, which occurs roughly halfway between successive periods during her menstrual cycle. Fertilization usually occurs in the upper one-third of one of the woman's fallopian tubes connecting the ovary to the uterus; upon entering the woman's vagina, sperm must travel through her cervix to the uterus and up the fallopian tubes, only one of which contains a released egg following ovulation.

Once fertilization has occurred, the first cell of the new individual, called a zygote, is slowly pushed by cilia down the fallopian tube and into the uterus. Along the way, the zygote undergoes several mitotic cellular divisions to begin the newly formed embryo, which at this point is a bundle of undifferentiated cells. Upon reaching the uterus, the embryo implants in the lining of the uterus. Hormonal changes occur in the woman's body to maintain the pregnancy. One of these hormones is human chorionic gonadotropin, which is the chemical detected by most pregnancy tests. Failure of the embryo to be implanted in the endometrium and subsequent lack of hormone production (specifically the hormone progesterone) will cause release of the endometrium as a bloody discharge; the woman will menstruate, and there will be no pregnancy. Therefore, menstrual cycles do not occur during a pregnancy.

The embryo will grow and develop over the next nine to ten months of gestation. The heart forms and begins beating at roughly five and one-half weeks following conception. Over the next several weeks and months, major organ systems begin to organize and develop. By the end of the first three months of the pregnancy, the developing human is considered to be a fetus. All the major organ systems have formed, although not all systems can function yet. The fetus is surrounded by a watery amniotic fluid within an amniotic sac. The fetus receives oxygen and nutrients from the mother and excretes waste products into the maternal circulation through the placenta. The fetus is connected to the placenta via the umbilical cord. During the second and third trimesters, full organ system development; massive cell divisions of certain tissues such as nervous, circulatory, and skeletal tissue; and preparation of the fetus for survival as an independent organism occur. The fetus cannot survive outside the mother's body, however, until the third trimester.

Changes also occur in the mother. Increased levels of the female steroid hormone estrogen create increased skin vascularization (that is, more blood vessels near the skin) and the deposition of fat throughout her body, especially in the breasts and the buttocks. The growing fetus and stretching uterus press on surrounding abdominal muscles, often creating abdominal and back discomfort. Reasonable exercise is important for the mother to stay healthy and to deliver the baby with relative ease. A balanced diet also is important for the nourishment of her body and that of the fetus.

Late in the pregnancy, the protein hormones prolactin and oxytocin will be produced by the woman's pituitary gland. Prolactin activates milk production in the breasts. Oxytocin causes muscular contractions, particularly in the breasts and in the uterus during labor. Near the time of birth, drastically elevated levels of the hormones estrogen and oxytocin will cause progressively stronger contractions (labor pains) until the baby is forced through the vagina and out of the woman's body to begin its independent physical existence. The placenta, or afterbirth, is discharged shortly thereafter.

Diagnostic and Treatment Techniques

The role of the obstetrician is to monitor the health of the mother and unborn fetus during the course of the pregnancy and to deliver the baby successfully at the time of birth. Once the fact of the pregnancy is established, the obstetrician is trained to identify specific developmental changes in the fetus over time in order to ensure that the pregnancy is proceeding smoothly.

The mainstay of diagnosis is the physical examination during prenatal visits. Early in the pregnancy, prenatal visits occur monthly, but they become more frequent as the pregnancy progresses. During these visits, the woman may receive counseling regarding a balanced diet, folic acid and iron supplementation, and substances or foods to avoid that may pose a risk to the pregnancy. The woman's growing uterus is measured to confirm proper growth, and, if indicated, a vaginal or cervical examination may be performed. After ten weeks of gestational age, fetal heart tones are also assessed at every prenatal visit using a simplified ultrasonic technique, to ensure that they are within the normal number of beats per minute. Fetal heart tones that are abnormally slow may indicate a fetus in jeopardy.

The other main component of diagnosis is through laboratory tests. Early in the pregnancy, the woman will receive a Pap test to screen for cervical cancer. Blood tests will be ordered to determine whether the mother is a carrier of the human immunodeficiency virus (HIV) or hepatitis B or C viruses, which can be transmitted to the fetus. In addition, the mother is checked for anemia, and the blood type of the mother is assessed. If the mother's blood type indicates that she is Rh negative, she will receive RhoGAM in the third trimester to prevent the development of a disease called isoimmunization, a condition that could be fatal to the fetus. An additional diagnostic test performed routinely during pregnancy is a screening test for diabetes, which pregnant women are at increased risk for.

Another important method of diagnosis in obstetrics is ultrasonography. Ultrasonography early in pregnancy can determine the gestational age of a pregnancy in cases in which a woman's last menstrual period is unverified. The correct development of the fetus and the presence of any birth defects can be assessed using this procedure. Ultrasound can also determine whether the placenta is growing in a safe location and whether the proper amount of amniotic fluid is found in the amniotic sac. Toward the end of pregnancy, ultrasound is an invaluable diagnostic tool for determining fetal well-being and the position of the infant in the uterus in preparation for delivery. Ultrasound is also a useful tool in guiding diagnostic procedures. For instance, amniocentesis can be extremely safe when performed under ultrasound guidance. Finally, one of the main methods of diagnosis in the third trimester is fetal heart monitoring. This technique involves following the heartbeat of the infant while in utero.

The heart rate of the infant is typically followed for twenty to thirty minutes. Any concerning dips in the heart rate may be indicative of a poor fetal state and a cause for increased monitoring or, in extreme cases, delivery of the infant.

Obstetricians have at their disposal a variety of treatment modalities. They are trained to turn manually fetuses that are in a breech (feet-first) position, a procedure called external cephalic version. In cases where the artificial induction of labor is desirable, the obstetrician may employ mechanical or hormonal means of cervical dilation, followed by infusions of a hormone called pitocin to stimulate contractions or the artificial rupture of the amniotic sac to promote natural contractions. When immediate delivery of the infant is needed and the chances of it emerging via the vaginal route are remote, then the obstetrician may perform a cesarean section. Common indications for cesarean section include fetal distress and lack of progress in labor.

Other treatments commonly used by obstetricians include the use of medications such as magnesium to relax the uterus in cases of premature labor and maternal steroid injections to induce fetal lung maturity when the fetus is premature but delivery is anticipated. When a woman experiences difficulty in the final stages of labor and the fetal head has descended almost to the vaginal opening, the obstetrician may employ forceps or vacuum devices to facilitate the delivery, particularly in cases of fetal distress. Obstetricians also treat the complications associated with childbirth, including postsurgical care after a cesarean section and repair of any lacerations of the vagina, cervix, or rectum after vaginal delivery.

Perspective and Prospects

Obstetrics is central to medicine because it deals with the very process by which all humans come to exist. The health of the fetus and its mother in pregnancy is of primary concern to these doctors. The field of obstetrics has blossomed as a sophisticated specialty, more likely to be practiced by obstetricians, certified nursemidwives, and specially trained and certified nurse practitioners, rather than the general practitioners who used to provide this care.

Advances in medical technology have enabled more precise analysis and monitoring of the fetus inside the mother's uterus, and obstetrics has therefore become a complex specialty in its own right. Technology such as ultrasonography and fetal heart rate monitoring, among other techniques, allows the obstetrician to collect a much larger supply of fetal data than was available to the general practitioner of the 1960s.

Increased data availability enables the obstetrician to monitor the pregnancy closely and to identify any problems earlier.

New advances in product development continue to improve the diagnostic ability of obstetricians. One example is the development of a test for fetal fibronection, which enables obstetricians to predict which patients are at low risk of premature delivery. This test involves a simple swab of the upper vagina. When negative, this test is highly reliable and allows the pregnant patient to leave the hospital and avoid prolonged and unnecessary hospitalization.

Advances in prenatal diagnosis and basic science have made it possible for parents to obtain information about their fetuses down to the molecular level. Through techniques such as amniocentesis and chorionic villus sampling (in which a small sample of placental cells is obtained early in pregnancy), genetic analysis has enabled the detection of chromosomal defects responsible for mental retardation and single-gene defects responsible for inherited diseases (such as cystic fibrosis). Amniocentesis has also made it possible to detect biochemical changes that may be indicative of major structural defects in the fetus, as well as to assess the developmental maturity of organs such as the lungs.

Advances in medical practice have dramatically decreased the morbidity and mortality of premature birth. For instance, with the introduction and widespread use of maternal steroid injections, the severity of serious diseases of prematurity, such as respiratory distress syndrome, has been dramatically reduced. The development of drugs against HIV has prevented the transmission of the virus from mother to infant in many cases.

The medical science of obstetrics continues to advance. There is ongoing research into the physiology and basic science of preeclampsia and eclampsia, common and potentially dangerous diseases peculiar to pregnancy. Fetal surgery programs at academic centers open the possibility that serious birth defects may be correctable while the fetus is in utero. Although many controversies currently exist in the field of obstetrics, an increased push toward medical practice grounded in scientific evidence promises many exciting advances in the future. It is hoped that many of these advances will result in improved outcomes and quality of life for patients.

Anne Lynn S. Chang, M.D.

Conversation With . . .
RACHEL FARRIS

MSN, RN
Director of Women and Newborn Care Center

Rachel Farris has been a nurse for fourteen years. She is Director of Women and Newborn Care Center, Baxter Regional Medical Center (BRMC) in Mountain Home, Arkansas.

1. What was your individual career path in terms of education/training, entry-level job, or other significant opportunity?

After graduating high school, I attended our local community college, Arkansas State University-Mountain Home, where I earned an associate degree in applied science in nursing. During a career fair in Hot Springs, I spoke with representatives from Baxter Regional Medical Center (BRMC), who recruited me to work as a nurse tech in the orthopedic unit while I finished my last year of nursing school. I really wanted to work in the obstetrical (OB) department, but they didn't have any positions available.

After working a few months on the orthopedic unit, I had the opportunity to work in OB one day when the staff was busy. The nurse manager asked if I would like to transfer to the department. My journey in the labor and delivery unit began that day.

After I graduated, I immediately started working on a temporary license until I passed my state boards and earned my registered nursing (RN) license. Working at a rural hospital, all nurses were cross-trained to perform in all areas in the Women & Newborn Care Center, which included antepartum, laboring, postpartum, newborns, and neonatal intensive care unit (NICU). I worked at bedside for seven years until I decided to go back and get my bachelor's degree in nursing (BSN) through an online program at Arkansas Tech University. Then the opportunity opened for my current role as the nurse director, which I have held for more than four years. After serving in this position for a year, I decided I needed to continue my education and go back to get my master's degree in nursing (MSN) so I could make sure I was educated on all aspects on nursing leadership. I earned my degree from Chamberlain University.

2. What are the most important skills and/or qualities for someone in your profession?

Caring, empathy, awareness, adaptability, communication, and decision-making are important, but probably the most important skill is critical thinking. The labor and delivery (L&D) nurse functions with a high level of autonomy, which is why critical thinking and decision-making skills are crucial. It is important to be able to adapt because situations can change. L&D units are similar to emergency rooms; you never know what will walk in, so you have to prepare for everything. You need to be able to communicate clearly with patients, families, and providers. Not all births end well, so having empathy for those who suffer the loss of their newborn is also crucial.

3. What do you wish you had known going into this profession?

I had no idea of the tragedy that can happen during childbirth. I never dreamt I would see so many mothers on drugs during their pregnancy, and witness the consequences of addiction. I wish I had been more mentally prepared for this.

I also never realized how much coaching and support was needed for not only the patient but for the patient's family. I never knew how much an L&D nurse meant to a mom who is in labor. You're forever ingrained into their memories and in photos of this special day. Being an L&D nurse is hard. And it really takes one to two years before you feel comfortable and confident with most situations.

4. Are there many job opportunities in your profession?

I never dreamed that when I started out as a nurse tech on the orthopedic unit, with a dream of working in OB, that one day I would be running the entire labor and delivery department. There are so many job opportunities as a nurse to grow in your career; that is one of the perks of being a nurse. One opportunity BRMC offers is a residency program for new RN graduates, which provides support and all the tools they need to be successful. If you are new to the nursing profession, I would highly recommend finding a facility that offers an RN residency program. Nursing is an excellent profession to grow your career due to ample opportunities.

5. How do you see your profession changing in the next five years, how will technology impact that change and what skills will be required?

In the next five years, I believe we will see many nurses with a higher degree than a BSN, and more nurses will gain certifications in their specialty areas. Technology will continue to impact L&D nurses with more wireless fetal heart monitoring. This will give the patients more control of their childbirth experience where they will be free to move around in various positions and provide different options for delivery.

6. What do you enjoy most about your job? What do you enjoy least about your job?

The most enjoyable part of being a labor and delivery nurse was when I saw the birth of babies I had been caring for all day—in utero—take their first breath when they enter the world and seeing the joy it brings to families.

The worst part of the job is those trying times when you have to care for a mother who has experienced a loss of a newborn. After working bedside for nine years as an

L&D nurse, this never got any easier. Every situation is very sensitive, and you just do your best to take care of your patient and her family. Now that my role has changed to director, I can enjoy taking care of my team and making sure they are equipped with all the tools and knowledge they need to care for our patients.

7. Can you suggest a valuable "try this" for students considering a career in our profession?

Get involved in your high school career academies if available, and look at the medical route. Students can also shadow at many places to see if this is an area of interest for them. In addition, they can get a certified nursing assistant (CNA) license prior to starting college and can work.

Perinatology

Perinatology is the branch of medicine dealing with the fetus and infant during the perinatal period (from the twenty-eighth week of gestation to the twenty-eighth day after birth).

Practitioners of perinatal medicine include physicians and advanced practice nurses with a specialty in perinatology (neonatal and pediatric nurse practitioners). They then complete additional training specifically related to the perinatal period (defined variously as beginning from twenty to twenty-eight weeks of gestation and ending one to four weeks after birth). The emphasis of perinatology is on a time period rather than on a specific organ system. The principal event of the perinatal period is birth. Prior to delivery, the perinatologist is concerned with the physiological status and well-being of both mother and fetus. Immediately after delivery, the perinatologist strives to maximize the newborn's chances for survival.

Diagnostic and Treatment Techniques

Prior to the birth, several diagnostic procedures are commonly employed by the perinatologist: ultrasonography, the measurement of fetal activity, and the evaluation of fetal lung maturity. Ultrasonography uses sound waves to create images. Sound waves are transmitted from a transducer that has been placed on the skin. Waves that are sent into the body reflect off internal tissues and structures, and the reflections are received by a microphone. Sound travels through tissues with different densities at different rates, which are characteristic for each tissue. Computers interpret the reflected sounds and convert them into an image that can be viewed. The images must be interpreted or read by someone with specialized training, usually a radiologist. Ultrasound does not involve radiation; thus it is not harmful to the fetus. Because sound waves are longer than radiation, the image generated is not as clear as that obtained with electromagnetic waves.

The measurement of fetal activity is important in evaluating fetal health. Fetal movement is normal; the earliest movement felt by the mother is called quickening. The diminution or cessation of fetal movement is indicative of fetal distress. Accordingly, movement is monitored by reports from the mother, palpation by the clinician, and ultrasound: Mothers report movements, individuals examining pregnant women can apply their hands to the abdomen and feel fetal movements, and ultrasonography can show breathing and other movements in real time using continuous video records of fetal movements.

Fetal lung maturity is assessed by measuring the relative amounts of lecithin and sphingomyelin in amniotic fluid. The concentration of lecithin increases late in fetal development, while sphingomyelin decreases. A lecithinsphingomyelin ratio that is greater than two indicates sufficient fetal lung maturity to ensure survival after birth.

Labor and delivery are the primary events of the perinatal period. Factors that can lead to difficulties include abnormalities of the placenta and prematurity. The placenta can be abnormally located (placenta previa) or can separate prematurely (placenta abruptio). Normally, the placenta is located on the lateral wall of the uterus. Placenta previa is defined as a placenta located in the lower portion of the uterus. The placenta is compressed by the fetus during passage through the birth canal. This compression compromises the blood supply to the fetus, which causes ischemia and can lead to brain or other tissue damage or to death. This condition is usually managed by a cesarean section. Placenta abruptio refers to a normal placenta that separates prior to fetal delivery. This condition is potentially life-threatening to both mother and fetus; immediate hospitalization is indicated.

Prematurity is defined as delivery before the fetus is able to survive without unusual support. Premature infants are placed in incubators. A lack of body fat in the infant leads to difficulty in maintaining a normal body temperature; special heating is provided to offset the problem. Lung immaturity may require mechanical assistance from a respirator. An immature immune system makes premature infants especially susceptible to infections; strict isolation precautions and prophylactic antibiotic therapy address this problem.

Many factors contribute to increasing the risks normally associated with pregnancy and delivery: maternal size and age; drug, tobacco, or alcohol use; infection; medical conditions such as diabetes mellitus and hypertension; and multiple gestations. A woman with a small pelvic opening may be unable to deliver her child normally; the solution in this case is a cesarean section. The risk of genetic abnormalities increases with advancing maternal (and, to a lesser degree, paternal) age. Counseling prior to conception is indicated. Once an older woman becomes pregnant, amniotic fluid should be obtained to test for genetic abnormalities. The degree of surveillance is dependent on maternal age: The recommended frequency of medical checks increases for older women.

Alcohol intake during pregnancy can result in an infant who is both developmentally disabled and mentally retarded; smoking during pregnancy frequently leads to an infant with a low birth weight. Drug usage during pregnancy can lead to anatomic or mental impairment. Avoiding the use of all substances is the easiest way to eliminate problems completely; any drug should be used only under the guidance of a physician. Some viral infections such as German measles (rubella) early in pregnancy can cause birth defects. Immunization prior to conception will avoid these problems.

Diabetes mellitus can cause abnormally large intrauterine growth and babies (frequently more than 10 pounds and referred to as macrosomic) who are too large for normal delivery. Diabetes that commonly develops during pregnancy is called gestational diabetes. Medical monitoring to detect diabetes early is prudent. Appropriate medical management of preexisting diabetes minimizes problems associated with pregnancy. A macrosomic infant must be delivered with a cesarean section. Hypertension can also develop during pregnancy. Like diabetes, it can compromise both mother and fetus. Appropriate and aggressive medical management, sometimes including complete bed rest, is needed to control high blood pressure during pregnancy. Multiple gestations (such as twins or triplets) strain the supply of maternal nutrients to the developing fetuses. Because space is limited, multiple fetuses are usually smaller than normal at birth.

Rhesus disease, also known as Rh incompatibility, can complicate pregnancy. It can occur only in the child of a father whose blood type is Rh-positive and a mother whose blood type is Rh-negative, and it affects the blood supply of a fetus. The treatment includes the identification of both maternal and paternal blood types and the administration of Rho(D) immune globulin to the mother at twenty-six weeks of gestation and again immediately after birth. An affected infant may require blood transfusions; in a severe case, transfusions may be needed during pregnancy.

Perspective and Prospects

Management of a pregnancy requires specialized skills. As the number of risk factors related to either mother or fetus increases, the problems associated with pregnancy also increase. The care of a pregnant woman and her fetus requires input from many individuals with specialized training. Consequently, perinatology is very much a team effort. Together, the team members can ensure a safe journey through the perinatal period for a pregnant woman and a healthy transition to life outside the womb for a newborn infant.

Fast Fact

Women have had help delivering babies for a long, long time: midwives were regulated under Moses. By the Middle Ages, surgeons argued that their techniques were better, and pushed to outlaw midwives. The first recorded caesarean section was performed in 1738 by Irish midwife Mary Donally.

Source: perigen.com

NEONATOLOGY

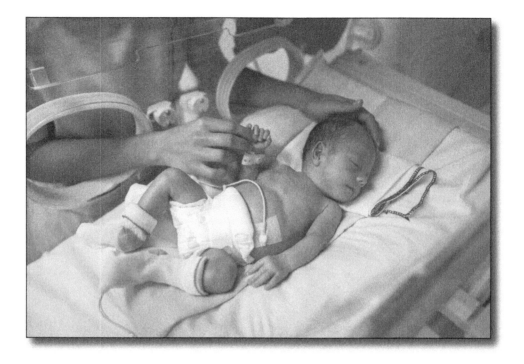

Science and Profession

Neonatology has grown dramatically since its beginnings in the late 1960s, and neonatologists have become an integral part of the obstetric-pediatric team at major medical centers throughout the world. In addition to being cared for by physicians who specialize in neonatology, some neonatal infants, in particular those who are critically ill or premature, are cared for by nurse practitioners with the specialty certification of neonatal nurse practitioner (NNP). In large part because of an ever-expanding technological base and marked advances in scientific research, these health care professionals have changed the outlook for premature and sick newborns.

As a subspecialty of pediatrics, neonatology is concerned with the most critical time of transition and adjustment-the first four weeks of life, or the neonatal period-whether the infant is healthy (a normal birth) or sick (as a result of genetic problems, obstetric complications, or medical illness). By the early 1970s, it became increasingly clear to health administrators that hospitals throughout the United States had varying abilities to care for medical and pediatric cases requiring the most sophisticated staff and equipment. Consequently, they developed a system that designated hospitals as either level I (small, community hospitals), level II (larger hospitals), or level III (major regional medical centers, also called tertiary care centers). It was in the last group that the most advanced neonatal care could be delivered. In these major centers, there are two types of nurseries, separating the normal healthy infant from the sick or high-risk infant: the routine nursery and the neonatal intensive care unit (NICU).

Routine nurseries are the temporary home of the vast majority of newborns. The services of the neonatologist are rarely needed here, and the general pediatrician or family practitioner observes and examines the infant for twenty-four to forty-eight hours to be sure that it has made a smooth transition from intrauterine to extrauterine life. These babies soon leave the hospital for their homes. Those neonates with minor problems arising from multiple births, difficult deliveries, mild prematurity, and minor illness are easily managed by a primary care physician in consultation with a neonatologist, perhaps at another hospital. It is in the neonatal intensive care unit, however, that the most difficult situations present themselves. Here several teams of pediatric subspecialists-surgeons, cardiologists, anesthesiologists, and highly trained nurses, along with many other health professionals-are led by a neonatologist, who coordinates the team's efforts. These newborns have life-threatening conditions, often as a result of extreme prematurity (more than six weeks earlier than the expected date of delivery), major birth defects (genetic or developmental), severe illness (such as overwhelming infections), or being born to drug- or alcohol-addicted mothers. They require the most advanced technological and medical interventions, often to sustain life artificially until the underlying problem is corrected. It is in this setting that the most dramatic successes of neonatology are found.

After hours of being inside a forcefully contracting uterus and sustaining the stress of passing through a narrow birth canal, the newborn emerges into a dry, cold, and hostile environment. The umbilical cord, which has provided oxygen and nutrients, is clamped and cut; the fluid-filled lungs must now exchange air instead, and the respiratory center of the infant's brain begins a lifetime of spontaneous breathing, usually heralded by crying. The vast majority of neonates make this extraordinary adjustment to extrauterine life without difficulty. At one minute and again at five minutes, the newborn is evaluated and scored on five physical signs: heart rate, breathing, muscle tone, reflexes, and skin tone. The healthy infant is vigorously moving, crying, and pink regardless of race. These Apgar scores, named for neonatology pioneer Virginia Apgar, evaluate the need for immediate resuscitation. A brief physical examination follows, which can identify other life-threatening abnormalities.

It is essential to remember that the medical history of a neonate is in fact the medical and obstetric history of its mother, and seemingly normal infants may develop problems shortly after birth. Risk factors include very young or middle-aged mothers; difficult deliveries; babies with Rh-negative blood types; mothers with diabetes mellitus, kidney disease, or heart disease; and concurrent infections in either the mother or the baby. Anticipating these problems of the healthy newborn by using the Apgar scores and the results of the physical examination allows the proper assignment of the infant to the nursery or NICU.

The NICU is a daunting place containing high-tech equipment, a tangle of wires and tubes, the sounds of beeps and alarms, and tiny, fragile infants. All this technology serves two simple purposes: to monitor vital functions and to sustain malfunctioning or nonfunctioning organ systems. Looked at individually, however, the machines and attachments become much more understandable. The incubator, perhaps the most common device, maintains a warm, moist environment of constant temperature at 37 degrees Celsius (98.6 degrees Fahrenheit). Small portholes with rubber gloves allow people to touch the child safely. Generally, the infants will have small electrodes taped on their chests, connected to video monitors that record the heart and breathing rates and that will sound alarms if significant deviations occur. These monitors will also record blood pressure through an arm or thigh cuff. To ensure immediate access to the blood, for delivering medications and taking blood for testing, catheters (plastic tubes) are placed into larger arteries or veins near the umbilicus, neck, or thigh (in adults, intravenous access is found in the arms).

The remaining equipment is used for the very serious business of life support, in particular the support of the respiratory system. Maintaining adequate oxygenation is critical and can be accomplished in several ways, depending on the baby's needs. The least stressful are tubes placed in the nostrils or a face mask, but these methods require that breathing be spontaneous although inadequate. More often, unfortunately, neonates with the types of problems that bring them to an intensive care unit cannot breathe on their own. In these cases, a tube must be connected from the artificial respirator into the windpipe (the endotracheal tube). Warm, moistened, oxygen-rich air is delivered under pressure and removed from the lungs rhythmically to simulate breathing. Tranquilizers and paralytic agents are used to calm and immobilize the infant. Sick or premature infants are also generally unable to feed or nurse naturally, by mouth. Again, several methods of feeding can be employed, depending on the problems and the length of time that such feedings will be needed. For the first few days, simple solutions of water, sugar, and protein can be given through the intravenous catheters. These lines, because of the very small, fragile blood vessels of the newborn, are seldom able to carry more complex solutions. A second method, known as gavage feeding, employs tubing that is inserted through the nose directly into the stomach. Through that tube, infant formula (water, sugar, protein, fat, vitamins, and minerals) and, if available, breast milk can be given.

As the underlying problems are resolved, the infant is slowly weaned, first feeding orally and then breathing naturally. Next, the infant will be placed in an open crib, and gradually the tangled web of tubes and wires will clear. With approval from the neonatologist, the baby is transferred to the routine nursery, a transitional home until discharge from the hospital is advisable.

Fast Fact

The smallest baby ever to survive and be discharged from a NICU was a twin girl born at 26 weeks and 9.2 ounces. Little Rumaisa Rahman was born in 2004.

Source: cbsnews.com

Diagnostic and Treatment Techniques

Neonatology has amassed an enormous body of knowledge about normal neonatal anatomy and physiology, disease processes, and, most important, how to manage the wide variety of complications that can occur. Specific treatment protocols have been developed that are practiced uniformly in all neonatal intensive care units. Short-term stays (twenty-four to forty-eight hours) are meant to observe and monitor the infant with respiratory distress at birth that required immediate intervention. Long-term stays, lasting from several weeks to months, are the case for the sickest newborns, most commonly those with severe prematurity and low birth weight (less than 1,500 grams), respiratory distress syndrome (also known as hyaline membrane disease), congenital defects, and drug or alcohol addictions.

Infants born prematurely make up the major proportion of all infants at high risk for disability and death, and each passing decade has seen younger and younger babies being kept alive. While many maternal factors can lead to preterm delivery, often no explanation can be found. The main problem of prematurity lies in the functional and structural immaturity of vital organs. Weak sucking, swallowing, and coughing reflexes lead to an inability to feed and to the danger of choking. Lungs that lack surfactant, a substance that coats the millions of tiny air sacs (alveoli) in each lung to keep them from collapsing and sticking together after air is exhaled, cause severe breathing difficulty as the infant struggles to reinflate the lungs. When premature delivery is inevitable but not immediate, lung maturity can be increased by administration of steroids to the mother. An immature immune system cannot protect the newborn from the many viruses, bacteria, and other microorganisms that exist. Inadequate metabolism causes low body temperature and inadequate use of food or medications. Neurological immaturity can lead to mental retardation, blindness, and deafness.

Aggressive management of the preterm baby begins in the delivery room, with close cooperation between the obstetrician and the neonatologist. Severely preterm infants, some born after only twenty weeks of pregnancy, require immediate respiratory and cardiac support. Placement of the endotracheal tube, assisted ventilation with a handheld bag, and delicate chest compressions similar to the cardiopulmonary resuscitation (CPR) performed on adults to stimulate the heartbeat are each accomplished quickly. Once the respiratory and circulatory systems have been stabilized, excess fluid will be suctioned, while a brief physical examination is performed to note any abnormalities that require immediate attention. As soon as transport is considered safe, the newborn is sent to the NICU. If the infant has been delivered at a small community hospital, this may involve ambulance or even helicopter transport to the nearest tertiary care center.

Once in the unit, the neonate will be placed in an incubator and attached to video monitors that record heart rate, breathing, and blood pressure. The endotracheal tube can now be attached to the respirator machine, and intravenous or intra-arterial catheters will be placed to allow the fluid and medication infusions and the blood drawing for the battery of tests that the neonatologist requires. Feeding methods can be set up as soon as the infant has stabilized. Within a short time after delivery, the premature newborn has had a flurry of activity about it and is surrounded by the most sophisticated equipment and staff available. Supporting the immature organs becomes the first priority, although the ethical issues of saving very sick infants must soon be addressed as complications begin to occur. Nearly 15 percent of surviving preterm infants whose birth weights were less than 2,000 grams have serious physical and mental disabilities after discharge. The majority, however, grow to lead normal, healthy lives.

Congenital defects are common, and it is estimated that the majority of miscarriages are a direct result of congenital defects that are incompatible with life. Many infants that do survive development and delivery die shortly after birth despite the most sophisticated and heroic attempts to intervene. The causes of such defects are arbitrarily assigned to two broad categories, although a combination of these factors is the most likely explanation: genetic errors (such as breaks, doubling, and mutations) and environmental insults (such as chemicals, drugs, viruses, radiation, and malnutrition). In the United States, among the most common birth defects that require immediate intervention are heart problems, spina bifida (an open spine), and tracheoesophageal fistulas and esophageal atresias (wrongly connected or incomplete wind and food pipes).

The birth of a malformed infant is rarely expected, and the neonatologist's team plays a key role in its survival. Congenital heart disease is the most prevalent life-threatening defect. During development in utero, the umbilical cord supplies the necessary oxygen; it is not until birth, when that lifeline is cut, that the neonate's circulatory and respiratory systems acquire full responsibility. At delivery, all may appear normal, and the one-minute Apgar score may be high. Several minutes later, however, the pink skin color may begin to darken to a purplish blue (cyanosis), indicating that insufficient oxygen is being extracted from the air. Immediately, the infant receives rescue breathing from the bag mask. Upon admission to the neonatal unit, the source of the cyanosis must be determined. A chest xray may provide significant information about the anatomy of the heart and lungs, but special tests are usually needed to pinpoint the problem. Catheters that are threaded from neck or leg vessels into the heart can reveal the pressure and oxygen content of each chamber in the heart and across its four valves. Echocardiograms, video pictures similar to sonograms generated by sound waves passing through the chest, enhance the data provided by the x-rays and catheterizations, and a diagnosis is made. Based on the physical signs and symptoms of the newborn, a treatment plan is devised.

Because of the nature of congenital defects and structural abnormalities, their correction generally requires surgery. Openings between the heart's chambers (septal defects), valves that are too narrow or do not close properly, and blood vessels that leave or enter the heart incorrectly are all common defects treated by the pediatric heart surgeon. Because of the delicacy of the operation and the vulnerability of the newborn, surgery may be postponed until the baby is larger and stronger while it is provided with supplemental oxygen and nutrients. The risk of such operations is high, and depending on the degree of abnormality, several operations may be required.

Another group of infants who have benefited from advances in neonatology are those born to drug-addicted women. The lives of these infants are often complicated by congenital defects and life-threatening withdrawal symptoms. For example, heroin-addicted babies are quite small, are extremely irritable and hyperactive, and develop tremors, vomiting, diarrhea, and seizures. The newborn must be carefully monitored in the unit, and sedatives and antiseizure medications are given, sometimes for as long as six weeks. Cocaine and its derivatives frequently cause premature labor, fetal death, and maternal hemorrhaging during delivery. Infants that do survive often have serious congenital defects and suffer withdrawal symptoms. The risk of acquired immunodeficiency syndrome (AIDS) adds another dimension to an already complicated picture.

Perspective and Prospects

Throughout human history, maternal and neonatal deaths have been staggering in number. Ignorance and unsanitary conditions frequently resulted in uterine hemorrhaging and overwhelming infection, killing both mother and baby. Highly inaccurate records at the beginning of the twentieth century in New York City show maternal death averaging 2 percent; in fact, the rate was probably greater, since most births occurred at home. Neonatal deaths from respiratory failure, congenital defects, prematurity, and infection loom large in these medical records. The expansion of medical, obstetric, and pediatric knowledge and technology that began after World War II has dramatically lowered maternal and infant mortality. It should not be forgotten, however, that nonindustrialized nations, the majority in the world, remain devastated by the neonatal problems that have plagued civilization for thousands of years.

Ironically, the problems associated with neonatology in Western nations are now at the other end of the spectrum: saving and prolonging life beyond what is natural or "reasonable." As neonatology advanced scientifically and technically, saving life took precedence over ethical issues. The famous and poignant story of Baby Doe in the early 1980s illustrates the dilemmas that occur daily in neonatal intensive care units. Baby Doe was a six-pound, full-term male born with Down syndrome and severe congenital defects of the heart, trachea, and esophagus. These malformations were deemed surgically correctable, although the underlying problem of Down syndrome, a disease characterized by intellectual disabilities and particular facial and body features, would remain. The parents did not agree to any operations and requested that all treatment be withheld. Baby Doe was given only medication for sedation and died within a few days. The case was later related by the attending physician in a letter to *The New England Journal of Medicine*, sparking enormous controversy. On July 5, 1983, a law was passed in effect stating that all newborns with disabilities, no matter how seriously afflicted, should receive all possible life-sustaining treatment, unless it is unequivocally clear that imminent death is inevitable or that the risks of treatment cannot be justified by its benefit. The legislators believed that Baby Doe had been allowed to die because of his underlying condition of Down syndrome.

Since then, attorneys, ethicists, juries, and courts have used the example of Baby Doe, and the law that grew from it, to interpret many cases that have come to light. Life-and-death decisions are made on a daily basis in the neonatal care unit. They are always difficult, but they usually remain a private matter between the parents and the neonatologist. These cases become public matters, however, when the family disagrees with the medical staff. Then the question of what is in the best interest of the child is compounded by who will pay for the treatments and who will care for the baby after it is discharged.

Such ethical dilemmas will continue as expertise and technology grow. A multitude of questions, previously relegated to philosophy and religion, will arise, and the benefits of saving a life will have to be weighed against its quality and the resources necessary to maintain it.

Connie Rizzo, M.D., Ph.D.,
Alexander Sandra, M.D.

Conversation With . . .
ELISSA RODRIGUEZ
RN
Neonatal Intensive Care Nurse

Elissa Rodriguez has been a neonatal intensive care nurse for twelve years. She currently works at Providence Saint Joseph Medical Center in Burbank, California, and the University of California, San Francisco.

1. What was your individual career path in terms of education/training, entry-level job, or other significant opportunity?

I participated in the Allied Health Science courses in high school in North Carolina, which gave me the opportunity to learn in depth about the health care field.

After high school, I attended North Carolina Agricultural & Technical State University, where I obtained a bachelor's degree in nursing (BSN). The first two years of undergraduate work were basic courses along with prerequisite classes for nursing. In my sophomore year, I applied to and was accepted by the university's College of Nursing for my final years of study.

At the College of Nursing, my courses focused on nursing with patient care clinicals. I took courses such as community health nursing, pediatric nursing, and medical-surgical nursing. After graduation, I passed the National Council Licensure Examination for Registered Nurses (NCLEX-RN). I had taken a prep class for the exam—a vital step in order to pass. Once I was an RN, I applied for jobs in the maternal child health field, which is labor and delivery, postpartum, and neonatal intensive care unit (NICU). I was offered a position as a new graduate staff nurse in the NICU. Once hired, I was required to complete an extensive sixteen-week orientation on the care of neonates. I cared for infants with a range of needs and conditions such as having been born after only twenty-three weeks' gestation, extremely low birthweight, congenital anomalies, and traumatic births.

2. What are the most important skills and/or qualities for someone in your profession?

People and customer service skills are the most important, along with compassion. It is also necessary for nurses to stay up-to-date on new, evidence-based practices within their specialty.

3. What do you wish you had known going into this profession?

I wish someone had told me the level of commitment and focus nursing school takes. You have to approach it like a job and spend the hours studying and preparing, or you will not succeed.

4. Are there many job opportunities in your profession? In what specific areas?

The field is always in need of nurses. A nurse can do many things within this profession. There is so much versatility and opportunity for growth. You can grow as a bedside nurse by learning more advanced procedures that qualified nurses perform. You can further your education and become a nurse practitioner in a specialty area. You can also leave the bedside and direct patient care and go into administration. You can prepare future nurses by becoming a nursing instructor.

5. How do you see your profession changing in the next five years, how will technology impact that change, and what skills will be required?

Nursing is changing and will require further education. Nurses will need to have a comfort level with computer charting and the use of machines that are used to simplify patient care in addition to helping diagnose illnesses.

6. What do you enjoy most about your job? What do you enjoy least about your job?

I enjoy the self-satisfaction that helping someone brings. When you get a genuine "thank you" from a patient's loved one or see a patient growing stronger, you have a sense of worth and accomplishment.

What I enjoy least about the job is that the long hours can be hard.

7. Can you suggest a valuable "try this" for students considering a career in your profession?

I recommend developing some customer service skills by having some type of job like a waiter. Also, read, read, read! Stay current with health issues.

NEPHROLOGY

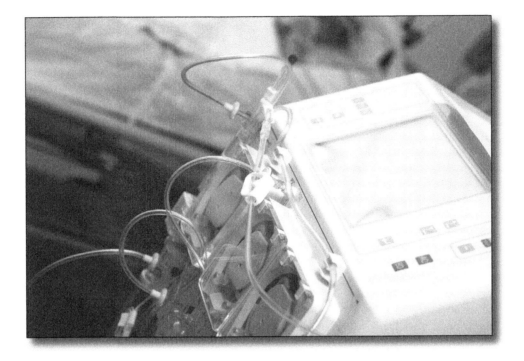

Science and Profession

Nephrology is the branch of medicine that deals with the function of the kidneys. As a consequence, a nephrologist frequently deals with problems related to homeostasis, that is, the maintenance of the internal environment of the body. The most obvious function of the kidneys is their ability to regulate the excretion of water and minerals from the body, at the same time serving to eliminate nitrogenous wastes in the form of urea. While such waste material, produced as by-products of cell metabolism, is removed from the circulation, essential nutrients from body fluids are retained within the renal apparatus. These nutrients include proteins, carbohydrates, and electrolytes, some of which help maintain the proper acid-base balance within the blood. In addition, cells in the kidneys regulate red blood cell production through the release of the hormone erythropoietin.

The human excretory system includes two kidneys, which lie in the rear of the abdominal cavity on opposite sides of the spinal column. Urine is produced by the kidneys through a filtration network composed of 2 million nephrons, the actual functional units within each kidney. Two ureters, one for each kidney, serve to remove the collected urine and transport this liquid to the urinary bladder. The urethra drains urine from the bladder, voiding the liquid from the body.

Each adult human kidney is approximately 11 centimeters in length, with a shape resembling a bean. When the kidney is sectioned, three anatomical regions are visible: a light-colored outer cortex; a darker inner region, called the medulla; and the renal pelvis, the lowest portion of the kidney. The cortex consists primarily of a network of nephrons and associated blood capillaries. Tubules extending from each nephron pass into the medulla. The medulla, in turn, is visibly divided into about a dozen conical masses, or pyramids, with the base of the pyramid at the junction between the cortex and medulla and the apex of the pyramid extending into the renal pelvis. The loops (such as the loop of Henle) and tubules within the medulla carry out the reabsorption of nutrients and fluids that have passed through the capsular network of the nephron. The tubules extend through the medulla and return to the cortical region.

There are approximately 1 million nephrons in each kidney. Within each nephron, the actual filtration of blood is carried out within a bulb-shaped region, Bowman's capsule, which surrounds a capillary network, the glomerulus. In most individuals, a single renal artery brings the blood supply to the kidney. Since the renal artery originates from a branch of the aorta, the body's largest artery, the blood pressure within this region of the kidney is high. Consequently, hypotension, a significant lowering of blood pressure, may also result in kidney failure.

The renal artery enters the kidney through the renal pelvis, branching into progressively smaller arterioles and capillaries. The capillary network serves both to supply nutrition to the cells that make up the kidney and to collect nutrients or fluids reabsorbed from the loops and tubules of the nephrons. Renal capillaries also enter the Bowman's capsules in the form of balls or coils, the glomeruli. Since blood pressure remains high, the force filtration in a nephron pushes about 20 percent of the fluid volume of the glomerulus into the cavity portion of the capsule. Most small materials dissolved in the blood, including proteins, sugars, electrolytes, and the nitrogenous waste product urea, pass along within the fluid into the capsule. As the filtrate passes through the series of convoluted tubules extending from the Bowman's capsule, most nutrients and salts are reabsorbed and reenter the capillary network. Approximately 99 percent of the water that has passed through the capsule is also reabsorbed. The material which remains, much of it waste such as urea, is excreted from the body.

Nephrology is the branch of medicine that deals with these functions of the kidney. Loss of kidney function can quickly result in a buildup of waste material in the blood; hence kidney failure, if untreated, can result in serious illness or death. Within the purview of nephrology, however, is more than the function of the kidneys as filters for the excretion of wastes. The kidneys are also endocrine organs, structures that secrete hormones into the bloodstream to act on other, distal organs. The major endocrine functions of the kidneys involve the secretion of the hormones renin and erythropoietin.

Renin functions within the renin-angiotensin system in the regulation of blood pressure. It is produced within the juxtaglomerular complex, the region around Bowman's capsule in which the arteriole enters the structure. Cells within the tubules of the nephron closely monitor the blood pressure within the incoming arterioles.

When blood pressure drops, these cells stimulate the release of renin directly into the blood circulation.

Renin does not act directly on the nephrons. Rather, it serves as a proteolytic enzyme that activates another protein, angiotensin, the precursor of which is found in the blood. The activated angiotensin, called angiotensin II, has several effects on kidney function that involve the regulation of blood pressure. First, by decreasing the glomerular filtration rate, it allows more water to be retained. Second, angiotensin II stimulates the release of the steroid hormone aldosterone from the adrenal glands, located in close association with the kidneys. Aldosterone acts to increase sodium retention and transport by cells within the tubules of the nephron, resulting in increased water reabsorption. The result of this complex series of hormone interactions within the kidney is a close monitoring of both salt retention and blood pressure and volume. In this manner, nephrology also relates to the pathophysiology of hypertension—high blood pressure.

The kidneys also regulate the production of erythrocytes, red blood cells, through the production of the hormone erythropoietin. Erythropoietin is secreted by the peritubular cells associated with regions outside the nephrons in response to lowered oxygen levels in the blood, also monitored by cells within the kidney. The hormone serves to stimulate red cell production within the bone marrow. Approximately 85 percent of the erythropoietin in blood fluids is synthesized within the kidneys, the remainder by the liver.

Since proper kidney function is related to a wide variety of body processes, from the regulation of nitrogenous waste disposal to the monitoring and control of blood pressure, nephrology may deal with a number of disparate syndromes. The kidney may represent the primary site of a disease or pathology, an example being the autoimmune phenomenon of glomerulonephritis. Renal failure may also result from the indirect action of a more general systemic syndrome, as is the case with diabetes mellitus. In many cases, the decrease in kidney function may result from any number of disorders, which poses many problems for the nephrologist.

Proper function of the kidney is central to numerous homeostatic processes within the body. Thus nephrology by necessity deals with a variety of pathophysiological disorders. Renal dysfunction may involve disorders of the organ itself or pathology associated with individual structures within the kidneys, the glomeruli or tubules. Likewise, the disorder within the body may be of a more general type, with the kidney being a secondary site of damage. This is particularly true of immune disorders such as lupus (systemic lupus erythematosus) or diabetes. Conditions that affect proper kidney function may result from infection or inflammation, the obstruction of tubules or the vascular system, or neoplastic disorders (cancers).

Immune disorders are among the more common processes that result in kidney disease. They may be of two types: glomerulonephritis or the more general nephrotic syndrome. Glomerulonephritis can result either from a direct attack on basement membrane tissue by host antibodies, such as with Goodpasture's syndrome, or indirectly through deposits of immune (antigen-antibody) complexes, such as with lupus. Nephritis may also be secondary to high blood pressure. In any of these situations, inflammation resulting from the infiltration of immune complexes and/or from the activation of the complement system may result in a decreased ability of the glomeruli to function. Treatment of such disorders often involves the use of corticosteroids or other immunosuppressive drugs to dampen the immune response. Continued recurrence of the disease may result in renal failure, requiring dialysis treatment or even kidney transplantation.

Activation of the complement system as a result of immune complex deposition along the glomeruli is a frequent source of inflammation. Complement consists of a series of some dozen serum proteins, many of which are pharmacologically active. Intermediates in the complement pathway include enzymes that activate subsequent components in a cascade fashion. The terminal proteins in the pathway form a "membrane attack complex," capable of significantly damaging a target (such as the basement membrane of a Bowman's capsule). Activation of the initial steps in the pathway begins with either the deposition of immune complexes along basement membranes or the direct binding of antibodies on glomerular surfaces. The end result can be extensive nephrotic destruction.

Nephrotic syndrome, which can also result in extensive damage to the glomeruli, is often secondary to other disease. Diabetes is a frequent primary disorder in its development; approximately one-third of insulin-dependent diabetics are at risk for significant renal failure. Other causes of nephrotic syndrome may include cancer or infectious agents and toxins.

Diagnostic and Treatment Techniques

Nephrologists can measure glomerular function using a variety of tests. These tests are based on the ability of the basement membranes associated with the glomeruli to act as filters. Blood cells and large materials such as proteins dissolved in the blood are unable to pass through these filters. Plasma, the liquid portion of the blood containing dissolved factors involved in blood-clotting mechanisms, is able to pass through the basement membrane, the driving force for filtration being the hydrostatic pressure of the blood (blood pressure).

The glomerular filtration rate (GFR) is defined as the rate by which the glomeruli filter the plasma during a fixed period of time. Generally, the rate is determined by measuring either the time of clearance of the carbohydrate inulin from the blood or the rate of clearance of creatinine, a nitrogenous by-product of metabolism. Though the rate may vary with age, it generally is about 125 to 130 milliliters of plasma filtered per minute.

Any significant decrease in the GFR is indicative of renal failure and can result in significant disruptions of acid-base or electrolyte balance in the blood. A decrease in the GFR can sometimes be observed through measurements of urine output. Healthy individuals usually excrete from 1 to 2 liters of urine per day. If the urine output drops to less than 500 milliliters (0.5 liter) per day, a condition known as oliguria, the body suffers a diminished capacity to remove metabolic waste products (urea, creatinine, or acids). Taken to an extreme, in which the filtering capacity is completely shut down and urine formation drops below 100 milliliters per day (anuria), the resulting uremia may cause death in a matter of days.

Anuria may have a variety of causes: kidney failure; hypotension, in which blood pressure is insufficient to maintain glomerular filtration; or a blockage in the urinary tract. As waste products, fluids, and electrolytes (especially sodium and potassium) build up, the person may appear puffy, be feverish, and exhibit muscle weakness. Heart arrhythmia or failure may also occur. Mediation of the problem, in addition to attempts to alleviate the reasons for kidney dysfunction, include regulation of fluid, protein, and electrolyte uptake. Medications are also used to increase the excretion of potassium and tissue fluids, assuming that the cause is not a urinary blockage.

The nephrologist or other physician may also monitor kidney function through measurements of serum analytes or through observation of certain chemicals within the urine. The levels of blood, urea, and nitrogen (BUN), nitrogenous substances in the blood, present a rough measure of kidney function. Generally, BUN levels change significantly only after glomerular filtration has been significantly disrupted. The levels are also dependent on the amount of protein intake in the diet. When changes occur as a result of renal dysfunction, BUN levels can be a useful marker for the progression of the disease. A more specific indicator of renal function can be the creatinine concentration within the blood. Serum creatinine, unlike BUN levels, is not related to the diet. In the event of renal failure, however, changes in BUN levels usually can be detected earlier than those of creatinine.

As the glomeruli lose their ability to distinguish large from small molecules during filtration, protein can begin to appear in the urine, the condition known as proteinuria. Usually, the level of protein in the urine is negligible (less than 250 milligrams per day). A transient proteinuria can result from heavy exercise or minor illness, but persistent levels of more than 1 gram per day may be indicative of renal dysfunction or even complications of hypertension. Generally, if the problem resides in the loss of tubular reabsorption, levels of protein generally are below 1 to 2 grams per day, with that amount usually consisting of small proteins. If the problem is a result of increased glomerular permeability caused by inflammation, levels may reach greater than 2 grams per day. In cases of nephrotic syndrome, excretion of protein in the urine may exceed 5 grams per day.

Measurement of urine protein is a relatively easy process. A urine sample is placed on a plastic stick with an indicator pad capable of turning colors, depending on the protein concentration. Analogous strips may be used for detection of other materials in urine, including acid, blood, or sugars. The presence of either red or white blood cells in urine can be indicative of infection or glomerulonephritis.

In addition to the filtration of blood fluids through the nephrons, the reabsorption of materials within the tubules results in increased urine concentration. A normal GFR within a healthy kidney produces a urine concentration three or four times as great as that found within serum. As kidney failure progresses, the concentration of urine begins to decrease, with the urine becoming more dilute. The kidneys compensate for the decreased concentration by increasing the amount of urine output: The frequency of urination may increase, as well as the volume excreted (polyuria). In time, if renal failure continues, the GFR will decrease, resulting in the retention of both analytes and water.

Determination of urine concentration is carried out following a brief period of dehydration: deprivation of fluids for about fifteen hours prior to the test. This dehydration will result in increased production by the hypothalamus of antidiuretic hormone (ADH), or vasopressin, a chemical that decreases the production of urine through increased renal tubule reabsorption of water. The result is a more concentrated urine. Following the dehydration period, the patient's urine is collected over a period of three hours and assessed for concentration. Significantly low values may be indicative of kidney disease.

A battery of tests in addition to those already described may be utilized in the diagnosis of kidney disease. These may include intravenous pyelography (in which a contrast medium is injected into the blood and followed as it passes through the kidneys), kidney biopsy, and ultrasound examinations. Diagnosis and course of treatment depend on an evaluation of these tests.

Fast Fact

The first human kidney transplant was tried in Ukraine in 1933 but failed. Twenty-one years later, Joseph E. Smith and his team successfully transplanted a kidney in Boston.

Source: thefactsite.com

Perspective and Prospects

The roots of modern nephrology date from the seventeenth century. In the early decades of that century, the English physician William Harvey demonstrated the principles of blood circulation and the role of the heart in that process. Harvey's theories opened the door for more extensive analysis of organ systems, both in humans and in other animals. As a result, in 1666, Italian anatomist Marcello Malpighi, while exploring organ structure with the newly developed microscope, discovered the presence of glomeruli (what he called Malpighian corpuscles) within the kidneys. Malpighi thought that these structures were in some way connected with collecting ducts in the kidneys that had recently been found by Lorenzo Bellini. Malpighi also suspected that these structures played a role in urine formation.

Sir William Bowman, in 1832, was the first to describe the true relationship of the corpuscles discovered by Malpighi to urine secretion through the tubules. Bowman's capsule, as it is now called, is a filter that allows only the liquid of the blood, as well as dissolved salts and urea within the blood, into the tubules, from which the urine is secreted. It remained for Carl Ludwig, in 1842, to complete the story. Ludwig suggested that the corpuscles function in a passive manner, in that the filtrate is filtered by means of hydrostatic pressure through the capsule into the tubules and from there concentrated as water and solutes that are reabsorbed.

The first definitive work on urine formation, *The Secretion of the Urine*, was published by Arthur Robertson Cushny in 1917. In the monograph, Cushny offered a thorough analysis of the data published on kidney function. Though Cushny was incorrect in some of his conclusions, the work catalyzed intensive research activity on the functions of the kidney. A colleague of Cushny, E. Brice Mayrs, made the first attempt to determine the glomerular filtration rate, measuring the clearance of sulfate in rabbits. In 1926, the Danish physiologist Poul Brandt Rehberg demonstrated the superiority of creatinine as a marker for glomerular filtration; the "guinea pig" for the experiment was Rehberg himself.

A pioneer in renal physiology, Homer William Smith, began his research while serving in the United States Army during World War I. Until he retired in 1961, Smith was involved in much of the research related to renal excretion. It was Smith who developed inulin clearance as a measure of the GFR; his later years dealt with studies on mechanisms of solute excretion.

With the newer technology of the late twentieth century, more accurate methods for analysis became available. These have included ultrasound scanning, intravenous pyelography, and angiography. In addition, better understanding of immediate causes of many kidney problems has served to control or prevent some forms of renal failure.

Richard Adler, Ph.D.

Conversation With . . .
LYNDA K. BALL

MSN, RN, CNN
Nephrology Nursing

Lynda K. Ball has been a nephrology nurse for thirty-two years and is currently the Quality Improvement Director for Health Services Advisory Group: ESRD Network 13 and President of the American Nephrology Nurses Association, 2018-2019.

1. What was your individual career path in terms of education/training, entry-level job, or other significant opportunity?

Nursing is a second career for me. Initially, I couldn't decide between nursing and teaching. I loved the outdoors and taught environmental science to elementary school students at a land laboratory while earning a bachelor's degree in conservation from Kent State University. I moved East and worked first at the Boston YMCA, then went on to teach environmental science at an environmental school in New Hampshire. I loved the work, but these were seasonal jobs that didn't pay well. The school's nurse wrote a letter of recommendation for me to go to nursing school, and I earned my associate degree in nursing (ADN) from Middlesex Community College in Bedford, Massachusetts.

My plan was to start my nursing career and then go back part-time and earn my bachelor's degree in nursing (BSN). I did complete an RN to BSN program nine years later, at Penn State University. And, nine years after that, I completed my master's degree in nursing education online at Walden University.

My first job was as staff nurse on a surgical unit at Akron City Hospital in Ohio, doing genitourinary, gynecology, and kidney transplants. I fell in love with transplant because, as a nurse, I could help people get their lives back. For example, kidney patients were off dialysis where they were tied to a machine three times a week. Typically, we had four patients on our unit at any given time. That required a lot of education, and it was the first time I realized I could combine teaching and nursing. I decided to become certified in nephrology nursing. I was required to have two years' experience in that field to take the national certification exam, or CNN for certified nephrology nurse. As soon as I was eligible, I sat for the exam.

After five years in transplant, I transferred to the dialysis unit because our transplant surgeon retired and I didn't want to lose my specialty certification. Dialysis offered even more opportunity for teaching, in this case, staff, patients, and families. I was assigned sixteen to twenty primary patients.

I next became an educator for a dialysis provider. This allowed me to impact approximately 300 patients as I trained new nurses. Then I became a quality improvement director for an End-Stage Renal Disease Network, or ESRD Network, that covered Alaska, Idaho, Oregon, Montana, and Washington. It was one of eighteen such positions in the United States. I monitored clinical indicators and created quality improvement activities for dialysis providers that impacted more than 10,000 patients. Today I work for another ESRD Network, which covers Arkansas, Louisiana, and Oklahoma and impacts more than 20,000 patients!

It's been twenty-six years since I was certified as a nephrology nurse, one of the best decisions I've ever made. Because I want to make a difference, in my spare time I now teach certification review courses all over the United States to encourage other nurses to become certified and realize their nephrology nursing opportunities.

2. What are the most important skills and/or qualities for someone in your profession?

Critical thinking, compassion, being nonjudgmental, caring, listening, and being sensitive to people's fears.

3. What do you wish you had known going into this profession?

I would have taken more courses on communication skills to learn how better to deal with different personalities. In addition, preparation to better organize and prioritize my workload would have been helpful.

4. Are there many job opportunities in your profession? In what specific areas?

There are many job opportunities, but some require advanced degrees. Several modalities exist in nephrology nursing: kidney transplant, chronic kidney disease (before you need dialysis or transplant), hemodialysis (at home or in a dialysis unit), and peritoneal dialysis. Nurses can work with acutely ill or chronic patients, and can be a case manager for a hospital, dialysis organization, or insurance company. There are opportunities to be an educator, director of nurses, nurse practitioner, or work in quality improvement. You could work in a hospital, a freestanding (non-hospital) setting, a college or university. Hemodialysis patients need to have their bloodstreams accessed for treatment, so vascular labs or freestanding access centers offer nursing positions. You could work in nursing informatics, designing programs, or supporting the operating systems for an organization.

5. How do you see your profession changing in the next five years, how will technology impact that change, and what skills will be required?

Health care continues to evolve. Today, the majority of providers use electronic medical records. Robots are being used in some settings to work in conjunction with nurses, and the use of artificial intelligence (computers and algorithms to interpret big data) continues to expand.

Nurses use apps on smartphones for many purposes, including medication management or signs and symptoms of diseases.

We're also seeing more simulation labs, which are great for teaching about disease, illness, or surgical procedures. These don't, however, replace the hands-on care and compassion of one-to-one communication.

6. What do you enjoy most about your job? What do you enjoy least about your job?

I most enjoy making a difference in the lives of patients, allaying fears, and helping them understand their disease. As you gather more experience and broaden your career path, you can have a positive impact on more and more patients.

What I enjoy least about my job is not interacting with patients face-to-face any longer. They are spread out over three states in more than 340 clinics. I miss connecting, getting to know them and their families, and learning their story.

7. Can you suggest a valuable "try this" for students considering a career in your profession?

If you are in a nursing program, see if you can spend a day in a dialysis facility shadowing a nurse. I used to love having nursing students come and spend the day with me. There were lots of teachable moments.

You could volunteer at a dialysis clinic or hospital unit. Of course, you would need to obtain permission from the facility/hospital administrator.

Finally, attend a local or national nursing association meeting. The American Nephrology Nurses Association (ANNA) has eighty-three local chapters and holds two national conferences annually. This is a great way to meet nephrology nurses who work in different settings and get the real scoop! You may meet a mentor, or bond with other nurses your age, or join groups within the organization that lead you in new directions for your career. Connecting like this can make all the difference for you in your career professionally, emotionally, everything.

PALLIATIVE MEDICINE

Science and Profession

While in the United States, The National Hospice and Palliative Care Organization (NHPCO) defines palliative care as: Treatment that enhances comfort and improves the quality of an individual's life during the last phase of life. No specific therapy is excluded from consideration. The test of palliative care lies in the agreement between the individual, physician(s), primary caregiver, and the hospice team that the expected outcome is relief from distressing symptoms, the easing of pain, and/or enhancing the quality of life. The decision to intervene with active palliative care is based on an ability to meet stated goals rather than affect the underlying disease. An individual's needs must continue to be assessed and all treatment options explored and evaluated in the context of the individual's values and symptoms. The individual's choices and decisions regarding care are paramount and must be followed.

Palliative medicine is a specialty that spans disciplines. The goal is to comfort and support patients as they face life-threatening illnesses, not only relieving their suffering but also addressing their emotional and spiritual needs. Although palliative medicine is typically associated with the final stages of life-threatening conditions, patients may also benefit from specialized care while they are still undergoing active treatment. In that case, symptom relief and other interventions to improve their quality of life help improve their strength and stamina to endure additional cycles of therapy.

Palliative care may be provided in a long-term care facility, a hospital, or the patient's home. Care is provided by a team consisting of primary care physicians, specialists in the patient's condition (for example, oncologists, cardiologists, or pulmonologists), palliative medicine specialist, nurses, social workers, mental health specialists (psychologists, psychiatrists, or counselors), nutritionists, and clergy. The level and type of care provided are guided by the wishes and needs of the patient. Pain management is often the greatest need, but the patient may also require relief of other symptoms associated with the condition or its treatment, such as nausea, vomiting, decreased appetite, inability to eat, dehydration, constipation or diarrhea, shortness of breath, malaise, fatigue, anxiety, depression, and altered consciousness.

Palliative medicine is recognized as a basic human right in the International Bill of Human Rights of the United Nations. The document declares that all people have the right to adequate health and medical care, and further states that patients with chronic and terminal illnesses have the right to avoid pain and die with dignity. Following these principles, Canada decreed that every citizen has the right to palliative care. The European Committee of Ministers and the South African Department of Health declared that palliative care is a right of all citizens. Palliative medicine is formally recognized as a specialty in Australia, France, Germany, Hong Kong, Ireland, New Zealand, Poland, Romania, Slovakia, Taiwan, the United States, and the United Kingdom.

Palliative medicine is an essential component of care for patients suffering from any chronic, life-threatening illness, but the specialty has taken on an added significance in the field of oncology. In the United States, the Institute of Medicine stated in 1997 that any comprehensive cancer care plan should include palliative care. A 2005 resolution of the 58th World Health Assembly to improve cancer care placed palliative medicine on equal footing with surgery, radiation, and medical oncology.

Although recognized as a medical specialty, palliative medicine relies on the unique contributions of numerous disciplines. Education in palliative techniques begins at the undergraduate level and is incorporated into the training of a number of medical specialties, such as oncology and gerontology. Continuing education programs focus on educating health care professionals in quality palliative care techniques. Other projects build on these efforts, using other health care professionals, such as nurse practitioners and physician assistants, to develop quality palliative medicine programs in their institutions.

The American Society for Clinical Oncology (ASCO) actively promotes continuing education in palliative medicine. Palliative care is incorporated into educational materials and programs developed by ASCO. The society published an educational curriculum for continuing medical education on palliative medicine, and it has a study program devoted to supportive care. Palliative medicine is included in the training for internists, as adopted by the American Board of Internal Medicine.

The National Consensus Project for Quality Palliative Care issued guidelines for palliative care to establish continuity of care across institutions. The clinical practice guidelines have been incorporated into the hospital accreditation standards of The Joint Commission (formerly the Joint Commission for the Accreditation of Hospitals). Institutions are assessed on the eight domains of palliative care: structure and process, physical aspects, psychological and psychiatric aspects, spiritual and religious aspects, cultural aspects, care of the imminently dying patient, the ethical aspects of care, and the legal aspects of care. Additionally, the Center for the Advancement of Palliative Care developed the State-by-State Report Card on Access to Palliative Care in Our Nation's Hospitals. The report card measures patient access to palliative care and to palliative medicine specialists, access of medical students to training in palliative care, and access of physicians to specialty training in palliative care. The report card emphasizes the importance of a multidisciplinary approach to palliative medicine.

Diagnostic and Treatment Techniques

Patient care is traditionally disease-oriented. Specialists in particular tend to focus narrowly on a specific organ or body system. Palliative care, however, takes a holistic, patient-centered approach. The emphasis is on communicating with the patient and family to assess the patient's specific needs and desires.

Palliative care can be divided into primary and secondary teams. The primary team, as defined by Medicare, is comprised by four core members (physician, nurse, social worker and spiritual counselor) and is responsible for assessing and managing symptoms, providing expertise regarding psychosocial services as well as communicating with the patient and family while involving the shared decision making model of care If, however, the patient's condition worsens and the primary team can no longer manage the symptoms, a palliative medicine specialist in the patient's condition is called. The palliative medicine specialist may be consulted on specific issues as needed or become a core member until the patient's death.

The whole-patient assessment begins with the patient's description of symptoms and level of function. Diagnostic tests may be used to evaluate symptom severity, but diagnosis is not the purpose. The emphasis is always on symptom relief.

Pain is a significant issue that must be managed properly. Inadequately controlled pain may reduce the effectiveness of treatment and wear the patient down psychologically. Proper pain management involves communication with and education of the patient and family members as well as continuous assessment of the effectiveness of pain medications. The World Health Organization (WHO) has developed an approach to pain for cancer patients, beginning with nonsteroidal anti-inflammatory drugs (NSAIDs), such as ibuprofen, and progressing through acetaminophen combined with an opioid medication, such as acetaminophen with codeine, and lastly to opioid medications such as morphine or oxycodone. The goal is to relieve pain while keeping the patient alert and in control.

The effect of the condition on the emotions and cognitive functioning of the patient is an important aspect of the palliative medicine assessment. Patients are facing serious issues while they battle their illnesses. They must cope with imminent death and the grief of their loved ones along with the fear of loss of control and dignity. Patients must be evaluated for depression and anxiety. Practical needs, such as relationship issues, legal affairs, and financial management, also need attention. The patient's spiritual needs should also be addressed. Spiritual counseling can be traditional religious advisement from a clergyperson or an informal discussion of personal beliefs, according to the desires of the patient.

Depression and anxiety are common among patients coping with life-threatening conditions. Feelings of sadness and depression are to be expected and should be managed appropriately even when they are not expected to be permanent. The members of the primary team who are in closest contact with the patient need to be alert for symptoms of depression that surpass the normal grieving process. Signs of major depression include persistent feelings of worthlessness, hopelessness, helplessness, and loss of self-esteem. Physical symptoms may include weight loss or changes in sleep habits, although these symptoms may also be attributed to the patient's underlying condition. Thoughts of suicide or requests by the patient to hasten death are not part of the coping process and are a sign of major depression. If the signs of depression fail to resolve after a few weeks, then the mental health specialists on the team are consulted and the depression should be treated.

Similarly, anxiety is an understandable and natural emotion as patients juggle financial concerns, family issues, medical concerns, and preparations for their own death. Anxiety may be managed through counseling or, if it is severe, with antianxiety medications.

The role of the palliative care team is not limited to the patient. The team assists family members in accepting the patient's condition, managing financial and insurance matters, and coping with grief. The health care team can advise family members on what to expect as the patient's condition deteriorates. Breathing difficulties, delirium or dementia, wasting, and incontinence can be upsetting for family members to experience if they are not properly prepared. After the patient's death, the palliative care team assists family members through the grieving process. The team follows up with the family through phone calls and home visits, providing grief counseling or referral to caregiver support groups or other mental health professionals when needed. Bereavement services often last for several months to a year after the patient's death.

Fast Fact

Cancer death rates are dropping: lung cancer rates declined 45 percent among men between 1990 and 2015, and 19 percent from 2002 to 2015 among women. Breast cancer declined 39 percent between 1989 and 2015.
Source: American Cancer Society

Perspective and Prospects

In the span of two decades, palliative medicine progressed from haphazard training through chance experiences to a recognized specialty. A 1998 member survey by ASCO revealed 90 percent of the oncologists who responded had no formal training in palliative medicine. Rather, they indicated they learned through "trial and error." Alarmingly, more than one-third claimed that their education in palliative medicine was from a "traumatic experience" with a patient. Most had little training in how to discuss a poor prognosis with patients and their families, and only 10 percent had completed clinical training in palliative care.

Since that survey, ASCO and other professional societies have incorporated palliative medicine into their continuing education curricula. More important, national and international groups have formally recognized the importance of palliative medicine in preserving the dignity and well-being of patients nearing the end of their lives. In recent years, palliative medicine has been incorporated as a routine part of comprehensive cancer care plans in the United States.

Despite these advances, much work remains. The need for palliative medicine is increasing. The population is growing older while the prevalence of cancer is rising. Cancer treatments are becoming more effective. Although cancer death rates are declining, more people are living longer with the disease, resulting in growing numbers of people who will benefit from palliative medicine.

To meet the growing need, health care practitioners must be educated in palliative medicine. Fellowships in palliative medicine (currently 93 in the United States), continuing education, and readily available educational resources are needed now more than ever. Formal certifications and national guidelines and standards of practice have been adopted to ensure consistency in the quality of palliative medicine across states and individual institutions. The concept of palliative medicine continues to be incorporated into care plans across medical disciplines. In 2006 the American Board of Medical Specialties approved the creation of Hospice and Palliative Medicine as a subspecialty to 10 medical disciplines, and after 2013, only those who have completed an accredited fellowship program will be able to be certified and practice this discipline.

Improving end-of-life care requires more than educational and quality control initiatives; it also requires political will. Unless palliative medicine is viewed as a priority by administrators and policy makers, quality care cannot be ensured.

Pain management is an integral piece of palliative medicine. Unfortunately, misconceptions remain among health care practitioners as well as the general public regarding the use of opioid medications. The fear of addiction frequently results in less than optimal pain control and patient suffering. The need for higher doses of pain medications does not indicate addiction; it is more likely a sign the pain is inadequately controlled or the condition is progressing. The United Nations elevated effective pain control to a fundamental human right. In a formal statement, the UN equated inadequate pain control with "cruel, inhuman, and degrading treatment" and called for nations to supply adequate pain medications to patients.

Collectively, the United Nations, individual countries, and medical societies are striving to ensure that all patients suffering from terminal illnesses receive compassionate and comprehensive care. The strength of palliative medicine is in considering the patient as a whole rather than focusing exclusively on a particular diagnosis. Palliative medicine breaks from traditional medical practice and creates a multidisciplinary team to care for the patient. The direction of care is dictated by the wishes of the patient and encompasses physical, emotional, and the spiritual needs of the patient and their families.

Cheryl Pokalo Jones,
Felix Rivera, M.D.

PEDIATRICS

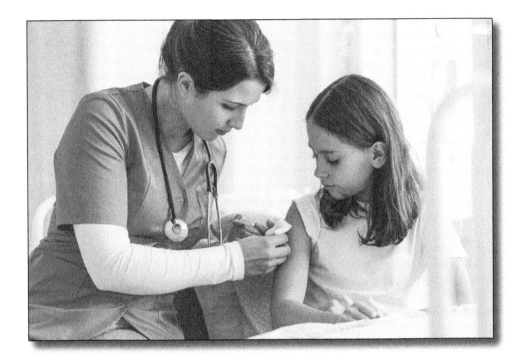

Science and Profession

The practice of pediatrics begins with birth. Most babies are born healthy and require only routine medical attention. Many hospitals, however, have a neonatology unit for babies who are born prematurely, who have disease conditions or birth defects, or who weigh less than 5.5 pounds (even though they may be full-term babies). All these infants may require short-term or prolonged care by pediatricians in the neonatology unit.

The problems of premature babies usually center on the fact that they have not fully developed physically, although other factors may also be involved, such as the health and age of the mother, undernourishment during pregnancy, lack of prenatal care, anemia, abnormalities in the mother's genital organs, and infectious disease. A past record of infertility, stillbirths, abortions, and other premature births may indicate that a pregnancy will not go to full term.

Low birth weight in both premature and full-term babies is directly related to the incidence of disease and congenital defects and may be indicative of a low intelligence quotient (IQ). Between 50 and 75 percent of babies weighing under 3 pounds, 5 ounces are mentally disabled or have defects in vision or hearing. Recent studies also indicate an increase in neurological problems such as attention-deficit hyperactivity disorder and autism in these children.

Because the lungs are among the organs that develop late in pregnancy, many premature infants are unable to breathe on their own. Some premature babies are born before they have developed the sucking reflex, so they cannot feed on their own.

Hundreds of congenital diseases can be present in the neonate. Some are apparent at birth; some become evident in later years. Some may be life-threatening to the infant or become life-threatening in later years. Others may be harmless.

The child may be born with an infection passed on from the mother, such as rubella (German measles) or human immunodeficiency virus (HIV), the virus that causes acquired immunodeficiency syndrome (AIDS). Rubella may also infect the child in the womb, causing severe physical deformities, heart defects, mental disability, deafness, and other conditions. Genital herpes affects about 1,500 newborns in the United States each year and may cause serious complications. A herpes infection during the second or third trimester of a woman's pregnancy may increase the chance of preterm delivery or cesarean section. Group beta strep (GBS) infections are another serious problem for one of every 2,000 newborns in the United States. GBS may cause sepsis (blood infection), meningitis, and pneumonia.

Among the most prevalent congenital birth defects is cleft lip, which occurs when the upper lip does not fuse together, leaving a visible gap that can extend from the lip to the nose. Cleft palate occurs when the gap reaches into the roof of the mouth.

Various abnormalities may be present in the hands and feet of neonates. These can be caused by congenital defects or by medications given to the pregnant mother. Arms, legs, fingers, and toes may fail to develop fully or may be missing entirely. Some children are born with extra fingers or toes. In some children, fingers or toes may be webbed or fused together. Clubfoot is relatively common. In this condition, the foot is twisted, usually downward and inward.

Many congenital heart defects can afflict the child, including septal defects (openings in the septum, the wall that separates the right and left sides of the heart), the transposition of blood vessels, the constriction of blood vessels, and valve disorders.

Congenital disorders of the central nervous system include spina bifida, hydrocephalus, cerebral palsy, and Down syndrome. Spina bifida is a condition in which part of a vertebra (a bone in the spinal column) fails to fuse. As a result, nerves of the spinal cord may protrude through the spinal column. This condition varies considerably in severity; mild forms can cause no significant problems, while severe forms can be crippling or life-threatening. In hydrocephalus, sometimes called "water on the brain," fluid accumulates in the infant's cranium, causing the head to enlarge and putting great pressure on the brain. This disorder, too, can be life-threatening.

Cerebral palsy is caused by damage to brain cells that control motor function in the body. This damage can occur before, during, or after birth. It may or may not be accompanied by mental disability. Many children with cerebral palsy appear to be mentally disabled because they have difficulty speaking, but, in fact, their intelligence may be normal or above normal. Down syndrome is one of the most common congenital birth defects, affecting 1 in 200 infants born to mothers over age thirty-five. It is caused by an extra chromosome passed on to the child. The distinct physical characteristics of Down syndrome include a small body, a small and rounded head, oval ears, and an enlarged tongue. Mortality is high in the first year of life because of infection or other disease.

Cystic fibrosis is one of the most serious congenital diseases of Caucasian children. Because the lungs of children with this disease cannot expel mucus efficiently, it thickens and collects, clogging air passages. The mucus also becomes a breeding ground for bacteria and infection. Other parts of the body, such as the pancreas, the digestive system, and sweat glands, can also be impaired. A common congenital disorder among African American children is sickle cell disease. It causes deformities in red blood cells that clog blood vessels, impair circulation, and increase susceptibility to infection.

One of the major problems of infancy is sudden infant death syndrome (SIDS), in which a baby that is perfectly healthy, or only slightly ill, is discovered dead in its crib. In 2010 in the United States, over 2,000 infant deaths were reported as SIDS. The cause is not known. The child usually shows no symptoms of disease, and autopsies reveal no evidence of smothering, choking, or strangulation. Research indicates that rebreathing of carbon dioxide as well as exposure to secondhand cigarette smoke and other forms of indoor air pollution may greatly increase the risk of SIDS.

Infectious diseases are more prevalent in childhood than in later years. Among the major diseases of children (and often adults) throughout the centuries have been smallpox, malaria, diphtheria, typhus, typhoid fever, tuberculosis, measles, mumps, rubella, varicella (chickenpox), scarlet fever, pneumonia, meningitis, and pertussis (whooping cough). In more recent years, AIDS and hepatitis have become significant threats to the young.

Certain skin diseases are common in infants and young children, such as diaper rash, impetigo, neonatal acne, and seborrheic dermatitis, among a wide variety of disorders. Fungal diseases of the skin occur often in the young, usually because of close contact with other youngsters. For example, tinea pedis (athlete's foot), tinea cruris (jock itch), and tinea corporis (a fungal infection that occurs on nonhairy areas of the body) are spread by contact with an infected playmate or by the touching of surfaces that harbor the organism. Similarly, parasitic diseases such as head lice, body lice, crabs, or scabies are easily spread among playmates. Some skin conditions are congenital. Between 20 and 40 percent of infants are born with, or soon develop, skin lesions called hemangiomas. They may be barely perceptible or quite unsightly; they generally resolve by the age of seven.

One form of diabetes mellitus arises in childhood, insulin-dependent diabetes mellitus (IDDM) or type 1. In the healthy individual, the pancreas produces insulin, a hormone that is responsible for the metabolism of blood sugar, or glucose. In some children, the pancreas loses the ability to produce insulin, causing blood sugar to rise. When this happens, a cascade of events causes harmful effects throughout the body. In the short term, these symptoms include rapid breathing, rapid heartbeat, extreme thirst, vomiting, fever, chemical imbalances in the blood, and coma. In the long term, diabetes mellitus contributes to heart disease, atherosclerosis, kidney damage, blindness, gangrene, and a host of other conditions.

Cancer can afflict children. One of the most serious forms is acute lymphocytic leukemia. Its peak incidence is between three and five years of age, although it can also occur later in life. Leukemic conditions are characterized by the overproduction of white blood cells (leukocytes). In acute lymphocytic leukemia, the production of lymphoblasts, immature cells that ordinarily would develop into infection-fighting lymphocytes, is greatly increased. This abnormal proliferation of immature cells interferes with the normal production of blood cells, increasing the child's susceptibility to infection. Before current treatment modalities, the prognosis for children with acute lymphocytic leukemia was death within four or five months after diagnosis.

In addition to the wide range of diseases that can beset the infant and growing child, there are many other problems of childhood that the parent and the pediatrician must face. These problems may involve physical and behavioral development, nutrition, and relationships with parents and other children.

Both parents and pediatricians must be alert to a child's rate of growth and mental development. Failure to gain weight in infancy may indicate a range of physical problems, such as gastrointestinal, endocrine, and other internal disorders. In three-quarters of these cases, however, the cause is not a physical disorder. The child may simply be underfed because of the mother's negligence. The vital process of bonding between mother and child may not have taken place; the child is not held close and cuddled, is not shown affection, and thus feels unwanted and unloved. This is seen often in babies who are reared in institutions where the nursing staff does not have time to caress and comfort infants individually.

Similarly, later in childhood, failure to grow at a normal rate can be caused by malnutrition or psychological factors. It could also be attributable to a deficiency in a hormone that is the body's natural regulator of growth. If this hormone is not released in adequate supply, the child's growth is stunted. An excess of this hormone may cause the child to grow too rapidly. Failure to grow normally may also indicate an underlying disease condition, such as heart dysfunction and malabsorption problems, in which the child does not get the necessary nutrition from food.

The parent and pediatrician must also ensure that the child is developing acceptably in other areas. Speech and language skills, teething, bone development, walking and other motor skills, toilet habits, sleep patterns, eye development, and hearing have to be evaluated regularly.

Profound mental disability is usually evident early in life, but mild to moderate disability may not be apparent until the child starts school. Slowness in learning may be indicative of mental disability, but this judgment should be carefully weighed, because the real reason may be impaired hearing or vision or an underlying disease condition. The diagnosis of neurological disorders, such as autism and attention-deficit hyperactivity disorder (ADHD), has greatly increased in recent years and poses a special challenge to both parents and pediatricians.

The battery of diseases and other disorders that may beset a child remains more or less constant throughout childhood. Puberty, however, begins hormonal changes that trigger new disease threats and vast psychological upheaval. As early as eight years of age in girls and after ten or eleven years of age in boys, the body begins a prolonged metamorphosis that changes the child into an adult. Hormones that were previously released in minimal amounts course throughout the body in great quantities.

In boys, the sex hormones are called androgens. Chief among them is testosterone, which is secreted primarily by the testicles. It causes the sexual organs to mature and promotes the growth of hair in the genital area and armpits and on the chest. Testosterone also enlarges the larynx (voicebox), causing the voice to deepen.

Girls also produce some testosterone, but estrogens and other female sex hormones are the major hormones involved in puberty. They cause the sexual organs to mature, the hips to enlarge and become rounded, hair to grow in the genital area and armpits, the breasts to enlarge, and menstruation to begin.

Many disease conditions can arise in association with the hormonal changes that occur during puberty, such as breast abnormalities and genital infections. Far and away the most common medical disorder at this time, however, is acne. Acne is a direct result of the rise in testosterone that occurs during puberty. About 85 percent of teenagers experience some degree of acne, and about 12 percent of these will develop severe, deep acne, a serious condition that can leave lifelong scars.

Important psychological changes also occur during puberty. The personality can be altered as the developing child begins to crave independence. Ties to the family weaken, and the teenager becomes closer to his or her peer group. Sexual feelings can be strong and difficult to repress. In modern Western society, this is usually the time when the teenager may begin to experiment with tobacco, alcohol, drugs, or other means of achieving a "high," although in some groups the use of these substances begins much earlier. Substance abuse is a major problem throughout society, but it is particularly devastating among young people.

Sexual activity among teenagers is widespread and, combined with inadequate education about health issues and limited access to care, has led to significant medical problems. The incidence of sexually transmitted infections (STIs) is higher among teenagers than any other group. Teenage pregnancy is one of the most challenging issues in modern society.

If the pregnant teenager who continues her pregnancy is from a disadvantaged family background, she is even more likely than other teen mothers to receive little or no prenatal care. Risks of delayed or absent prenatal care can include a fetus that is not properly nourished. Additional risks can arise from a mother who smokes, drinks alcohol, or takes drugs throughout the pregnancy. In these cases, the child often may be born prematurely, with all the physical problems that premature birth involves. Hospital care of these infants is extremely costly, as is the maintenance of the mother and child if the baby survives.

Another important issue of teenage sexuality is the rapid spread of HIV, both as a sexually transmitted infection and as an infection passed from mother to baby.

Famous First

The nation's first nursing school based on Florence Nightingale's principles, the Training School for Nurses, opened at Bellevue in 1873. Sister Helen Bowdin of the All Saints Sisterhood in London was the first Superintendent. Sister Bowdin remained a faithful All Saints sister, later nursing for the community in South Africa.

Source: http://allsaintssisters.org/Who/OurHistory.aspx

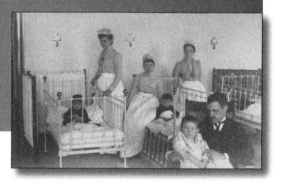

Diagnostic and Treatment Techniques

Pediatrics is one of the widest-ranging medical specialties, embracing virtually all major medical disciplines. Some pediatricians are generalists, and others specialize in certain disease areas, such as heart disease, kidney disease, liver disease, or skin problems.

Doctors and nurses specializing in neonatology, including advanced practice nurse practitioners with specialty certification in pediatrics or neonatology, have radically improved the survival rates of premature and low-weight babies. In neonatal care of the premature, the infant may have to be helped to breathe, fed through tubes, and otherwise maintained to allow it to develop.

Infectious diseases passed from the mother to the newborn child are a particular challenge. In some cases, such as with GBS and herpes infections, appropriate antibiotics and antiviral agents can be given. In others, such as with babies born with HIV, support measures and medications that help prevent the progress of the disease are the only procedures available.

Many birth defects and deformities can be repaired or at least ameliorated. Disorders such as cleft lip or palate, deformities of the skeletal system, heart defects, and other physical abnormalities often can be remedied by surgery. Certain structural malformations may require prosthetic devices and/or physical therapy.

The treatment of spina bifida depends on the seriousness of the condition; surgery may be required. With hydrocephalus, medication may be helpful, but most often a permanent shunt is implanted to drain fluids from the cranium. Before this technique was developed, the prognosis for babies with hydrocephalus was poor: More than half died, and a great many suffered from mental disability and physical impairment. Today, 70 percent or more live through infancy. Of these, about 40 percent have normal intelligence; the others are mentally disabled and may also have serious physical impairment.

There are no cures for cerebral palsy, but various procedures can improve the child's quality of life, exercise and counseling among them. Neither is there a cure for Down syndrome. If mental disability is profound, the child may have to be institutionalized. When a child with Down syndrome can be cared for at home in a loving family, his or her life can be improved.

SIDS continues to be a problem both in hospitals and in the home. The American Academy of Pediatrics' Back to Sleep campaign, in which parents are encouraged to place babies on their backs for sleeping, has been extremely successful, however, and has resulted in a decrease in the incidence of SIDS by 70 to 80 percent.

Managing the infectious diseases of childhood is one of the major concerns of pediatric providers, who are often called on to treat infections, for which they have a wide variety of antibiotics and other agents. Pediatric providers also seek to prevent infectious diseases through immunization. Medical authorities now recommend routine vaccination of all children in the United States against diphtheria, tetanus, pertussis, measles, mumps, rubella, poliomyelitis, pneumococcal pneumonia, *Hemophilus influenzae*, varicella, and hepatitis Aand B. Vaccines are also available against rabies, influenza, cholera, typhoid fever, plague, and yellow fever; these vaccines can be given to the child if there is a danger of infection. Vaccines for diphtheria, tetanus, and pertussis are generally given together in a combination called DTaP. Measles, mumps, and rubella vaccines are also given together as MMR. Repeated doses of some vaccines are necessary to ensure and maintain immunity.

Skin disorders of childhood, including teenage acne, are usually treated successfully at home with over-the-counter remedies. As with any disease, however, a severe skin disorder requires the attention of a trained provider.

Patients with diabetes mellitus type 1 are dependent on insulin throughout life. It is necessary for the pediatrician or attending nurse to teach both the parent and the patient how to inject insulin regularly, often several times a day. Furthermore, patients must monitor their blood and urine constantly to determine blood sugar levels. They must also adhere to stringent dietary regulations. This regimen of diet, insulin, and constant monitoring is often difficult for the child to learn and accept, but strict adherence is vital if the patient is to fare well and avoid the wide range of complications associated with diabetes.

Other serious conditions are now considered to be treatable. Modern pharmacology has greatly improved the prognosis of children with leukemia. Similarly, many children with growth disorders can be helped by treatments of growth hormone.

Medications and other treatment modalities for the mental disorders of childhood have improved in recent years. Mentally disabled children can often be taught to care for themselves, and some even grow up to live independently. Children with behavioral problems may be helped by clinicians specializing in child psychology or psychiatry.

The problems of sexuality, sexually transmitted infections, and pregnancy among teenagers have provoked a nationwide response in the United States among medical and sociological professionals. Safer-sex programs have been launched, and clinics specializing in counseling for teenage girls are in operation to stem the rise in teenage pregnancies.

Fast Fact

What's the age limit for a child being cared for by pediatric medical practitioners? It's an issue that has been studied. In 2017, the American Academy of Pediatrics made it official: cutting off care at 21 may not work for everyone.
Source: pediatrics.aappublications.org

Perspective and Prospects

Pediatrics affects virtually every member of society. Diseases that once raged through populations of all ages are now being controlled through the mass immunization of children. Some diseases of childhood are not yet controllable by vaccines, but research in this area is ongoing.

Childhood health is directly related to economics. Middle-class and upper-class children have ready access to professional care for any problems that may arise. The medical and psychological needs of disadvantaged children, however, especially those who live in inner cities, are often neglected. Many of these children are not being immunized fully and remain susceptible to diseases that are no longer a problem among the middle and upper classes.

In an effort to improve the medical care of disadvantaged children, some vaccines are being made available at low or no cost to inner-city families. Programs educate parents and teachers about the need for a child to receive the full dosage of vaccine. Computerized records allow authorities to keep track of the immunization status of individual children and to alert their parents when a follow-up inoculation is due.

The psychological problems of inner-city children, as well as children who live in disadvantaged rural areas, are at least as serious as the bodily diseases that threaten them. They may live in a universe of violence, deprivation, and drug addiction, and they might lack a stable family environment and opportunities for advancement. Pediatric providers at all levels can advocate for these youth by becoming involved in medical, psychological, and sociological outreach programs to help disadvantaged children.

C. Richard Falcon,
Lenela Glass-Godwin, M.W.S.

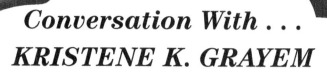

Conversation With . . .
KRISTENE K. GRAYEM

MSN, CNS, PPCNP-BC, RN-BC
President-Elect
American Academy of Ambulatory Care Nursing

Kristene K. Grayem has been a nurse for twenty-nine years and is currently Vice President of Population Health Management at Akron Children's Hospital in Akron, Ohio.

1. What was your individual career path in terms of education/training, entry-level job, or other significant opportunity?

I liked helping people and wanted a career where I could have a family and flexibility, so I entered nursing, which allows that. I earned a bachelor's degree in nursing (BSN) from the University of Akron. During my last semester, I worked with a preceptor in pediatrics and fell in love with pediatric nursing and the medical environment. I started as a staff nurse in the neonatal intensive care unit (NICU) at Akron Children's Hospital.

I have spent my entire career in the same organization. While in the NICU, I returned to school and received my master's degree in nursing (MSN) on a clinical nurse specialist (CNS) and pediatric primary care nurse practitioner (PNP) track. I was the first person to hold either role in my hospital's NICU. As a pediatric nurse practitioner, I cared for sub-intensive care patients—kids with chronic diseases such as respiratory problems.

Among my leadership roles, I served as a manager in our NeuroDevelopmental Center, in which we brought together neurology, physiatry, developmental pediatrics, and neuropsychology under one umbrella. We had a number of children with chronic conditions who needed those combined services. We formed a number of multidisciplinary clinics in the center, such as a cerebral palsy clinic. This allowed the kids to be seen by multiple specialists in one location.

Over time, my administrative roles increasingly moved into the area of ambulatory care, which is care delivered outside a hospital in outpatient settings. I worked with nurses and other health care professionals to develop and oversee outpatient facilities and programs.

Nationally, we have a movement toward value-based care and population health. This means the emphasis is on preventing illness, and the shift in payment is moving from a fee for service model—where we get paid for the things we do for patients—to being paid for keeping populations healthy. My current role allows me to lead my hospital in this shift. We have begun to partner with the community to address the social determinants of health –conditions in the environment that occur outside of health care such as employment, social support, housing, and transportation.

After serving on several of its task forces and its board of directors, I've recently become president-elect of the American Academy of Ambulatory Care Nursing, the only national organization committed to advancing the art and science of this nursing specialty. The organization has enhanced my personal and professional growth, and provided me with access to numerous resources, practice standards, and leadership education.

2. What are the most important skills and/or qualities for someone in your profession?

When I think of the skills that are important for nurses in the ambulatory care setting, I think of three C's: compassion, communication, and critical thinking. These nurses are the link between patients, families, caregivers, medical professionals, and the community. It is important that they have strong communication skills to make all of these connections and advocate for their patients. Being compassionate allows the nurse to feel a connection to patients and have sympathy for what they are going through. Ambulatory care nurses respond rapidly to high volumes of patients in a short span of time. Critical thinking skills allow the nurse to quickly assess the patients' situations and anticipate their needs.

3. What do you wish you had known going into this profession?

I talked with many individuals before entering the profession, so I do not think there is anything I wish I had known. Through my research, I decided to go the BSN route even though many diploma schools of nursing existed at the time. Sometimes there are reasons to do a two-year-degree such as if you work for an organization that will pay for you to earn a four-year degree. Nationally, a big push is underway for nurses to earn four-year degrees.

4. Are there many job opportunities in your profession? In what specific areas?

Overall, there are a lot of nursing positions. However, it can be a challenge at times for new graduates entering the pediatric market. Because of the nursing shortage, most pediatric organizations have developed a pipeline or feeder system for hiring nurses. If you're interested in pediatrics, nursing school is a great time to explore that opportunity early on.

Because 85 percent of health care occurs in the ambulatory setting, more and more opportunities are opening up for ambulatory care nurses. Settings are varied, such as hospital-based outpatient clinics/centers, solo/group medical practices, telehealth call centers, university hospitals, community hospitals, military and VA settings, managed care/HMOs/PPOs, colleges/educational institutions, patient homes, and freestanding facilities. Many ambulatory care nurses work from home and provide care to patients and families remotely. Ambulatory care nurses provide services ranging from wellness and prevention to illness and end-of-life care. Patients span all populations and age groups.

5. How do you see your profession changing in the next five years, how will technology impact that change, and what skills will be required?

As I mentioned, we are moving from fee-for-service to value-based pay. The adult care world already has been living in that space for a while. In conjunction, the ambulatory care nurse's role is constantly expanding. Ambulatory care has become increasingly complex as health care continues to shift from the inpatient to the outpatient setting. In the next five years there will be a greater focus on care coordination and transition management (CCTM). The registered nurse will play a key role in filling CCTM needs because patients can so easily fall through the cracks in today's health care system. Nurses are the health care providers who will help them navigate safely and get back home.

As the focus on decreasing health care costs continues, ambulatory care nurses will need to continue to bring care closer to where their patients and families live and work. Technology will play a major role in making that happen. It will not be feasible or sustainable to take the current in-person model to every neighborhood.

For pediatrics, this shift means we have a unique opportunity to influence young patients about how to take care of themselves, as well as to educate their parents and families. A big piece of pediatrics is teaching: discussing healthy environments and changes you can make to protect your health. We have the opportunity to think longterm about health and teach young people how to prevent diseases from forming now and worsening into adulthood.

6. What do you enjoy most about your job? What do you enjoy least about your job?

I love pediatric ambulatory care nursing! I love the changing environment and the population health shift we are experiencing, with the goal of keeping people healthy and out of the hospital. As a pediatric nurse practitioner, I have found that this model lines up perfectly with my training and personal philosophy. If we begin to use health care resources to prevent diseases from occurring in the first place, we will be a healthier population overall. I love helping patients and families reach their full potential. I love educating them about their conditions and how to manage them. I love helping them coordinate their care, teaching them to navigate the health care system, and advocate for themselves. I love helping others, and I appreciate the respect that our profession has with the public.

We have a unique opportunity to influence young people on how to take care of themselves as well as influence their parents and families. Pediatrics is both about disease prevention and disease management. The percentage of disease prevention is just much greater in pediatrics than in adults, and the proportion of disease management is significantly less in pediatrics than when dealing with adults.

What I like least about my job is the volume of work that occurs in the ambulatory care setting. Sometimes it feels like there is always more work than time to get it done, and I do not like feeling that I don't have enough time to give patients and families what they need.

7. Can you suggest a valuable "try this" for students considering a career in your profession?

Because it's difficult to shadow a nurse due to the privacy laws that protect patients and families, spend time talking with experienced nurses and asking them any questions you may have. If you enter nursing school, think about working as a nurse's aide in a setting where you think you may want to practice nursing. This will give you exposure to the profession and allow you to learn what it may be like to practice in that particular setting.

PREVENTIVE MEDICINE

Science and Profession

Modern preventive medicine is considered to exist at three levels within the health-care community. The initial level also known as primary prevention, has as its purpose to maintain health by removing the causes of or by protecting the community or individual from agents of disease and injury. These activities are no longer limited to the prevention of infection; yet they now include improvement in the environment and behavioral changes to reduce risk factors that contribute to chronic disease and injury. Examples of primary prevention are immunization programs. Other examples include risk reduction. For example, to reduce the risk of heart attack, one should refrain from smoking, be active, and reduce dietary fat intake-all wise primary prevention actions. Environmental risk reduction includes halting the loss of atmospheric ozone, reducing air and water pollution, and developing environmentally friendly technologies.

Secondary prevention seeks to detect and correct subclinical, adverse health conditions before they become manifest as disease, by reversing, halting, or retarding the disease process. A frequently used secondary prevention technique is health screening. Examples of secondary prevention aimed at detecting disease and early pathological changes include blood pressure measurement for hypertension (high blood pressure), fasting blood sugar screening for diabetes, mammography for breast cancer, PSA levels that detect prostate cancer, and glaucoma screening. In industry, a hearing test is used as a tool to prevent noise-induced hearing loss among the workforce. Once a potential health problem is identified, clinical preventive medicine techniques can be instituted to reverse the condition or prevent further progression.

Tertiary prevention attempts to minimize the adverse effects of conferred disease and disability. Coronary bypass surgery, vocational rehabilitation following a cerebrovascular accident (CVA), and treatment of an incapacitating mental illness are examples.

Specialists in the field of preventive medicine typically focus their efforts within the paradigms of primary and secondary prevention. In epidemiological terms, primary prevention results in a reduction of the incidence of a disease (the new cases occurring over time). Secondary prevention, on the other hand, results in a reduction of the prevalence of a disease (the number of actual people suffering from a particular illness at a given point in time).

Most health providers practice some degree of preventive medicine services. Pediatricians and pediatric nurse practitioners are practicing preventive medicine when they conduct "well-baby evaluations" and ensure that immunizations are current. Family medicine and primary care providers are promoting such services when they perform Pap testing or order mammograms. When smoking cessation is discussed as part of a clinical management plan and health care providers prescribe nicotine-patch regimens, that too is preventive medicine.

In the United States, approximately one thousand physicians specialize in general preventive medicine. Some use epidemiological methods to design and develop prevention programs that may feature a single intervention or may constitute a strategy that includes a multitude or matrix of screening technologies and interventions. Other preventive-medicine specialists including physician assistants and advanced practice nurses, provide services in a clinical setting by ordering a history and physical examination, which may include age- and gender-specific screening tests. The clinical preventive medicine specialist then can counsel the patient on lifestyle alterations recommended to preserve or improve health.

Within the United States, another field in preventive medicine is occupational medicine. Practicing in industry or private clinic settings, specialists in this field are concerned about preventing injury and illness as a result of the physical, biological, and chemical hazards that are present in the workplace. Should workers be injured or made ill as a result of their employment, the occupational health providers manage their treatment, rehabilitation, and return to work. Aerospace medicine providers limit their practice to those involved in the aeronautical and space transportation fields, including flight crews, support personnel, and passengers. The major task of these providers is to protect this population group from the adverse environmental conditions of flight, including pressure changes, reduced availability of oxygen, thermal stressors, accelerative forces, and psychosocial factors that might compromise performance.

Famous First

Sydney Hospital is a major hospital in Australia, located on Macquarie Street in the Sydney central business district. It is the oldest hospital in Australia, dating back to 1788, and has been at its current location since 1811. It first received the name Sydney Hospital in 1881.

Many of the 736 convicts who survived the voyage of the First Fleet from Portsmouth, England arrived suffering from dysentery, smallpox, scurvy, and typhoid. Soon after landing Governor Phillip and Surgeon-General John White established a tent hospital along what is now George Street in The Rocks to care for the worst cases. Subsequent convict boatloads had even higher rates of death and disease. A portable hospital which was prefabricated in England from wood and copper arrived in Sydney with the Second Fleet in 1790.

Source: https://en.wikipedia.org/wiki/Sydney_Hospital

Diagnostic and Treatment Techniques

An example of the application of preventive medicine is a comparison of the leading causes of death in the United States in 1900 with those in 2000. There was a major shift from deaths attributable to infectious disease at the beginning of the twentieth century to deaths attributable to chronic diseases that are often a reflection of individual lifestyle. Preventive medicine has proven itself effective in altering both the cause of death and the age at which death occurs. Accompanying this increased shift to chronic diseases such as cancer and heart disease, moreover, is a significant increase in the life expectancy of the population during the same century. Preventive medicine's focus is now on reducing morbidity and mortality from chronic diseases and accidents, particularly those in which an individual's lifestyle increases the risk for illness and death.

Disease prevention and health promotion are the two pillars supporting the discipline of preventive medicine. Beginning in 1987, a consortium was convened to begin to address a preventive medicine strategy to improve the health of Americans. The Institute of Medicine of the National Academy of Sciences worked with the US Public Health Service and numerous organizations to formulate health objective goals to be attained by the beginning of the twenty-first century. Once goals and objectives were established, the next task was to devise methods, technologies, and strategies to achieve the objectives by the year 2000. The resulting report was titled *Healthy People 2000: National Health Promotion and Disease Prevention Objectives* (1991).

The implementation of what was then known about disease prevention and health promotion was the central challenge. Good health is the result of reducing needless disease, injury, and suffering, resulting in an improved quality of life. A strategy of *Healthy People 2000* was to combine scientific knowledge, professional skills, community support, individual commitment, and the public will to achieve good health. This plan required reducing premature death, preventing disability, preserving the physical environment, and enabling Americans to develop healthy lifestyles. Three broad goals were detailed in *Healthy People 2000*: first, increase the healthy life span for Americans; second, reduce health disparity among Americans; and third, achieve access to preventive services for all Americans. A number of examples of the types of programs required to attain these goals were provided.

Tobacco use is the most important single preventable cause of death in the United States, accounting for more than four hundred thousand deaths annually. This loss of life is the equivalent of crashing two commercial jumbo jet airliners filled with passengers every day throughout the year. Smoking is a major risk factor for heart and lung disease; cancer of many organs, including the lungs, pancreas, and bladder; and stomach ulcers. Passive or environmental tobacco smoke is a recognized cause of cancer for exposed nonsmokers, and children in smoke-filled homes experience more ear infections. Tobacco use during pregnancy increases the risk of prematurity and low birth weight.

More than 3 million injuries occur annually in the US private sector, according to the Bureau of Labor Statistics; preliminary reports for 2013 indicate that more than four thousand deaths were attributable to work-related injuries. The occupations with the highest injury rates include mining, construction, agriculture, and transportation. The prevention of occupational disease and injury requires engineering controls, improved work practices, use of physical protective equipment, and monitoring of the work environment to identify emerging chemical and physical hazards.

In 2011 in the United States, nearly 575,000 people died from cancer. Nearly one in three Americans will experience a form of this disease. Research has helped to identify many risk factors related to cancer causation, such as tobacco use, low fiber intake, excess fat intake, sunburn, alcohol use, and exposure to chemical carcinogens. Information, education, and early detection have important roles in reducing both the incidence and the prevalence of cancer. Pap sampling, prostate examinations, mammography, and oral examinations are secondary prevention procedures that allow for early diagnosis and treatment. Such screening procedures, coupled with education and lifestyle changes, have the potential to reduce cancer rates significantly.

Healthy People 2010 (2000), like its predecessors, was developed through a broad consultation process, built on scientific knowledge and designed to measure programs over time. Its two primary goals included helping individuals of all ages increase life expectancy and improve their quality of life and eliminating health disparities among different segments of the population. The healthy life expectancy at birth increased slightly from 2000-1 to 2006-7 from about seventy-seven years of age to about seventy-eight among the overall population. There were no significant changes in health disparity across race and ethnicity in 70 percent of the objective areas. *Healthy People 2020* includes similar objectives to previous *Healthy People* reports, but also includes several new areas of focus, including adolescent health; lesbian, gay, bisexual, and transgender health; and sleep health. Improvement in health disparities tracked in Quality & Disparities Report 2014 has demonstrated improvement from 2010 to 2015 among uninsured adults from 18-64 years across all racial and ethnic groups and poverty levels (Cohen & Martinez, 2015; Access and Disparities in Access to Health Care, 2016).

Achieving the many objectives of *Healthy People* requires the dedicated commitment of preventive medicine specialists and the broader medical community. Enhanced effectiveness and efficiency of clinical preventive services, screening procedures, immunizations, consultation, and counseling can be achieved only through close relationships between the physician and both the community and the individual. To assess whether the goals and objectives for the prevention of disease and health promotion for the year 2010 were realistic, it would be helpful to review a success in the application of preventive medicine. Many of the objectives for 2010 were not met, but pesticide exposure, for example, was one area that showed marked improvement, from more than twenty-three thousand doctor's office visits in 1998 to less than fifteen thousand in 2008, though the total fell short of the 2010 target of less than twelve thousand visits. Another area in which preventative medicine seemed to be effective was the reduction of adolescent pregnancies, specifically among the black population. In 1996, the rate of pregnancy per one thousand girls between the ages of fifteen and seventeen was about 130; by 2005, the rate was less than eighty.

Coronary artery disease and its resultant heart attacks are preventable. A large national clinical trial of preventive medicine procedures known as MRFIT (multiple risk factor intervention trial) not only demonstrated the value of risk factor reduction in preventing disease but also demonstrated that the impact of established disease could be reversed. A subgroup of the MRFIT population made up of those who had established coronary artery disease at the start of the study had 55 percent fewer fatalities than did the control group when both were followed over seven years.

Preventive medicine interventions are not only cost-effective but relatively inexpensive as well. For example, coronary artery bypass surgery or a heart transplant costs many times more than preventive medicine rehabilitation and lifestyle modification programs. The same advantages also accrue for the prevention of strokes. Reducing salt intake, controlling high blood pressure, correcting obesity, performing regular exercise, and quitting smoking reduce the risk of stroke. The evidence clearly shows that preventive medicine reduces the death rate for heart attack and stroke and enhances quality of life.

Clinical preventive services have been designed based on the best available scientific evidence to promote the health of the individual while remaining practical and cost-effective. The 1989 publication of the *Guide to Clinical Preventive Services* (a document that has been updated several times) by the US Preventive Services Task Force was a major milestone on the road toward reducing premature death and disability. It has been well established that the majority of deaths among Americans under the age of sixty-five are preventable. The guide is the culmination of more than four years of literature review, debate, and synthesis and provides a listing of the clinical preventive services that clinicians should provide their patients. More than one hundred interventions are proposed to prevent sixty different illnesses and medical conditions. The guide is intended to be used by preventive medical specialists and other primary care clinicians. The recommendations are based on a standardized review of current scientific evidence and include a summary of published clinical research regarding the clinical effectiveness of each preventive service.

Although there have been sound clinical reasons for emphasizing prevention in medicine, studies have repeatedly demonstrated that physicians often fail to provide these services. Busy clinicians frequently have inadequate time with the patient to recommend or deliver a range of preventive services. Furthermore, until the publication of this guide, considerable controversy had existed within the medical community as to which services should be offered and how often. In the past, there was skepticism regarding the value of certain preventive interventions and their ability to reduce morbidity or mortality significantly. One result of this review process has been the clear evidence that reducing the incidence and severity of the leading causes of disease and disability is dependent on the personal health practices of individuals. The periodic health examination was once frequently referred to as an annual examination.

The *Guide to Clinical Preventive Services* tailors this examination to the individual needs of the patient and considers factors such as age, gender, and risk. Consequently, a uniform health examination is not recommended. The examination for those between forty and sixty-four years of age is scheduled on a one- to three-year basis, with the more frequent examinations scheduled for those in high-risk groups. Although the examination is not comprehensive, it is focused on identifying the leading causes of illness and disability among people in this age group. During the physical examination, particular attention would be paid to the skin of those individuals at high risk for excessive exposure to sunlight or with a family or personal history of skin cancer. A complete oral cavity examination would be appropriate for individuals using tobacco or consuming excessive amounts of alcohol. Counseling would be provided on such items as diet and exercise, substance abuse, sexual practices, and injury prevention.

According to the National Diabetes Clearinghouse, approximately 28 million persons in the United States suffer from diabetes; however, 7 million of them are unaware of their condition. Diabetes is the seventh leading cause of death in the United States, accounting for nearly seventy thousand deaths per year. In addition, it is the leading cause of kidney failure, blindness, and amputations. The detection of diabetes in asymptomatic persons provides an opportunity to prevent or delay the progress of the disease and its complications. The *Guide to Clinical Preventive Services* recommends an oral glucose tolerance test for all pregnant women between the twenty-fourth and twenty-eighth weeks of their pregnancy. Routine screening for diabetes in asymptomatic nonpregnant adults, using blood or urine tests, is not recommended. Periodic fasting blood sugar measurements may be appropriate in persons at high risk for diabetes mellitus, such as the markedly obese, persons with a family history of diabetes, or women with a history of diabetes during pregnancy.

Fast Fact

Infection is expensive: infectious diseases acquired in a health care setting cost US hospitals between $28.4 and $45 million every year.

Source: silverbook.org

Famous First

Kate Marsden (13 May 1859 – 26 May 1931) was a British missionary, explorer, writer and nursing heroine. Supported by Queen Victoria and Empress Maria Fedorovna she investigated a cure of leprosy. She set out on a journey from Moscow to Siberia to find a cure, creating a leper treatment centre in Siberia. In 1895, Marsden founded a charity, still active today, now known as the St Francis Leprosy Guild. In 1897, she returned to Siberia where she opened a hospital for lepers in Vilyuysk. She never fully recovered from her journey but she recorded all the details in her book *On Sledge and Horseback to Outcast Lepers*, published in 1893. She died in London on 26 March 1931, and was buried in Hillingdon cemetery in Uxbridge on 31 March. Her grave had been overgrown for many years and covered in bushes. These have now been cleared and her grave, and the ones nearby are now accessible.

Source: https://en.wikipedia.org/wiki/Kate_Marsden

Perspective and Prospects

In the mid-nineteenth century, John Snow provided one of the best examples of preventive medicine by applying what could be called observational epidemiology. During a rather severe cholera epidemic in London, Snow observed an unusual pattern of disease that appeared to be dependent on the particular water supply company providing water to the neighborhood. Recognizing that there was a high incidence of cholera in the Broad Street area, he was able to determine that most of the disease was associated with those families depending on the Broad Street pump for their drinking water. It has been said that he simply removed the handle on the pump and was able to control the epidemic in that area. His discovery occurred before there was a clear understanding of the relationship of bacteria or germs to infectious disease.

Another historic example of the application of preventive medicine was the control of smallpox. In the late eighteenth century, Edward Jenner observed that the milkmaids in the English countryside were not scarred by the scourge of smallpox. On further examination, he determined that these young women had years earlier been infected with cowpox and thus had been spared the more serious smallpox infection. He then advocated intentional infection with the cowpox vaccine. Years later, using this preventive medicine application, the World Health Organization was able to institute a worldwide eradication of smallpox. The last case of smallpox reported in the world was in October, 1977, marking the first time that a major human disease had been eradicated. Neither the control of cholera in London by Snow nor the eradication of smallpox resulted from medical or surgical treatment of a disease. These results were obtained because of the application of the principles of preventive medicine and public health.

Roy L. DeHart, MD, MPH,
Carolynn Bruno

Conversation With . . .
VICKI ALLEN

MSN, CIC
Infection Prevention Director
CaroMont Regional Medical Center
Gastonia, North Carolina

*Vicki Allen has been a nurse for twenty-four years and has worked in the area of
infection control for twenty years.*

1. What was your individual career path in terms of education/training, entry-level job, or other significant opportunity?

When I was growing up, women were basically teachers or nurses, and I just always
thought I was going to be a nurse. I went into practical nursing after high school with a
one-year degree from the Watts Hospital School of Nursing in Durham, North Carolina.
After I entered the field, I realized there is a lot more to nursing, but one benefit of
practical nursing is being in a clinical setting from the beginning.

After my family moved to Pennsylvania, I worked in an acute-care rehabilitation facility,
but after a few years I realized I needed more advanced education. Starting with an
associate degree in nursing from Excelsior College, an online program, I completed my
clinical in Syracuse, New York. As I looked for more opportunity as a registered nurse
(RN), an employee health and infection control position opened up. I had never heard
of it. One of the nurses I knew who worked in that area was interested in my coming to
work with her. I did, and I liked it.

My job duties included employee health, worker's comp, and risk management. I liked
the interaction with employees. The nurse I worked for was focused only on infection
control. I attended her meetings but the things that were discussed—pathogens,
organisms, cultures—were not topics nurses learn in-depth in nursing school. I
became more involved in the infection control world by covering for her when she was
on vacation.

When my family moved to northwest Arkansas, I acquired a job as an infection control
and employee health nurse for an acute-care rehab hospital. In that capacity, I quickly
learned that I needed to collaborate with other nurses to learn the job, so I began
to network with infection control nurses in that region. During that time, one of the
infection control practitioners—a microbiologist with whom I'd become acquainted—
left her position to go back to research. I applied for her job and was hired at an acute-
care hospital. That led me into full-time focused work on infection control. I earned
my CIC certification (Certified in Infection Control) through the Certification Board of
Infection Control and Epidemiology. It's one of the few nursing certifications that require

retesting of the certification exam boards every five years. By the time we left Arkansas ten years later, I had been the infection prevention program coordinator for an acute-care hospital system for six years.

My husband and I moved back East briefly, and I stayed in infection prevention and control in acute-care settings. During this time, I earned my bachelor's degree in nursing science from Kaplan University, and then moved to Texas to acquire management experience and finish my master's degree in nursing education at the University of Texas at Tyler. I also was employee health manager for a four-hospital system. In 2008, we relocated to Charlotte, North Carolina, where I was hired as the manager for the Infection Prevention Program at a community 435-bed acute-care hospital, where I am still employed.

In the past, infection prevention nurses focused on culture surveillance and identifying events, but there wasn't a lot done with the information outside of reporting to internal committees. For instance, how many positive urine cultures were associated with a Foley catheter? Not a lot of benchmarking or corrective action was performed.

Then federal and state laws began to require mandatory reporting of health care-associated events and started to penalize hospitals for subpar benchmarks. This change got the attention of senior management and hospital leaders, who began the shift in focus from infection control to infection prevention. Infection preventionists (IPs) became significantly more focused on education of infection prevention geared toward patients and visitors, staff, physicians, students, and volunteers. Currently, this education remains a primary element of infection prevention.

Infection prevention is everyone's responsibility, so needless to say in a health care setting, there is a tremendous amount of collaboration needed across the continuum to assist with writing policies, developing signage for various infection prevention measures such as visitor restriction, and conducting required orientations, training, and workshops. IPs may be called upon to provide clarification to patients at the bedside.

2. What are the most important skills and/or qualities for someone in your profession?

Flexibility is a requirement. You may have an agenda for the day but, depending on what's happening, you may have to put it on hold. You must have the ability to work autonomously. Many people do not understand the job of an IP or the focus on evidence-based practice, recommendations, and rules and regulations. You must also be able to collaborate with people in other departments in the hospital. You may write the policies and procedures, but you are dependent on others to follow the parameters they set.

3. What do you wish you had known going into this profession?

It would be helpful if educational entities would provide more focus on the importance of infection prevention and the elements involved in a health care setting to protect patients and staff. Initially, I did not have much of an idea what was involved, or an understanding of how much infection prevention affects all areas of a hospital.

4. Are there many job opportunities in your profession? In what specific areas?

Currently, the opportunities are limited but growing. There will be more opportunities expanding hospital programs and in health care industry outside hospitals in an effort to maintain the same standard of care. More and more recruiters and headhunters specialize in finding and placing IPs. Infection prevention specialists are increasingly entering into the community health setting. There is a lot of growth in clinical settings including doctor's offices due to the expectation that they maintain the same standard of care as a hospital. There are increased opportunities as an IP consultant to do such tasks as filling in for someone on medical or maternity leave, or for preparing for a site visit by an accrediting agency.

5. How do you see your profession changing in the next five years, how will technology impact that change, and what skills will be required?

Primarily, I see more community-based clinical integration. Some larger organizations have IPs traveling from clinic to clinic. A lot of health care that was previously performed in hospitals is moving to ambulatory settings such as surgical centers. We may see more home-based surveillance.

6. What do you enjoy most about your job? What do you enjoy least about your job?

The variety and autonomy are my favorites. IP is a very rewarding job. I enjoy the collaboration and integration with other personnel and departments throughout the hospital system.

I least like the paperwork. But, overall, there's not a day that I think that I just don't want to come to work.

7. Can you suggest a valuable "try this" for students considering a career in your profession?

One of the most valuable tools for students is job shadowing. I've had experience with interns, and they are always surprised at how broad our reach and obligations are within the organization. Some have even elected to further their education and/or change their major focus based on what they've learned in our department.

There is a tremendous amount of information available online for health care personnel and consumers on infection prevention, including the website for the Association for Professionals in Infection Control and Epidemiology at www.apic.org, as well as www.cdc.gov.

PRIMARY CARE

Health care system

Primary care is a patient's entry point into the health care system. A primary care practitioner can be one of several different types of medical professionals and usually provides for the patient's basic medical care and coordinates care with other providers for more complex health situations. The primary care practitioner is the one the patient sees for routine exams and common conditions such as ear or throat infections. It is usually the primary care practitioner who diagnoses more serious and/or chronic conditions such as heart disease or diabetes and refers the patient to a specialist for specific care for these conditions.

Background

A primary care practitioner is usually the person individuals refer to as their "doctor". This medical practitioner may be a physician, an internist, a nurse practitioner, or a physician's assistant. Some patients choose a primary care provider often referred to as a PCP—who has the educational background to deal with specialized populations. These may include pediatricians for children, family health providers, adult health providers and individuals specializing in gerontology for older adults. The PCP provides for all of the patient's primary health care needs. These include well-checks or check-ups, routine immunizations, screening, and care for common illnesses such as viruses, muscle and joint pains, skin eruptions and other infections. The primary care provider will also be the first point of contact for many sudden illnesses or injuries that do not require emergency room care.

It is often the primary care provider who diagnoses more serious illnesses or determines that a person's health concern requires a specialist's care. For instance, a patient who complains of foot pain may be referred to a podiatrist for more in-depth care. The routine tests ordered by a primary care provider either as part of an annual medical exam or in response to a health issue can also identify more serious illnesses that require follow-up with a specialist.

A primary care practitioner may also treat a patient for certain chronic conditions, such as high blood pressure, diabetes controlled or uncontrolled gastric problems, musculoskeletal issues, and others. It is important to keep your PCP involved in your care especially if you are referred to a specialist. This involvement provides coordination of care that can help prevent errors and improve health outcomes.

Overview

The focus of primary care is on the overall health of the individual rather than on one particular system or part of the body. The PCP coordinates care for the patient, directing the patient to specialists when needed while serving as a central point of contact that can avoid duplication of care and help prevent errors. For example, a patient who has pain in both a foot and a shoulder may see a podiatrist for the foot problem and an orthopedic specialist for the shoulder. If the two specialists are coordinating with the PCP, they might discover that both are prescribing similar pain medications for the patient, which could lead to medical complications.

The PCP is also an advocate for the patient when that patient is enmeshed in the larger health care system. A hospitalized patient who has concerns that are not being addressed by a surgeon and a patient who is having difficulty getting a health insurance claim paid can both benefit from the knowledge and intervention of the primary care provider.

Another important function of a primary care provider is a focus on prevention. Their emphasis on the overall health of the patient means that the PCP makes a point of being aware of what routine tests or immunizations the patient may need. They can also take note of other potential health risks, such as smoking, alcohol consumption, and weight issues, and provide guidance and care to help the patient avoid future health issues.

Medical fields include more primary care physicians than specialists. This means that PCPs help provide greater accessibility to health care for a wider portion of the public. They can also provide some level of specialized care for those who would otherwise go without, such as patients without insurance or low-income patients who lack the funds for copayments for specialists. This helps to increase access to care and improve the overall quality of health care available in an area.

The intervention of the PCP can also help to minimize the number of specialist visits that are required, either by identifying and initiating treatment for conditions before they become serious or by performing some of the follow-up that might otherwise be handled by a specialist. This care helps to improve the patient's overall health and reduce health care costs. The level of trust that can be built between a practitioner and a patient he or she sees regularly can also benefit health care outcomes by encouraging patient cooperation with treatment.

While primary care can be an important facet of improved health care availability and outcomes, reduced costs, and greater patient satisfaction, some potential issues exist. One is the lack of available PCPs. The need for more primary providers is outstripping the supply of new practitioners in the United States,. It can also be difficult to attract primary care providers to rural areas where income levels and the scarcity of specialists and medical facilities makes the need greatest.

Janine Ungvarsky,
Geraldine Marrocco

Industries

COMPLEMENTARY AND ALTERNATIVE HEALTH CARE INDUSTRY

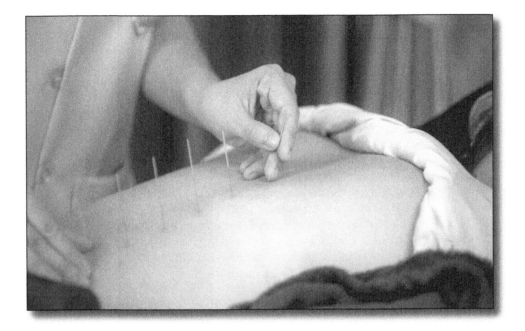

The complementary and alternative health or medical care (CAM) industry produces and applies a wide range of herbal, vitamin, and food remedies; patient-practiced therapies; and practitioner services. They are not considered part of conventional medical practice, although complementary care may be used along with it. Alternative health care, by contrast, is used in place of conventional medical care and can interfere with it. For example, herbal therapy could interact with conventional medications. Patients turn to CAM therapies when conventional medical care is not relieving their symptoms, such as chronic pain. In the United States, these therapies are most often used by well-educated Caucasian women.

History of the Industry

Some CAM therapies have been in practice since the beginning of human civilization. Herbs have been used to treat and prevent illness for at least as long as the concept of an herb has existed. Midwives, or their ancient equivalent, were most likely the first nonfamily members to assist in the delivery of infants. The ancient Chinese developed a medical system that included acupuncture for the treatment of their health problems.

Early physicians were not interested in delivering infants. As a result, untrained midwives delivered all infants until the 1700's. If a mother had complications of delivery, she often died because midwives lacked medical skills. In the 1700's, surgeons began to deliver infants for the wealthy. New York City began to require that midwives be licensed. In 1799, doctors Valentine Seaman and William Shippen opened a school to train midwives. In the early 1800's, physicians began to take over the delivery of infants for the middle class. The practice of midwifery declined. Increasingly, mothers delivered their infants in hospitals.

In the 1970's, women clamored for the opportunity to demedicalize childbirth and to deliver their infants at home. Nursing schools began to offer programs in nurse-midwifery. Both nurse-midwives and nonnurse midwives received formal training. Physicians fought to hold onto childbirth, and laws were created to limit the practice of midwifery. Many states required that midwives practice only under the supervision of physicians. Other states licensed nonnurse midwives and permitted them to practice independently.

There is evidence that acupuncture has been practiced for at least eight thousand years. From 650 to 692 c.e., the development and practice of acupuncture increased, and acupuncture schools were established. In 1911, Western medicine was introduced to China, and acupuncture and herbal medicines experienced a decline. In 1950, the Chinese merged Western medicine with acupuncture. Gradually, acupuncture came to the United States. Starting in 1971, acupuncture began to be well known in the United States, and by 1997, it was widely available.

Chiropractic care was recognized as a medical treatment in 1895. It was introduced by Daniel David Palmer. Spinal adjustment is the basis of chiropractic medicine, and it is used to treat a wide variety of conditions. It is thought that spinal adjustment has been practiced since ancient times. Palmer defined the practice of chiropractics and started a training school. In the early 1900's, states began regulating and licensing chiropractors.

Homeopathy was developed by a German physician, Samuel Hahnemann, in 1796. It was introduced to the United States in 1828 by John Franklin Gray. It was quite popular with patients in the early 1900's, in part because conventional medical treatments were often ineffective. Homeopathy is frequently criticized by conventional medicine as being ineffective. Very little research has been done to establish its effectiveness.

Naturopathy was introduced to the United States in the late 1800's by Benedict Lust, although it had been practiced in Germany earlier. In the early 1900's, it was widely accepted, but after that it experienced a decline in popularity. Beginning in the 1970's, there has been increased interest in natural treatments such as those proposed by naturopaths.

Hypnosis was originally performed as part of the system of Chinese medicine. It was not studied and practiced until the 1800's. James Braid, a Scottish surgeon, began this exploration. Subsequently, the study of hypnosis became popular in France. One of the students of the French school of hypnosis was Sigmund Freud. Hypnosis was first studied in the United States in 1933 by Clark L. Hull.

The Industry Today

CAM is fairly popular today, in part because conventional medical care is sometimes impersonal and fragmented. Consumers want to be treated as whole people, not just body parts. Stress-related symptoms are common in contemporary society. Some conventional medical treatments do not cure patients or treat their symptoms effectively. CAM practitioners practice holistic medicine, meaning that they base their treatments on the total needs of each individual patient, rather than concentrating only on the particular system or body part that demonstrates symptoms. Patients' medical and psychological histories, body types, and family histories are all considered when treating them. CAM providers have been successful in treating some health issues that conventional medicine has been unable to cure.

Acupuncture is used to treat a wide variety of conditions, such as depression, chronic pain, and the nausea caused by chemotherapy. An acupuncturist inserts many very fine needles into various locations on the body to assist the flow of chi, or life energy. Acupuncturists work in individual or group practices, and some are employed by hospitals in their integrative therapy clinics. Persons with no medical training must have at least two thousand hours of acupuncture training in order to practice acupuncture. Some physicians, dentists, and other medical practitioners train in the practice of acupuncture. If they use it in their regular practices, they need one to two hundred hours of training. If they plan to devote their practices solely to acupuncture, they require fifteen hundred hours of training. Most states require licensure for acupuncturists.

Acupuncture is used to treat a wide variety of conditions, such as depression, chronic pain, and the nausea caused by chemotherapy. (©Dreamstime.com)

Most midwives choose to become nurse-midwives to avoid the legal limitations placed upon nonnurse midwives. Nurse-midwives have master's degrees in nursing with majors in midwifery. They are usually employed by either physician practices or hospitals. In physicians' offices, nurse-midwives provide pre- and postnatal care, and they also assist in delivery rooms. They perform only normal vaginal deliveries. If there appears to be a complication during childbirth, a physician takes over the delivery. Nurse-midwives do not perform surgery. They are permitted to prescribe medications in some states. Some states permit nurse-midwives and nonnurse midwives to have their own practices and to participate in home childbirth.

Chiropractors practice either alone or with other chiropractors. They can also practice as part of hospital-based integrative medical clinics, but this is not as common. Chiropractors work on the musculoskeletal and nervous systems. Frequently, they use spinal realignment as a treatment to improve nerve conduction. Potential chiropractors must have at least ninety semester hours of undergraduate study, or bachelor's degrees, before they can enter chiropractic programs. Such programs provide four years of training in the medical sciences and public health, and they grant the degree of doctor of chiropractic (DC). Licensure is required for the practice of chiropractic in all U.S. states and the District of Columbia.

The basis of the practice of homeopathy is the belief that "like cures like" and that the body is able to heal itself of symptoms by confronting similar symptoms. Homeopaths use very dilute solutions of substances that come from plants, minerals, or animals to treat their patients. Homeopathy is often used to treat allergies, rheumatoid arthritis, irritable bowel syndrome, minor injuries, and muscle sprains. It is never used to treat persons with severe, acute injuries or serious illnesses such as heart disease or cancer. Homeopaths may be medical doctors who have taken homeopathy courses, or they may be nonphysicians who have taken four-year courses in homeopathy. Only three states license homeopaths: Arizona, Connecticut, and Nevada. Licensure for homeopathy does not include standards for practice.

Naturopaths believe that an imbalance in one's life is the cause of illness and that by restoring a natural balance, the illness can be cured. The balance is restored by natural treatments and improvements in lifestyle. Naturopaths do not perform any surgical procedures. They are trained as general practitioners or primary care providers and are able to treat a wide range of conditions. A bachelor's degree, including completion of premedical courses, is required for admission to a school of naturopathy. Naturopathy students study for four to five years. Often, the fifth year of study is devoted to a specialty such as obstetrics. There are only three or four schools of naturopathy in the United States and Canada. A number of states have licensure requirements and standards for practice. These standards include education and passing the Naturopathic Physicians Licensing Examinations (NPLEX). The areas requiring licensure are Alaska, Arizona, California, Connecticut, Hawaii, Idaho, Kansas, Maine, Montana, New Hampshire, Oregon, Utah, Vermont, Washington, the District of Columbia, Puerto Rico, and the U.S. Virgin Islands.

Hypnosis consists of guided relaxation and focused attention that induces a trancelike state in which the subject blocks out external stimuli. It is thought that hypnosis increases suggestibility and helps subjects change their thoughts. Not everyone is susceptible to hypnosis. Hypnosis is used to achieve weight loss and to treat addictions to cigarettes, alcohol, and drugs; insomnia; anxiety; asthma; and irritable bowel syndrome. Hypnosis has been successfully used to alleviate the pain of childbirth. There are no educational requirements for hypnotists in the United States, so consumers must evaluate hypnotists themselves. Some psychologists, counselors, psychiatrists, and dentists are trained in hypnosis. Four states—Colorado, Connecticut, Indiana, and Washington—require licensure for hypnotists, and some other states regulate their practice.

An important issue for CAM providers and recipients is health insurance coverage. Many health insurance plans do not cover any CAM therapies. Of the classes of those therapies, chiropractic and acupuncture are the most likely to be covered by health insurance, but insurance plans may limit the number and frequency of treatments for which they will pay. Other plans may contract with specific CAM providers and obtain discounts for their members. Most CAM treatments must be paid for directly by patients.

In the past, some animosity has existed between CAM providers and conventional medical providers. While some research has been done to evaluate CAM practices, it has not been adequate to reach definitive conclusions. Moreover, some existing studies do not validate their hypotheses. If a patient chooses a CAM treatment over conventional medical treatment for a serious condition, the patient's life can be at risk. Some efforts are being made by the National Center for Complementary and Alternative Medicine (NCCAM) to increase CAM research. Meanwhile, some conventional medical institutions such as hospitals are setting up CAM clinics in order to integrate CAM therapies with conventional medicine, and some conventional medical providers use CAM treatments in their practices.

Industry Market Segments

Unlike most industries, CAM providers fall entirely within two segments: small or large. CAM providers either operate small practices of one or several providers or they operate as part of hospitals or hospital systems. Thus, there are no midsize businesses in this industry.

Small Businesses

The majority of CAM providers are employed in small businesses. The typical model for a CAM practice is an office with one to five providers of the same type of CAM care and, possibly, some support staff. Some CAM providers go into practice with other CAM providers in holistic care clinics. CAM provider offices are most commonly located in cities. Nurse-midwives may work in physician practices, which are also small businesses.

Clientele Interaction. CAM providers tend to form close relationships with their patients because of the holistic nature of their practices. One of the draws of these practitioners is the time that they spend with their patients and the individualized treatment they provide. Typically, CAM providers spend thirty minutes or more getting to know their patients. Since they often provide regular, frequent services, they rely on having good relationships with their clients to maintain their businesses.

Typical Number of Employees. In order to keep business costs low, CAM providers have few employees. A practice usually consists of one to five providers and three or fewer support staff. Providers may have receptionists to make appointments, or they may make their own appointments. They may use answering machines in lieu of phone staff. With the exception of nurse-midwives and possibly chiropractors, many CAM providers operate cash-only businesses, so they do not require billing staffs either. Those providers that need to bill health insurers generally must hire billing persons and purchase computer software to keep track of their bills. They are likely to order their own supplies and equipment and perform their own marketing. They are likely to advertise on the Internet, at health fairs, at grocery stores, at health food stores, at beauty salons or day spas, or in smaller, alternative newspapers or magazines.

Nurse-midwives who are employed by physicians are not involved with running their offices unless they are very small. Many physician practices have staffs of six to ten persons who work as receptionists, billing staff, and medical assistants to each physician. Some practices may have business managers. Each physician practice either has a single billing person or uses a professional billing service, depending on its size. Larger physician groups may have their own billing services. They send claims to health insurers for most of the services that they provide. Chiropractors tend to operate in a similar manner to physicians. They usually have receptionists and several medical assistants. They accept cash payments from some patients, but they also require either billing persons or billing services.

Traditional Geographic Locations. CAM providers tend to have offices in locations where physicians and other medical providers have offices. Most of their offices may be in cities, but they also may be in the suburbs. They are less likely to be located in rural areas, since they want to be conveniently accessible to their clients. Holistic health clinics with multiple CAM providers are frequently located in college towns, where residents are thought to be more open-minded about nontraditional health care providers. Hospital-based CAM clinics are usually in separate office buildings owned by their parent hospitals, usually on or near the hospitals' campuses. Physician offices where nurse-midwives may be employed are often in large medical office buildings near hospitals.

Pros of Working for a Small Practice. Practitioners working in small practices have significant control over their business. They are, generally speaking, their own bosses. Even in partnerships of five or six providers, few decisions—such as hiring receptionists or choosing a location—need to be made jointly. Otherwise, each provider maintains responsibility for his or her own patients and is ultimately answerable only to him- or herself. They set their own hours and determine their own workloads—although nurse-midwives and chiropractors are more likely to work typical business hours. In addition, practitioners working in small practices usually are able to develop closer and better relationships with their clients, since they are not insulated from them by office staff. Nurse-midwives who work in physician practices and chiropractors in practice with more than three other chiropractors are exceptions to this principle because such practices usually place several staff members between clients and their providers.

Cons of Working for a Small Practice. The owners of a small practice are at significant risk of financial loss if they cannot operate profitably. One- or two-person practices cannot afford to hire many staff. As a result, they must fulfill many business roles, including accountant, secretary, receptionist, supply clerk, marketer, business manager, and possibly housekeeper. These additional responsibilities increase practitioners' working hours. All CAM practitioners must meet state licensing requirements, including those for education. Malpractice insurance is necessary for all medical providers, including CAM providers, and it can be a significant expense. In the provision of health care, malpractice is always a risk.

Clientele Interaction. CAM providers strive to achieve supportive and caring relationships with their patients. The goal of CAM providers is to care for patients as complex, whole entities, and this can only be achieved if they take the time to get to know each patient individually. Typically, patient care sessions are scheduled to last thirty minutes to one hour. Much CAM business is repeat business, and new patients are often referred by friends who use the provider, so maintaining good relationships is necessary.

Pros of Working for a Hospital. Large businesses such as hospitals are departmentalized, allowing each employee to perform a single job role and concentrate on a narrow area of expertise. CAM providers at such facilities need only provide care and need not attend to financial record keeping, patient scheduling, or ordering supplies. CAM providers working in hospitals usually enjoy government-mandated benefits, paid vacation, and sick time. Nurse-midwives can count on consistent paychecks, and, in integrative care departments, providers may also receive consistent paychecks, depending on their contracts. Hospitals provide continuing education for their staffs, so employees may have access to free classes on a wide variety of topics, including computer software. Hospitals always have employee cafeterias, and they sometimes subsidize the cost of the food.

Cons of Working for a Hospital. Hospital workloads may be inconsistent. Employees in labor and delivery units may wait with nothing to do at some times, only to find themselves facilitating multiple simultaneous births at other times. Similarly, in integrative care departments, providers may not be very busy part of the day, but then, at other times, they may be overloaded, forcing patients to wait for care. This occurs because hospitals experience peak hours, as patients often come before or after work, or on their lunch hour. Hospital employees must all generally work on-call shifts, and they may not be able to leave work on schedule.

Hospitals are dramatically more bureaucratic than small practices. Business decisions are made by administrators at a level that is unrelated to direct patient care. Thus, staffing may be reduced, and hours and policies may be changed by hospital executives without consulting providers. Individual employees in large organizations may have relatively little control over their work lives. It is unusual for professional providers, such as CAM providers, to be unionized, even if other hospital employees are.

Organizational Structure and Job Roles

There are two settings where CAM providers are employed, private practices and general hospitals. In smaller offices, either providers themselves or office managers must fulfill multiple roles to keep the businesses running. In larger offices, several staff members will fulfill these roles. A majority of CAM practitioners work in private practices.

Some CAM practitioners are employed by general hospitals. Some work in integrative medicine departments, while nurse-midwives are generally employed in labor and delivery departments. In hospitals, most business functions are performed by hospital staff.

The following umbrella categories apply to the organizational structure of businesses in the complementary and alternative health care industry, including general hospitals that employ CAM providers:

- Management
- Public Relations
- Marketing
- Human Resources
- Housekeeping
- Maintenance
- Information Technology
- Nursing
- Billing

Nursing

Some CAM providers employ nurses to assist them in caring for patients in their offices. Not all CAM offices have nursing staffs. CAM office nurses may be registered nurses (RNs), licensed practical nurses (LPNs), or nurses' aides.

Hospital nursing staffs provide direct patient care throughout their hospitals. Hospitals employ nurse managers, nursing supervisors, staff nurses, and patient care assistants. Nursing supervisors and nurse managers must have bachelor's and master's degrees in nursing or related fields, as well as experience in nursing, usually including emergency care. Nurse clinicians and nurse midwives have master's degrees in nursing. Staff nurses have completed accredited nursing programs. Nurses are usually paid by the hour, although some nursing supervisors and nurse managers are paid annual salaries.

Patient care assistants are trained by hospitals to assist nursing staffs. They are taught technical skills, such as taking electrocardiograms and drawing blood for testing. They also provide direct care to patients. LPNs are trained in one-year programs and lack the medical science knowledge that RNs have. Nurses' aides are trained by hospitals, nursing homes, or technical schools in programs that last several months. Patient care assistants, LPNs, and nurses' aides are paid by the hour.

Nursing occupations may include the following:

- Office Nurse
- Nursing Supervisor
- Nurse Manager
- Nurse Clinician/Nurse Midwife
- Registered Nurse
- Licensed Practical Nurse
- Patient Care Assistant

Industry Outlook

The outlook for this industry shows it to be in decline in the United States. From 1997 through 2007, the use of CAM practitioners decreased by about 50 percent, although self-care CAM measures increased. CAM practitioner visits, among survey respondents in 2007, totaled 1,592 visits per 1,000 adults. One-third of out-of-pocket dollars spent on CAM services were for practitioner visits. Acupuncture did not follow this general downward trend: Acupuncturist office visits increased during the same period and reached a total of 17.6 million visits in 2007. This rise in the number of acupuncture treatments may be due to an increase in the number of acupuncturists, as well as increased media discussion of acupuncture and increased health insurance coverage for acupuncture.

Several factors could affect the long-term outlook of the CAM industry. The U.S. population continues to age, and large numbers of baby boomers are turning 62 and becoming eligible to receive Social Security payments. The recession of 2007-2009 significantly decreased the retirement savings of many Americans. The Patient Protection and Affordable Care Act of 2010 (PPACA) is expected to lead to more than 30 million uninsured Americans gaining health insurance. More than 20 million Americans will still lack insurance, however. Because CAM treatments may be less expensive than conventional treatments but may also be ineligible for health insurance coverage or reimbursement, these events may have unpredictable and conflicting effects upon the CAM market. However, in general, health care utilization of all sorts is expected to increase after 2014 when the major provisions of the PPACA go into effect.

Market analyses may also be distorted by a lack of data on nurse-midwives and nonnurse midwives. Nurse-midwives, who most often work within the realm of traditional medicine, may not be perceived as CAM practitioners. Surveys may also be distorted if they include only participants who are either middle- or upper class. Working-class Americans are less likely to respond to surveys, and they are more likely to use nonnurse midwives, than are members of other classes. Survey respondents may also be reluctant to admit to visiting CAM practitioners as a result of social stigmas against those practitioners in some groups. Nevertheless, it appears that the demand for treatment by CAM providers other than acupuncturists and possibly midwives is in decline.

In other countries, the use of herbal medicines represents the highest percentage of CAM treatments. International data on CAM use, other than herbal treatments, is limited, particularly for less affluent countries. The World Health Organization reports that in countries other than the United States, traditional medicine is responsible for at least 80 percent of medical care. China embraces the practice of acupuncture. Great Britain and Australia provide some data on their use of CAM practitioners.

Employment Advantages

Americans' consumption of acupuncture is increasing, and acupuncture is increasingly being covered by health insurers, as research is published demonstrating its effectiveness. Acupuncturists require significantly less training and less financial investment than do medical doctors, and they may be able to develop better relationships with their patients than many doctors are able to. Careers in midwifery may appeal to people who wish to support maternity patients who dislike conventional medical techniques for delivery. It can be very exciting to assist women in childbirth and witness one of the major events of life. Nurse-midwives may have significantly greater career options than nonnurse midwives, however, especially given that nonnurses are not allowed to practice midwifery in many states.

While other CAM providers are less in demand, people who are able to succeed in such careers may find them rewarding. CAM providers help people with health problems who cannot or do not wish to seek conventional medical treatment. They often develop close relationships with their patients because they are committed to treating whole people rather than symptoms.

The demand for complementary and alternative care services, with the exception of midwifery, is related to the availability of disposable income, since services must often be paid for in cash, and to the incidence of chronic health problems. Americans, particularly educated Americans, have a fair amount of disposable income. As the U.S. population ages and health reforms mandated by the PPACA are implemented, the demand for CAM services is likely to increase. With annual expenditures at $33.9 billion in the United States, there appears to be a continued demand for CAM providers.

It is difficult to determine the demand for CAM services in the international health care market. There are few data on current expenditures on CAM services. Developing countries are unlikely to increase their use of CAM services. They are also unlikely to report the use of these services. Lack of education and scarcity of conventional medical care make it unlikely that interest in alternative medicine will increase. Countries such as Australia, Great Britain, Japan, and China may demonstrate increased interest in CAM services as their populations increase in wealth, education, and age.

Related Resources for Further Research

American Holistic Medicine Association
23366 Commerce Park
Suite 101B
Beachwood, OH 44122
Tel: (216) 292-6644
Fax: (216) 292-6688
http://www.holisticmedicine.org

Global Institute for Alternative Medicine
3822 Lake Ave.
Wilmette, IL 60091
Tel: (800) 410-0612
Fax: (888) 201-4186
http://www.gifam.org

National Association for Integrative Health Care Practitioners
9201 Edeworth Dr.
P.O. Box 5631
Capital Heights, MD 20791
Tel: (757) 292-7710
http://aihcp-norfolkva.org

National Center for Complementary and Alternative Medicine, National Institutes of Health
9000 Rockville Pike
Bethesda, MD 20892
Tel: (888) 644-6226
Fax: (866) 464-3616
http://nccam.nih.gov

Christine M. Carroll

Education and training of CAM practitioners

Overview

The education and training of practitioners of complementary and alternative medicine (CAM) are widely varied, as these practices encompass any type of therapy that is not considered conventional or scientifically proven. Many of these therapies, however, have a long history in other cultures. CAM education and training may involve rigorous courses of study similar to those for a medical degree or for postdoctoral training. However, some CAM education consists of only minimal training, such as a six-week course that leads to a certificate. Even within the same discipline, training and certification requirements may vary widely from state to state, because there is no national regulatory body to oversee the process.

The education and training of CAM practitioners are the focus here, so the discussion will cover only those areas of unconventional therapy with standard educational or training programs. Covered here are acupuncturists, chiropractors, homeopaths, massage therapists, naturopaths, and integrated medicine programs that combine conventional medicine with CAM practice.

Many other types of CAM practitioners, such as aromatherapists, crystal therapists, reflexologists, reiki practitioners, and native or indigenous healers, study for long periods with experienced experts in their field. However, no particular training programs, educational courses, recognized requirements, or state or national certifications are available in the United States for these practitioners.

Practitioners

Acupuncturist. Acupuncture is a standard accepted practice in the Chinese medicine tradition; however, it is relatively new in the United States and, as such, varies from state to state in education and certification requirements and venues. About forty states have established criteria for persons seeking to practice acupuncture. Nonmedical professionals, to become licensed as an acupuncturist, must take a four-year course of study and a board examination. Persons with a medical background, such as medical doctors, dentists, nurses, and chiropractors, must often complete a rigorous course of study too, including classroom study (a minimum of three hundred hours) and clinical acupuncture practice, before becoming licensed.

Courses in acupuncture focus on anatomy, physiology, and other areas that are typical for any type of medical practice. Courses also include detailed study of the nervous and vascular systems so that a practitioner has a thorough understanding of needle insertion and the body's reaction to it. A practitioner of acupuncture may also be trained in other aspects of Chinese traditional medicine.

Two bodies certify and accredit acupuncture colleges and practitioners in the United States: the Accreditation Commission for Acupuncture and Oriental Medicine and the American Board of Medical Acupuncture. These organizations provide continuing education and examinations for practitioners and oversight for educational programs in the United States. They also provide standards for acupuncturists trained in other countries who wish to practice in the United States.

Chiropractor. This branch of CAM may be one of the most highly regulated in the United States. The Council on Chiropractic Education (CCE) is an accreditation body for chiropractic schools, and its accreditation criteria are recognized by the U.S. Department of Education. CCE regulates all training programs for chiropractors. The American Chiropractic Association, a leading professional organization for chiropractors, provides continuing medical education and other resources to practitioners.

A chiropractic training program must include a minimum of 4,200 hours of class time, laboratory work, and clinical experience and must include courses in orthopedics, neurology, and physiotherapy (all with a focus on clinical practice of manipulation and spinal alignment). Chiropractors may also pursue studies in a specialty, such as orthopedics, sports medicine, or rehabilitation.

After completion of a doctor of chiropractic (D.C.) program, student practitioners must pass a four-part examination from the National Board of Chiropractic Examiners and must pass a state examination to be licensed. In some areas, the state examination takes the place of the national examination.

Homeopath. The education and training of a homeopath can take varied courses. Programs designed for medical doctors or others with medical training tend to focus on homeopathy and its application, assuming that those with a medical degree would already have a basic background in medicine and medical practice. Other courses, geared to those who do not have a medical background, focus more on medical education, such as anatomy and physiology, but also train students in homeopathy practices and principles.

A few states in the United States offer training in homeopathy (Arizona, California, Colorado, Florida, Massachusetts, and Utah, and the District of Columbia). Admission requirements for courses of study vary widely; some require a medical doctor (M.D.) or similar degree, and others enroll students with little or no medical background. Because homeopathy itself is not regulated in the United States, anyone can use the word "homeopath" to describe themselves or their type of work. However, a person cannot identify himself or herself as a homeopathic doctor or imply to the public that he or she is practicing medicine if he or she does not hold a medical license.

Several programs offer homeopathic education, but no single certification is recognized throughout the United States. Each state has its own standards for licensing this type of care. Some homeopaths are licensed in a conventional type of medicine and may hold a degree as an M.D. or as a nurse practitioner. In Arizona, Connecticut, and Nevada, M.D.'s and D.O.'s (doctors of osteopathy) can be licensed as homeopathic physicians. Homeopathic assistants, who practice under the supervision of a homeopath, are licensed in Arizona and Nevada.

Organizations such as the Council for Homeopathic Certification and the American Board of Homeotherapeutics offer certifications to homeopaths who have completed certain requirements: for example, M.D.'s or D.O.'s who pass oral and written exams in homeopathy. Upon completing these exams, the successful candidate is awarded a diplomate of homeotherapeutics (D.Ht.). Even though the Department of Education does not recognize any one organization as a certifying body, homeopathic practitioners use the standards upheld by these organizations to maintain competency and to encourage self-regulation.

Massage therapist. Most U.S. states regulate the practice of massage therapy in some way with a type of governing board providing certification or licensure. Usually, a massage therapist must complete some course of training and pass a board examination to be licensed. However, the requirements vary widely from state to state. Education provided in massage therapy schools typically requires about five hundred hours of study and involves courses in anatomy, physiology, motion and body mechanics, and clinical massage practice. Licensure also may involve passing a nationally recognized test, such as the National Certification Examination for Therapeutic Massage and Bodywork or the Massage and Bodywork Licensing Examination.

Naturopath. There are two basic types of naturopath: traditional and naturopathic physicians. Education and training for traditional naturopaths vary from nondegree certificate programs to undergraduate degree programs. After completion of a degree program, a traditional naturopath can certify with the American Naturopathic Medical Certificate Board and become a naturopathic consultant. Traditionally, these types of naturopaths do not practice medicine and thus do not require a license.

A naturopathic physician must have a doctor of naturopathic medicine (N.D., or N.M.D. in Arizona) degree from an accredited school of naturopathic medicine. Only four schools in the United States (in Washington, Oregon, Arizona, and Connecticut) are accredited for this type of education. The N.D. involves four years of graduate-level study in a standard medical curriculum, with added courses in natural therapeutics. Practitioners must then pass a state board licensing examination. (In the state of Utah, naturopathic doctors must complete a residency before starting a practice.)

Practitioners often work as primary care clinicians, but some states do not recognize the D.M. degree, so practitioners in these areas cannot legally practice medicine. Generally, they may still practice traditional naturopathic medicine. Two states, South Carolina and Tennessee, specifically prohibit the practice of naturopathy in any form.

The Council of Naturopathic Medical Education is a governing body that provides accreditation for education in naturopathy. The American Naturopathic Certification Board provides testing and continuing education for this profession.

Famous First

Regarding nursing in ancient and medieval world: Women therapists of all social classes were conveyors of knowledge of the medicinal properties of herbs and 'drug' preparation. They actively continued these traditions and applied knowledge in the care of sick women throughout the medieval period. Until the thirteenth century BCE, despite the already established persecutions, women continued to work either as therapists or as caregivers. During the 13th CE it is estimated that in Europe approximately 200,000 nuns and commoners, provided organized care services under the auspices of the church.

Source: "Nursing and Caring: An Historical Overview from Ancient Greek Tradition to Modern Times" by Dimitrios Theofanidis and Despina Sapountzi-Krepia. *International Journal of Caring Sciences*, Volume 8:3 (2015)

CAM Education and Training in Mainstream Institutions

As the practice of CAM becomes more widespread and integrated into society, many medical colleges in the United States have begun to offer courses in CAM. One area of complementary medicine that is often taught in integrative medicine courses is pain management. CAM courses often teach conventional physicians how CAM methods can be incorporated into, and can truly complement, conventional medicine.

The University of Arizona College of Medicine teaches a program of integrative medicine that critically examines branches of alternative medicine and trains clinicians in practices that it finds helpful and that cause no harm. Other such programs include Mayo Clinic Complementary and Integrative Medicine, the Integrative Medicine Program at MD Anderson Cancer Center, and University of Michigan Integrative Medicine.

Marianne M. Madsen, M.S.

CRIMINAL JUSTICE AND PRISON INDUSTRY

Summary

Prisons are places where persons convicted of crimes are held in order to meet the goals of punishment or rehabilitation. Persons are physically confined, so they cannot harm others, and they are deprived of freedom, so they will be deterred from future crime. The prison industry has also become a business where prisoners are used for work. Prison-run programs for inmates can be public or private and bring in revenue for the industry.

History of the Industry

Prisons constitute one subsection of the criminal justice system, which is made up of three major parts: police, courts, and corrections. The act of imprisoning individuals is based on the notion of incapacitation, or making one physically unable to commit a crime. Imprisonment throughout history has been used to confine criminals, who would be subject to corporal punishment or even death.

Prisons were established in London under the ideas of Jeremy Bentham, who was a classical theorist. He believed, along with Cessare Beccaria, that crime could be deterred if the punishment for violations of the law were swift, certain, and severe. They both believed that punishment could prevent persons from committing crime if the consequences outweighed the benefits. During the nineteenth century, prison became a form of punishment, rather than a place to hold a criminal until he was punished.

The first prison in the early nineteenth century was based on the penitentiary movement. Individuals were supposed to reflect upon their behavior, and do penance for their crimes. The term "prison" is often used interchangeably with "jail." However, they really are different terms, associated with the severity of the crime and the length of time for which one is incarcerated. A prison can be run by the state or federal government and is a place where criminals are held for more than a year. State prisons are reserved for serious criminals, and federal prisons are reserved for those who violate federal laws, such as white-collar criminals. Jails are run by municipalities or counties and are reserved for individuals who have been convicted of less serious crimes or for those awaiting trial. The longest amount of time spent in jail is one year.

While incarcerated, prisoners are required to work and exercise. They also have the option of participating in recreational activities. This not only keeps them busy and out of trouble but also gives them skills they can use on release. In addition, they can obtain high school equivalency credits and get the therapy and treatment necessary for success outside the prison walls. Prisoners have to earn the right to work in the more desirable areas of the prison and are paid (very little) for their work. They can use their earnings to buy items for themselves at the commissary.

The prison industry has become an important revenue stream for prisons. Often, inmates are hired out to work in factories, where they produce goods to be sold to the federal government. They are cheap labor, so profit margins increase at companies that use them, and prisons earn money by lending out their inmates as laborers. In addition, the work helps inmates feel they are accomplishing something during the course of their day, and sometimes they learn usable skills. Even if they are performing tedious labor, the more they work, the lower the likelihood they will be involved in criminal behavior.

The Industry Today

Prisons and jails continue to hold those awaiting trial and those convicted criminals serving time as part of their sentences. Some facilities have thousands of beds, while others have only two cells. Many have education, vocational, and treatment programs that help meet the special needs of inmates. Since jails hold prisoners for relatively short periods of time, the therapeutic and recreational programs offered in such facilities are minimal. Jails must still provide care and treatment in a safe environment, however. Thus, they need employees, food service, laundry service, attorneys, therapists, and other workers, as well as security personnel and managers. The physical environment ranges in size from small, one-to-two-cell local jails to massive prisons run like hotels at the state and federal level. Prisons may operate through public or private funding.

Some jails are found in small towns and municipalities and offer few services. They typically have relatively small staffs, comprising local police officers. These locations are used only to hold offenders for twenty-four to forty-eight hours. In mid-2009, local jails held 767,620 persons awaiting trail or serving sentences, according to the Bureau of Justice Statistics (BJS).

Midsize prisons might be found in larger counties and smaller states. They must provide for all of the basic needs of offenders, although they may not be able to offer all of the services of a large prison. For example, larger prisons might offer drug treatment and counseling, as well as vocational training in many areas. Midsize prisons might not have the room or the budget for such services. Facilities for women only, tend to offer even fewer services. Although food, security, and medical services are imperative, treatment opportunities and useful vocational training might be lacking.

Large institutions, especially those located in states with a high number of inmates, such as California, are run as big businesses. They have all the necessary housekeeping services, as well as administrative, educational, and vocational programs. These prisons can house serious violent offenders in separate locations on the prison grounds and offer opportunities for offenders to work on-site or have inmates hired out by private companies to produce goods to be sold or services to be offered outside the prison walls.

Prisons have undergone a significant evolution since the 1700's. They operate more like businesses and even earn profits by selling products made by inmates. Prisons are now focused on rehabilitation and deterrence, in addition to retribution and punishment. Today's prisons have better criminal record keeping, forensic analysis, fingerprint analysis, quicker access to records, and automation of records, as well as decreased delays in processing information. At midyear 2008, state and federal prison authorities had over 1.6 million prisoners under their jurisdiction. Today, there are more than 2.3 million people behind bars. Those numbers are expected to go up as the penalties for certain crimes, especially drug offenses, go up. In addition, tougher state and federal sentencing laws have increased the population of minority offenders in particular.

Another major change has been the use of private prisons. Today, about 10 percent of U.S. prisons and jails have been privatized. They have become for-profit businesses that reduce essential services within the prison. The private contracting of prisoners for work is a booming business because it allows prison workers to supply the market with goods that are cheap to produce. Federal prison industry workers produce almost all U.S. military and war supplies and assemble many products and appliances. The three major private firms in the United States that offer security services to private corporations are the Corrections Corporation of America, Wackenhut, and Esmor. There are a few others that operate correctional or detention facilities, and the big three also have facilities in Australia, England, and Puerto Rico.

Interestingly, private prisons were common over one hundred years ago. Prisoners were hired out as slave labor and were exposed to horrible conditions. They were worked to death, and there was no concern for their physical safety. Today, legislation regulates private contractors running correctional facilities. Most of those run by private firms are low- to medium-security level. The number of private prisons is likely to increase in the near future.

Changes in the programs offered to inmates have occurred during the early twenty-first century. Faith-based programs have been added, and restorative justice efforts are being incorporated into the prison mentality. Programs that promote positive behavior, as opposed to punishing deviant behavior, are projected to be a new focus. In addition, technological changes will play a major role in communication and offender tracking, detection, and monitoring. Biometrics—the identification or verification of identities via measurable physiological and behavior traits—will be used more. Examples could include retinal and facial recognition, voice- and fingerprint identification, and thermal imagery. Global Positioning System devices will begin to be used with more regularity as well.

Industry Market Segments

Prisons can be designated as minimum-security, medium-security, and maximum-security facilities. Sometimes, a prison has sections devoted to one or another security level, but these designations are used to protect offenders from one another and to make management of the prison run more smoothly.

Minimum-Security Facilities

Minimum-security prisons are reserved for the least serious offenders. They are often set up like small camps and might be located in or near military bases. The prisoners live in less secure dormitories, and they are usually surrounded by a single fence. The facilities are most often located in rural areas, and the offenders are usually nonviolent. Inmates usually participate in community-based work assignments and in prerelease transition programs.

Medium-Security Facilities

Medium-security prisons house offenders who require more secure facilities than those housed in minimum-security facilities. They are often set up like maximum-security facilities but have fewer controls over the freedom of the inmates. The prisoners live in secure, barred cells within fortified perimeters. The rooms can be set up in dormitories or bunk beds, with communal showers, toilets, and sinks. Medium-security facilities often house fifty inmates per officer, and some might be designed with "dry cells," with no toilet fixtures in the dormitory. There is a single cell unit set aside for punishment of inmates. The facilities are most often located in rural areas, and the offenders are less violent than maximum-security inmates. Inmates usually participate in work assignments, education, and vocational training, as well as faith-based programs and prison industry. There is less supervision in regard to internal movement of prisoners, but the dormitories are locked at night (and are thus more secure than minimum-security facilities).

Maximum-Security Facilities

Maximum-security prisons are reserved for the most serious offenders. They are often set up to confine the most dangerous offenders, for long periods. Thus they need to have a highly secure perimeter. The facilities are most often located in rural areas, and the offenders are usually violent. Inmates have strict controls placed on them, and routines are highly regimented.

Organizational Structure and Job Roles

The organizational structure within a prison is typically based on law and policy. Wardens are likely to handle most of the major decision making because they are prisons' administrators. Wardens make arrangements for prisoners to be placed in certain positions, based on trust, qualifications, and need. They delegate to assistant wardens and to correctional officers the coordination of moving prisoners. Correctional officers keep their sites safe. In addition, there are companies that provide private correctional and detention management.

The following umbrella categories apply to the organizational structure of institutions in the criminal justice and prison industry:

- Administration
- Correctional Officers
- Clerical Support
- Program Staff
- Maintenance
- Food, Beverage, and Laundry
- Groundskeeping

Program Staff

Program staff in prisons are responsible for encouraging prisoners to participate in educational, vocational, and recreational opportunities. Advanced degrees are required for teachers and counselors, who generally have teaching certificates, and possibly master's or Ph.D. degrees. Teachers need to have knowledge of curriculum design, and if they are teaching English as a second language (ESL), they need knowledge of the English language, including grammar and spelling. Inmates can also be taught the skills necessary to run a business, how to apply for jobs, or how to improve parenting skills. Teachers must be able assess learning styles and work with the resources available in prisons. They also need to keep the environment safe by monitoring the inmates' behavior.

Correctional officers are responsible for keeping the staff safe. Clerical staff make sure that program staff members have proper credentials. Inmates can earn general education diplomas (GEDs) and college credits by taking classes from program staff. They can get the drug treatment and mental health counseling they need to be healthy and emotionally secure. Depending on the security level of their facilities, inmates can also obtain vocational skills in construction, heating, air-conditioning, landscaping, or even painting in the community. Programs are offered in small-appliance repair, culinary arts, forklift operations, floor care, pest control, typing, and even certification in alcohol and substance abuse counseling. In addition, inmates can participate in prison industry, making goods to be used by the government.

Program staff occupations may include the following:
- Psychologist
- Psychiatrist
- Physician
- Nurse
- Teacher
- Counselor
- Recreational Instructor
- Religious Counselor/Chaplain

Related Resources for Further Research

American Correctional Association
206 N Washington St., Suite 200
Alexandria, VA 22314
Tel: (703) 224-0000
Fax: (703) 224-0179
http://www.aca.org

American Jail Association
1135 Professional Ct.
Hagerstown, MD 21740
Tel: (301) 790-3939, ext. 24
http://www.corrections.com/aja

Federal Bureau of Prisons
320 1st St. NW
Washington, DC 20534
Tel: (202) 307-3198
http://www.bop.gov

U.S. Bureau of Justice Statistics
810 7th St. NW
Washington, DC 20531
Tel: (202) 307-0765
http://bjs.ojp.usdoj.gov

U.S. Department of Justice
950 Pennsylvania Ave. NW
Washington, DC 20530-0001
http://www.justice.gov

Gina M. Robertiello

International Association of Forensic Nurses

The International Association of Forensic Nurses is the only international professional organization for registered nurses that works to develop and support the science of forensic nursing and to publicize the work of forensic nurses nationally and internationally.

The International Association of forensic Nurses (IAFN) was established in 1992 when a group of sexual assault nurses held their first national convention in Minneapolis, Minnesota. By 2008, the organization had grown to twenty-six state chapters in the United States and a membership of more than two thousand, including nurses and other professionals in more than sixteen nations around the world. Members include students, forensic scientists, emergency medical technicians, and physicians as well as nurses.

The IAFN is devoted to promoting the practice of forensic nursing and disseminating information about the field of forensic nursing science. Forensic nursing encompasses activities in many areas in which the nursing profession and the legal system intersect, particularly the areas of child and elder abuse, domestic violence, and emergency trauma. For example, forensic nurses may investigate and collect evidence in incidents involving trauma and questionable deaths; treat perpetrators and victims of violence, abuse, and traumatic accidents; conduct physical and mental health examinations; provide consultation services to health, medical, and legal agencies; and serve as expert witnesses regarding adequacy of health care and services. Forensic nurses practice in diverse roles, including as members of disaster response teams, as sexual assault nurse examiners (SANEs), as legal nurse consultants and attorneys, as medicolegal death investigators, as nurse educators, and as researchers.

The IAFN has established standards of ethical conduct for forensic nurses and works to improve forensic nursing practice, to promote and encourage the exchange of ideas among members and others in the profession, and to develop knowledge in the field of forensic nursing by offering educational opportunities for nurses and professionals in related disciplines. Toward these ends, the association holds an annual international conference at which issues of forensic nursing practice are discussed. The organization is also involved in an effort to integrate prevention strategies to stop interpersonal violence around the world.

Sharon W. Stark

Law and medicine

The use of medicine in legal contexts-to determine whether a person has been injured by the act of another, the extent of such an injury and its treatment, and whether a defendant was physically or emotionally capable of committing a crime or tort-and in related ethical and philosophical contexts-to determine when life begins (in the abortion debate) or how one evaluates "quality of life" (the euthanasia debate).

Key terms

Medicine as it relates to law is referred to as forensic medicine. Forensic medicine plays a part in three basic areas of the law. The first two involve the practical application of medicine in civil law and in criminal law. The third area involves the use of medical science to help in defining philosophical or ethical issues, such as when life begins and ends. Ethics in medicine, also called bioethics, refers to a set of moral standards and a code for behavior that govern people's interactions with one another and with society. Bioethics deals with moral issues and problems that have arisen as a result of modern medicine and research. Bioethical principles focus on autonomy (self-determination), beneficence (doing good), nonmaleficence (avoiding evil), and justice (the fair distribution of scarce resources).

In a civil case, a private party, the plaintiff, files a complaint in court against another party, the defendant, requesting that a judge or a jury settle a dispute between the two parties. A party to a civil suit can be an individual, a corporation, an association, a government organization, or any other group. A civil suit differs from a criminal case in that neither party is claiming that a crime (such as theft, kidnapping, or murder) was committed and that someone should be put in jail. Instead, the plaintiff in a civil suit can ask that the defendant pay some amount of money to the plaintiff to compensate for damages that the plaintiff has suffered because of something the defendant did.

In a criminal case, however, the government, on behalf of "the people," files a complaint with the court claiming that the defendant committed a crime, and the government seeks to have a judge or jury determine the guilt or innocence of that defendant. If the defendant is determined to be guilty, the judge has the authority to punish the defendant, usually by imposing a fine, by requiring community service, by setting a jail sentence, or rarely, in some states, by having the defendant put to death. In both civil and criminal cases, medical science is called upon to provide evidence that can be used to prove or disprove a party's case. In a civil case, the parties will often turn to medical experts to determine the extent of a plaintiff's mental and physical injuries. These experts act as witnesses in their areas of expertise and testify in a court of law. For example, a plaintiff in a civil suit might claim that he or she was born with birth defects as a result of drugs that the mother had taken during pregnancy and may present evidence of that injury and its cause in the form of testimony of doctors and medical research experts specializing in those related areas of medicine. This testimony, supported by current medical knowledge, would be presented to the jury to bolster the plaintiff's claim that the drug caused the plaintiff's birth defect.

Medical science, through the discovery of disease causality and pathophysiology, has created more distinct medical specialties. This trend is reflected in the increasing number of expert witnesses: At the beginning of the twentieth century, a general practitioner was considered qualified to testify on most areas of medicine; today, the courts require expert witnesses to be specifically qualified in the area of medicine about which they testify.

The practice of using highly qualified and specialized doctors as expert witnesses has long been accepted by courts as an effective way to educate a jury regarding the extent, cause, and treatment of the injury in question. However, there are some limitations on the use of such testimony. In order for the court to allow a medical expert to testify as to specific facts from which conclusions are to be drawn, the facts must be outside what is considered to be the general or common knowledge of a lay jury. For example, a court may not allow a party to use a medical expert to explain commonplace injuries, such as sprained ankles. The court would, however, allow a medical expert to explain toxic shock syndrome, because the existence, causes, and effects of that impairment are not common knowledge. The reasoning behind this limitation is that the jury members are supposed to form their own opinions when such opinions do not involve or require specialized knowledge. Only when it is necessary or helpful to the jury to be educated in a specialized area of knowledge is expert testimony usually allowed. In contrast to a lay witness, an expert witness is permitted to testify about the ultimate issue in the case. The medical expert in an accident case, for example, may testify about the proximate cause of injury, that is whether the accident caused the plaintiff's injury that is subject of the lawsuit. Lay witnesses are not permitted to testify along these lines because they do not have the expertise to do so.

The court also recognizes a distinction between testimony from a medical expert and testimony from the plaintiff's treating doctor. Whereas the former educates the jury regarding an area of medicine that is relevant to the case, the latter does not. Instead, the treating doctor is called to testify to actual events or facts of the case that the doctor personally witnessed: that the plaintiff was examined on a certain date, the extent of his or her injuries, and so on. Thus, although an expert witness may not be allowed by the court to educate the jury on the subject of a sprained ankle or other topic of common knowledge, the fact that the plaintiff sustained a sprained ankle and was treated for it may be testified to by the treating doctor.

In a civil suit, the plaintiff must prove that he or she was injured by some act of the defendant. That injury can be economic (the loss of property or money), physical (such as a torn muscle or broken leg), or mental (stress or anxiety). Over the years, more and more types of injuries have become recognized as compensable injuries in civil cases. The term "pain and suffering" has been used to describe physical and emotional symptoms that a plaintiff may claim were caused by the defendant. Medical facts can help determine the existence and extent of all these types of injury.

Sometimes the expert will testify only hypothetically. In the hypothetical question, the expert may be asked to render an opinion based on certain assumptions concerning a hypothetical case that closely resembles the case at bar. The hypothetical question provides an opportunity for counsel to summarize his or her client's position. Sometimes, however, a medical expert will need to examine a plaintiff. It is not unusual for such examinations to take place years after the injury occurred, and the doctor will have to determine whether the injury exists, the extent of the injury, the cause of the injury, what (if any) limitations are caused by the injury, the treatment that is indicated, and the probable duration of the injury (perhaps based on the average rate of recovery for such an injury).

In the criminal justice system, medical experts may testify on a variety of scientific and medical issues. In the case of a murder, for example, it may be necessary to identify blood, tissue, bone, or some other human remains and to determine the source of those remains-namely, whether the remains belong to the alleged victim or perpetrator of the crime. Doctors who specialize in forensic medicine are often called upon to conduct special tests, such as DNA testing, to identify whose blood or tissue was found at the scene of a crime or on a murder weapon. Forensic experts can also determine the approximate time and cause of death. Testimony on these issues helps a jury determine the guilt or innocence of the accused.

Criminal cases occasionally also require the testimony of a forensic psychiatrist, who is an expert in mental and emotional disorders as they relate to legal principles. Testimony from such an expert assists in determining whether the defendant is "insane." According to section 4.01 of the Model Penal Code, a person is insane if he or she "lacks substantial capacity either to appreciate the criminality [wrongfulness] of his conduct or to conform his conduct to the requirements of the law." Not every state follows the Model Penal Code. Other variations of the insanity defense exist that deal with a person's ability to distinguish right from wrong. Psychiatric evaluations of the accused are performed to determine whether the defendant fit this definition at the time the crime was committed. Testimony regarding the defendant's insanity would significantly affect the case's outcome and sentencing.

A separate issue, unrelated to the defendant's mental condition at the time of the crime, is the defendant's "competency" to stand trial. According to Black's Law Dictionary (9th ed., 2008), a defendant is competent to stand trial if he or she has "the capacity to understand the proceedings, to consult meaningfully with counsel, and to assist in the defense." The law ensures that an accused person's rights are protected by requiring that the defendant be capable of understanding these proceedings and their implications before he or she is allowed to stand trial. If either of the attorneys, or the judge, asserts that the defendant is not competent to stand trial, the court will hold a competency hearing to decide whether the defendant is "competent." In determining the competency of the defendant, the court will hear the testimony of psychiatric experts. If the defendant is determined to be incompetent at the time of the trial, the defendant will not be tried but may instead be sent to a mental institution until such time as he or she is competent to stand trial.

In addition to being used in civil cases and criminal cases, medical science is used to provide scientific information to support or disprove wholly nonscientific determinations. Such philosophical and ethical issues include abortion and euthanasia. In the long-running debate over the legality of abortion, for example, many issues and circumstances come into play, including rape and the possibility that pregnancy may endanger the woman's life. One central and hotly contested question, however, is "When does life begin?" This question may also involve an equally difficult and controversial one: "What is life?" The courts and various state legislatures have turned to medical science to address these profound, and possibly unanswerable, questions. Medical science has identified two key concepts to answer these questions: the concept of "viability" (that is, the ability of the fetus to survive outside the womb) and the distinction between the first, second, and third trimesters of a pregnancy. The distinction of trimesters was originally based on the concept of viability: A fetus generally could not survive outside the womb during the first trimester (that is, was not viable), while a fetus was generally considered viable during the third trimester. Thus, the courts and legislature would often use the concept of trimesters in determining a cutoff date after which an abortion could not be performed.

These concepts have been used as the basis for legislation to regulate and authorize abortions. Medical science is, however, a rapidly evolving field. Because it is now possible for a human egg, once fertilized, to become viable outside the womb, the legal foundation upon which abortions are based is becoming unstable.

Another important area that has emerged from late twentieth and early twenty-first century technology concerns the use of human embryonic stem cells. Widely acknowledged as extremely valuable in assisting scientists in understanding basic mechanisms of embryo development and gene regulation, stem cell research holds the promise of enabling scientists to direct stem cells to grow into replacement organs and tissues to treat a wide variety of diseases. Embryos are valued in research for their ability to produce stem cells, which can be harvested to grow a variety of tissues for use in transplantation to treat serious illnesses such as cancer, heart disease, and diabetes.

The Applications of Medical Testimony

Medical experts in almost every field of medicine have played a part in civil cases, criminal cases, and controversies involving philosophical and ethical issues. Sometimes, the interaction between medicine and the law has spawned new medical or legal subspecialties. In fact, medical expert testimony has become a field and an occupation in itself, supporting an entire group of medical professionals to the exclusion of actual medical practice. This phenomenon has occurred in large part in response to the greater acceptance by the courts of medical expert testimony and the increased reliability of recent medical testing.

Personal injury cases afford a good example of all the different types of testimony that come into play in civil suits. A physical injury case, as the name suggests, is based on a physical (or mental) injury, as opposed to a purely financial injury, suffered by the plaintiff. A physical injury case may involve an automobile accident and its resulting injuries. In such a case, doctors who are experts in the field of muscle damage, neurology (for head and nerve injuries), orthopedic surgery, and countless other areas could be called as experts, depending on the extent of the injuries.

Another type of case, called a product liability case, will often use expert medical testimony. A product liability case is one in which a person has been injured by a specific product on the market and sues the manufacturer, and often the seller, claiming that the product was defective. Famous examples of product liability cases include claims filed against manufacturers of asbestos products, certain tampons (for causing toxic shock syndrome), contraceptive devices such as the Dalkon Shield, and some generic or prescription drugs, such as thalidomide and Halcion. All these cases required medical experts in recently developed fields of medicine. Prior to the product liability suits filed against some tampon manufacturers, few people had heard of toxic shock syndrome. The testimony of medical experts was required to prove a link between an allegedly defective product and the resulting injury that was claimed. Without expert medical testimony in these cases, it would be impossible to prove that the defective products caused the injuries of which the defendants complained.

Another example of the medical profession developing to suit the law is in the area of workers' compensation. The California legislature, like the legislatures of many states, has established by statute (Labor Code section 3600 and following) a method by which to compensate any employee who has suffered a job-related injury. An employer is required by law to carry workers' compensation insurance, which will compensate an injured employee. If an employee is injured on the job in any manner, that employee is supposed to file a claim notifying his or her employer of the injury. The claim is then submitted to the workers' compensation insurance carrier. If the employer and the carrier accept liability, necessary treatment is provided to the employee. If the carrier denies further treatment or denies that an employee is disabled, the employee may file a claim with the Workers' Compensation Appeal Board. Once such a claim is filed, a judge will review all the medical reports of the injured worker. Additional medical evidence and testimony may be introduced to prove or disprove the employee's claim of injury or disability. The award of the Workers' Compensation Appeal Board is determined by the medical condition of the person claiming the injury. The growing popularity of workers' compensation has spawned an entire field of medicine, that of work-related injuries.

California courts routinely allow damages for "mental distress" in almost every type of tort action. Accordingly, psychiatrists and psychologists are routinely called upon to testify regarding whether a plaintiff has suffered such an injury. Emotional distress is not a specific medical condition, but rather a general emotional state, which may include anger, fear, frustration, anxiety, depression, and similar symptoms. Although psychiatric or psychological testimony is not required by the court for the plaintiff to recover damages for mental distress, it can be very effective in explaining to the jury the extent of the injuries and the effect of those injuries on the plaintiff's future life.

If a jury determines that the plaintiff suffered a physical or mental injury caused by the defendant, then, based on the medical testimony-of either the medical witness or the treating doctor-the jury may award any medical fees incurred, as well as anticipated medical fees and costs and compensation for the pain and suffering of the defendant. The jury may also award further damages not related to the medical condition of the plaintiff, if the case warrants such damages.

In a criminal case, particularly a case of homicide, forensic medicine often provides the key and fundamental evidence upon which the entire case is based. During the investigations of the assassination of President John F. Kennedy in the 1960s, the forensic evidence played a vital, although controversial, role. The testimony presented by the doctors who examined the president's body was used to reconstruct the crime. Forensic science was used to interpret the angle of entry of the bullets that killed Kennedy and thereby to extrapolate the source of the shots. Furthermore, forensic science was called upon to demonstrate how many shots were fired and the paths of the bullets upon entering the bodies of the president and Governor John Connally. Using medical evidence, along with other evidence, the Warren Commission concluded that the bullets all came from the book depository building behind the presidential caravan. Also using medical evidence and experts, critics of the Warren Commission's findings have alleged that the injuries suffered by the president could have been caused only by a bullet entering from the front of the president's neck and exiting the rear of the skull.

In another case, forensic evidence was able to reach a conclusive determination that certain bones were those of the Nazi war criminal Josef Mengele, known as the Angel of Death. In 1992, forensics experts discovered, using DNA testing, that some bones retrieved from a grave in Brazil were those of Mengele. To make this determination, doctors compared the DNA found in the blood of Mengele's son with DNA from the bones found in the grave. They found that the DNA from both sources matched. Because DNA constitutes a "genetic fingerprint" that remains the same from parent to offspring, the doctors were able to conclude that the remains found in Brazil were those of Mengele.

DNA testing is now also commonly used in suits to determine the father of an infant. According to the Genetics Institute, DNA testing is at least 99.8 percent accurate. Medical science has so refined its ability to chart DNA "fingerprints" that the chance of coming upon two identical DNA patterns is approximately one in six billion. Prior to DNA testing, a blood testing method called human leukocyte antigen (HLA) typing was used to determine paternity, but this typing was only 95 percent accurate.

Some medical or scientific tests, while accepted by the courts, remain subject to much controversy. The Breathalyzer test, used to determine blood alcohol levels, is one such test. While the courts regularly accept the results of such tests to determine whether a suspect was intoxicated, the test is based on several assumptions and averages. Based on the alcohol content in the suspect's breath, the test extrapolates a probable amount of alcohol in the suspect's blood. The reliability of this test depends on the correct calibration of the equipment and the care of the person taking the readings. Since the tests are taken by nonmedical or nonscientific personnel in the field, mistaken readings are not uncommon. Furthermore, if the suspect used a spray breath freshener just before the test, the readings may be skewed, since such breath fresheners are usually alcohol-based.

Fast Fact

Forensic nurses are involved in a number of criminal-related cases, but they're also called upon during disasters. Among their potential duties, sadly, is working on a disaster mortuary operational response team, which works to identify victims.
Source: International Association of Forensic Nurses

Perspective and Prospects

Medicine has always played some role in the outcome of court cases, but this relationship did not come into full flower until relatively recently. In the early twentieth century, courts placed strict limitations on the type and amount of medical testimony allowed into evidence. Often, certain types of medical evidence were not admissible because the science was not deemed reliable-there was too much room for error. The polygraph (lie detector), for example, could not be relied upon to reveal consistently whether a person was telling the truth, since it simply measured galvanic skin response, respiration rate, and other factors that only tend to be correlated with the subject's feelings of guilt. Most other evidence presented by medical experts concerned the likelihood of events or outcomes and therefore usually constituted opinion, rather than fact.

With the advent of new technologies in the later part of the twentieth century, medical science began to present "hard" (more precise) data that became more frequently accepted by the courts as reliable and relevant evidence. Even so, it took some time before medical scientists were able to present enough data to persuade the courts that the evidence of such methods as DNA "fingerprinting" was truly reliable. The acceptance of DNA testing, for example, was a long and hard-fought battle among legions of medical experts on both sides of the issue. Finally, DNA testing was accepted by the courts as a reliable source of evidence. As forensic medicine advances, no doubt its contribution to the law will also advance. The ability of the medical and other scientific professions to determine reliable conclusions relating to court cases is progressing rapidly with increases in scientific knowledge, methods, and technology.

Ironically, medical progress may cloud other areas of the law. In the early twentieth century, for example, few could have dreamed of the technology that makes life support possible. With the advent of kidney dialysis machines, pacemakers, respirators, and other life-support devices, medical science has achieved the ability to prolong an individual's bodily functioning. Whether this functioning alone is sufficient to define "life," however, remains a question that cannot be addressed by medical science alone but must be considered in the light of philosophical, ethical, and other values. Medicine is consequently becoming an area in which the law must adapt. Issues that have challenged existing laws include abortion and the point at which life begins, euthanasia, the individual's right not to have life extended, the right to reveal an individual's genetic predisposition toward disease, egg implantation, and genetic engineering. Medical science has propagated these dilemmas but may also be called upon to solve them.

Larry M. Roberts, J.D.;
updated by Joshua Lampert, MS-III, and Amanda Grannis, B.A.

> # Conversation With . . .
> # CARRIE EDWARDS
> PhD, RN, CA/CP SANE, AFN-BC
> Assistant Professor, Texas Tech University
> Health Sciences Center School of Nursing

Carrie Edwards has been a registered nurse (RN) for twenty-four years and a forensic nurse for fourteen years. She is Founding Director of Forensic Nurse Staffing of West Texas in Lubbock, Texas.

1. What was your individual career path in terms of education/training, entry-level job, or other significant opportunity?

I graduated from Ursuline Academy of Dallas in Texas and then attended a four-year university, Texas Tech University Health Sciences Center (TTUHSC). I graduated early—in three-and-a-half years—as a registered nurse (RN) with a bachelor's degree in nursing (BSN) and then began working in an intensive care unit and the emergency room of Covenant (formerly Methodist) Hospital. After earning my master's degree in nursing (MSN), I began teaching at TTUHSC and obtained my PhD in nursing. I noticed all faculty members seemed to have specialized in a specific area of nursing, so I chose forensic nursing because I found it so interesting, and I loved interacting with other disciplines such as law enforcement, lawyers, or advocates. Forensic nursing also seemed to best fit my personality and love for adventure and mystery. My state offered a state certification for Sexual Assault Nurse Examiners (SANEs) through the Attorney General's Office, as do some other states. For states that do not offer certification, there is the option of certifying through the International Association of Forensic Nurses (IAFN). Many universities now offer degrees in forensic nursing.

The city where I lived did not have a forensic nursing program at the time, so I met with significant city leaders and hospital administrators to create forensic nursing opportunities. Our medical examiner hired a forensic nurse, and I formed a nonprofit organization to provide forensic nursing services to the city and county hospitals called Forensic Nurse Staffing of West Texas. Additionally, I began practicing as a legal nurse consultant for medical malpractice attorneys. Legal nurse consulting is another subspecialty of forensic nursing, and as I became more involved in the forensic community, attorneys called on me for my nursing expertise and my experience in testifying. Legal nurse consulting allows me to work independently and rely on my critical thinking skills to formulate expert opinions. This line of work is much like putting pieces of a puzzle together; it keeps me challenged, stimulates my brain, keeps me current in my practice, and makes me a better practitioner, as I can learn from others' mistakes.

2. What are the most important skills and/or qualities for someone in your profession?

Flexibility, patience, compassion, empathy, strong communication skills, and the ability to work with others and solve problems. This subspecialty of nursing has a high rate of burnout, so it is important to have a strong support system in place. Burnout can happen in any job when you work long hours or take calls for both day and night hours. Forensic nurses are at a higher risk for burnout because of the patients they treat: victims of violent crimes. These patients come to the hospital at their most vulnerable state, and the stories they tell can put their health care provider at risk for secondary or vicarious traumatization.

3. What do you wish you had known going into this profession?

I had no idea what I was getting myself into, and I don't think anyone really knows until they start training. Forensic nursing is very different from other specialties in the field because you are dealing with vulnerable patients who have been through extreme trauma. The reality of how cruel life can be is oftentimes very stressful and draining. Many nurses get halfway through training only to realize this isn't the path for them, and that is okay. It is important for any nurse considering this specialty to remember to recharge their batteries often and take time out frequently. Many forensic nurses work on-call and all hours of the night, which can be hard on families. It's important to recognize your loved ones at home and be sure they are onboard because their lives will inevitably be impacted as well.

4. Are there many job opportunities in your profession? In what specific areas?

Forensic nursing has a variety of subspecialties. They include sexual assault nurse examiner (SANE), specially trained nurses providing medical forensic examinations, treatment, and evaluations; they also collect forensic evidence from victims of sexual assault or abuse. In addition, the field has legal nurse consultants who are retained by either the prosecution or defense to provide expert opinions and/or testimony in medical malpractice or forensic cases; correctional health nurses practice in correctional facilities. Forensic nursing opportunities vary by location, but new programs are starting all the time. Lastly, using a SANE for sexual assault exams is quickly becoming the standard of care.

5. How do you see your profession changing in the next five years, how will technology impact that change, and what skills will be required?

Just like anything in medicine, forensic nursing is constantly changing and evolving. Forensic nursing started in the '70s, and I think the specialty will continue to grow during the next five years. In the fourteen years I have practiced, we have changed our equipment three times and gone from paper to electronic charting. Texas, where I practice and teach, is currently working on a standardized evidence collection protocol while changes are being made in the crime labs that will impact our practice.

Forensic nurses will be challenged to keep up with technology and collaborate with other disciplines in addition to working with the changes.

6. What do you enjoy most about your job? What do you enjoy least about your job?

I love working and collaborating with multidisciplinary teams. I love the challenge that most cases bring and never knowing what your shift is going to be like. Every day is different. Just when you think you have seen it all, you see something completely unbelievable. This area of nursing challenges me in ways I never knew were possible. It is my passion, my greatest joy, and biggest heartbreak at times, but I can't imagine anything I would rather do or where I could make a bigger difference.

What I enjoy least is that forensic nursing isn't in every hospital, and so, many times, it seems like there are too many outside factors determining the type of exam a sexual assault victim will receive instead of hospitals simply providing the highest level of care for all.

7. Can you suggest a valuable "try this" for students considering a career in your profession?

I would highly recommend volunteering at a hospital to see if nursing is the right fit. Once someone is a nurse, I would suggest shadowing a forensic nurse or volunteering for a rape crisis center prior to going through the training. Most programs require two years' nursing experience before a nurse is eligible for certification as a SANE. There is a certification available for legal nurse consultants, but most attorneys are simply looking for a nurse with higher education and years of experience in a certain specialty. Many law firms employ nurses, and they are good resources for advice.

HOSPITAL CARE AND SERVICES

Summary

Hospitals provide medical, diagnostic, and treatment services that are delivered by physicians, nurses, and other medical services staff. Specialized accommodations required by inpatients are more costly to provide than are outpatient services, and they represent the primary expense for entities delivering these services. Hospitals have traditionally provided outpatient services as a secondary activity, but their focus has shifted in the twenty-first century (largely driven by cost). Hospitals admit fewer patients to beds, and they provide more care on a nonadmission basis, either through the hospitals proper or through their ancillary clinics. Contemporary outpatient, or ambulatory, services provide greater revenue opportunities than do inpatient services. This situation represents a distinct change that occurred over the first decade of the twenty-first century.

The American Hospital Association (AHA) defines a hospital as a facility in which at least six inpatient beds are available for admission and occupancy twenty-four hours a day, seven days a week. A hospital must have on staff fully licensed physicians and other medical professionals authorized to provide inpatient oversight and care. Diagnostic services, some invasive, ranging from pathology to radiology are delivered by physicians, nurses, and ancillary staff. Inpatient services are highly specialized and require substantially greater facility and equipment expenditures and highly trained nursing support. Hospitals, however, must also provide some ambulatory services, such as emergency care, in order to meet criteria required to call themselves hospitals.

There are three overarching categories of hospitals that admit patients for care: general hospitals, specialty (tertiary) hospitals, and psychiatric hospitals. Specialty hospitals provide higher-acuity services—specialized facilities, medical specialists, and enhanced technologies—that general hospitals do not. Private and public hospitals in the United States employed over 5.5 million people in 2006, according to the U.S. Bureau of Labor Statistics (BLS). Some 35 percent of the U.S. health care workforce works in a hospital setting. Of that number, 70 percent work in facilities with more than one thousand employees.

Health care reform and efforts to curb prohibitive costs have resulted in a push to deliver more services on an ambulatory basis. For example, years ago it was common practice to admit newly diagnosed diabetics to hospitals for at least several days to start insulin therapy and educate the patients about their condition and treatment. In the twenty-first century, an admission of this sort is likely to be denied payment by most insurers, who expect such patients to be treated in doctor's offices or clinics on an outpatient basis. Hospitals have become places where only the sickest and most resource-intense patients are admitted, leaving outpatient care to doctors' offices and clinics.

Many physicians (internists and specialists) establish relationships with hospitals so that when their patients are sick, they can send them to those facilities. Traditionally, doctors in private practice would communicate with relevant hospital staff to coordinate their patients' care, visiting the hospital either before or after their workdays to gauge their patients' progress and issue orders for patient care. However, a new physician specialty, the hospitalist, has developed. A hospitalist works solely within a hospital and assumes care for patients during their course of treatment. While hospitalists consult with their patients' primary care physicians, the responsibility for those patients' care rests with their hospitalists.

History of the Industry

Hospitals, or communal places where the sick might go to receive treatment, can be traced back to ancient cultures in Sri Lanka, India, and the Persian Empire. Later, in Europe, the Roman Catholic Church, through monasteries staffed with monks and nuns, assumed responsibility for the care of the sick. In eighteenth century England, independent hospitals developed, usually through the efforts of wealthy benefactors.

The U.S. hospital system originated around the time of the Civil War, when sterilization and modern medical treatments were being developed. In these early years, hospitals were public or not-for-profit; they treated all comers and were staffed by physicians and nurses. By the 1920's, public hospitals were viewed in some circles as service providers for the working class. A transition occurred, as some not-for-profit hospitals began to offer limited services for those who could afford them. This transition represented a response to a social demand for services of a presumed higher quality than those offered by public hospitals. People who could afford these better and costlier health care services, and who were willing to pay for them, brought much-needed revenue streams to the limited-access not-for-profits.

In the 1950's, during the baby-boom generation's birth, American families were living more financially secure lives than they had during previous generations. People began to move away from the centers of towns and cities, taking their wealth with them. Public hospitals, located in the center of many communities, began to suffer even more financial pressure, as their patients tended to be without means. It was not until 1965, though, with the passage of the Social Security Act that public hospitals began to have more secure sources of funding to treat the aged and the poor. As the years have progressed, public hospitals have not disappeared. In fact, public hospitals often play an important role as teaching institutions. Losing paying customers to not-for-profits, however, has presented an ever-growing challenge to the sustainability of these vital public institutions.

In the 1970's, federal legislation designated public hospitals serving a preponderance of poor and indigent persons as "disproportionate care hospitals." Both federal dollars and a commitment to the population that public hospitals serve have maintained the livelihood of these hospitals. Together with private and other not-for-profit hospitals, they provide a network of medical services to an American population that demands top quality, patient-centered care.

The Industry Today

There are nearly six thousand hospitals registered in the United States today. Over the years, hospital-delivered inpatient care has become more specialized, and designated units have been established to serve specific populations. These include pediatrics wards, cardiac care units, and neurology units specializing in seizure and epilepsy patients, among many others. Medical specialties started to emerge in the latter part of the twentieth century, and general practitioners who once took care of everyone in the hospital have began to specialize in any number of limited areas, such as orthopedics or emergency medicine. Nursing has begun to follow suit, as the medical community recognizes that consistency in care and highly skilled area-specific expertise results in better patient outcomes.

Hospital inpatient care has historically been paid by Medicare and other insurance companies under a formula based on a hospital's reported costs to deliver service. Today, most hospitalizations are paid on a per event basis, using a concept known as a "diagnostic related group." Physicians, nurses, and care managers—everyone involved in patient care—work toward one goal: to discharge the patient, either in an improved state or in a manner that allows for successful care at home. People working in hospital care today face greater expectations for efficiency and economy, working with enough people to deliver quality care but, ideally, not so many as to cause financial hemorrhage to the organization. Registered nurses supervise direct inpatient care with support from nonlicensed patient-care technicians or licensed nursing assistants. Some hospitals employ licensed practical nurses (LPNs) for inpatient work, while some limit the LPN role to the ambulatory setting. Phlebotomists, radiology technicians, ultrasonographers, and respiratory therapists are just a few of the numerous professionals employed to care for patients in an inpatient setting.

Hospitals, according to the BLS, constitute only 1 percent of health care establishments, despite being one of the largest employers in the industry. The majority of health care services revenue is driven by pharmaceutical utilization, the long-term care industry, and ambulatory care, not by inpatient hospital activity.

Common partnership industries to hospital care are primarily service driven. They include pharmaceutical companies and providers of medical technology for both patient care and information system infrastructure. Long-term care or rehabilitation facilities, which often serve those recovering from severe injury or illness, may be owned and operated alongside a parent hospital, or they may be privately owned. Transitioning patients too sick to go home but too well to stay in the hospital into such facilities is critical to medical professionals and their patients. Keeping patients in the hospital too long increases costs and can prevent the admission of patients needing immediate and more intense treatment by limiting bed availability.

Industry Market Segments

Hospitals may be small, community-based institutions that tend only to the needs of the local populations, or they may be large urban centers of treatment, research, and instruction of medical students. Some hospitals that specialize in a particular highly demanding service, such as cardiac or brain surgery, receive patients from all over the world seeking the best care available. Other, smaller hospitals may have no specialties to speak of, acting as general medical centers for relatively small populations.

Small Hospitals

The Internal Revenue Service (IRS) categorizes smaller hospitals as those in the gross revenue range of $25 million or less annually. Many smaller hospitals are not-for-profit institutions that closely manage costs. In the early twenty-first century, many rural and small hospitals have been purchased by larger hospital systems, often those centered in nearby metropolitan centers. For instance, University Hospitals in Cleveland, Ohio—a large teaching institution affiliated with Case Western Reserve University Medical School—decided to expand its geographical reach. To that end, University Hospitals developed alliances with smaller hospitals outside the Cleveland area, expanding ambulatory services in these facilities. The benefit to smaller hospitals from such arrangements is an increase in the services they can offer, the ability to negotiate higher payments from insurers, and access to capital in order to purchase equipment and technology and to expand facilities.

Clientele Interaction. Patients receiving services in a hospital setting, particularly during an inpatient stay, are in a highly vulnerable state and are often frightened, in addition to suffering the malady for which they are being treated. Patients rarely arrive alone, and employees of the hospital must be cognizant of extended family's pressures and fears. Financial worries, child care, lost wages, and social concerns for the patient and the family require providers of care to have compassion, understanding, a good sense of timing, and empathy. Hospital staff, from physicians to housekeepers, must maintain professional and respectful decorum; they should promote the hospital's quality to help allay fears and aid recovery, and they must always be aware of the need to protect patients' privacy and confidentiality.

Amenities, Atmosphere, and Physical Grounds. Cleanliness and a calm atmosphere are critical in hospitals. Entering the hospital should be made relatively simple, with such measures as sufficient parking and clear signage. Within the hospital, an attended receiving area should assist in allaying patients' anxiety. Probably the most important consideration within care-delivery areas is the comfort of patients. Controlled humidity and temperature, rigorous attention to modest noise levels, utmost attention to privacy and confidentiality, and minimal odors are all important. Employees in hospitals can expect to undergo an orientation that highlights these important patient-care factors.

Typical Number of Employees. Small hospitals employ up to one thousand staff members and often represent the largest employer in their small communities. These hospitals provide strong economic stability in their locales, offering positions from entry level all the way up to professional physician staff and chief operating officers.

Traditional Geographic Locations. Small hospitals are likely to be located in rural communities (with populations under fifty thousand). It is not uncommon to find these hospitals colocated with long-term care facilities (the next step for many patients no longer sick enough to be hospitalized in acute hospital settings or for those, such as the elderly, needing full-time care). While staff are drawn primarily from the immediate locale, specialty services and providers travel to small rural hospitals from other areas to provide services. Patient transportation to larger hospitals can be cost prohibitive, so many smaller local hospitals work hard to staff additional service deliverables for their consumers. These enhancements might include telemedicine, which leverages patients' ability to receive specialty services without leaving their hometown and can help smaller hospitals increase revenue and retain patients.

Pros of Working for a Small Hospital. Providing local care at a small, local hospital allows employees to work in a more intimate community atmosphere. Direct health care providers see many types of diagnoses and are exposed to variation in their work, providing them with learning opportunities. Working in a smaller setting will likely subject employees to less bureaucracy than they would encounter at larger hospitals. Larger hospitals have more pronounced cultures, or politics, which can be challenging to penetrate or change. Small hospitals provide full-service medical care, including emergency services, yet they rely on larger medical centers to treat complex patients who require specialty consultation and care.

Cons of Working for a Small Hospital. Many small hospitals do not have the financial resources of their larger counterparts. Capital investment in advanced equipment, facility enhancements, or structural expansion is limited. Smaller hospitals can have trouble recruiting and retaining trained staff, including physicians. Lack of resources and inability to match the salaries of larger organizations are two primary drivers behind these staffing challenges. The hospitals' purchasing power and negotiated prices for employee benefits are not as robust as those of larger institutions, which have better risk ratings and can likely offer employees more and better benefit options. In addition, small hospitals primarily provide general medical services, so health care providers working in this setting should not expect to see highly complex patients requiring specialty services. For some, this lack of specialty services may be limiting. These are the many reasons that smaller hospitals seek relationships with larger systems.

Midsize Hospitals

A midsize hospital's gross revenue is likely to be more than $100 million; net income after expenses, however, varies widely depending on the amount of charity care provided, the mix of insurance payers (including Medicare and Medicaid), expenses, and overhead. A hospital's profit margin can be very small after the impact of many factors, including the strength of the national and local economies. In terms of employee annual earnings, professional staff can expect to be paid on a salary basis at a level commensurate with similar positions in similar benchmark organizations. Some professionals work under a base salary with incentive opportunities for additional bonuses. Incentive drivers can include, but are not limited to, productivity or quality metrics for patient-care outcomes. Nonsalaried staff members are paid hourly, and wages are generally competitive.

Clientele Interaction. For the most part, hospitals' core function is fairly consistent: Providing inpatient hospital care and ambulatory services. Working purely in a service industry, staff must be customer-focused, possess excellent communication skills, and truly desire to be in a hands-on, interactive, and caring industry. Midsize hospitals are likely to be general-service facilities and have a critical need to provide service to referring physicians trying to admit patients to the facility. Maintaining positive relationships with those individuals and groups who refer their patients for care is critical to an organization's success.

Amenities, Atmosphere, and Physical Grounds. Usually located in suburbs or small cities, midsize facilities must have adequate parking, secure storage for medical records, privacy in the waiting area, an information technology infrastructure, sufficient support staff, and a commitment to quality patient care. Clinicians should have control over their own office area, and attention to patients' comfort and physical safety should be a priority.

Typical Number of Employees. The number of employees in a midsize hospital will vary by size and service lines offered. General hospitals, specialty hospitals, psychiatric hospitals, and rehabilitative hospitals vary by service line and number of beds. The staff can extend into the thousands depending on the facility. Though defining hospitals by size is challenging, there is evidence that those housing two hundred or more beds are considered to be midsize. If centralized functions such as billing, contracting, collections, and communications systems are contracted externally rather than in-house, the number of employees will be dramatically different.

Traditional Geographic Locations. Midsize facilities are typically located near more populated areas, though there are exceptions. A hospital-service-area population of fifty thousand or more in an urban setting would support a midsize facility. Referrals from medical providers are the lifeblood of these organizations. The closer they are to referring physicians, the greater the likelihood of visibility for such referrals. Professional engagement with the hospital's physician staff and private-practice physicians should be paramount. Socioeconomics in the area can play a role in a hospital's viability. The ability to access inpatient care without onerous travel for patients can contribute to the need for midsize facilities to situate in more populated locales.

Pros of Working for a Midsize Hospital. Well-established organizations provide employment security, and their purchasing power may allow them to offer better benefits at a more favorable rate for their employees that can smaller facilities. Midsize hospitals can provide the infrastructure for scheduling, human resource services, contracting, billing, managing day-to-day facility operations, and financial performance. Employees in this setting have access to health insurance for themselves and their families at group rates, which are more favorable than those a smaller hospital might be able purchase. Pay incentives may be available in these settings, usually based on productivity and expense controls. Shared responsibility for being on call at night and on weekends is more likely to be available than at smaller hospitals, given that more professionals are available to share this responsibility.

Cons of Working for a Midsize Hospital. Midsize hospitals are more complex organizations than their smaller counterparts. This greater complexity can entail more communication challenges and less autonomy, which can pose a challenge for professional medical service workers. Hours and work output are likely to be defined by employers with minimum expectations, even for professional staff. Round-the-clock staffing is required, so working weekends and holidays is likely to be required. The organizational structure of the hospital may require worthy individuals and units within the organization to compete for limited resources.

Large Hospitals

According to an IRS study of over five hundred not-for-profit hospitals, the largest U.S. organizations accommodate over 100,000 visits annually, including inpatient, outpatient, and emergency services combined. An example of a large hospital is one housing sufficient inpatient beds to meet the needs of service and referral areas, a twenty-four-hour emergency department, and surgical and medical services. Typically, such an institution employs many thousands of people, ranging from physicians, nurses, and administrators to support staff, security, and housekeeping personnel. The organization may draw its business from patients within up to a one-hundred-mile radius, depending on competition and patient willingness to travel for services. Competition exists in the health care industry, and grappling for market share while maintaining sufficient staffing for a large hospital is a constant challenge.

Clientele Interaction. Larger organizations offer more diversity and opportunity for medical professionals. Concentrating on inpatient care, long-term care, or ambulatory care may be an option for professionals entering a large hospital setting. An example of a large organization would be an academic medical center with an embedded psychiatry department that offers both inpatient and outpatient services to adults, children, and employees. Daily interactions in such a hospital may involve patients and their families, as well as medical students, nursing students, insurance providers, social service providers, Medicare or Medicaid representatives, vendors, and myriad other stakeholders in the health care delivery system.

Each physician or nurse in this type of setting is part of a large group of similar professionals. All of them are expected to share in on-call (after hours and weekend) duties. Professionals represent their organization and their colleagues whenever they interact with clients, so they are expected to be available and responsive when they are on call. Nonprofessional staff members play just as pivotal a role in supporting excellent and timely care and safety for patients, so they must have the utmost integrity when committing themselves to a career in the health services industry.

Amenities, Atmosphere, and Physical Grounds. Large organizations are typically freestanding, with sizeable grounds and many users. Open space, clear and visible signage, and friendly and helpful staff should be evident to make encounters favorable and stress-free for consumers and employees. Facilities maintenance is critical for patient health and continued patronage. Additionally, facility expansion (on-site or at a satellite location) is often desirable and necessary for large institutions, as many expand their services within their campuses, within a larger urban neighborhood of medical facilities, or into suburban locations.

Typical Number of Employees. Large health care facilities employ thousands of people, including medical, administrative, financial, operations, and support staff. From the first phone call, to patient admission, to patient discharge and followup, hundreds of staff members representing the hospital come in direct or indirect contact with patients. It takes a synergistic, well-coordinated staff to meet the needs of the patients and fulfill the mission of the hospital.

Traditional Geographic Locations. Large hospital facilities, particularly academic ones, are generally located in metropolitan, highly populated areas. A sufficient population base with the promise of growth is critical to the livelihood of such a medical facility.

Pros of Working for a Large Hospital

Large health care facilities offer many people the opportunity for advancement. Throughout their careers, employees can work hard to develop leadership skills and move into growth positions, such as administrative or management roles, especially if they are motivated and committed to learning. Larger organizations tend to have the financial capacity to develop employee skills, particularly if their mission includes academic instruction or research alongside clinical care. The hospital industry, embedded in the overarching and mammoth health care industry, offers job security and opportunities for advancement.

Cons of Working for a Large Hospital

Employees of a large hospital can expect the bureaucracy and delays inherent to decision making within any large organization. Sometimes, it can take what seems a very long time to move initiatives forward. No area of the hospital is exempt from these challenges: Leadership and managers must advocate regularly for resources in order to receive them. Money plays a role in investments. Anyone searching for a position in a large hospital should pay close attention to the mission and vision of the organization and its current employees' satisfaction with their work. Potential employees should feel empowered to ask these questions when applying for a position.

The health care industry is somewhat more conservative than are other major industries: Hospitals do not tend to be on the cutting edge of progress when compared to large corporations or technology-based companies in other sectors. However, large hospitals with robust surgical and medical services need to remain competitive. Investment in organizational and facility growth is an ongoing expectation; information technology is exploding in hospitals, with patients demanding more immediate access to their medical information. Surgical and diagnostic advances represent major capital investments, but without them a hospital can lose its competitive edge. Computer and technology staff are always in high demand in this fast-paced environment.

Organizational Structure and Job Roles

Any size entity providing hospital services must function as a business, no matter what its nature and mission are. Particularly important in the hosptial industry is keeping patient care and safety paramount. The need to provide a positive operating margin to sustain the mission of a hospital drives its financial stewardship. It can be very challenging for administrative and financial professionals to keep their hospitals going concerns while maintaining favorable relations. Hospitals rely greatly on their primary revenue producers (physicians and medical staff) for financial viability. They are highly complex, integrated systems that require many key critical roles to be filled.

The following umbrella categories apply to the organizational structure of hospitals:
- Business and Operations Management
- Medical Staff
- Contracting and Reimbursement
- Human Resources
- Customer Service/Risk Management
- Marketing and Public Affairs
- Information Technology and Communication Systems
- Facilities and Security
- Housekeeping
- Nutrition

Medical Staff

Hospitals are defined by the quality and professionalism of those providing medical care, from surgeons to radiologic (X-ray) technicians. Successful organizations thrive on high standards of care, excellent communication, and a shared understanding of best practices in providing patient care. The range of medical staff is wide, including highly trained specialists, staff nurses, medical technicians, physical therapists, and nursing aides or orderlies.

Famous First

The Blessed Gerard (c. 1040 – 3 September 1120) was a lay brother in the Benedictine order who was appointed as rector of the hospice in Jerusalem in 1080, and who, in the wake of the success of the First Crusade in 1099, became the founder of the Order of St John of Jerusalem (Knights Hospitaller, which received papal recognition in 1113). During the Siege of Jerusalem (1099), when the Christian population had been expelled from Jerusalem, Gerard was able to remain behind with some fellow serving brothers to tend to the sick in the hospital.

After the success of the First Crusade and the establishment of the Kingdom of Jerusalem, Gerard continued his work at the hospital. By 1113, the hospital was a wealthy and powerful organization within the kingdom of Jerusalem, and Gerard expanded its operations far beyond the limits of the city, establishing daughter hospitals at Bari, Otranto, Taranto, Messina, Pisa, Asti and Saint-Gilles, placed strategically along the pilgrim route to Jerusalem.

Source: https://en.wikipedia.org/wiki/Blessed_Gerard

Occupation Specialties

Medical and Health Services Manager
Specialty Responsibilities

Chief dietitians: Direct institutional departments that provide food service and nutritional care. They provide direction for menu development, food preparation and service, purchasing, sanitation, safety procedures, and personnel issues.

Coordinators of rehabilitation services: Plan and direct the operation of health rehabilitation programs, such as physical, occupational, recreational, and speech therapies.

Dental services directors: Administer dental programs in hospitals and direct department activities. They are responsible for establishing training programs, setting up policies and procedures, and hiring and promoting employees.

Nursing service directors: Administer nursing programs in hospitals, nursing homes, or other medical facilities. They maintain standards of patient care and advise other medical staff about the nursing services provided.

Pharmacy services directors: Coordinate and direct the activities and functions of a hospital pharmacy. They implement policies and procedures, hire and train interns, and aid in the development of computer programs for pharmacy information management systems.

Medical staff occupations may include the following:
- Physician
- Specialized Physician
- Advanced Practice Nurse
- Registered Nurse
- Licensed Practical Nurse
- Radiologic Technician
- Phlebotomist
- Physical Therapist
- Laboratory Technician

The outlook for the hospital care industry shows it to be on the rise. Demand for workers and career opportunities are favorable. Growth is rapid, with total health care expenditures representing 17 percent of the U.S. gross domestic product (GDP). With the largest aging population in the nation's history on the cusp of old age, growth in terms of services is inevitable, and with the passage of the Patient Protection and Affordable Care Act (2010), 34 million more Americans are projected to acquire health insurance and thereby gain greater access to health care services. By 2019, the health care sector is projected by the Department of Health and Human Services to represent 21 percent of GDP.

Challenges for those entering this industry will include greater competition for college-educated professionals, with a bachelor's degree as bare minimum. Those with advanced degrees will have greater prospects in this highly competitive service industry. The industry will look for those who are self-directed and have highly honed interpersonal skills. In the past, health care was not considered a business, so service, rather than finance, was its focus. Today, nurses and physicians are increasingly augmenting their education with finance and business operations training.

In terms of hospitals' financial stability, unemployment has led more customers to be covered under federal and state insurers (specifically Medicare and Medicaid), with insufficient reimbursement to hospitals to cover their costs. Pressures to reduce both the costs and the length of patient stays in the hospital, as well as to lower nurse-to-patient ratios, have occurred as a result of financial constraints on these health care facilities. The projected growth of the medical industry will make working in a hospital a secure career choice. The industry, however, is not immune to economic pressures. Difficult financial times can result in unexpected hiring freezes or reductions in force for "noncritical" positions. Direct patient care positions are mission-critical and are some of the most secure in the industry during economic downturns.

Academic excellence is a sure stepping stone for entry into this competitive market, particularly for skilled, white-collar positions in the hospital setting. Students should actively search for internship opportunities to gain hands-on exposure to the hospital environment during their academic training. Early exposure is invaluable and a strong self-marketing tool.

Employment Advantages

People who work in hospitals will recognize job security as a strong attractor in a global economy that threatens other industries, such as manufacturing. Health care, particularly inpatient services, cannot be outsourced and demand for them will only grow over time. Health care professions are vast and disparate. In an industry of increasing federal oversight and legal compliance regulations, specialization in career avenues is inevitable. Hospital service offerings are increasingly focused on specific populations and medical conditions, such as geriatrics, adolescent care, mental health care, and other segments.

Because of growing specialization, and because the work of hospitals is to help people gain wellness, the opportunities for a rich, diverse career are numerous. Care and treatment of patients, as well as teaching and professional research in academic settings, are all intriguing opportunities for professionals to explore. Strong communicators who excel at helping others and who are emotionally competent will find themselves well-suited for health care careers. Working within a hospital provides great satisfaction to the professional who enjoys working face-to-face with customers and who enjoys being part of a vital community asset.

Annual Earnings

With an aging U.S. population, the hospital industry is seeing an increasing number of older patients demanding more intense and costly services. Technological and pharmacological advances continuously offer new treatments to meet this demand to extend quality of life well into patients' eighties and nineties, as well as the demands of an American public that has come to expect positive health outcomes.

Parsing out earnings in the hospital industry, nationally or globally, is speculative at best. Hospitals employ 35 percent of all people working in the health care industry, according to the BLS. Annual earnings in the hospital setting are no longer a metric of direct relevance to the BLS. Hospitals' gross revenues have historically been calculated based on what they bill insurers, and net revenues have been calculated based on what insurers actually pay, adjusted to reflect the hospitals' reported costs to render service. However, quality and medical outcomes have become the financial metric of success and are quickly becoming the core basis on which payment is made to hospitals for both inpatient and outpatient services. A unit of service is an admission, and payment is based not only on how patients fare in terms of health but also on how efficiently and cost-effectively the hospital rendered service. The BLS projects that health care and insurance revenues will grow by $547 billion by 2016. As the baby boomers continue into retirement, the demand for hospital services is expected to grow.

Fast Fact

It's a rare occurrence, but it does happen: patients under anesthesia can wake up during surgery. It's called anesthesia awareness, and when it happens patients may remember their surroundings or pressure or pain.

Source: Medicaldaily.com

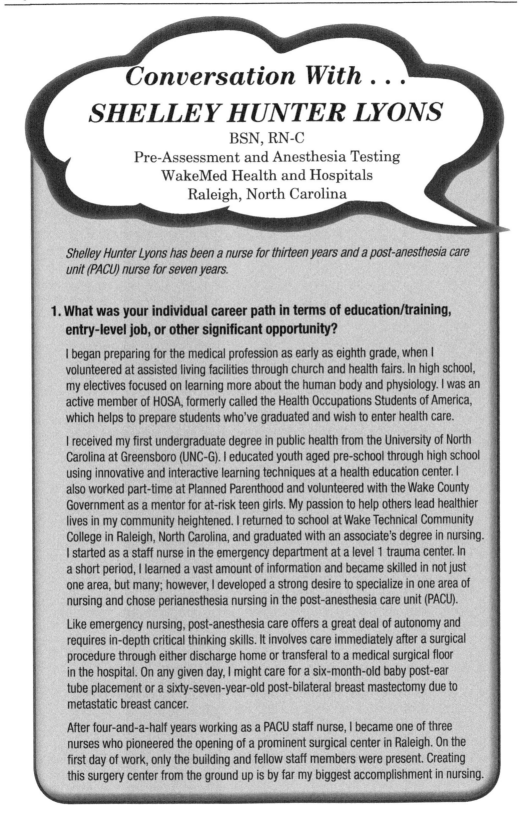

Conversation With . . .

SHELLEY HUNTER LYONS

BSN, RN-C
Pre-Assessment and Anesthesia Testing
WakeMed Health and Hospitals
Raleigh, North Carolina

Shelley Hunter Lyons has been a nurse for thirteen years and a post-anesthesia care unit (PACU) nurse for seven years.

1. What was your individual career path in terms of education/training, entry-level job, or other significant opportunity?

I began preparing for the medical profession as early as eighth grade, when I volunteered at assisted living facilities through church and health fairs. In high school, my electives focused on learning more about the human body and physiology. I was an active member of HOSA, formerly called the Health Occupations Students of America, which helps to prepare students who've graduated and wish to enter health care.

I received my first undergraduate degree in public health from the University of North Carolina at Greensboro (UNC-G). I educated youth aged pre-school through high school using innovative and interactive learning techniques at a health education center. I also worked part-time at Planned Parenthood and volunteered with the Wake County Government as a mentor for at-risk teen girls. My passion to help others lead healthier lives in my community heightened. I returned to school at Wake Technical Community College in Raleigh, North Carolina, and graduated with an associate's degree in nursing. I started as a staff nurse in the emergency department at a level 1 trauma center. In a short period, I learned a vast amount of information and became skilled in not just one area, but many; however, I developed a strong desire to specialize in one area of nursing and chose perianesthesia nursing in the post-anesthesia care unit (PACU).

Like emergency nursing, post-anesthesia care offers a great deal of autonomy and requires in-depth critical thinking skills. It involves care immediately after a surgical procedure through either discharge home or transferal to a medical surgical floor in the hospital. On any given day, I might care for a six-month-old baby post-ear tube placement or a sixty-seven-year-old post-bilateral breast mastectomy due to metastatic breast cancer.

After four-and-a-half years working as a PACU staff nurse, I became one of three nurses who pioneered the opening of a prominent surgical center in Raleigh. On the first day of work, only the building and fellow staff members were present. Creating this surgery center from the ground up is by far my biggest accomplishment in nursing.

I also have obtained certification as an ambulatory perianesthesia nurse (CAPA) from the American Board of Perianesthesia Nursing and board certification in emergency nursing (CEN). At age forty-one, I returned to UNC-G and earned my bachelor of science degree in nursing.

Recently, I have transitioned to more of an administrative role in perianesthesia, which is preoperative education and assessments for patients scheduled for surgical procedures. My main goal is to optimize the patient's safety for surgery. I review medical history, ask appropriate questions to close gaps, and order appropriate lab and diagnostic testing. I review and advise on continuing and discontinuing medications while collaborating with surgeons and primary care providers. I also obtain medical and cardiac clearances for patients with health problems who are about to undergo surgery. I help alleviate patients' fears and anxiety surrounding surgeries. My experience working in the community molded me to perform this position effectively and with ease and confidence.

My current job also has a more predictable schedule, allowing me to spend more time at home with my seven-year-old daughter.

My ultimate goal is to become a family nurse practitioner with a focus in women's health. Personally, it's time for me to evolve. The health of my community matters to me, and I desire to make a significant impact in my community. To do so, I must broaden my scope of practice. I am confident that I am capable of providing well-informed, evidence-based nursing to my community.

2. What are the most important skills and/or qualities for someone in your profession?

Efficient time management skills and critical thinking. A nurse must have empathy, yet function within ethical and moral boundaries. At times, you have to meet patients where they are and proceed from there. Respect their wishes even if you don't agree. A nurse must remain nonjudgmental, respectful of other cultures and beliefs, be willing to continue learning and accept change gracefully. The health care field is constantly evolving.

A PACU nurse also needs to be a strong advocate for patients post-surgery, as they are sedated and unable to express needs effectively. Be assertive and an excellent verbal communicator with the patient, family, surgeons, and the anesthesia staff. You are the patient's voice.

3. What do you wish you had known going into this profession?

Nursing can be very emotionally demanding and physically taxing. You're not only a nurse at work but to family, friends, and even to strangers who see you in your work attire. I didn't realize the many holidays I would spend at work away from my family because health care is always needed. At times, I have risked my life in inclement weather (hurricane, disasters, snow, and ice) to save lives. I wouldn't change it. I love it! Nursing is the core of my being.

In addition, my last instructor in nursing school shared a memorable piece of advice when I was trying to decide my path as a new graduate. She told me not to become too comfortable in any nursing position. When this happens, you make life-altering mistakes because tasks become habitual. Her true takeaway message? Take the time to challenge yourself. Enroll in a class, attend national-level nursing conferences, or join a professional organization and be an active member. Ultimately, do not become complacent, jaded, or bitter in nursing. You can choose otherwise. Change can be uncomfortable, but nothing in this life remains the same.

4. Are there many job opportunities in your profession? In what specific areas?

The nursing profession is vast! A nurse can work in home health, a hospital, clinical research, and more. Other positions in PACU include nurse educator/supervisor, nurse manager, director of nursing, and multiple other positions that require advanced degrees.

5. How do you see your profession changing in the next five years, how will technology impact that change, and what skills will be required?

Technology is a major factor at this time; most advanced degrees are earned 100 percent online.

6. What do you enjoy most about your job? What do you enjoy least about your job?

I enjoy the autonomy and respect from other coworkers and practitioners. I enjoy medicine and health. I also attend health fairs and conferences to learn new information in my profession. Lastly, I find joy talking with patients while making a difference in my community.

My least favorite is the high demand for nurses without reciprocal gratitude and a lack of monetary return.

7. Can you suggest a valuable "try this" for students considering a career in your profession?

Volunteer or spend time with various populations of age groups such as nursing homes, daycares, different floors at hospitals, The American Red Cross, YMCA, and even The Salvation Army. Research medical-related clubs and organizations to join such as HOSA. Keep your options open. Never say never. The one area of medicine/health you may think is "not for you" may just be your niche.

Related Resources for Further Research

American Academy of Medical Management
Crossville Commons
560 W Crossville Rd., Suite 103
Roswell, GA 30075
Tel: (770) 649-7150
Fax: (770) 649-7552
http://www.epracticemanagement.org

American College of Healthcare Executives
1 N Franklin, Suite 1700
Chicago, IL 60606-3529
Tel: (312) 424-2800
Fax: (312) 424-0023
http://www.ache.org

American Counseling Association
5999 Stevenson Ave.
Alexandria, VA 22304
Tel: (703) 823-9800
Fax: (800) 473-2329
http://www.counseling.org

American Hospital Association
155 N Wacker Dr.
Chicago, IL 60606
Tel: (312) 422-3000
http://www.aha.org

Healthcare Financial Management Association
2 Westbrook Corporate Center, Suite 700
Westchester, IL 60154
Tel: (708) 531-9600
Fax: (708) 531-0032
http://www.hfma.org

Medical Group Management Association
104 Inverness Terrace East
Englewood, CO 80112-5306
Tel: (303) 799-1111
http://www.mgma.com

National Association of Public Hospitals and Health Systems
1301 Pennsylvania Ave. NW, Suite 950
Washington, DC 20004
Tel: (202) 585-0100
Fax: (202) 585-0101
http://www.naph.org

Nancy Sprague

INSURANCE INDUSTRY

The business of insurance affects nearly every transaction that can be quantified in the world, as it offers protection to individuals and businesses from potential financial risks through automobile, casualty, disability, health, home, liability, life, and property insurance. In exchange for a sum of money—called the premium—policyholders receive the promise of reimbursement from insurers for small and large losses due to a variety of hazards, including car accidents, property theft, fire damage, medical ailments, and loss of income resulting from disability or death. The insurance industry is regulated in most cases by state governments rather than the federal government. The insurance industry offers full- and part-time employment in several occupations at different levels.

History of the Industry

Although the concept of risk management can be traced as far back as the third millennium b.c.e. among Chinese merchant traders attempting to encourage the safe arrival of goods, the practice of insuring officially began in the United States in the seventeenth century. Great Britain and its American colonies were heavily involved in commercial trade of spices, tea, sugar, dyes, fabrics, and other goods. Given the treacherous seas, Britain developed a system of insuring the risks of loss of, or damage to, cargoes through Lloyd's of London.

Insurance offers protection to individuals and businesses from potential financial risks through automobile, casualty, disability, health, home, liability, life, and property insurance.

In 1688, Edward Lloyd opened a coffee shop that attracted many shipowners and merchants. These traders began to transact business in the shop, so Lloyd also began offering marine insurance. By the end of the eighteenth century, Lloyd's had become the first modern-day insurance company. Today, Lloyd's is still a leader in the international insurance market, providing specialist services to businesses in more than two hundred countries and territories.

Another branch of the insurance industry also developed in Great Britain and America during the same period. Fire represented a growing danger in urban areas, where there was no running water and many structures were constructed of wood. In particular, the Great Fire of London, which devastated more than thirteen thousand houses in 1666, prompted a more serious interest in protecting buildings against this risk. Mutual fire protection services, in which residents and businesses pledged to help fight local fires, began to form.

In 1752, Benjamin Franklin and a group of prominent citizens started the Philadelphia Contributionship for the Insurance of Houses from Loss by Fire in South Carolina, which became known as the first property insurance company in the American Colonies. Franklin had personal experience with fire and wanted to ensure protection for others. The contributionship now includes five subsidiaries that still specialize in property insurance but cover much more than the loss of homes by fire. Franklin also organized the first life insurance company—the Presbyterian Ministers' Fund—in 1759.

From the eighteenth century forward, insurance companies became common business ventures in America. The industry diversified greatly in the United States during the nineteenth and twentieth centuries. For example, lenders required farmers to take out crop insurance when securing mortgages on their property to obtain crop loans. Additionally, the invention of the automobile led to the need for automobile insurance.

In many cases, purchasing insurance is not voluntary. Mortgage lenders require homeowners to insure their property as a condition of lending them money. Similarly, states require drivers to purchase automobile insurance. On the other hand, life insurance is usually voluntary.

Many societal factors have contributed to the evolution of the insurance industry, including the passage of workers compensation laws and the advent of the Industrial Revolution. Quite possibly the biggest growth area in the insurance industry has been in medical services and health insurance. Technology has prompted many developments in medicine, and the population has continued to grow. Both situations have increased the cost of health care, creating the need for a middleman to manage its utilization. Further, an aging population has sprouted new needs, such as long-term care insurance. Health insurance will continue to change as a result of the

Patient Protection and Affordable Care Act (PPACA) of 2010 and the Health Care and Education Reconciliation Act of 2010.

Besides new coverage options, the standard policy language across most of the segments of the insurance industry has also changed through the years. Insurance coverage for some kinds of tangible losses is generally clear, but gray areas and exclusions remain that are decided on a case-by-case basis. So as long as there are transactions between members of society, there will always be insurance to minimize an individual's or a business's risk.

The Industry Today

There are a great many insurance companies in the United States today, and the insurance industry has grown to be one of the top five industry sectors in the twenty-first century. Some insurance companies have strong national presences, while others are regional businesses. Some offer all types of insurance, while others specialize. The industry is still mostly regulated at the state level, and even the PPACA designates the states as the primary regulators of the health insurance exchanges.

For the most part, the concept of insuring has not changed. An insurer agrees to shoulder a risk on behalf of an individual or business (the insured) for a set fee (a premium). Through the underwriting process, the insurer evaluates the circumstances surrounding the measurable risk and produces a policy, or contract, stating the risks it will insure against and how much it will guarantee as a reimbursement to the insured if the risk occurs. Policies also include lists of exclusions, or things that are not insured against, and these policies can be quite complex.

The most common segments of the industry are property and casualty insurance (for automobiles, homes, and businesses), health insurance, and life insurance. Until the 1950's, each U.S. company was restricted to selling only one type of insurance. Today, firms can underwrite several insurance types each.

Beyond the main areas of coverage, insurance protection can be purchased for just about any measurable risk. Insurance companies generally fall into two categories— life insurance or nonlife insurance. Life insurers sell life insurance, annuities, and pension products, while nonlife companies sell all other types of coverage.

Disability insurance provides financial assistance to individuals when they are unable to work because of a disabling illness or injury. Similarly, workers' compensation insurance—purchased by employers—replaces all or part of emloyees' lost wages and accompanying medical expenses after job-related injuries. For businesses, disability overhead insurance reimburses for the overhead expenses experienced by businesses when their owners are unable to work.

Besides developments in society leading to greater coverage niches and industry opportunities, several outside factors have changed the modern-day insurance market. For example, technology has had both negative and positive effects on the insurance industry. Customers can use Web browsers to access account and billing information, submit claims, view insurance quotes, and purchase policies. Communication among sales agents, adjusters, and insurance carriers has also improved through the Internet. These functions may reduce paperwork and allow companies to keep better track of their customers, thus increasing productivity and decreasing costs. Claims adjusters may no longer need to visit the site of their customer's damage; instead, they can rely on satellite imagery to evaluate claims.

At the same time, the availability of information and services on the Internet has adversely affected some insurance occupations, such as insurance sales agents, who may be less necessary to businesses that can make sales online. Insurance offerings for property, casualty, and automobiles are relatively straightforward, and online resources allow customers to compare and purchase insurance products on their own. They thus eliminate the need to meet face-to-face with a live agent, although some customers still prefer to do so. Further, software upgrades have automated some jobs, such as that of an underwriter. The ability to compare rates online and identify the cheapest rate has also increased competition within the industry.

Jobs in the insurance industry range from agents and brokers to appraisers to underwriters to claims adjusters to actuaries, again working across several insurance coverage types. In addition to these industry-specific roles, there are administrative and executive opportunities in the industry. Overall job growth within the industry has been slowed by industry consolidation, corporate downsizing, new technology, and increasing direct mail, telephone, and Internet sales. In particular, the recession of 2007-2009 caused declining revenues, investment losses, and credit rating downgrades, as it did in many other industries.

Health Insurance

Health insurance covers the costs of medical care, as well as loss of income due to illness or injury. Dental care and long-term disability also fall under the umbrella of health insurance. Health insurance coverage varies from the most basic (covering only catastrophic events, or what used to be called "major medical") to the most comprehensive (covering preventive, inpatient, and outpatient care). The amount of coverage determines a person's premium, deductible, and coinsurance. Under the PPACA and its companion legislation, the Health Care and Education Reconciliation Act of 2010, health insurance will be required of most Americans beginning in 2014. Health insurance is offered through the private and public sectors and by both for-profit and nonprofit private entities.

Pros of Working in Health Insurance. Growth is probably the biggest advantage in the health insurance segment. The PPACA will increase the market for health insurance by roughly 30 million people, opening a number of new opportunities for insurance agencies. The law's nationwide mandate to purchase health insurance will also increase sales. Industry reports indicate that approximately 5 percent of health insurers plan to increase the number of full-time employees on their payrolls by more than 20 percent.

Increasing life expectancy has had a positive impact on health insurance and will continue to do so in the future. This trend creates a greater need for health and long-term care insurance. Coupled with new discoveries and developments in medical care, the health insurance segment remains very dynamic.

Another pro is the niche found in the health insurance segment. Claims examiners play an important and unique role, offering a specialty in the field. These workers review claims to see whether costs are reasonable based on their corresponding services and diagnoses. A second specialty is in the actuary career path. Actuaries help companies develop health and long-term-care insurance policies by predicting the likelihood of occurrence of heart disease, diabetes, stroke, cancer, and other chronic ailments among particular groups of people, such as those living in a certain area or sharing a family history of illness. Actuarial work can be beneficial to both consumers and companies because the ability accurately to predict the probability of a particular health event among a certain subgroup ensures that premiums are assessed fairly based on the risk to the organization.

Cons of Working in Health Insurance. The PPACA poses a number of challenges for the health insurance industry. Health insurance will become more regulated as the law is phased in. In addition to the individual insurance mandate and the mandate for companies to provide insurance, the law restricts the behavior of health insurance companies. Companies will no longer be allowed to deny coverage or charge higher fees because of preexisting medical conditions, and they will be required to offer particular levels of coverage if they wish to offer plans to individuals through insurance exchanges. All health plans will be required to cover preventive care. Although these changes are being phased in over a ten-year period, the industry will look very different at the end of the process than it did before the reforms were passed. Thus, working in the health insurance segment may become more complicated, especially in the short term.

Also, because medical care is always changing, coverage issues arise easily. Health insurance policies differ tremendously, and it is difficult for customers to read the fine print. It may be difficult even for insurance agents to keep up with all the changes.

The following umbrella categories apply to the organizational structure of businesses within the insurance industry:

- Office and Administrative Support
- Management, Business, and Financial Operations
- Sales
- Medical, Legal, and Actuarial Staff
- Information Technology
- Human Resources

Medical, Legal, and Actuarial Staff

Some 11.4 percent of insurance personnel are members of companies' medical and legal staff. Lawyers represent their companies in litigation, responding to suits and bringing actions against clients and other companies as necessary. Doctors and nurses advise insurance companies in managed care health plans.

Actuaries represent a small portion of insurance employment but are essential. An actuary is an insurance professional who calculates probabilities for the purpose of setting policy premiums, providing statistical data for records, and developing new products for a company. This occupation is considered one of the top one hundred fastest-growing jobs. Actuaries have degrees in actuarial science, mathematics, statistics, or business-related fields and must take a series of national exams to attain full professional status, which takes five to ten years. Most actuaries work traditional workweeks of forty hours. In 2009, the mean annual salary for actuaries was $96,080 for those employed by carriers and $98,630 for those employed by agencies and brokerages.

Medical, legal, and actuarial occupations may include the following:
- Actuary
- Attorney/Counsel
- Title Examiner/Abstractor/Searcher
- Paralegal
- Nurse
- Physician

Health care reform and the changing face of health insurance will create new opportunities for health insurers. Advances in the medical and pharmaceutical fields will also affect health insurance, inspiring new coverage options. The aging of the American population will result in more people needing insurance for longer periods of time. The resulting greater demand will apply to all areas of insurance, including health and automobile coverage. In addition to growth, employment opportunities exist because of continuous turnover. Companies will always need to replace workers who leave or retire.

Conversation With . . .
KEVIN D. HOLT

BA-Education, AND, RN, COHN-S (inactive)
Retired Ooccupational Nurse

Kevin D. Holt was an occupational nurse for ten years and retired as the corporate health and wellness director for a manufacturing corporation in Eastern North Carolina.

1. What was your individual career path in terms of education/training, entry-level job, or other significant opportunity?

My background is in science, anatomy, and physiology. I went to the University of North Carolina at Chapel Hill and graduated with a bachelor's degree in health and physical education. I looked for coaching jobs but there were none, so I became health and fitness director at a YMCA for six years. From there I did sales with a small manufacturing company for a number of years, but it was a family-run company with no upward mobility. My job got stale. At the time I was reading article after article about a huge shortage of nurses. My wife said, "You could do that." I was forty years old with two kids, but still I went to over to the local school, Edgecombe Community College, and spoke with a counselor who looked at my background. I had a number of college credits, such as in anatomy, that were still good and transferred. It was a year-and-a-half program. I thought on that for a little while and decided to take a chance, and went on to earn my associate degree in nursing.

Initially, I looked at being an operating room nurse and did my first clinical there. They ran twelve-hour shifts, no nights, and no weekends. After graduating, I was offered an occupational health position at a pharmaceutical plant, so I took that.

Most occupational nurses are in large manufacturing plants. You've got many different rules and regulations to follow. You handle all the injury and with that, no matter how bad the injury, you still have to work with workers' compensation. You also do medical surveillance. Say it's a noisy plant. You have to test employees' hearing every year, make sure they have proper ear plugs, and train, train, train. People who run a forklift have to pass a physical. There's a lot of medical testing, including for drugs, and we also do eye exams. As the nurse, you have to document everything.

My last job was at a large paper manufacturer, which makes brown craft paper sent to twenty-five cardboard manufacturing plants where they make boxes. I was the corporate health and wellness director, and managed health and work-related injuries, workers' compensation, and the wellness program. I also audited plants with the safety team. I ended up traveling almost every week, all over the country. After several years, I decided to retire.

2. What are the most important skills and/or qualities for someone in your profession?

You've got to be observant and able to assess a health situation. You need very good math skills. You must document, so you need to learn medical language.

3. What do you wish you had known going into this profession?

I didn't realize how many different types of nurses there were. If I'd known that ten years earlier, I probably would have gone to nursing school sooner.

4. Are there many job opportunities in your profession? In what specific areas?

There's a tremendous, tremendous amount of opportunity and demand for nursing of all kinds. Occupational nursing doesn't tend to grow that much; typically, only the larger companies use them.

5. How do you see your profession changing in the next five years, how will technology impact that change, and what skills will be required?

All the documentation is computer-oriented, but you've got to observe and understand what's happening with the person you're seeing. So it's a hands-on job.

6. What do you enjoy most about your job? What do you enjoy least about your job?

I enjoyed helping people change and lead a healthier lifestyle. With these big businesses, you get to meet all the new hires. They come through the human resources department as well as the nursing office. I enjoyed creating or implementing health and wellness programs, like smoking cessation or weight loss programs. When you get somebody in one of those programs and they lose twenty to thirty pounds, that's pretty exciting.

It was a rare day I went home unhappy. This work was something I could relate to. In my last position, the travel became wearing after a while. Also, there's a lot of administrative paperwork.

7. Can you suggest a valuable "try this" for students considering a career in your profession?

The easiest way is to shadow someone. There may be days all the nurse does is physicals, or they're out in the plant doing a safety inspection on a piece of equipment. When I got into occupational nursing, the average age of nurses was mid-fifties, so as a group, there were a lot of experienced nurses drawn from different specialties. Also, contact your state occupational health nurses' association for additional information.

Related Resources for Further Research

American Council of Life Insurance
101 Constitution Ave. NW, Suite 700
Washington, DC 20001-2133
Tel: (202) 624-2000
http://www.acli.com

American Insurance Association
2101 L St. NW, Suite 400
Washington, DC 20037
Tel: (202) 828-7100
Fax: (202) 293-1219
http://www.aiadc.org

American Risk and Insurance Association
716 Providence Rd.
Malvern, PA 19355
Tel: (610) 640-1997
Fax: (610) 725-1007
http://www.aria.org

Independent Insurance Agents and Brokers of America
120 S Peyton St.
Alexandria, VA 22314
Tel: (800) 221-7917
Fax: (703) 683-7556
http://www.iiaba.net

Insurance Information Institute
110 William St.
New York, NY 10038
Tel: (212) 346-5500
http://www.iii.org

National Association of Insurance and Financial Advisors
2901 Telestar Ct.
Falls Church, VA 22042
Tel: (877) 866-2432
http://www.naifa.org

National Association of Insurance Commissioners
444 N Capitol St. NW, Suite 701
Washington, DC 20001
Tel: (202) 471-3990
Fax: (816) 460-7493
http://www.naic.org

National Association of Professional Insurance Agents
400 N Washington St.
Alexandria, VA 22314
Tel: (703) 836-9340
Fax: (703) 836-1279
http://www.pianet.com

Society of Actuaries
475 N Martingale Rd., Suite 600
Schaumburg, IL 60173
Tel: (847) 706-3500
Fax: (847) 706-3599
http://www.soa.org

Patrice La Vigne

PUBLIC HEALTH SERVICES

The public health industry addresses health issues that face both individuals and entire communities. The industry is multifaceted, comprising public safety officials, elected and appointed government leaders, emergency personnel, medical professionals, and scientists and researchers. The mission of this industry is threefold. First, it assesses and monitors the health of populations and groups in order to identify and gauge the extent of health problems. Second, it creates policies by which these issues may be remedied. Third, it studies and promotes the use of health systems.

History of the Industry

Public health concerns and policy have been manifest for millennia. Two thousand years before the first century c.e., ancient civilizations in northern India, and later in Egypt, built cities complete with drainage systems designed to draw away unclean water runoff and sewage from pedestrian walkways and roads. For many of these ancient civilizations, cleanliness was a religious tradition, giving rise to the expression or principle "cleanliness is next to godliness."

Still, epidemics and transmissions of communicable diseases have been prevalent throughout human history. During the great "liberation of thought" in the fourth and fifth centuries b.c.e. in Greece, considered one of the major milestones in the history of human thought, a serious study of the causes of disease and epidemics was undertaken. Prior to this, disease and epidemics were largely attributed to the meddling of otherworldly beings and gods. The new school of thought in Greece, spearheaded by great philosophers such as Hippocrates (c. 460-370 b.c.e.), sought more earthbound causes. (Hippocrates himself is often referred to as the "father of medicine."

The collapse of the Roman Empire around 476 c.e. brought with it a corresponding collapse of public health infrastructures. The Romans, who were famous for their water management and public health systems, suffered defeats by invading forces from European and Arab nations, both in Rome and throughout their realm. Lacking attention, the aqueducts and water systems that characterized the Roman Empire fell into disrepair. The Byzantine Empire, to which much of the former Roman regime migrated after Rome's fall, assimilated many of the ancient Greek and Roman writings on public health practices. Europe, however, reverted to religious-based thought, and the Dark Ages followed.

During the Dark Ages, sanitation and health issues in Europe increased, exacerbated by the development of large, crowded cities. In fact, Rome's collapse was immediately followed by a plague. In the centuries that followed the Dark Ages—from which Europe emerged in the eleventh century—European governments began implementing strict cleanliness policies. These policies were designed to keep waste off the streets and to keep markets clean, not only to protect the public health but also to attract traveling consumers.

This renewed focus on public health did not prevent devastating pandemics, particularly as humanity grew closer together through trade and exploration. In the early fourteenth century, the disease known as Black Death arrived in Italy from central Asia. This pandemic originated in China then spread to India, moving along trade routes via fleas that resided on both rats and human travelers. In only a few years, about one-third of the entire population of Europe was dead, having succumbed to the violent illness. The root causes of the illness remain shrouded in mystery. Naturalists at the time speculated that the disease was born in the swamps adjacent to large cities. Later scientists believed it was an outbreak of the bubonic plague, which had appeared on numerous occasions throughout history. Others believed it was a hemorrhagic fever akin to Ebola. The disease itself remains a mystery, as did its cessation: It abruptly disappeared in 1351.

During the era of exploration, European sailors introduced new diseases to the New World. Among these virulent strains was smallpox, a disease prevalent for millennia prior, but not present in either North nor South America. Millions of Native Americans were exposed and died as a result. It was believed that many of the items brought with these Europeans contained the agents of this disease.

In 1918, another public health crisis erupted, this time in an industrialized society. Soldiers returning from World War I had been exposed to countless contaminants and germs while living in the trenches. This exposure was due to the close quarters and unsanitary conditions of the battlefield. Veterans returned home to the United States and elsewhere with coldlike symptoms. Those symptoms erupted into a far more significant and threatening illness—influenza. Influenza would eventually affect one-fifth of the human population. Over a two-year period, 675,000 Americans died of the illness, a number that surpassed the combat deaths in World War I.

The number and severity of the pandemics and outbreaks that have occurred throughout human history have led to an evolution of public health services. Over time, medical experts and political leaders have been joined by policy makers, educators, emergency personnel, and public safety officials seeking to combat threats to public health. Agencies such as the Centers for Disease Control and Prevention (CDC) have been created not only to assess public health risks but also to trace the roots of diseases as they occur. Agencies such as the CDC work alongside the numerous local, state, and national public health departments.

The Industry Today

The public health services industry is a vast network of interconnected agencies, businesses, and institutions. According to the American Public Health Association (APHA), the industry is dedicated to meeting ten goals:

- Monitoring the public's health status to identify community health problems
- Diagnosing and investigating risks and threats
- Informing, educating, and empowering the public
- Mobilizing community partnerships
- Developing policies and plans that protect and maintain public health
- Enforcing public health laws and regulations
- Providing links and information to people with personal health needs
- Ensuring a competent public health workforce
- Evaluating and reporting on the industry's effectiveness
- Conducting research to develop new insights into public health threats and innovative solutions to those threats

Because the health of individuals is often connected to the health of others (which is the very principle behind the concept of public health), medical practitioners such as doctors, nurses, and allied personnel are but one part of the broad public health services industry. In fact, the total population of people who work in public health, either directly or indirectly, is innumerable. The APHA, for example, has 500,000 public health workers in its ranks, which does not include its local, state, and federal government partners and associated groups.

Educational opportunities for training in public health are equally innumerable, and there are dozens of major public and private universities that offer advanced degrees in public health. Harvard University, for example, offers one of the country's leading programs. The program features students from a wide range of backgrounds, including doctors, nurses, researchers, and social scientists. The field of public health entails an equally broad combination of disciplines, including epidemiology (tracing diseases to their sources), sociological analysis, statistics, environmental studies, and even history.

Although the field of public health services is broad and multifaceted, it is not without connectivity. In fact, it is designed to be a network, taking into account elements that previous fields could not because of their historical limitations. Today's public health services industry is organized in such a way that it can quickly assess public health risks and dangers, trace them back to their foundations, isolate and treat illnesses, implement protective government policies, communicate with the public on the issues at hand, and even introduce programs designed to prevent further spread of the negative agent or illness.

Industry Market Segments

There are several major components to the modern public health industry. Among the longest-standing members of this network are the health care provider and institution. Doctors, nurses, and other medical professionals in hospitals, community health centers, private practices, and local clinics are at the forefront in the effort to combat public health dangers. In many cases, these health care professionals treat those afflicted with disease and other health conditions before their afflictions are known to represent community-wide risks. Because of their role in public health arenas, hospitals and medical facilities have also been focal points of health care reform proposals in the United States. This is particularly true because many poor and uninsured people turn to hospital emergency rooms for treatment of ill health, rather than seeking preventive care from primary care physicians.

Another important component of the public health services industry is the government. Most political systems at their various levels (national, state, county, or municipal) have entities dedicated to initiating programs to promote good health, enforcing public health laws within their jurisdictions, and quickly assessing and reporting epidemiological risks and threats as they arise. Legislators and executive agencies are often on the tail end of public health issues, reacting to risks after the fact and issuing public policies designed to contain risks or to promote alternative behaviors that will mitigate them. The U.S. federal government has four agencies dedicated to public health, while a number of other agencies (such as the Department of Defense and the Environmental Protection Agency) also address public health as part of their functions. The military may be called in during disaster situations from which public health dangers may arise.

Additionally, the contributions of the nonprofit sector to the public health services industry are invaluable. Nonprofit organizations are myriad in nature, and many of them have access to information about their constituencies that medical practitioners and researchers (as well as sociologists) may not. Some, such as the American Red Cross, the American Diabetes Association (ADA), and the AIDS Coalition to Unleash Power (ACT UP), may have data and perspectives on their respective constituents that may suggest better vehicles for preventing public health risks.

The industry also relies heavily on the research of academic institutions. Schools of public health, medical schools, and other such programs conduct studies of existing public health systems and the dangers thereto. These studies help the industry as a whole not only address those dangers but also evolve in response to the altered conditions of an ever-changing population. Often, these schools and programs use grant monies from corporations and governments to conduct their research.

Finally, the role of the public safety agencies in public health services cannot be discounted. Paramedics, police officers, and firefighters are invaluable agents of quick containment in the event of a public health emergency. They are typically the first responders to a disaster scene, such as a fire, earthquake, or severe weather event, all of which may create peripheral health risks even after the event has ended.

The public health services industry is a vast network whose total population of workers is difficult to gauge. The constant evolution and adaptation of this industry to changing environmental conditions in the twenty-first century remain invaluable to the well-being of residents.

Medical Practitioners

Nurses, along with doctors and other health providers, are often the first to encounter emergent public health threats. In the course of treating patients, they note patterns of illness and unusual symptoms, and they are responsible for notifying public health agencies of any worrisome anomalies. In addition, in the twenty-first century, it is possible for groups of medical practitioners to identify patterns accidentally: Reports of symptoms observed at clinics, hospitals, and other sites are aggregated and analyzed by agencies such as the CDC, so no individual front-line doctor needs to recognize an anomaly in order to sound the alarm. Conscientious reporting of seemingly innocuous data may be enough.

Pros of Working for a Medical Facility. A medical facility such as a hospital, medical practice, or physician group offers employees a fast-paced workplace with numerous challenges. There is no typical work schedule, as medical workers encounter an unpredictable environment in which the treatment required for each patient is different. Medical facilities also make available to employees a wide range of resources, such as medical labs, libraries, and medical technologies. Such facilities also present medical professionals with candidates for case studies and, as a result, opportunities to write and publish scholarly articles.

Cons of Working for a Medical Facility. Medical facilities are bound by budgetary constraints that are dictated by the revenues generated by patients and their insurance carriers. In medical facilities that administer to poor patients, reimbursement by the government is considerably less than reimbursement from insured patients. Budgets are therefore often very tight in such instances, limiting medical professionals' ability to earn higher salaries, as well as the resources available to address public health needs. Additionally, nurses are often part of a union, which means that salaries and benefits must be negotiated at the end of every contract. Medical professionals also work long hours, as patients may require around-the-clock care.

Government Agencies

Federal and local governments monitor public health and formulate and implement plans to safeguard and improve health, both over the long term as a matter of policy and in response to short-term crises and disasters.

Traditional Geographic Locations. Departments of public health and other government agencies dedicated to addressing public health concerns are located throughout a given political system. Federal agencies in the United States are based in Washington, D.C., but they have offices in each of the states in order to coordinate with Washington. County and regional governments usually have public health departments located in the largest city or town in the area, usually a county seat. The CDC is headquartered in Atlanta, Georgia.

Pros of Working for a Government Agency. Government agencies and public health departments have access to a wide range of resources that may be of great use to them in their pursuits. This range extends to Washington, D.C., in the case of the United States, where many of the nation's public health policies and regulations are created. This point is important, as it means that even local government employees have the same information available to them. Benefits may also be above competitive levels, since governments negotiate reasonable rates for employee insurance, investment strategies, and other benefits.

Cons of Working for a Government Agency. Because national, state, and local laws and regulations pertaining to public health are either uniform or expected to be compatible with one another, it may be a challenge to implement a new regulation in an area that may not fit the profile of the regulation. Regulations that are broadly imposed may not be easily enforced by a given local agency as a result of geography, sociological differences, or other factors. As a result, public health agents may become frustrated in their attempts to implement strategies that are not specific to their regions' demographics. Additionally, funding for programs is not always consistent or equitably distributed among agencies. Some cities receive more money from a state or national government than do others for a number of reasons, and this imbalance of distribution may affect an agency's ability to meet its goals and requirements.

Nonprofit Organizations

Nonprofit organizations relating to public health range from professional advisory organizations, such as the American Heart Association, to political advocacy groups, such as ACT UP, to nongovernmental organizations, such as the Red Cross. All attempt to improve public health, whether by demanding that more public resources be spent on a particular health problem or constituency, by disseminating useful information to the public, or by administering directly to those in need.

Clientele Interaction. Nonprofit public health organizations usually spend the bulk of their time working with clients, communicating with them directly via local or regional meetings. Such an approach gives an organization opportunities to have a more intimate relationship with the people it serves and therefore helps it increase its impact on those people. Client interaction is therefore essential for nonprofit organizations.

Traditional Geographic Locations. Nonprofit organizations are often located in major urban centers and capital cities, as many of them have vested interests in social and budget policy decisions at the government level. Additionally, many are found in areas heavily populated by those with whom they work, such as Native American reservations and other impoverished regions where public health issues may become manifest.

Pros of Working for a Nonprofit Organization. Individuals who work at nonprofit public health organizations enjoy an ability to interact more directly and consistently with affected clients than do the employees of hospitals and government agencies. Those with a passion for addressing a specific public health issue—such as acquired immunodeficiency syndrome (AIDS), cancer, or childhood obesity—may enjoy the one-on-one interaction with clients that nonprofits create. Additionally, the relative informality of many nonprofit organizations may appeal to those who do not wish to wear professional clothes to work or be bound by strict professional codes of conduct.

Cons of Working for a Nonprofit Organization. Nonprofit public health organizations are often hampered by a lack of donations or government grant monies, particularly during economic downturns. In the light of this fact, many of their programs may be cut short by budgetary constraints. Similarly, employees tend to have lower salaries and more limited benefits than do workers in other sectors of the industry. The relatively small size of many nonprofits limits opportunities for upward career mobility.

Academic Institutions

Academic institutions conduct research critical to understanding the nature of illnesses and other public health and safety threats. Like nonprofit organizations, academic institutions' activities are often funded on a project-by-project basis by specific government or private grants. Indeed, academic scholars in the sciences are expected to conduct research precisely because it brings funding into their home institutions.

Pros of Working for an Academic Institution. Academic institutions offer a wide range of resources, often across the spectrum of public health (including economics, sociology, environmental engineering, and public policy, as well as medicine). Public health researchers may therefore enjoy an ability to conduct research that encompasses a broader perspective than they might find in a hospital or as part of a government agency. Many of these work environments are not as formal in terms of professional decorum, which may appeal to those who prefer to work in a less structured environment.

Cons of Working for an Academic Institution. One of the most difficult challenges of working on a public health-related project within an academic institution is the fact that such projects rely on grants, endowments, and government-imposed budget earmarks that may not be renewed from one year to the next. A team may thus go from operating with a sizable budget to working under extremely strict conditions (if its project does not lose funding altogether). Additionally, those personnel who prefer a degree of client interaction may not find a solely academic setting conducive to such interaction. Finally, those who are used to working in a corporate or government setting that establishes strict benchmarks and goals may find the flexibility and informality of academic work frustrating.

Clientele Interaction. Police, firefighters, paramedics, and other first responders encounter and aid people in crisis. In the event of a dangerous public health event, they are typically the first units to arrive on the scene. Client interaction is therefore a constant component of the job. Because such personnel are called upon to intervene in emergency situations, the interaction between them and private citizens can be of a confrontational nature.

Typical Number of Employees. Public safety departments vary in size based on the size of the jurisdiction covered. For example, major cities such as New York and Chicago each employ thousands of police officers, while many smaller communities employ only a few dozen. The number of paramedics in a particular location also depends on the size of the community, as well as the nature of the department (some are privately owned and operated, while others are publicly operated through fire departments).

Traditional Geographic Locations. Police, fire, and paramedic personnel are located in or near every municipality and county in the country. In most urban and suburban locations, there are a number of fire stations. In many cities, there are multiple police district offices in addition to the main police headquarters. In rural environments, public safety departments are usually based in county seats or larger municipalities, and personnel patrol outlying areas.

Pros of Working for a Public Safety Department. Working as a police officer, firefighter, or paramedic can involve a great deal of excitement. Such employees often place themselves at great risk to protect the lives of others. When they retire, they and their families generally receive strong retirement benefits, including insurance.

Cons of Working for a Public Safety Department. Public safety work is dangerous. In public health situations, officers may be exposed to dangerous chemicals or fumes, virulent diseases and blood, and violent patients and situations. Additionally, police and firefighters are paid by way of contracts negotiated with the cities or counties in which they operate; when budget dollars are short, they may lose pay or even their jobs as a result of budget austerity. Many officers, paramedics, EMTs, and firefighters experience trauma in their daily work that can have serious psychological repercussions over time.

Organizational Structure and Job Roles

The organizational structure of the public health services industry is both compartmentalized and designed to interconnect its various components based on the demands of a given situation. For example, in the event of a natural disaster, emergency response, government, and health practitioners must all work in such a way that each segment is synchronized with the others. In the event of a disease outbreak or epidemic, government, health practitioners, and nonprofit organizations may work together to combat emergent illnesses, as well as to prevent dangerous behavior that might perpetuate the spread of such illnesses.

The following umbrella categories apply to the organizational structure of entities providing public health services:

- Leadership
- First Responders
- Research and Analysis
- Communications and Public Affairs
- Policy Making
- Medical Care

Leadership

Those who lead public health organizations, both public and private, are skilled administrators who are capable of organizing groups of people with diverse backgrounds and professional skills. They manage the overall operations and organizational structure of their agencies and institutions, and they oversee all aspects of an organization's endeavors. They set goals and strategies, assign tasks to personnel, draft and implement budgets, and review all data and information that is to be issued to the public.

Public health leaders generally earn higher salaries than anyone else in their organizations. Their job is to manage the overall functions of an agency or association, address systemic issues, guide any political activities when necessary, and ensure that all departments function effectively to address all relevant public health concerns. In most cases, they are also the public faces of their agencies, issuing statements and fielding questions from the media.

A public health leader is generally well educated, usually holding a master's degree in public health or business administration or a medical degree. Nonprofit leaders may not have such advanced degrees, but they often have undergraduate degrees and advanced training in organizational management. Public safety officials are also well educated in law enforcement training and disaster response.

Leadership occupations may include the following:

- President/Chief Executive Officer (CEO)
- Executive Director
- Secretary
- Board Chair
- Department Chair
- Department Chief

Research and Analysis

Public health researchers and analysts are called upon to compile and study data pertaining to public health risks and threats. They may study social behaviors and environmental conditions. In the case of epidemiologists, they may trace the occurrences of disease outbreaks back to their sources. These workers analyze the effects of treatments, outreach programs, and public policies pertaining to the cessation of a health danger, gauging their effectiveness.

Policy Making

The responsibility for formulating public health policy falls to government legislators and executive departments. Legislators write laws to regulate businesses, protect the environment, govern health care reporting and services, and provide emergency funds to mitigate disasters and epidemics (such as outbreaks of H1N1 and avian flu). Executive departments implement and enforce these laws by establishing oversight mechanisms and writing the regulations authorized by the laws. Lawmakers and executive department leaders are generally well educated, with advanced degrees in public policy and administration, law, business, or health care. Salaries vary widely, depending on the level of government, the individual's professional experience, and government-set pay scales.

Medical Care

Hospitals, medical centers, clinics, and group practices play an integral role in the public health services sector. Doctors, nurses, and related medical staff are fully trained in the causes, transmission, and treatment of disease and other public health conditions, so they are able to work with patients to mitigate health risks. Medical professionals work as a team, caring for urgent care patients, drawing blood for tests, treating symptoms, and providing patients with information about the prevention of public health dangers.

Medical professionals have advanced degrees in their fields, such as M.D.s, nursing degrees, D.D.S.s (doctors of dental surgery), and physician assistant or master's degrees. Some have vocational training in medical assistance, such as medical technology, phlebotomy, or physician assistance. Salaries vary based on the field involved, the individual's amount of experience, collective bargaining arrangements (for those positions that are managed by unions), and the geographic location of the position.

Medical care occupations may include the following:
- Physician
- Registered Nurse
- Dentist
- Licensed Nurse Practitioner
- Nursing Assistant
- Physician Assistant
- Medical Technologist

- Phlebotomist
- Laboratory Technician

Overview

The public health services industry is a diverse and complex network, composed of a number of large individual industries. Its composition is reflective of the complexity of public health itself. Public health services do not focus entirely on treating epidemics of disease or other emergencies; they also take into account lifestyle issues, such as obesity, diet, tobacco use, sexual activity, and alcohol abuse, because such issues can create social groups whose conditions affect others in the community.

Additionally, public health has a political significance. Many government social services are geared toward those with health conditions who cannot afford treatment. Increased volumes of people with tobacco-related illnesses (such as lung cancer and emphysema) who receive health care through Medicaid and other government care programs increase the financial strains on such programs. Furthermore, because public health emergencies warrant emergency money and services, political leaders have a vested interest in implementing preventative public health policies and regulatory measures.

The public health industry continues to grow. Several of its components form some of the largest industries in the world. In 2006, for example, the U.S. health care industry provided about 14 million jobs, and it is expected to add 3 million more jobs by 2016. Nonprofit organizations that focus on public health, already one of the largest sectors of the nonprofit industry, account for as much as half of the entire industry's revenue and employment, with millions of jobs and hundreds of billions of dollars in revenues for more than thirty thousand American nonprofit organizations.

In the United States, public health is expected to hold the spotlight both as a political issue and as a critical public service. In the early 1990's, the Bill Clinton administration attempted to pass comprehensive reform of the health care system, citing the need to provide affordable health care to all American citizens. The Barack Obama administration renewed this effort, successfully passing through Congress the Patient Protection and Affordable Care Act of 2010. It was repeatedly pointed out throughout the yearlong debate over this measure that total health care expenditures in the United States account for approximately one-sixth of the entire U.S. economy.

The continuing emergence of viruses and diseases in the integrated global community gives rise to a continued need for public health outreach. The so-called swine flu (also known as H1N1), eastern equine encephalitis (EEE), Creutzfeldt-Jakob disease (the human form of "mad cow disease"), and fears of transmission of avian flu to humans provide evidence of the ongoing need for active public health services in the twenty-first century. Similarly, the fact that so many developing nations are still experiencing communicable diseases in nearly epidemic proportions represents an imperative for public health services to continue to work with poor countries to combat the spread of HIV/AIDS, tuberculosis, hemorrhagic fever, and other epidemics. These diseases, which may be treatable and curable, if left unchecked can afflict large populations and ultimately spread to the rest of the world, as residents of affected regions travel to other countries.

The public health services industry will most likely continue to remain one of the most vibrant industries, not just in the United States but also across the globe. The continuing need to protect against epidemics and outbreaks, coupled with the recognition that dangerous lifestyles have an impact on entire communities, leads to the conclusion that public health services remain an important part of the twenty-first century global community.

Employment Advantages

The diversity of the public health services industry offers potential employees an extremely broad range of subfields in which to operate. Employees in this industry may have backgrounds in politics, medicine, sociology, environmental studies, education, public relations, or law enforcement. While this diversity allows for a great deal of individual career growth, people who work within the industry are part of a network, working as an interconnected team either in the event of a public health emergency or when addressing ongoing public health issues. As was the case in both ancient Greece and Rome, this network is integral to ensuring that public systems and infrastructures do not create public health dangers.

While public health work requires a focus on the individual tasks of each component of the industry, public health services personnel also have the benefit of taking a broader view of the effects of certain conditions and behaviors on communities at large. Individual patients are important, but the systematic effects of their conditions on finances, emergency capabilities, and response times are equally critical in the eyes of public health professionals. This distinction is notable because such a broad focus can help prevent major public health crises from beginning or spreading.

Fast Fact

Gaming has come to public health: the CDC makes apps, including a free one called Health IQ, that's designed to help educate the general public on health. It uses health gamification. Also in on the trend: the American Red Cross, which has a number of apps including one designed to help prepare children for emergencies.

Source: imedicalapps.com

Conversation With . . .
DEIRDRE ARVIDSON

RN, BSN, SANE
Public Health Nurse
Barnstable County, Massachusetts

Deirdre Arvidson has been a nurse for twenty-six years and a public health nurse for nine years.

1. What was your individual career path in terms of education/training, entry-level job, or other significant opportunity?

Originally, I wanted to become a nurse because I admired and was inspired by Mother Theresa. Before I made it to nursing school, I earned a bachelor's degree in literature and writing at the University of California, San Diego. Toward the end of that degree I realized I still wanted to be a nurse. So I went to a community college and earned my associate degree.

After graduation, I got a job in a smaller hospital doing neuro rehab for stroke victims. I then moved to a larger hospital and was a floor nurse on an intermediate care unit. I had always wanted to do labor and delivery, and got into a preceptor program at a hospital in San Diego. Unfortunately, my preceptor turned out to be a bully, I lost confidence in my skills, and I left. It can be tough, especially when you are learning and not totally confident in something you've just learned. I went on to work for a temp agency as a medical-surgical nurse while raising my first two sons. Then my family moved to Cape Cod, Massachusetts. After my third son was born, I wanted a change: to work outside a hospital.

I worked at a number of facilities, including a skilled nursing facility, as an adult family care nurse, and as a dosing nurse in a methadone treatment clinic. I also worked as a substitute school nurse, which worked well with my children's schedule.

Then a time came when I needed to work full-time. I had worked as a contractor to the Barnstable County Department of Health and Environment conducting flu clinics, saw an opening for the county health nurse, and applied. It was very fortuitous to be hired in the midst of a recession.

When I started, we provided services such as TB testing, and flu and other immunizations to public safety workers; education in tick and Lyme disease to school children; and sun safety prevention programs. I continued to do those in order to get out into the community but saw other needs as well.

I wanted to reach vulnerable populations, but out here on the Cape it's not like a city where people are clustered. So I started a program called Ask a Public Health Nurse at a single food pantry. I set up a table, offered free blood pressure screenings, flu shots, and health information. I worked with a collection of food pantries called the Hunger Network, and the program grew to the point where I needed to use my contract nurses. Now we're in food pantries and soup kitchens all along Cape Cod. I also started a public immunization program and do everything, including travel immunizations. We clearly fill a gap. We provide preventative health screenings at health fairs and other events across the county. There are no charges for our services.

I'm also working on an online master's degree as a psychiatric nurse practitioner to prepare for the future. There's a lot of demand in that area and, unfortunately, a government job like this is not necessarily as secure.

2. What are the most important skills and/or qualities for someone in your profession?

You need to have basic skills in nursing and feel comfortable with them. Public health nurses work very autonomously and need to be creative—to think outside the box to find solutions.

3. What do you wish you had known going into this profession?

I wish I'd known how to manage a budget better. I had never been in a position before where I had to handle a large budget.

4. Are there many job opportunities in your profession? In what specific areas?

Unfortunately, public health nurses, including school nurses, are at the bottom of the pay scale for nursing. You're not going to find a lot of people gravitating toward that initially. But it is a great job to get out and help people be healthier in their communities. There is a lot of health teaching involved. I've literally had people ask me, "Why am I taking this medication?" The most opportunity is likely to be in a city or larger community.

5. How do you see your profession changing in the next five years, how will technology impact that change, and what skills will be required?

I think it's important to be able to somehow harness the data you're collecting. We collect it, but don't have time to put it into some meaningful form. It's important to do that because it demonstrates the value of your programs and helps you get grant money. However, this is an in-person job that requires compassion and care. I don't think we're going to be replaced by AI anytime soon.

6. **What do you enjoy most about your job? What do you enjoy least about your job?**

I most enjoy my patients who come into my office. They all have stories from all different places, and they are traveling all over the world. I play a role in helping them stay safe when they travel. Most leave with a smile.

I least enjoy the politics involved in a local government position.

7. **Can you suggest a valuable "try this" for students considering a career in your profession?**

I volunteered in a hospital first, but you can also volunteer in public health agencies. Also, talk to people who work in these areas and start taking some courses. As you learn more, you'll be more confident in your decision.

Related Resources for Further Research

American Diabetes Association
1701 N Beauregard St.
Alexandria, VA 22311
Tel: (800) 342-2383
http://www.diabetes.org

American Public Health Association
800 I St. NW
Washington, DC 20001-3710
Tel: (202) 777-2742
Fax: (202) 777-2534
http://www.apha.org

Centers for Disease Control and Prevention
1600 Clifton Rd.
Atlanta, GA 30333
Tel: (800) 232-4636
http://www.cdc.gov

Harvard School of Public Health
677 Huntington Ave.
Boston, MA 02115
Tel: (617) 384-8990
Fax: (617) 384-8989
http://www.hsph.harvard.edu

U.S. Department of Health and Human Services
200 Independence Ave. SW
Washington, DC 20201
Tel: (202) 619-0257
http://www.hhs.gov

World Health Organization
Ave. Appia 20
1211 Geneva 27
Switzerland
Tel: 41-22-791-2111
Fax: 41-22-791-3111
http://www.who.int

Michael P. Auerbach

RESIDENTIAL MEDICAL CARE INDUSTRY

Summary

The residential medical care industry serves patients who require skilled medical or rehabilitative care but who do not carry an illness or injury burden serious enough to qualify for acute hospital care. Residential care facilities are also known as skilled nursing facilities (SNFs). Their primary mission is to provide professional nursing care in an inpatient setting, with a goal of discharging patients to their homes or other appropriate residential environments.

SNFs offer a full spectrum of rehabilitative and recovery services, including occupational therapy, physical therapy, and speech therapy. Registered nurses (RNs) and physicians oversee the care plan of each patient. Twenty-four-hour care is a feature of this care delivery system. Sometimes diagnostics, such as phlebotomy and radiology, may be available on-site; if not, they may be brought via mobile unit, or patients may have to be transported to external testing facilities. Treatments and care are delivered by a number of professionals, from licensed care technicians to RNs and pharmacists.

Limited access to hospitals, cost issues, and advances leading to better survival rates for the chronically ill have led to the development of the specialized services of SNFs. These facilities deliver skilled care much more economically than do acute care facilities, and most insurance companies now mandate transfer to such facilities when patients no longer meet hospital criteria. SNFs pay rigorous attention to the appropriateness of the care they provide, and patients must meet a minimum level of illness severity to qualify for insurance coverage of SNF care. This is especially true of those covered by Medicare.

The residential medical care industry serves patients who require skilled medical or rehabilitative care but not acute hospital care.

There are over fifteen thousand SNFs in the United States. This number is projected to grow as a result of the aging of the U.S. population and the longer life spans made possible by medical technology. Health care reform and escalating costs have resulted in a push to deliver more services in SNF settings when appropriate. Medicare and Medicaid, both governmental insurance programs, are the primary payers in the residential care industry, modifying their reimbursement schemata to save their programs from financial crisis. As one example, patients on assisted ventilation used to remain hospitalized until they were weaned from their ventilators. Now, these same patients go to SNFs, whose care and technological expertise has been shown to be successful in achieving more rapid patient recoveries and discharges. In short, hospitals have become places where only the sickest and most resource-intense patients are admitted, and acute inpatient recovery care is being redirected to SNFs. Jobs opportunities in this sector are many and growing.

History of the Industry

In the early twentieth century, senior citizens and others who needed continual care were either housed in private institutions that had been established by ethnic or religious communities or left to their fates in state-supported almshouses. Private institutions had strict criteria for entrance, usually based on moral character, financial means, or social standing, and they housed only a small portion of the people who needed their services. For the rest of the population, who relied on almshouses for care, no regulations or criteria for wellness or illness were established. To call them nursing facilities would be to employ a misnomer; often, people went to almshouses to live out their lives in meager and substandard conditions. Workers staffing these facilities were unskilled and often were not even qualified to offer custodial care. Medical care was not available, and mortality rates were high.

In 1935, the federal government instituted Old Age Assistance (OAA), a program for retired workers. As residents in almshouses could not qualify for OAA funds, private institutions began to spring up whose residents would be eligible for OAA payments, which they used to pay for their care. By the end of World War II, governmental oversight structures for elderly care facilities began to mandate that such facilities receive licenses and meet codified standards of care in order to qualify for OAA payments.

In the mid-1950's, federal monies started to become available to construct more standardized nursing care facilities. The residents of such facilities had greater needs for regular medical treatment and attention than they had had in the past, so the facilities evolved to embrace more medical missions. They became recognizable as health care institutions and were no longer treated just as elderly homes for the impoverished. Nurses, physicians, and other skilled personnel composed the labor force in these more advanced facilities.

Both the law and federal funding provisions continued to evolve over time; reforms to payment mechanisms occurred, and some monies were withdrawn in response to funding crises. These spending cuts caused difficulties for people who had previously qualified for support and found themselves newly uninsured. Many frail and elderly persons faced barriers to obtaining medical care outside of acute care hospitals. Federal regulatory mandates grew unpopular, and the large number of uninsured citizens was widely publicized. As a result, a new category of "intermediate" care facilities was created to serve elderly and disabled patients and provided federal funding support. Intermediate care facilities had to meet rigorous standards to be paid, and care standards suffered when funding decreased. As a result, more administrative positions were created to monitor and report on facilities' adherence to federal standards.

In 1965, Medicare was enacted to provide health care to senior citizens. SNFs were eligible to receive Medicare reimbursements for their services. More strict eligibility requirements for patient coverage emerged, along with even more strict regulatory oversight of facilities. Nurses, physicians, and administrators ran their facilities and cared for patients, but they found themselves spending increasing amounts of time on compliance and reporting to the government.

The SNF designation was not established until the early 1990's. Originally, these entities were referred to as extended care facilities. SNFs are not custodial care facilities. The federal Medicare regulations spell out the difference between reimbursed medical care and unreimbursed custodial care.

The projected growth of the medical industry will make employment in an SNF a secure career choice for the foreseeable future. The industry, however, is not immune to economic pressures, and difficult financial times can result in unexpected hiring freezes or reductions in noncritical positions. Direct patient care positions are mission-critical and are some of the most secure in the industry. The average age of nurses in the United States is in the mid- to late forties; with an aging workforce and smaller numbers of younger people, jobs will continue to open up as baby boomers retire.

The Industry Today

SNFs are sometimes referred to as nursing homes, a broad term for facilities that offer skilled residential care in combination with restorative or custodial care. Of the sixteen thousand SNFs registered in the United States, about two-thirds are owned by for-profit companies, with the remaining portion owned by not-for-profit organizations. Fewer than 10 percent are owned by the federal government.

Some patients are admitted to SNFs for short-term medical recuperation or rehabilitation; costs of this recuperation are generally borne by a patient's private health insurance carrier. Elderly persons who are unable to care for themselves at home pay for assisted living facilities privately, often through pensions, retirement savings, or the proceeds of selling personal assets such as homes. Those needing more extensive medical care may find that paying for care in skilled nursing facilities becomes more complex, based on medical conditions, functionality, and financial means. In spite of the complex nature of SNF revenue sources, Medicaid is the primary payer for the SNF population in the United States. However, many people qualify for Medicaid only after they have expended their private assets.

People working in residential care facilities currently face stringent expectations for efficiency and economy. Most facilities operate with just enough staff to deliver quality care in a timely manner, and are accountable to the economic bottom line. Because life expectancies are increasing, medical and long-term care costs are rising significantly toward the end of life. Compounding the issue is the fact that aging slows one's recovery processes in general and can make going home immediately posthospitalization challenging.

For these reasons—and because extended families are no longer the norm in the United States—SNF care represents a burgeoning business. RNs with associate's degrees can find supervisory and direct medical positions within SNFs. Licensed patient care technicians or licensed nursing assistants, under the supervision of RNs, provide custodial care and medical treatments within the scope of their licensure.

Phlebotomists, radiology technicians, ultrasonographers, and respiratory therapists are just a few of the numerous professionals who may be employed or contracted to care for patients in the residential medical care industry.

SNF employment opportunities are growing faster than are opportunities in acute hospital care facilities. Gone are the days when patients were admitted to hospitals for weeks or months. Exceptional costs preclude long hospital stays, increasing the demand for skilled recuperative care in appropriate and fiscally responsible settings.

Common partnership industries to residential medical care include long-term residential care facilities. Long-term care facilities and residential care facilities may be owned and operated alongside parent hospitals, or they may be privately owned. Transitioning patients too sick to go home but too well to stay in the hospital is of key importance to hospitals. Keeping patients in the bed too long increases costs and can prevent admissions of sicker patients by limiting bed capacity. Allowing patients who recover well to return home is certainly desirable, but when doing so proves impossible, residential care facilities allow hospitals to shift as much nonnecessary inpatient care as possible to an outpatient setting as soon as it can be done safely.

Industry Market Segments

Individual skilled nursing facilities range in size from small establishments with only a few beds to large facilities with more than one hundred beds. These facilities may be individual private entities, or they may be owned and managed by larger corporations. For example, Genesis HealthCare Corporation operates more than two hundred SNFs in thirteen states. Some corporations specialize in managing SNFs, whereas others may also own and operate hospitals and private medical office buildings, among other properties.

Small Skilled Nursing Facilities

Small SNFs have fewer than fifty beds and employ as few as twenty-five people full time. They are often rural facilities, since most urban areas support significantly larger establishments.

Clientele Interaction. Patients, their families, government payers, federal facility surveyors, colleagues, referring hospitals, and vendors are the primary clients for SNFs. Patients in SNFs, as inpatients, are often in a highly vulnerable state, frightened and suffering maladies of various sorts. Many arrive at SNFs from independent homes and find themselves in unfamiliar surroundings, feeling a loss of autonomy and self. Patients rarely arrive alone, and employees of SNFs must be cognizant of extended families' pressures and fears.

Financial worries, child care, lost wages, and social concerns for the patient and the family require care providers to have compassion, understanding, a good sense of timing, and empathy. SNF nursing staff face particular challenges posed by competing demands for their time. High levels of bureaucracy and regulated oversight of staff make it all the more important for them to make the effort to connect directly with their patients. Everyone, from physicians to housekeepers, must maintain professional and respectful decorum; they should promote the quality of their SNFs to help allay fears and aid recovery, and they must be ever aware of the need to protect patients' privacy and confidentiality. In short, taking on the responsibility of working in health care requires employees to provide the medical, social, and psychological support necessary for recovery.

Amenities, Atmosphere, and Physical Grounds. Cleanliness and a calm atmosphere are critical in the SNF setting. Surgical-patient recovery requires sterility and designated treatment areas. Increasingly, SNFs are developing a patient-centered approach, with innovative designs that strive to be more "homelike," as comfort and peace of mind speed the recovery and discharge processes. Facilities seek to make access for family members relatively simple, providing sufficient parking and clear signage. Within an SNF, an attended receiving area assists in quickly routing visitors. However, the most important consideration within the care delivery areas is the comfort of the patients. Controlled humidity and temperature, rigorous attention to maintaining modest noise levels, and utmost attention to privacy and confidentiality are important to recovery.

Typical Number of Employees. Small SNFs of less than fifty beds generally employ a total of around twenty-five persons. They are often situated in sparsely populated areas, so they may find it difficult to find sufficient staffing for even those few positions. However, these smaller SNFs are likely to be fairly near acute-care facilities, and they provide strong economic stability in their locales, employing staff of all grades, from entry-level personnel to professional physicians and chief operating officers.

Traditional Geographic Locations. Small facilities are likely to be located in rural communities, with populations of under twenty thousand within their service areas. It is not uncommon to find such SNFs colocated with hospitals. While staff are drawn primarily from the immediate locale, higher-level administrative positions are attractive for their growth potential, and SNFs cast wide nets when recruiting for such positions. Finding physicians to staff SNFs can be challenging, because such a high proportion of the facilities' payments are made through Medicare and Medicaid, which have relatively low reimbursement rates. Contracts are required to reimburse physician travel time to small rural facilities.

Pros of Working for a Small Residential Care Facility. Providing local care at a small SNF allows employees to work in a more intimate community atmosphere. Direct health care providers at such facilities see many types of diagnoses and are exposed to stimulating technical and cognitive challenges in their work. Small SNFs are therefore attractive to many who value the unique learning opportunities they provide.

Smaller facilities often involve less bureaucracy and greater personal relations for employees with patients and their families. The U.S. Centers for Disease Control and Prevention Nursing Home Statistics Database suggests that smaller facilities have higher staff-to-patient ratios than do larger facilities. This higher ratio is likely to decrease stress levels and facilitate better distribution of workloads among caregivers. Small SNFs are likely to provide more intimate settings for staff and patients than do large SNFs, and those seeking close relationships with their patients should seek facilities housing no more than fifty to seventy-five beds.

Cons of Working for a Small Residential Care Facility. One challenge that professional staff face in an SNF is the lack of continuous and personal relationships with patients, given the technical resource requirements of their jobs. Nurses, therapists, and others delivering skilled services spend much time attending to medications, technologically administered treatments, and oversight of less skilled staff. Time spent in a nurturing role can be limited, which can be a dissatisfying situation.

Small SNFs may not have the financial resources of their larger counterparts, depending on whether they are run for profit. For-profit facilities tend to seek lower staff-to-patient ratios, raising concerns over patient safety and staff burnout due to stress and overwork. Capital dollars to improve equipment or enhance facilities may be more limited than at larger facilities. Additionally, small SNFs may have trouble recruiting and retaining trained staff, including physicians. Their lack of resources and inability to match the salaries of larger organizations are two primary drivers behind staffing challenges.

At small SNFs that lack sufficient depth in their work pools, employees are at risk of being required to work extra shifts or, at times, to work on shifts that are short-handed. The purchasing power that comes with a large workforce can also be compromised at small facilities, and employee benefits may not be as robust at smaller SNFs as they are at larger SNFs. Larger organizations have better risk ratings and can likely offer employees more and better benefit options. However, small SNFs that are part of larger chains may be able to offer the benefits common at larger organizations. Small SNFs provide high-level medical and procedural services, but health care providers who value the opportunity to work with the latest technology, with critically ill patients, or with younger populations may not feel fully challenged in these facilities.

Midsize Skilled Nursing Facilities

Midsize SNFs have bed capacities of from fifty to one hundred. Net income after expenses varies widely, depending on the amount of bad debt burden, insurance payments (including Medicare and Medicaid, which pay poorly compared with private pay or other insurers), direct and indirect expenses, and overhead. SNFs' margins can be very small as the result of external factors; the broader economy plays a role, especially in driving competition to obtain privately paying patients who can afford skilled care.

Clientele Interaction. For the most part, the core mission of an SNF is to deliver medical and rehabilitative services. Working purely in a service industry, staff must be customer-focused, possess excellent communication skills, and have a desire to work in a hands-on, interactive, and caring industry. Midsize SNFs are likely to have lower staff-to-patient ratios than do small facilities, putting more pressure on care staff to maintain a safe and personal environment for their patients. The reputation of a facility is public knowledge because Medicare survey results on safety and quality are publicly accessible. Similarly and importantly to businesses, word-of-mouth referrals are more likely when personal service and good client interaction are delivered. Facilities have far too many overhead expenses to be able to leave beds unfilled, so reputation and interaction are priorities.

Amenities, Atmosphere, and Physical Grounds. Cleanliness and a calm atmosphere are critical in the SNF setting. Surgical-patient recovery requires sterility and designated treatment areas. Increasingly, SNFs are developing a patient-centered approach, with innovative designs that strive to be more "homelike," as comfort and peace of mind speed the recovery and discharge processes. Facilities seek to make access for family members relatively simple, providing sufficient parking and clear signage. Within an SNF, an attended receiving area assists in quickly routing visitors. However, the most important consideration within the care delivery areas is the comfort of the patients. Controlled humidity and temperature, rigorous attention to maintaining modest noise levels, and utmost attention to privacy and confidentiality are important to recovery.

Typical Numbers of Employees. A midsize SNF of up to one hundred beds will likely employ fifty to sixty staff members. Patient-to-staff ratios need to be explicitly understood, so employees are ensured of a responsible and manageable workload. A major factor in total staffing numbers is the centralization of functions or external contracting of services such as billing, collections, and communications systems.

Traditional Geographic Locations. Midsize facilities are typically located near populated areas. Two-thirds of SNFs are located in metropolitan areas. This makes sense, given that a sufficient population density is needed to support such a facility. Most U.S. SNFs are located in the Midwest and the South. (Retirement to warmer climes and older populations in these areas probably explain this distribution.) Many SNF admissions come from discharges following surgery or medical service; the closer it is to referring physicians and hospitals with technology and ancillary services, the more attractive an SNF will be to investors (if privately run) and to patients. Close links to physician staff and private-practice physicians should be paramount to maximize referral sources. While socioeconomics in the SNF's local area can play a role, the demand for easily accessible SNFs can bring midsize facilities to more populated locales despite sour economic conditions. Reputation and quality reports play a much larger role than location in an organization's sustainability, however.

Pros of Working for a Midsize Residential Care Facility. Well-established organizations provide employment security, and their purchasing power allows them to offer better benefits at more favorable rates for their employees, especially if they are part of larger chains of privately owned nursing facilities. Employees of midsize SNFs have access to health insurance for themselves and their families at group rates, which are more favorable than those a smaller employer might be able to offer. Pay incentives may be available as well, usually based on productivity and expense controls. Every employee of an SNF is responsible for contributing to the financial bottom line of the organization.

Physicians, nursing leaders, and administrators generally share responsibility for being on call at night and during weekends. Midsize and larger facilities are able to spread this responsibility out over larger staffs, making the burden less onerous on each individual. Any facility providing service twenty-four hours a day, seven days a week faces unique staffing challenges, but skilled employees are in high demand, creating a favorable scenario for job seekers.

Cons of Working for a Midsize Residential Care Facility. Midsize SNFs are more complex organizations than their smaller counterparts. Their higher patient-to-staff ratios can contribute to staff dissatisfaction. With complexity comes increased communication challenges and, potentially, less autonomy; this situation is sometimes challenging for medical service professionals. When ratios are low, staff can become antagonistic to coworkers who call in sick or are not seen as pulling their weight. The danger of overwork, including mandatory overtime, is one of many factors affecting employee retention and satisfaction.

Multiple equally worthy individuals and units may have to compete for limited resources. Thus, medical staff—in addition to already demanding jobs—may need to be strong advocates for themselves and their clients when confronting their own institutions' bureaucracies. Pressures to be more efficient and work with fewer staff while providing excellent care will be felt.

Large Skilled Nursing Facilities

Large SNFs have more than one hundred in-patient beds. Their patient demographics and staffing qualifications are identical to those of small and midsize SNFs. Patient-to-staff ratios tend to be higher in large SNFs, likely as a result of economies of scale, though larger SNFs that are privately owned are known to cut staffing and costs to improve their financial bottom lines. Higher patient-to-staff ratios can raise safety and quality concerns. Large facilities can draw business from up to 100 miles away or even further, depending on competition and patient willingness to travel. Competition exists in the health care industry, and grappling for market share while maintaining sufficient staffing is a constant challenge for a large SNF.

Clientele Interaction. Larger organizations offer more diversity and opportunity for professionals. SNF care, which can be long term (months), can force patients to spend months away from their homes and familiar environments. Removing patients from familiar settings and family can delay recovery, however. Physicians, nurses, and other staff can become surrogates for family, and they must have excellent interpersonal caring skills. Staff should advocate for patients and encourage their families to assign guardians or family advocates to closely monitor patient care and progress.

Physicians and nurses employed by large SNFs work as part of a large group of similar professionals, sharing on-call duties. Collaboration and patience are required, and staff may face challenges scheduling their obligations around holidays and school vacations. Professionals represent their organizations and their colleagues when they interact with clients, and they are expected to be available and responsive when they are on call.

Amenities, Atmosphere, and Physical Grounds. Large SNFs are typically freestanding, with sizable grounds. Investments in aesthetics are important to develop client security and trust in an organization, which in turn is important for maintaining the organization's client base. Open space and a trend toward less clinical environments are common, as the focus of those designing amenities and interiors lies more on patient comfort than on optimal medical-care-delivery design or the convenience of deliverers.

Typical Number of Employees. Large health care facilities employ thousands of staff members, including medical, administrative, financial, operations, and support staff. From the first phone call, to patient admission, to patient discharge and follow-up, numerous staff members representing a given SNF come in direct or indirect contact with patients. This size and structure requires a synergistic, well-coordinated effort to meet the needs of patients and to fulfill the mission of the SNF.

Traditional Geographic Locations. Large SNFs are generally located in densely populated areas, mostly in the Midwest and the South. A sufficient population base, with actuarial promise of growth, is critical to the livelihood of a medical facility. Unlike a business that relies on product sales through the Internet, for example, a health care facility provides a face-to-face service to its clients.

Pros of Working for a Large Residential Care Facility. Large health care facilities offer many people the opportunity for advancement. Throughout their careers, people working in SNFs can develop leadership skills and move into growth positions, such as administrative or management roles. Large SNFs provide significant areas for growth, especially if employees are motivated and committed to learning. Larger organizations tend to have the financial capacity and structure to promote such advancement, particularly if their missions include academic opportunities alongside clinical care. The SNF industry, embedded in an overarching and mammoth health care industry that contributes nearly 20 percent of the U.S. gross domestic product (GDP), offers job security and strong opportunities for advancement.

Cons of Working for a Large Residential Care Facility. Internal politics become more evident in larger service organizations. The employees of large SNFs can expect more bureaucracy and delays inherent in decision making; sometimes, it can take what seems a very long time to move initiatives forward. The higher ratio of patients to each nurse creates employee tension, as well as higher risks for patients. While minimum staffing ratios are set by oversight bodies such as Medicare, the higher the ratio of patients to staff members, the longer recovery will take for patients.

No area of SNFs is exempt from financial challenges: Leadership and managers must advocate regularly for resources and be mindful of staff burnout and overwork. Working in any large organization can cause employees to feel unnoticed or underappreciated. Large SNFs with robust postsurgical and medical services must remain competitive. Investment in facilities for growth is a priority. Information technology, for example, is exploding in SNFs, as diminishing revenues force greater efficiency and rapid management to discharge. Surgical and diagnostic advances represent major capital investments, but without them SNFs can lose their competitive edge.

Organizational Structure and Job Roles

Any size entity providing medical services has to function as a business. An SNF represents a complex, integrated system that requires many key critical functions to interrelate daily. At small facilities, multiple functions and roles may be filled by the same individual. Large facilities are more likely to employ specialists in each role.

The following umbrella categories apply to the organizational structure of businesses in the residential medical care industry:

- Business and Operations Management
- Medical Staff
- Contracting, Reimbursement, and Billing
- Human Resources
- Customer Services/Risk Management
- Public Affairs and Marketing
- Facilities and Security
- Housekeeping
- Nutrition
- Information Technology and Communication Systems

Medical Staff

SNFs depend heavily on their reputations, which can make or break them. The quality and professionalism of those providing medical care, from doctors to health aides who work directly with patients, determine the greatest share of their facilities' reputations. They have the most direct contact with patients and guide their care. Successful organizations thrive on high standards of patient care, excellent communication, and a shared understanding of best practices in providing care.

- Medical staff occupations may include the following:
- Physician
- Nurse Practitioner
- Registered Nurse
- Licensed Practical Nurse
- Home Health Aide

Industry Outlook

The outlook for the residential medical care industry shows growth to be an ongoing trend. Demand for workers and career opportunities are very favorable. Growth in this industry is steady, with health care contributing 17 percent to the U.S. GDP. Contributing to this growth is the largest aging population in U.S. history. Americans expect to live longer and are treating illnesses aggressively, creating a market for skilled nursing facilities that will extend for a significant portion of the early twenty-first century. Threats to the industry come from diminishing Medicare and Medicaid funds. State-run Medicaid funding is also under threat, as the recession of 2007-2009 threatens the financial health and stability of state governments across the country.

Employment and job security in this sector are strong. Challenges for those entering the industry include greater competition for college-educated professionals in direct care positions and some administrative roles. Physicians, psychologists, pharmacists, and other direct care providers with advanced degrees should see greater opportunities in this highly competitive job market. SNFs seek those who are self-directed and have an affinity for the elderly and disabled.

SNFs have the potential to earn significant profits if managed closely and efficiently. Troublesome trends are emerging, however, in which investors purchase facilities and then cut corners in terms of cost and quality. Whether privately or publicly owned, regulatory complexity and declining Medicare funds suggest challenging times for SNFs. Overall, nursing homes collected more than $75 billion in revenues from federal (Medicare) and state (Medicaid) funding, money that presents an attractive opportunity for investors. The aging U.S. population will keep SNFs in business, but astute management will be of utmost importance for them to remain financially viable.

Employment Advantages

Positions in medicine, nursing, and pharmacology are in demand. Whether part-time or full-time, these positions are often salaried and very secure relative to the general economic environment. Those interested in medical technical work will find much opportunity, as complex treatments require increasing use of medical technology in the industry. Shortages in key professional positions help keep salary and benefits competitive.

Additionally, SNFs hire skilled, white-collar workers in such fields as administration, finance, and management. Professionals in such careers may find SNFs to be rewarding settings in which to work. Caring for the elderly or debilitated provides the personal reward of seeing patients through to recovery and back home. The challenges in this area lie in the balance of providing excellent care while managing operating expenses.
SNFs offer work experiences that were once found only in hospitals. Nursing and medical students will likely find themselves doing clinical rotations in these settings, but they may find that working in acute-care hospitals initially after graduation will hone their skills and confidence prior to working in SNFs. Clinical academic rotations can only give a flavor of the independence that professionals may enjoy in SNFs. Today, one of the greatest advantages of SNF work is job security, as millions of baby boomers are aging and demand in this area is growing.

Fast Fact

Globally, mental and substance use disorders are the leading cause of disability. They account for about 23 percent of all years lost due to disability.

Source: World Health Organization

Related Resources for Further Research

AARP
601 E St. NW
Washington, DC 20049
Tel: (888) 687-2277
http://www.aarp.org

American College of Healthcare Executives
1 N Franklin, Suite 1700
Chicago, IL 60606-3529
Tel: (312) 424-2800
Fax: (312) 424-0023
http://www.ache.org

American Hospital Association
155 N Wacker Dr.
Chicago, IL 60606
Tel: (312) 422-3000
http://www.aha.org

Healthcare Financial Management Association
2 Westbrook Corporate Center, Suite 700
Westchester, IL 60154
Tel: (708) 531-9600
Fax: (708) 531-0032
http://www.hfma.org

Medical Group Management Association
104 Inverness Terrace East
Englewood, CO 80112-5306
Tel: (303) 799-1111
http://www.mgma.com

Nancy Sprague

What Are Your Career Interests?

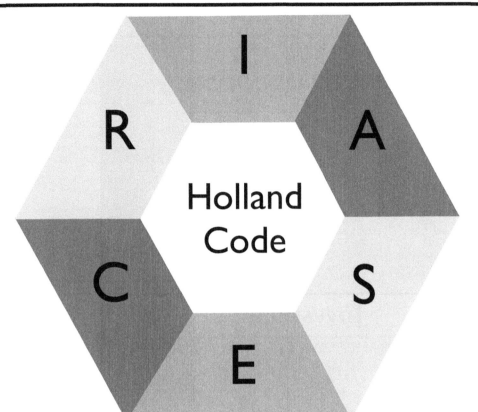

This is based on Dr. John Holland's theory that people and work environments can be loosely classified into six different groups. Each of the letters above corresponds to one of the six groups described in the following pages.

Different people's personalities may find different environments more to their liking. While you may have some interests in and similarities to several of the six groups, you may be attracted primarily to two or three of the areas. These two or three letters are your "Holland Code." For example, with a code of "RES" you would most resemble the Realistic type, somewhat less resemble the Enterprising type, and resemble the Social type even less. The types that are not in your code are the types you resemble least of all.

Most people, and most jobs, are best represented by some combination of two or three of the Holland interest areas. In addition, most people are most satisfied if there is some degree of fit between their personality and their work environment.

The rest of the pages in this booklet further explain each type and provide some examples of career possibilities, areas of study at MU, and co-curricular activities for each code. To take a more in-depth look at your Holland Code, take a self-assessment such as the SDS, Discover, or a card sort at the MU Career Center with a Career Specialist.

Realistic *(Doers)*

People who have athletic ability, prefer to work with objects, machines, tools, plants or animals, or to be outdoors.

Are you?		Can you?	Like to?
practical	independent	fix electrical things	tinker with machines/vehicles
straightforward/frank	ambitious	solve electrical problems	work outdoors
mechanically inclined	systematic	pitch a tent	be physically active
stable		play a sport	use your hands
concrete		read a blueprint	build things
reserved		plant a garden	tend/train animals
self-controlled		operate tools and machine	work on electronic equipment

Career Possibilities
(Holland Code):

Air Traffic Controller (SER)	Dental Technician (REI)	Laboratory Technician (RIE)	Property Manager (ESR)
Archaeologist (IRE)	Farm Manager (ESR)	Landscape Architect (AIR)	Recreation Manager (SER)
Athletic Trainer (SRE)	Fish and Game Warden (RES)	Mechanical Engineer (RIS)	Service Manager (ERS)
Cartographer (IRE)	Floral Designer (RAE)	Optician (REI)	Software Technician (RCI)
Commercial Airline Pilot (RIE)	Forester (RIS)	Petroleum Geologist (RIE)	Ultrasound Technologist (RSI)
Commercial Drafter (IRE)	Geodetic Surveyor (IRE)	Police Officer (SER)	Vocational Rehabilitation
Corrections Officer (SER)	Industrial Arts Teacher (IER)	Practical Nurse (SER)	Consultant (ESR)

Investigative *(Thinkers)*

People who like to observe, learn, investigate, analyze, evaluate, or solve problems.

Are you?		**Can you?**	Like to?
inquisitive	intellectually self-confident	think abstractly	explore a variety of ideas
analytical	Independent	solve math problems	work independently
scientific	logical	understand scientific theories	perform lab experiments
observant/precise	complex	do complex calculations	deal with abstractions
scholarly	Curious	use a microscope or computer	do research
cautious		interpret formulas	be challenged

Career Possibilities
(Holland Code):

Actuary (ISE)	Chemical Engineer (IRE)	Geologist (IRE)	Physician, General Practice (ISE)
Agronomist (IRS)	Chemist (IRE)	Horticulturist (IRS)	Psychologist (IES)
Anesthesiologist (IRS)	Computer Systems Analyst (IER)	Mathematician (IER)	Research Analyst (IRC)
Anthropologist (IRE)	Dentist (ISR)	Medical Technologist (ISA)	Statistician (IRE)
Archaeologist (IRE)	Ecologist (IRE)	Meteorologist (IRS)	Surgeon (IRA)
Biochemist (IRS)	Economist (IAS)	Nurse Practitioner (ISA)	Technical Writer (IRS)
Biologist (ISR)	Electrical Engineer (IRE)	Pharmacist (IES)	Veterinarian (IRS)

Artistic *(Creators)*

People who have artistic, innovating, or intuitional abilities and like to work in unstructured situations using their imagination and creativity.

Are you?
creative
imaginative
innovative
unconventional
emotional
independent
Expressive

original
introspective
impulsive
sensitive
courageous
complicated
idealistic
nonconforming

Can you?
sketch, draw, paint
play a musical instrument
write stories, poetry, music
sing, act, dance
design fashions or interiors

Like to?
attend concerts, theatre, art
 exhibits
read fiction, plays, and poetry
work on crafts
take photography
express yourself creatively
deal with ambiguous ideas

Career Possibilities
(Holland Code):

Actor (AES)
Advertising Art Director (AES)
Advertising Manager (ASE)
Architect (AIR)
Art Teacher (ASE)
Artist (ASI)

Copy Writer (ASI)
Dance Instructor (AER)
Drama Coach (ASE)
English Teacher (ASE)
Entertainer/Performer (AES)
Fashion Illustrator (ASR)

Interior Designer (AES)
Intelligence Research Specialist
 (AEI)
Journalist/Reporter (ASE)
Landscape Architect (AIR)
Librarian (SAI)

Medical Illustrator (AIE)
Museum Curator (AES)
Music Teacher (ASI)
Photographer (AES)
Writer (ASI)
Graphic Designer (AES)

Social *(Helpers)*

People who like to work with people to enlighten, inform, help, train, or cure them, or are skilled with words.

Are you?
friendly
helpful
idealistic
insightful
outgoing
understanding

cooperative
generous
responsible
forgiving
patient
kind

Can you?
teach/train others
express yourself clearly
lead a group discussion
mediate disputes
plan and supervise an activity
cooperate well with others

Like to?
work in groups
help people with problems
do volunteer work
work with young people
serve others

Career Possibilities
(Holland Code):

City Manager (SEC)
Clinical Dietitian (SIE)
College/University Faculty (SEI)
Community Org. Director
 (SEA)
Consumer Affairs Director
 (SER)Counselor/Therapist
 (SAE)

Historian (SEI)
Hospital Administrator (SER)
Psychologist (SEI)
Insurance Claims Examiner
 (SIE)
Librarian (SAI)
Medical Assistant (SCR)
Minister/Priest/Rabbi (SAI)
Paralegal (SCE)

Park Naturalist (SEI)
Physical Therapist (SIE)
Police Officer (SER)
Probation and Parole Officer
 (SEC)
Real Estate Appraiser (SCE)
Recreation Director (SER)
Registered Nurse (SIA)

Teacher (SAE)
Social Worker (SEA)
Speech Pathologist (SAI)
Vocational-Rehab. Counselor
 (SEC)
Volunteer Services Director
 (SEC)

<u>E</u>nterprising *(Persuaders)*

People who like to work with people, influencing, persuading, leading or managing for organizational goals or economic gain.

Are you?		**Can you?**	**Like to?**
self-confident	ambitious	initiate projects	make decisions
assertive	agreeable	convince people to do things	be elected to office
persuasive	talkative	your way	start your own business
energetic	extroverted	sell things	campaign politically
adventurous	spontaneous	give talks or speeches	meet important people
popular	optimistic	organize activities	have power or status
		lead a group	
		persuade others	

Career Possibilities
(Holland Code):

Advertising Executive (ESA)	Credit Analyst (EAS)	Foreign Service Officer (ESA)	Politician (ESA)
Advertising Sales Rep (ESR)	Customer Service Manager	Funeral Director (ESR)	Public Relations Rep (EAS)
Banker/Financial Planner (ESR)	(ESA)	Insurance Manager (ESC)	Retail Store Manager (ESR)
Branch Manager (ESA)	Education & Training Manager	Interpreter (ESA)	Sales Manager (ESA)
Business Manager (ESC)	(EIS)	Lawyer/Attorney (ESA)	Sales Representative (ERS)
Buyer (ESA)	Emergency Medical Technician	Lobbyist (ESA)	Social Service Director (ESA)
Chamber of Commerce Exec	(ESI)	Office Manager (ESR)	Stockbroker (ESI)
(ESA)	Entrepreneur (ESA)	Personnel Recruiter (ESR)	Tax Accountant (ECS)

<u>C</u>onventional *(Organizers)*

People who like to work with data, have clerical or numerical ability, carry out tasks in detail, or follow through on others' instructions.

Are you?		**Can you?**	**Like to?**
well-organized	practical	work well within a system	follow clearly defined
accurate	thrifty	do a lot of paper work in a short	procedures
numerically inclined	systematic	time	use data processing equipment
methodical	structured	keep accurate records	work with numbers
conscientious	polite	use a computer terminal	type or take shorthand
efficient	ambitious	write effective business letters	be responsible for details
conforming	obedient		collect or organize things
	persistent		

Career Possibilities
(Holland Code):

Abstractor (CSI)	Claims Adjuster (SEC)	Elementary School Teacher	Medical Records Technician
Accountant (CSE)	Computer Operator (CSR)	(SEC)	(CSE)
Administrative Assistant (ESC)	Congressional-District Aide (CES)	Financial Analyst (CSI)	Museum Registrar (CSE)
Budget Analyst (CER)	Cost Accountant (CES)	Insurance Manager (ESC)	Paralegal (SCE)
Business Manager (ESC)	Court Reporter (CSE)	Insurance Underwriter (CSE)	Safety Inspector (RCS)
Business Programmer (CRI)	Credit Manager (ESC)	Internal Auditor (ICR)	Tax Accountant (ECS)
Business Teacher (CSE)	Customs Inspector (CEI)	Kindergarten Teacher (ESC)	Tax Consultant (CES)
Catalog Librarian (CSE)	Editorial Assistant (CSI)		Travel Agent (ECS)

GENERAL BIBLIOGRAPHY

Ackley, Betty J. *Nursing Diagnosis Handbook: An Evidence-Based Guide to Planning Care*. Mosby, 2019. Print

Alfaro-Lefevre, Rosalinda. *Critical Thinking. Clinical Reasoning and Clinical Judgement: A Practical Approach*. St Louis: Mosby, 2016. Print.

Austin, Paul. *Something for the Pain: Compassion and Burnout in the ER*. New York, NY: W.W. Norton & Co, 2009. Print

Barkin, Laurie. *The Comfort Garden: Tales from the Trauma Unit*. San Francisco: Fresh Pond Press, 2011. Print.

Berman, Audrey, Shirlee Snyder, Geralyn Frandsen, Audrey Berman, and Barbara Kozier. *Kozier and Erb's Fundamentals of Nursing: Concepts, Process and Practice*. , 2018. Print.

Bluni, Rich. *Inspired Nurse Too*. Fire Starter Publishing, 2016. Print.

Bowen, Will. *A Complaint Free World: How to Stop Complaining and Start Enjoying the Life You Always Wanted*. , 2013. Print.

Buppert, Carolyn. *Nurse Practitioner's Business Practice and Legal Guide*. Jones & Bartlett Learning, 2018. Print.

Bureau of Labor Statistics, Nurse Anesthetists, Nurse Midwives, and Nurse Practitioners, on the Internet at https://www.bls.gov/ooh/healthcare/nurse-anesthetists-nurse-midwives-and-nurse-practitioners.htm (visited *January 04, 2019*).

_____, Nurse Anesthetists, Nurse Midwives, and Nurse Practitioners, on the Internet at https://www.bls.gov/ooh/healthcare/nurse-anesthetists-nurse-midwives-and-nurse-practitioners.htm (visited *January 04, 2019*).

_____, Registered Nurses, on the Internet at https://www.bls.gov/ooh/healthcare/registered-nurses.htm (visited *January 21, 2019*)

Bureau of Labor Statistics, U.S. Department of Labor, *Occupational Outlook Handbook*, Licensed Practical and Licensed Vocational Nurses, on the Internet at https://www.bls.gov/ooh/healthcare/licensed-practical-and-licensed-vocational-nurses.htm (visited *January 13, 2019*).

Cardillo, Donna W. *Your First Year As a Nurse: Making the Transition from Total Novice to Successful Professional*. Roseville, Calif: Prima Pub, 2001. Print.

Cherry, Barbara, and Susan R. Jacob. *Contemporary Nursing: Issues, Trends, & Management*. , 2018. Print.

Dellasega, Cheryl. *When Nurses Hurt Nurses: Recognizing and Overcoming the Cycle of Nurse Bullying*. Indianapolis: Sigma Theta Tau International, 2014. Print.

Dolan, Josephine A, M L. Fitzpatrick, and Eleanor K. Herrmann. *Nursing in Society: A Historical Perspective*. Philadelphia: W.B. Saunders, 1983. Print.

Donahue, M. Patricia. *Nursing: The Finest Art*. 3d ed. Maryland Heights: Mosby Elsevier, 2011.

Dunham, Kelli S, and Staci J. Smith. *How to Survive and Maybe Even Love Your Life As a Nurse*. Philadelphia, Penns: F.A. Davis, 2005. Print.

Estes, Mary E. Z, Pauline Calleja, Karen Theobald, and Theresa Harvey. *Health Assessment and Physical Examination*. , 2016. Print.

Fraser, Robert. *The Nurse's Social Media Advantage: How Making Connections and Sharing Ideas Can Enhance Your Nursing Career*. Indianapolis, IN: Sigma Theta Tau International, 2011. Print.

Gallen, Bademan E. *Daybook for Critical Care Nurses*. Indianapolis: Sigma Theta Tau International, 2014. Internet resource.

Garavaglia, Jan. *How Not to Die: Surprising Lessons on Living Longer, Safer and Healthier from America's Favourite Medical Examiner*. London: Marshall Cavendish, 2009. Print.

Gawande, Atul. *Complications: A Surgeon's Notes on an Imperfect Science*. , 2008. Print.

Glazer, Greer L, and Joyce J. Fitzpatrick. *Nursing Leadership from the Outside in*. New York: Springer Pub. Co, 2013. Print.

Gray, Stuart A. *A Paramedic's Diary: Life & Death on the Street*. Rugby: Monday Books, 2007. Print.

Groopman, Jerome E. *How Doctors Think*. Boston: Houghton Mifflin, 2011. Print.

Gulanick, Meg, and Judith L. Myers. *Nursing Care Plans: Diagnoses, Interventions, & Outcomes*. Elsevier, 2017. Print.

Gurian, Michael, and Barbara Annis. *Leadership and the Sexes: Using Gender Science to Create Success in Business*. Hoboken: John Wiley & Sons, Inc, 2010. Print.

Gutkind, Lee. *I Wasn't Strong Like This When I Started Out: True Stories of Becoming a Nurse*. InFact Books, 2013. Print.

Hardin, Sonya R, and Roberta Kaplow. *Cardiac Surgery Essentials for Critical Care Nursing*. , 2020. Print.

Heron, Echo. *Intensive Care: The Story of a Nurse*. London: Warner Books, 1993. Print.

Hill, Michael O. *Conspiracies of Kindness: The Craft of Compassion at the Bedside of the Ill*. Topanga, CA: Hand to Hand Publishing, 2010. Print.

Iwasiw, Carroll L, Mary-Anne Andrusyszyn, and Dolly Goldenberg. *Curriculum Development in Nursing Education*. , 2020. Print.

Johnson, Spencer, Bruce Bracken, L D. Johnson, Al Lowenheim, and David A. Hamby. *Who Moved My Cheese?*Orem, UT: Spencer Johnson/Red Tree, 2010.

Jones, Sherry Lynn. *Confessions of a Trauma Junkie: My Life As a Nurse Paramedic, 2nd Edition*. Place of publication not identified: Modern History Press, 2017. Print.

Journal of Nursing Administration: Jona. Hagerstown, Md: Lippincott, Williams & Wilkins, 1971. Internet resource.

Karch, Amy M. *Lippincott Nursing Drug Guide*. Wolters Kluwer, 2015. Print.

Karels, Carol. *Cooked: An Inner City Nursing Memoir*. United States: Full Court Press, 2005. Print.

LeMone, Priscilla, and Karen M. Burke. *Medical-surgical Nursing: Critical Thinking in Client Care, Single Volume Value Package (includes Study Guide for Medical-Surgical Nursing: Critical Thinking in Client Care, Single Volume)*. Upper Saddle River, N.J: Pearson/Prentice Hall, 2008. Print.

Luka, Rob, and Olson Huff. *Fearless Medicine: Helping Children and Adults Overcome Fear in a Medical Setting : a Guide for Healthcare Professionals.* , 2014. Print.

Maheady, Donna C. *Leave No Nurse Behind: Nurses Working with Disabilities*. Lincoln, NB: iUniverse, 2006. Print.

Maria, Dancing H. *The Last Adventure of Life: Sacred Resources for Living and Dying from a Hospice Counselor*. Findhorn, Forres: Findhorn Press, 2008. Print.

Merritt, Connie. *Too Busy for Your Own Good: Get More Done in Less Time-with Even More Energy*. New York: McGraw-Hill, 2009. Print

Millman, Dan. *Way of the Peaceful Warrior: A Book That Changes Lives*. Solon, Ohio: Playaway Digital Audio, 2009. Sound recording.

Myers, Ehren. *RNotes: Nurse's Clinical Pocket Guide*. F.A. Davis Company, 2018. Print.

Nightingale, Florence, and Maureen S. Kennedy. *Notes on Nursing: What It Is and What It Is Not*. Wolters Kluwer, 2020. Print.

Oliveira, Robin. *My Name Is Mary Sutter*. Penguin Books, 2012. Print.

Pagana, Kathleen D. *The Nurse's Communication Advantage: How Business-Savvy Communication Skills Can Advance Your Nursing Career*. Indianapolis, IN: Sigma Theta Tau International, Honor Society of Nursing, 2011. Print.

Pausch, Randy, and Jeffrey Zaslow. *The Last Lecture*. Hachette Books, 2018. Print.

Potter, Patricia A, Anne G. Perry, Amy Hall, and Patricia A. Stockert. *Fundamentals of Nursing*. 2017. Print.

Pregerson, Brady. *Think Twice!: Don't Try This at Home #2. More Lessons from the E.R. Pocket Version: Volume 1 of 2*. hinkTwiceBooks.com, 2004. Print.

Quan, Kathy. *The Everything New Nurse Book: Gain Confidence, Manage Your Schedule, and Be Ready for Anything (new Nurse Book)*. Adams Media, 2011. Print.

Rundio, Al. *The Nurse Manager's Guide to Budgeting & Finance*. Sigma Theta Tau International, 2016. Print.

Sanders, Lisa. *Every Patient Tells a Story: Medical Mysteries and the Art of Diagnosis*. New York: Broadway Books, 2010. Print.

Skloot, Rebecca. *Immortal Life Of Henrietta Lacks*. S.L.: Picador, 2018. Print.

Summers, Sandy, and Harry Summers. *Saving Lives: Why the Media's Portrayal of Nurses Puts Us All at Risk*. New York: Kaplan Pub, 2010. Print.

Ulrich, Connie M. *Nursing Ethics in Everyday Practice: A Step-by-Step Guide*. Indianapolis: Sigma Theta Tau International, 2014. Prin

Venes, Donald, Clarence W. Taber, and Clarence W. Taber. *Taber's Cyclopedic Medical Dictionary*. F.A. Davis Company, 2017. Print.

Vorvick, Linda J. "Types of Health Care Providers." MedlinePlus, August 14, 2018.

Waugh, Anne, and Allison Grant. *Ross & Wilson Anatomy and Physiology in Health and Illness*. Elsevier, 2018. Print.

Young, Amy Y. *Bedlam Among the Bedpans: Humor in Nursing*. St. Louis, MO: Mosby Elsevier, 2007. Print

GLOSSARY

ambulatory care: nurses who practice in a setting other than a traditional inpatient arena such as a hospital are called ambulatory care nurses: group practice or health center; medical office; university, community, or private hospital; military clinic; community health centers; free-standing facilities, such as a surgical center; home health setting; school; telehealth/call center; government institution; managed care payors, such as an HMO or insurance company

clinical nurse specialist: nurse with experience, education, or an advanced degree in a specialized area of nursing. Some examples are geriatrics, infection control, oncology, orthopedics, emergency room care, operating room care, intensive and coronary care, quality assurance, and community health. Nurses who function in such specialties carry out direct patient care; teach patients, families, and staff members; act as consultants; and sometimes conduct research to improve methods of care.

floor nurse: generally referred to as a medical-surgical or med-surg nurse; responsible for the basic care of patients (medication and shots, setting up IVs, informing the patient of his condition and diagnosis, and providing emotional support). Also maintain and update patient medical records.

nurse administrator: functions at various levels of management in the health care field. Depending on the position held, advanced education may be in business or hospital administration. The administrator is directly responsible for the operation and management of resources and is indirectly responsible for the personnel who give patient care.

nurse anesthetist: nurse who has also successfully completed a course of study in anesthesia. Nurse anesthetists make preoperative visits and assess patients prior to surgery, administer and monitor anesthesia during surgery, and evaluate the postoperative condition of patients.

nurse educator: nurse with a master's or doctoral degree, who teaches or instructs in clinical or educational settings. This nurse can teach both theory and clinical skills.

nurse midwife : nurse who has successfully completed a midwifery program. The nurse midwife provides prenatal care to expectant mothers, delivers babies, and provides postnatal care after the birth.

nurse practitioner: nurse with an advanced degree who is certified to work in a specific aspect of patient care. Nurse practitioners work in a variety of settings or in independent practice. They perform health assessments and give primary care to their patients.

nurse researcher: has an advanced degree and conducts special studies that involve the collection and evaluation of data in order to report on and promote the improvement of nursing care and education.

preceptor: an experienced staff nurse who serves as a role model and point person for newly employed staff nurses, student nurses, or new graduate nurses.

scrub nurse: prepares the instruments for the surgeon or surgeons in a hospital operating room; provides the correct instruments to the surgeon during surgery and handles the used items afterwards. Usually a registered nurse, though similar duties are performed by surgical technicians.

travel nurse: nurse who is hired to work in a specific location for a limited amount, typically work 13-week periods who move around the country depending on where they are needed.

triage nurse: in emergency rooms, triage nurses decide the order that patients receive treatment; telephone triage nurses answer patients' questions over the phone and advise patients on whether they need to go to the emergency room.

ORGANIZATIONS & RESOURCES

Academy of Medical-Surgical Nurses
amsn.org

Accrediting Bureau of Health Education Schools
www.abhes.org/

American Academy of Ambulatory Care Nursing
www.aaacn.org

American Academy of PAs. What is a PA?
www.aapa.org/what-is-a-pa/

American Association of Colleges of Nursing
www.aacnnursing.org/

American Association of Medical Assistants
www.aama-ntl.org/

American Association of Nurse Anesthetists
www.aana.com/

American Association of Nurse Practitioners
www.aanp.org/

American Board of Surgical Assistants
www.absa.net/

American College of Health Care Administrators
achca.memberclicks.net/

American College of Healthcare Executives
www.ache.org/

American College of Nurse-Midwives
www.midwife.org/

American Health Information Management Association
www.ahima.org/

American Medical Certification Association
www.amcaexams.com/

American Medical Technologists
www.americanmedtech.org/

American Midwifery Certification Board
www.amcbmidwife.org/

American Nephrology Nurses Association
www.annanurse.org

American Nephrology Nurses Association
www.annanurse.org

American Nurses Association
www.nursingworld.org/

American Nurses Credentialing Center
www.nursingworld.org/ancc/

American Optometric Association
www.aoa.org/

American Society of Podiatric Medical Assistants
aspma.org/

American Society of Registered Nurses
www.asrn.org/

American Society on Aging
www.asaging.org/

Association for Professionals in Infection Control and Epidemiology
apic.org

Association of American Medical Colleges. Careers in medicine
www.aamc.org/cim/specialty/exploreoptions/list/

Association of Surgical Technologists
www.ast.org/

Association of University Programs in Health Administration
www.aupha.org/

Commission on Accreditation of Allied Health Education Programs
www.caahep.org/

Commission on Accreditation of Healthcare Management Education
www.cahme.org

Emergency Nurses Association
www.ena.org

Gerontological Advanced Practice Nurses Association (GAPNA)
www.gampna.org

Hospice & Palliative Nurses Association
https://advancingexpertcare.org

Institute for Credentialing Excellence
www.credentialingexcellence.org/

International Association of Forensic Nurses
www.forensicnurses.org

Johnson & Johnson
Nurses change lives, nursing.jnj.com/home

Joint Commission on Allied Health Personnel in Ophthalmology
www.jcahpo.org/

Medical Group Management Association
www.mgma.com/

Medical-Surgical: Academy of Medical-Surgical Nurses
amsn.org

National Association for Home Care & Hospice
www.nahc.org/

National Association of Clinical Nurse Specialists
nacns.org/

National Association of Health Care Assistants
www.nahcacna.org/

National Association of Licensed Practical Nurses
nalpn.org/

National Association of Long Term Care Administrator Boards
www.nabweb.org/

National Board of Certification and Recertification for Nurse Anesthetists
www.nbcrna.com/

The National Board of Surgical Technology and Surgical Assisting
www.nbstsa.org/

National Center for Competency Testing
www.ncctinc.com/

National Commission for the Certification of Surgical Assistants
www.csaexam.com/

National Council of State Boards of Nursing
www.ncsbn.org/

National Healthcareer Association
www.nhanow.com/

National League for Nursing
www.nln.org/

National Network of Career Nursing Assistants
cna-network.org/

National Student Nurses' Association
www.nsna.org/

Oncology Nursing Society
www.ons.org

Paraprofessional Healthcare Institute
phinational.org/

Pediatric Nursing Certification Board
www.pncb.org/

Professional Association of Health Care Office Management
www.cms.gov

INDEX

WITHDRAWAL